Journals of an Expat

Journals of an Expat

Judith Whitworth

Memory Lane

First published in Great Britain by Memory Lane

ISBN 978-0-9563076-7-5

Typeset by TW Typesetting, Plymouth, Devon

Printed and bound by Good News, Ongar, England.

*This book is dedicated to Stamos,
without whom none of this would have happened,
and Maria.
May we meet in our next lives.*

Contents

Contents

Book III

Foreword

Judith Tripos Whitworth, a handsome woman, lady, wife, mother-earth, farmer, vet, cook, spinner, weaver, breadwinner, writer, disciplined, austere, resourceful, inventive and unusually loyal friend above all.

When she did me the great honour to ask me to write the introduction to her book, this book – my mind immediately jumped to Sir Patrick Leigh Fermor (who, as a young British officer, kidnapped General Kreippe, the German military governor on the island of Crete, during World War II – 65 years ago) when I asked him to do the same for the book I was writing on my wartime experiences, back in the 90s, his answer was, I quote, 'Alas I am a broken reed as to introductions. I have let myself in to do two, and it is a task I find extremely difficult and forbidding.'

So my first reaction to Judith's request was to answer likewise. A broken reed though I am myself but having had the privilege of knowing Judith for some forty years, and her remarkable endeavours to make the best out of God's blessings wherever she happens to be on the planet, I cannot but venture a few – of a million words I could put on paper about this exceptional lady writer.

Most of all I will never forget her amazing talent after she married Stamos, in 'resurrecting' and re-organizing a dying farm near Corinth in Greece. In spite of fierce opposition from all sides, she did achieve the impossible. Her warm relationship with the neighbouring peasants uplifted her, and her able help with their animals made her a good friend to them all.

She was also blessed to have given birth to four magnificent sons, ranging from six feet three inches to six feet six inches (which, incidentally, qualifies them to be admitted to the Grenadier Guards, a matter of utmost importance to me personally) very handsome and healthy they are too.

But, let me blah-blah no more, let me say that when you read this book, many other characteristics that illustrate in bright colour the unique personality of my dear friend Judith, will emerge between the lines.

Frederick V Carabott
Akrate/Archaia, Greece. August 2009

BOOK I

Chapter 1

Arrival in Corinth

The first time Stamos took me to Argos market was a perfect, spring Saturday. We set off early to catch the action. In those days the road was tortuous and winding, yet we happily sped along, through Solomos, leaving the sea and the great hump of Akro Corinth behind us. Inland, through Xiliomothi, Ayios Vassilis and Fihtio, all ugly, new, straggling, ribbon developments.

Here on this big road lived the middle aged, generally running businesses. Huddled in the hills above, lay the villages, where the old and the young lived. The lovely clusters of old houses seemed grown, not built, out of the rocky hillsides. In splendid disarray they jostled for space in steep, narrow streets, quite unfit for modern traffic. The original villagers lived here where they had always been safe in past and dangerous times. Yet, above them, higher still, barely visible after years of wind and weather, lie even more ancient villages. All that remains of them now are broken toothed towers, dominating straggly walls and piles of rock where once there had been scores of houses, hundreds, maybe thousands of years ago. Undoubtedly, if one did DNA tests from the bone fragments which litter lost graveyards, it would prove that there had lived the forebears of present day families.

Above all, far from the rush of modern life, were the shepherds, who kept their flocks on high pastures near ancient and working wells.

Vulgar, bright, exotic spring, with bluest sky, vivid wild flowers embedded in luxuriant green, sped past, and for us, the secret delight in each other and our blossoming relationship.

Suddenly in a bend in the road, way ahead in a fold in the land, revealed the far off citadel of Argos. Impressive, intriguing from a distance, it dominated the great spread of the town laid out under it in a shallow basin. As we entered the narrow streets, the glorious chaos of market day unfolded before my eyes. Struggling through hordes of humanity and every kind of vehicle, we were all swept along in one direction, the market square. My first of very many visits to Argos market, it was and still is marvellous.

Huge, bordered with fine buildings, it is as perfect a market place as I have ever seen. Probably the existing buildings around the square are replacements of the ancient. For they are really handsome, not to be compared with the usual, and ghastly, concrete boxes. Open onto the square, the fine ceramic tiled roofs are edged with acanthus leaves, Hermes and Zeus. Serious business goes on in there, for they are more warehouses than market stalls, what we might call Cash & Carry, supplying, no doubt, every kind of shop for miles around.

In the square itself, stalls were spread before us, mostly just tables, but some with awnings, for although early spring, it became quite hot by midday.

It seemed as if but everything was sold there. In one area you would find cloth, household linen and clothes. In another, household utensils. Tools. Splendid baskets, ranging from the huge grape carriers, to tiny ones for children. Fresh flowers and plants. Plastic goods of every sort including, colourful, fantasy flowers, many of which would end up littering the cemeteries, there to fade eventually from the garish splendour of the Far East, into a muted, sunburnt apology. There were all kinds of shoes and the equivalent of our gum boots, the rubber sandals, beloved of country people. Pots and pans. Religious pictures and incense together with hideous nick-nacks to tempt the foolish. In fact, all the ghastly imported junk so beloved by peasants the world over. And food, every kind of food in abundance.

The vegetables had obviously been dug up and scrubbed the night before and left sitting in buckets of water, for they looked bright and wonderfully fresh. Dark skinned Rom, the original Romanies, stood yelling from the backs of their trucks, parked along one side, selling five kilo bags of potatoes and onions. Meanwhile their brightly-dressed women swung gaily through the crowds, flashing the occasional precious gold tooth, a trail of children behind them. Locals sold whatever they had, and being early spring, it was mostly leafy greens of all kinds.

We slowly made our way along one side of the square where the individual sellers stood. I learned that they might come every week, or once a month. Or, when they urgently needed money, for some special cause. Medicines. A court case. Seed. A big bill. A daughter getting married. They had left the hills and far flung villages in the chill of early morning, hitching a ride as they could. They simply stood there without a table, their wares spread on a sheet at their feet and waited like predators, ready to pounce.

By then, Stamos and I had realised that we would probably stay together. We had met mere months before, but a lovely bond held us, and a happy man again, he delighted in showing me his country.

My original shock at his farm was gradually receding from memory. Always a worker, the few short weeks I had been there were already showing results. It was to take a long time to undo the previous years of dreadful neglect, but ever optimistic, I believed we would do it. One of the first tasks I learned was to prune trees, first the desperately hard citrus wood, which gave me fine calluses, then the softer apricots. It was not just the pruning either, there was the

5

hauling away of the often substantial prunings, a job and a half alone. The Forth Bridge, if I had but known it. No wonder Stamos had given up, it was far too much work for one man. So it was during those halcyon days of early spring I realised that the one thing the farm needed, was animals. For the grass was amazing. Lush, green, full of wonderful herbs and flowers, an abundance in a dry land and oh shame, no creatures to eat it.

Which is why we had come to Argos, to buy a lamb. Little acorns grow into big oak trees.

We slowly walked along the rows of vendors taking in the variety of wares and being subjected to noisy entreaty.

'Good one!' they shrieked, 'I am all attention.' and thrust whatever, right under our noses.

There were huge hay lined baskets of eggs. Plastic tubs of olives and cheese. Gleaming jars of golden honey. Vine leaves in brine. Great baskets of horta, my first experience of the hand picked wild greens of Greece. Sacks of almonds and walnuts. Old Coke bottles filled with deep green olive oil, or the local, pink retsina. Beautifully tied bunches of every type of herb. Fluffy white fleeces to spin and splendid chunks of rough, home made olive oil soap.

Further down the line, stood the sellers of livestock. Amidst the racket, their varied wares lay, silent and dazed with shock, legs bound, panting in pathetic leggy heaps. Hens, ducks, turkeys, rabbits and finally, the kids and lambs. My heart bled, for of course, I wanted to buy them all. Their short lives suddenly shattered with removal from their dam, no doubt a dreadful journey to market, they made no sound now, utterly exhausted. Quickly the vendors realised that here was a potential buyer. Rowdily they jostled for place in front of us, thrusting their lambs at me, upside down. It hadn't taken them long to realise that here was a foreigner (therefore rich and easily cheated). Helpless I watched as they brandished and prodded their poor wares, shouting their attributes till Stamos intervened and equally loudly, demanded peace.

Trying to act cool, I walked up and down the row, trying to look professional. Their combined determination that I should buy their lamb again grew to crescendo. However, it did not take me long to decide on my baby. It probably helped that she was not being carried upside down, but lay comfortably on the arm of the young shepherd. Coal black with a white blaze on her head, the farmer in me noted her bright eye and clean back side. Having decided, quietly I told Stamos my choice.

If the racket before had shocked me, it now grew two fold. Momentary disappointment at not having made a sale, as one, they swept in to assist the shy young shepherd. Indeed I can say there were only two silent people in that throng, he and I. I observed him, a handsome dark haired, dark eyed young fellow with a surprisingly fresh complexion. Later I would learn that he was a Sarakatzany, an interesting nomadic tribe which extends from Romania to Crete.

Now the bargaining had begun. Having been born in the East, I am certainly not against it, indeed enjoy it. But this! It was quite shocking. I watched my gentle mate and love of my life, yelling and gesticulating like a lunatic. What he gave alas, came back ten fold. Lambs dumped without ceremony on the ground, arms were raised, fingers spread. Stamos took them all on while we two stood and watched.

Unable to agree on the price, my beloved grasped me by the elbow and smartly marched me off. As one, they dragged us back and battle commenced again. I was truly appalled. For a paltry sum, we seemed to have taken on half the market place. Stamos stood firm, price named and refused to budge. Later he explained to me that seeing that I was a foreigner, they assumed he must be wealthy, or worse, a fool. Nothing doing.

Symphony! That beautiful Greek word, meaning – in harmony. We agreed on the price, indeed, the correct price. Every eye watched as the notes were counted into the hand of the successful vendor.

The lamb now safely in my arms, her back legs un-hobbled, she rested her head on my shoulder. Sweet, dumb thing, little did she realise her destiny. The chosen one, for she would indeed lie on the Greek equivalent of a bed of roses.

But! It seemed it was not yet finished. Honour intact, my love, happy now with my happiness and his success, asked with a gleam in his eye, 'How much for the rope?'

With a whoop, as the Pied Piper, Stamos led the way to the nearest kaféneon. What money we had spent on the lamb was now doubled with buying drinks for everyone. Honour was restored.

It is the earliest of my warm memories. Rickety, bright blue painted tables were dragged forth onto the pavement. Equally rickety chairs followed. While the proprietor prepared our orders, our new found friends set to with loud enthusiasm, questioning Stamos about me and where had he found me? Peasant curiosity overflowing, they wanted to know everything. The tiny glasses of ouzo appeared accompanied with thick little white plates of olives and octopus on tooth picks. It was a merry little party, glasses raised, good health, prosperity. Each one wished us luck with the lamb, which they generously praised. Soon, all smiles, happy at least to have something unusual to recount back home that evening, they left with optimism to return to their pitches and duty.

Later, on the way back to the car, I spotted the young shepherd walking with a bonny young woman, presumably his wife. Carried in her arms was a great, bright red, rolled up bundle. It was easy to see from her glowing eyes, she was immensely pleased. Stamos explained that she must have taken her own spun and dyed wool to the weaver to have it made into a flokati, a traditional thick shaggy blanket. We guessed that the lamb had paid the weaver, so all happy, we went our various ways.

Back at the farm, our first lamb answered to the name of Come-along and was a good baby. We agreed that while I did the house first thing, prepared the meal and so forth, she should accompany Stamos out on the land where he had begun farming again. I joined him when my chores were done, and I usually gave her the bottle.

When it rains in the Corinthia, it rains, the same in three months as in London in one year. I found the earth became like a quagmire, the fine sandy soil sucked you down, so rubber boots were essential. Thus I learned more of life, or at least lambs. One night Come-along refused to come into the hall where she normally slept. I was perplexed, tempting her with an extra bottle, I tried to coax her inside. Yet she refused, returning to her chosen place. Then I realised with delight, that she was curled up beside our muddy boots on the door step. We had got it all wrong. We were not her mother, the wellies were. So boots moved just inside the front door, Come-along followed meekly and settled down again. Later, when sandals replaced rubber boots and she was full grown, she changed her allegiance from the boots to me. Whenever she could, unaware of course of the heat and prickly burrs, she often got onto my lap, draped like a shaggy blanket. Head outstretched, I would be obliged, suffering, to scratch her neck. While recognising her affection, I still found it extremely hot, smelly and most uncomfortable.

Despite having learned to read and write Greek, I had great difficulty in speaking it. Probably I started learning it when I was too old for I was incredulous and admiring of the youngsters who picked it up so easily. At any rate, somehow just getting my tongue around the words seemed hard. With two husbands, both excellent linguists, always being afraid to try, I was very slow to learn. Thinking that if I watched the news on the television I might, was a non-starter. They spoke so fast, it was impossible.

So I just strung a row of words together, never mind about grammar. Most of the time anyway, I barely needed Greek. As we were always together, I left the talking to Stamos. The breakthrough came about indirectly through our opposite neighbours.

The Petropolous were shepherds without land, so they had to walk their sheep every day where there was unfenced grazing. It was from them I began to learn Greek, long distance, as it were.

During the spring lambing, the mothers and babies were left together to bond for perhaps twenty four hours. Then the mother would have to go out walking with the flock, leaving the hungry, lonely and yelling lamb behind. Feed was far too expensive to leave them together for longer, especially where there was no home grazing. So mornings and evenings, were a nightmare of noise. As Mitsos, Mr Petropolous, walked out with the mothers, they and the lambs would call to each other frantically, until out of hearing. As the cries of the mothers faded in the distance, the lambs cried even louder. Poor little things; they cried till too exhausted to cry any more, then collapsed to sleep till evening when the mothers came home. Then, the racket began, all over again, even worse. The mothers having grazed all day, were full-uddered, and desperate to get back to their very hungry babies. The turmoil of the search for the right mouth/udder was amazing. At last, all satisfied, blessed silence fell, till the morning when it began all over again.

During the day, Angiliki, Mrs Petropolous, stayed at home with the lambs, her children all being off and away to work or school or the army. If I, from a distance, went mad with the noise, it must have been far worse for her, being on the spot. So she solved the problem by putting on the TV or radio at its absolute loudest, to drown out the wailing. Sixty odd lambs really could produce an impressive racket. So I got them both, lambs and music, top decibel, the full works.

While their mothers were out, they would sometimes escape from their tiny pens where they were incarcerated for safety and company. Then I used to hear Mrs Petropolous crying, adding her bit to the rest of it, 'I can not, I can not, I am too old!' While she tore around trying to catch the escapee.

'Then borrow, then borrow, eamia pew megali!' I turned it around my mouth. Tested it, spoke it, and was pleased, progress.

Occasionally, the senior Petropolous would go away for the day, or even a night and two days – and very occasionally it was, thank goodness, probably to relatives for a wedding or funeral, in their mountain village.

Then I really did miss them, for the two sons were left in charge and if it had been chaos before, it was merry hell now. They were totally incompetent, having turned their backs on their family occupation, they worked with cars. The noise was always louder and longer as they struggled with the unfamiliar tasks. Thus I knew the elders were away. The flock, creatures of habit, seemed to just go to pieces without their familiar and calm shepherd.

Above the farm on the south border, is a curious little canal, usually dry but which, in good years, brings water from the mountains. Many was the time I heard escapee lambs actually in it. So I fished them out to return them to sometimes unknowing, surprised, yet highly relieved boys.

During my many hours pruning, I often heard Mr Petropolous walk by along the ridge with the sheep, warbling his marvellous songs. They sounded so ancient, oriental, a curious keening, crooning sound, quite fascinating and beautiful. Not like some of the young shepherds I observed walking in the hills, with their portable radios clamped to their ears.

There had been, sadly, some unpleasantness between Eleni, Stamos' ex wife, and the innocent Petropolous. Eleni and the children had been picking almonds on the front of the farm by the road and, job finished, apparently they had gone back to the house, leaving the sacks of almonds, probably awaiting collection. Undoubtedly the Rom or some other opportunist, spotting the sacks, speedily made off with them. Sadly the Petropolous were blamed, and to this day, deeply hurt, hotly refute responsibility. Hence Stamos did not allow them in with their sheep to graze, and naturally, with three daughters to marry they could not afford to offer to pay so they never asked. Whether Stamos was at home or not, they would never dream of letting the sheep in, just skirt the farm. Of course quite frequently, the odd crafty sheep could not resist

11

the temptation and dashed in to snatch a quick mouthful of good grass. Mitsos, his name was Dimitrios, a veritable David in fact, would then half heartedly sling a stone to get her back in line.

It was without too much effort I persuaded Stamos to consider the very real advantages of inviting our excellent neighbours, onto the land to graze their sheep.

Free manure liberally spread on the land with fine pointed little hooves helping to dig it in. Surely that could do nothing but good, all the while mowing the grass, which we didn't need anyway, and cost us nothing. 'Goodwill,' I hammered Stamos, 'is gold itself,' with excellent neighbours who would act as guardians of house and farm if we were away. Nothing but good could come of the relationship, give and take. He listened and acted.

Good? It became the warmest, most loyal, mutual relationship one could ever wish for and which still continues to this day.When Come-along grew up, she joined the Petropolous flock, but to Mitsos astonishment, she always came when I called. Briefly touching my hand, and my heart, dim memories of babyhood stirring, she then turned away and went back to the flock, just an ordinary sheep. Yet she turned out to be a good sheep, producing twins every year. Mitsos used her milk for fetta together with that of his own sheep. He kept one twin to sell with his lambs at Easter and always gave us the other one to rear for ourselves.

After the lambs were sold, both the Petropolous used to walk with the flock every day. They were an amazing and deeply loving couple. He was always smiling, gentle and quiet, loving and loved by all, especially children. She was quite the opposite, a wonderful, passionate, hard-working and often ferocious woman.

One day I called at their little house across the road to find some sort of crisis. Mrs Petropolous was sitting in the yard, wailing and nursing her leg, while Mitsos and their two sons stood beside her, silent, just wringing their hands. I took one look at the leg and was appalled. It was very swollen, black and oozing.

'Hospital?' I asked.

'Whatever for?' she shouted in reply, her face grey with pain. I had a closer look and asked, horrified, for warm water and cloths. Seeing they had none I went home, collected my medical kit and rushed back, still with the full intention of taking her to the local hospital some three kilometres away. Some hope.

She was adamant she would not go. She gritted her teeth while I cleaned the leg, which was indeed septic and quite horrible, but at least I found out that the black was not from within. It was from the mixture of soot and oil which she had anointed herself with. (Soot and oil? Oh! Now that was a new one for me.)

'If you leave it much longer they will have to cut your leg off.' I told her quite seriously.

Obviously I was making some sense for she was indignant.

'So,' she replied furiously, 'I will have one leg.'

'And what good is a one legged wife to a shepherd?' I struggled on.

'Then he will have to find another wife,' came the prompt reply. Her mouth set in a stubborn line, she continued to nurse her leg and rock in pain.

We were desperate, Mitsos and I. For the first time I saw his face without a smile. Gently he appealed to her to listen to me. Rocking with more vigour she yelled back that she would not go to the hospital. Then more quietly, she trotted out that she was not yet ready to die.

This was my first experience of the terror many peasants had of hospital. You only went there to die, so it must be avoided at all costs. Mitsos told me that he had alone safely delivered their six children in the mountains. They had no need of hospitals in those days, he announced firmly, as do the foolish young women of nowadays.

I can't remember how long it took to convince her, it seemed a long battle. Eventually she accepted, still with a very poor grace, that something must be done. Relieved to have succeeded, I rushed back to the farm for the car. But I need not have hurried for I found on return that, no, they were not yet ready. For of course no peasant would ever go anywhere, let alone to hospital, except in their best clothes. I had to wait while they thoroughly washed at the hose, Mitsos tenderly assisting his wife, then changed into their Sunday best.

Oh heavens! I was exhausted with effort and emotion, worried too and quite incredulous.

We drove quickly there and I, with a scheme up my sleeve, tore ahead to find the sister in charge of Outpatients.

By happy chance I knew her. I had recently had a tetanus shot, and as usual, leaving my boots at the door, had walked in just in my socks. Which happened to be some crazy, charming and colourful socks, with each toe like a glove finger. Apparently this had so impressed the sister, remembering me or the socks, she greeted me warmly, as a long lost relative. Quickly I struggled to explain to her what had happened and to please, please help me, by making a big thing of it.

'Scold her.' I entreated. 'Insist she never leaves such a wound so long again. Give her hell. Please!'

We grinned at each other as conspirators and delighted to cooperate, she held forth at length while I listened outside in the corridor with satisfaction. Eventually, an unusually chastened lady limped out and I drove a very sober couple home.

It was a great privilege for me to get to know those simple and excellent Greeks right at the beginning. They were and still are, always there for me, true and loyal, even in the dark days years later, when Greece and Greeks turned their backs on me.

But why and how did I meet Stamos? Back to the beginning.

Chapter 2

The Perivoli Tripou /
(The Orchards of the Tripos)

The first time I visited the farm was on a late February night. Bitterly cold and raining, it was hardly encouraging. Thinking back, why I went at all is something of a mystery still. I had several other invitations for Easter, the big day in Greece.

My three sons were coming from Britain for the holidays. I badly needed to be with them, for it had not been a happy time for any of us since I had left their father. Although I never saw much of them during term as they were boarding, school holidays had been special. We had always spent their vacations doing mad and exciting things, not only in Britain, but in a camper, the length and breadth of Europe. I tried to rent a little house by the sea. Various invitations to exciting places were being sorted out in my mind. At the same time I was pretty sure if I accepted any, there would be a price to pay, which did not appeal. (Well, I was beginning to learn, nothing is free in life.)

Then Stamos appeared. Fate was at work.

My hosts in Athens lived in a fascinating, big old family house. Emilios approached me one day, hands in supplication.'

15

'Sister-in-law.' (I was not in fact, but we enjoyed the fantasy.) 'Dear sister-in-law. I owe hospitality to about one hundred people. Please, please will you cook curry for them.'

At that time, 1974, there was no Indian restaurant in the whole of Athens. Having been born in India, it was always assumed I could cook curry. Having left India, hating curry, aged nine, I could not. Having spent many years in school, indeed I could cook little. So in fact, I began to cook at about twenty, and with trial and error, now actually liking curry, soon became a dab hand at making it.

Of course I would cook for him. It was arranged. About every two weeks there was a dinner party for about twenty. They were fun, and the curries were much appreciated as most of the guests were widely travelled. My host was most happy.

At one of these Do's, Stamos appeared, the 'uninvited guest'. Apparently he had been walking in the centre of Athens with a friend when they met Emilios. Ever the perfect gentleman, on reminding Pandias he was expected that evening, Stamos was automatically included in the invitation. Emilios used to tell me that the goddess Athena was the goddess of hospitality and he certainly lived by that maxim.

So my life changed in a twinkling of an eye, with a clashing of cymbals.

Well, not quite, for I barely noticed the silent, hungry man in brown who just sat and ate. Much later he even told me he did not like curry. This surprised me as he had gate crashed every subsequent dinner. Anyway, I was too busy dishing up to the throng and at that time I was certainly off men in a big way.

My elder sister, who was then working in Athens, was to have her fortieth birthday. Such a milestone needed celebrating and another party was arranged. Amongst others, the Quiet Man in Brown, was invited, and, I recall, I even had the temerity to tell him to come 'dressed up'.

Well he didn't. He arrived, as usual, all in brown, with his shoes gleaming. Alas I remember gently chiding him for his casual clothes, as all the other guests were in black tie. He just nodded smiling. I was beginning to discover he was quite deaf, so thought he probably hadn't heard a word of what I was saying. I also discovered much later to my shame, that he had no other clothes, these were indeed, his best.

As ever, searching for a husband for my sister, I did pay him rather more attention on that occasion. I had learned that he had been separated from his wife for some years, that he had three teenage children, and that he lived on a farm near Corinth.

'Do you speak French?' he pleaded.

'Badly,' I honestly replied. So badly, he realised, he quickly decided his English would be better. It was, though slightly archaic, correct and with his wonderful deep voice, oh so charming. We conversed thereafter, in English.

Ah, but the best laid plans and all that. He did not, as they say, fancy my sister. It soon became apparent that I was the object of his attentions.

So it was, having heard that my three sons would be coming out for Easter, he invited us to all go to spend it with him and his children at his farm.

'It is,' he told me earnestly in his lovely voice, 'Rather morose.' (Pronounced as in French – More-roze.)

I often wonder what would have happened if I had not gone. I had a house to go back to in Somerset which was being restored. I had an interesting job in a Cordon Bleu College waiting for me. But my heart went out to that quiet man, he was so lonely, so needing company. Pity is a strange word to use in this connection, but for lack of other good enough, I use it. I did pity him. When I saw his home, my pity magnified. I went because I felt so very sorry for him. I stayed because he needed me. And I was rewarded with a wonderful marriage and a great, if occasionally stormy, love.

We bowled along through the night, west along the motorway. Not only was he quite deaf, he was blind in one eye. So he kept twisting around to see me, to hear me. I was terrified, he drove with his mind on me rather than on the road, he drove as a madman. I did not know then that he had never taken a driving test, but had, as is often the norm in Greece, somehow bluffed his way into getting a driving license.

There had been several splendid stories about the loss of his eye. A duel was the one I liked best. Indeed it was even possible as he had a reputation of being quite lunatic. In fact it was a medical matter, nothing romantic or dramatic. Sadly before penicillin, at birth, an infection in the eye, caused it to be removed when he was about ten. Despite his terrifying driving, he managed amazingly well with his one eye.

We did not go straight to the farm as I expected. As yet not into the Mediterranean way of a siesta, I was exhausted. He announced that we had to go to visit his sister's holiday home in Loutraki. A lovely old family house, recently done up, it was being undermined by the building of a new block of flats next door. He left me in the house while he went out into the dark, wind and rain to 'see' the foundations.

Having been told he was very poor, I had brought a meal and so produced it in the charming, beautifully equipped kitchen.

Later, a Greek friend of Stamos laughingly explained why, the charade of a detour had taken place.

Pride would not allow him to show me his sad home without first giving me to understand, that, some of his family were well heeled. We both had a lot to learn about each other and our cultural differences.

One thing which he said, moved me so much, that I never, ever forgot it. As the years passed and life often became almost unbearable, and he sometimes, almost unbearably impossible, I made myself remember. His frailty. His pathetic (and if he did but know, unnecessary) need to impress me.

'I have,' he said, 'the French Consulship of the Corinthia.'

Remembering his words in times of stress, always took me back to the beginning. That lovely, lonely man. So I always felt the healing surge of tenderness, however ghastly the current crisis.

At last we careered up a terrible bumpy drive and drew up before a gaunt house surrounded with great dripping walnut trees. The one thing which fixed in my mind was the terrible stink of rotten oranges. It was to take me some time to realise that he barely farmed. Occasionally he rushed out to fill some sacks of oranges to pay a bill. Otherwise his wonderful fruit was stolen or fell to the ground and rotted. Thereafter I could tell when we had arrived, by that horrible, cloying smell.

He seemed past caring about the condition of his farm. While he raged if anyone stole his fruit to sell, he was most philosophical about people helping themselves to eat on the spot.

A month or so later, we drove west along the coast road, then up into the foot hills, to a pleasant village. The view north was glorious, across the Gulf of Corinth to the snowcapped mountains on the other side. He parked his van in the little platea and we found a table and chairs in the sunshine, slightly protected from the cold wind. The café owner came out and took our orders. It was pleasant and relaxing sitting there, as yet without the pressures of farming bearing down on us. As we rose to go, the owner approached with a bill and stood scrutinising the van.

Now it is the law, if you are a farmer, or whatever, to have your name and province painted on your vehicle. For tax reasons I think.

'Are you,' the young man asked, 'Mr Tripos of Corinth?'

'Indeed,' replied Stamos.

'Is your farm on the road to Examilia past the army camp?'

'Indeed,' again.

With a splendid and theatrical gesture, the young man tore up the bill and cast it to the wind 'Then today you are my guests, in thanks for the many excellent oranges I stole from you when I was in the army.'

How we laughed and after much hand shaking and goodwill, we drove off.

'It could be,' joked the happy Stamos, 'that every village in Greece owes us a drink.' And I am sure he is right.

Gradually I learnt that The Perivoli Tripou – The Orchards of the Tripos – situated roughly between old and new Corinth, was very well known for two reasons. Firstly because the family, having been there for a long time, were the 'squires', if such a thing exists in Greece. Secondly because the Tripos men were always avant-garde in their farming methods. They seemed always to be the first. Theirs was a rare courage in a harsh land. They led the way, they took the risks. I'm happy that even as late as my day, Stamos was still the forerunner of several enterprising, if alas, more often than not, unsuccessful schemes.

It was I believe, Uncle Frederikos who, taking a caique to Turkey, brought back many varieties of citrus tree. I later discovered them in an orchard so overgrown, it reminded me of Mordor. Going through the Peloponnese today with its endless orange groves, it is amazing to realise that he was the first citrus farmer. That until his courageous experiment, there were no citrus orchards on mainland Greece. Possibly almost every orange and lemon tree originated from our farm.

Stamos told me that when he'd removed every stone from the fields, only then could he leave. He never did. Yet by the average standard, it was a fine farm, with level land, good wells and an underground irrigation system, with really very few stones. Having trained in France as an Agricultural Engineer, he installed it himself, and, he told me grinning, spent his first years at the farm, mainly underground. It was, he assured me, the most modern farm in the whole district. I had no reply, for after the tidy, well run farms of Britain, I regarded the neglect and muddle in some sort of shock.

He was an honest man. When I asked him how many men he had working the farm, he replied after some hesitation,

'One.'

I was soon to discover that one, was he.

He told me it had belonged to his grandfather, who was buried by the church. I was quietly amused by his pride in the size of his farm. Over 130 stremata, it was considered huge. To me, it was a mere small-holding, about thirty acres, nothing by UK standards. Later, when I began to learn about the local 'farms', which are anything from 5 to 50 stremata, where families lived, worked and prospered, I understood.

That first night I was horrified. 'Morose,' he had called it.

Morose? It was desolate. Grim. Cheerless. Freezing. While he rushed about, I stood helpless, gazing around, shocked at the lack of comfort, very tired and cold. It was a large, high-ceilinged room which rather resembled a railway station waiting room. There were some long sofas and a few chairs. Everything was dull and utility. The room was dominated by a ping-pong table under which dust lay, thick in a neat rectangle.

He flung open some French doors and disappeared into the night to return with a huge barrow loaded with wet wood. Next, he ripped pages from the phone book, pushed them into the gaping fireplace, smashed wet orange boxes on his knee and tried to light the fire.

Kindly he asked me if I would also like the electric fire on all night, but mindful of his reported poverty and the high cost of electricity, I refused. He made up a bed for me, right there, in the big saloon and disappeared up the wide creaking stairs. I later discovered he had given me his own bed.

He was, surprisingly, absolutely correct. The perfect gentleman. Which is no doubt, in the end, why he won me.

It was a dreadful night. The fire sulked and smoked. It certainly gave off no heat. Cold, exhausted and miserable, ever the poor sleeper, I lay wondering what on earth I was doing there.

No sooner, with the first streaks of dawn, did I finally get to sleep, he appeared, woke me up and offered me coffee. The thought of a huge hot mug so appealed, I gratefully accepted.

21

A tiny cup of foul black liquid appeared. Having drunk it, all I wanted to do was sleep again, but he had other ideas. He wanted to find out about my politics!

So, we had our first disagreement. I flatly told him I was apolitical. He was aghast, and proceeded to assault me with all the reasons why I was foolish.

It would be some time before I understood the passion most Greek men have for politics. Due to their centuries of harsh history, there had never been time for hobbies. Eat, if they were lucky, sleep, work and talk. That was about it. Hence the delight of sitting over a coffee or an ouzo, thrashing over that, to me at least, oh so boring topic.

In fact in a previous visit to Greece I had found the general attitude to politics unbelievable. I had suffered, as had most of the population of Athens, the recent overthrowing of the latest tyrants, the colonels, and the return of Karamanlis from France. Car horns blew a welcome literally all day and half the night, as ecstatic citizens roared around announcing their joy. It was exhausting, one just could not escape from the noise.

Later, when I was confident enough to question him about the dreadful neglect of his farm, he told me that he had been so miserable, his courage nil, he could not work. So he sat all day instead and read about politics. This was another difference between us. When I am depressed, I hurl myself into work. Stamos just stopped.

In his loneliness, he had developed another habit. Of going to the cinema very frequently. This was, he told me, 'to feel humanity about me.' So sad.

Indeed he tried to persuade me to join him, which I did once or twice, but it soon palled. Poor or aged films, dreadful sound, and heating which was turned off the moment they started. Eventually I told him, that he must go alone. Despite this, being a garrison town, the most awful film was splendidly perked up by the audience, three quarters of whom were ribald soldiers, escaping from the camp for

22

the evening. Although I understood very little Greek then, their bawdy comments were quite clear. Anyway, about five minutes into the film, Stamos went to sleep. It was exactly the same when his sister gave us some interesting pieces of furniture. Amongst them was a mammoth TV. No sooner was it on and he was settled in front of it, he dozed off.

That first morning, I was glad when he announced that he had to return to his sister's house. Wryly I thought, he might be able to see the foundations in daylight, and, thankfully, it broke up discussions on politics.

As often happens in Greece, the weather changed overnight. The morning was sunny and glorious. A halcyon day. The sky was cloudless and blue, the warmth causing the puddles to rise in drifts of steam. I peered out to see a perfect day, courage re-entering my soul.

My explorations of the house showed me a nice big kitchen with bathroom off. Stamos had built on this two room extension. Later, during earthquakes, this is where we ran for safety. For, as was his way, it was splendidly well built. The huge fridge was impressive by being almost empty. A packet of margarine and a tin each of sardines and evaporated milk graced the fine shelves. The bathroom was big and rather cold with mildewy walls. The shelves appeared to be full of medicaments for the bowels. Up the creaking handsome wooden stairs, I came to a big square landing with four bedrooms off. If I had thought the downstairs desolate, upstairs was far worse. Broken windows had allowed the floors to be strewn with autumn leaves. A few beds and the odd cupboard gave the feel of an abandoned house. Later I found this to be virtually so, for a few years earlier, Stamos' wife had left, taking the children and much of the furniture. Hastily I retreated down the stairs, guilty but grateful that my poor host had given me his bed.

The rectangle of dust under the ping-pong table caught my eye, so I found a broom and swept. What I tell now will no doubt bring forth all kinds of skepticism even criticism. There must be few people who understand what it is to be – 'a sensitive'. So I tell it as it happened. It was not a new experience for me and by now I could just about handle it. Yet each time, it was unexpected, and of course I was totally unprepared.

My breathing slowed, the broom in my hands became heavy, so I gradually stopped working. The sun blocked out, there was no sound. A tall, big man, well dressed all in black with a white cravat, stood with his back to the fireplace. We gazed at each other for some moments. Very courteously, in English, he asked me who I was and what I was doing.Now understand this. Not one word was spoken, no voice, no sound. This conversation was with the minds. I told him my name, that I was British, and, foolishly, that I was sweeping. He nodded, apparently absorbing what I had said. We surveyed each other further. I have no idea if all this took minutes or seconds. Eventually, coward that I am, I asked if he minded, if I got on. Again, with great courtesy, he excused himself, indicating with a hand that I continue with my work, and was gone.

Light and sound came back slowly, filtering into my numb brain. Like waking from a faint, or a deep sleep. Birdsong and sunlight. Slowly, I finished sweeping, gathering my wits, thinking about the tall man, guessing it must have been Stamos' grandfather who I knew had lived there.

Next, I began a tour of the farm. The back door from the kitchen led straight out into an overgrown yard facing north. There was nowhere to leave muddy boots, no porch, or shelter outside the door. Just from in to out. Or out to in. Most impractical and inconvenient. The thick glass in the kitchen door had a large slice missing, which made it easy to open the door from outside. I supposed that the neighbours were honest. However, there was indeed all too little within the house worth stealing, so good luck to them.

A small, faded blue tractor was parked nearby, dejected, wet and dripping. So I assumed that there was no barn, or garage either. What, sort of a farm was this, I thought?

No farm buildings, just the house. Originally, it must have been a fine building, square, big and high, The walls a jigsaw of cracked, dirty white plaster. The roof, undulating in places, and uneven along the eaves, was laid with the huge red ceramic tiles, generally used in the Mediterranean.

Picking my way through puddles and wet grass, I wandered about, then approached a small tumbledown stone building, south of the house. With difficulty, I pushed the broken door open, and I realised in amazement, that it was a church. The roof was on the floor, a mess of timbers and broken tiles. The incredible blue sky was framed by high, broken walls. The bright sun shone down, on the destruction and the old icons still hanging, damp on the walls.

Fear gripped my heart. Having my own idea of God, I was not particularly religious, but nonetheless with a deep sense of right, I was appalled. To be privileged to have a tiny, ancient church on ones land, and treat it thus! My mind reeled. I was truly shocked. I remember it as if it were yesterday.

'Flee!' an inner voice told me. 'Flee now!' Myriad thoughts whirled in my head. I spoke no Greek. Stuck, car-less in the country, how would I get back to Athens? How could I just walk out on that poor lonely man? He who seemed so happy to have my companionship?

I could not. I did not. Although ever since I have wondered why. Especially when the scales of life tipped me down.

Destiny I suppose. To give Stamos some happiness at last. To create another life perhaps, another fine Frederikos? Unknown, it lay before me as I stood in the sunlit ruins, in the warm embrace of Saint Nicholas of Bari.

Stamos returned hours later. If he had a watch, he never used it. As his wooing of me progressed, I was often put out at his inability to keep appointments on time. I considered it poor manners, indeed uncaring, to keep me waiting. Later, when I knew more of Greece, I discovered that this lackadaisical attitude to timekeeping is quite the norm.

It was a happy weekend. We spent some time on Akro Corinth, enjoying the fine views and talking. Trying to be casual, I asked him if his grandfather had been a tall, handsome big man. He replied, 'No.' That had been his Uncle Frederikos, the first time I heard the name. His grandfather had been a short man. Ah.

At the time, I did not think too deeply about that strange encounter, but as the years passed, I understood that I had a role to play.

Our nearest village, Examilia, was founded during the Roman occupation as Hexamillion, the six mile fort. There had been walls, roads and forts and the tiny village of Examilia is all that remains of one of them.

Pleased with my interest, Stamos told me a wonderful story about his Uncle Frederikos which became a family joke. Years before, when he was visiting America, he was invited to some large function. As he entered, he was asked by the Master of Ceremonies, his name and home town.

'Frederikos Tripos, from Examilia.' (The name is pronounced Treepos, not Tripos/Trypos, as from Cambridge.) Whereupon the master announced in a great voice: 'Mr Fred-er-ick Try-pos, from Exa-Miles City!'

That scruffy little one-horse village being called a city. Splendid, and by no means the only reason why that excellent man will be remembered by many, for a very long time.

Chapter 3

Easter

Examilia is just a village strung along a small road. As with most country villages in Greece, it is a huddle of houses, apparently dumped at random, without any planning whatsoever. Built of whatever was to hand at the time, stone, or half stone, sun-dried mud bricks, and even a sort of lath and plaster. Inevitably there were some proud new monsters, evidence of the wealth accumulated by emigrants who had returned to their home village. As well as the huge new church, an edifice of wild expenditure and poor taste, there is the odd shop, bakery, kaféneon and petrol station. Most farmers live in the village, going out every day to their plots of land. In the past, it was too dangerous to live isolated on your farm. Safety in numbers I suppose. Generally, farms are not only small but are scattered, fields being here and there, and rarely in one whole piece. Perhaps the lack of daughters in the Tripos family accounted for their farm being intact, for the dowry system was generally the cause of splitting up of land. Unfortunately, only rarely do neighbouring farmers agree to simplify things for themselves and re-shuffle their plots.

Part of Examilia, a rocky hill scorched by sun, blasted by wind and utterly wretched, is the Rom village. They are not called Rom there, but that is what they call themselves, and of course, they are true Romany, for no one would marry into what is the poorest segment of society. The Greeks call them either gyftis, which they are not, or tzingania. They are hated, mistrusted and always in trouble with the law. It is quite something to be Rom, even if down-trodden and utterly despised by others, which they are. There are endless, many no doubt illegal, shacks on that rocky hill, having no sanitation or running water. Amongst rusting and rotting rubbish of every kind, hordes of gorgeous and grubby children run wild, often totally naked.

There is also, for obvious reasons, constant war between the villagers and the Rom, who have no conscience about thieving from outsiders, and even each other.

Above the farm, there is an area called Saint Theodore, where all that remains of a small village is a tiny Byzantine church. It must have been occupied for centuries for there is water there, and, after ploughing, I used to find flakes of obsidian in abundance, showing just how ancient.

On the maps, indeed even on our electricity bill, the area around the farm is known as, 'Pyrgos', in English, 'Tower'. I often wonder where it was. When I first arrived at the farm, there was the 'big' house, the ruined church of Saint Nikolaos and above that a long, low 'little' house known as the spitaki. Spiti = house, aki = little; spitaki, the little house. The Petropolous family had lived there when first they came down from the hills, and while their little house was being built.

Old photographs show that it was once a lovely country estate with vineyards which bullocks used to plough. There was even a small swimming pool, surrounded by rose arbours and with changing rooms, to accommodate the many important people who visited the estate in its heyday.

A large staff ran the perivoli. Some of the old people, delighted when I arrived with a Landrover, still spoke of Uncle Frederikos. After years of driving his little pony trap around, he was the first to have an automobile, like mine, a jeep. Although there is little evidence to show for it now, it had once been a gracious small estate.

There is a postcard of a very fine stone building, alas now gone, which was the distillery which had a large cellar. The rising and falling fortunes of the family were thus reflected. Stamos demolished the ruined distillery and converted its cellar into a large agricultural cistern. Not only did this enable him to irrigate the land, but it provided a wonderful, if often icy, swimming pool. On one side is a small platform, originally the square tank where the grapes were trodden. There, still visible, are two stone spouts from where the must, the juice, flowed.

On the south border of the farm there is a cave. When I first went there it was barely visible, the trunk of a huge, sick plane tree blocking the entrance, brambles barring the way. It wasn't until much later when we had a consignment of seed potatoes with nowhere to keep them, that we finally cleared it and it became a useful cool, dim, store-room.

At the back of the cave is a tunnel with water in it, said to run three kilometres into the hills. Reputedly, it was created in the second century by the Emperor Hadrian, that very organised campaigner. Apparently, wherever he travelled, he used to send his engineers ahead to make sure there would be sufficient water for his horses and entourage. They certainly did a good job, for after two thousand years there is still water there. Whether it is three kilometres long is questionable. Sadly, time and earthquakes make it very unstable, and I fear it is gradually collapsing, as have the many other caves along that ridge.

Those of us who live in areas of moderate rainfall can have no conception of how it is to be without water. A Greek farmer never asks another how many acres he has. Land is useless without water. Instead he asks the far more important question – 'Have you water?'

We were lucky, Stamos, had laboured mightily during his early years to dig out his wells, and in nine years out of ten, they provided ample water.

Even then, he was very afraid of the condition of the cave and tunnel, and never allowed his children to explore it. During my time however, he relaxed, and there were many daft and filthy excursions inside the tunnel, and though we did not learn much from our efforts, it was all great fun. It was only possible to go into the cave during dry years and even then there was amazing, slimy mud. Inevitably there were never enough torches to go around, or some idiot dropped his. The conditions were really ghastly, with very low, back-breaking headroom, bats, frogs, and even snakes. At one point the tunnel must lie directly under the road to Examilia, for we could hear the traffic thundering overhead.

It was then, a good water source and that must have been why the land at its mouth had always been a fine farm. Stamos told me that Hadrian, yes, the same one who built The Wall, actually camped on the land, although I do not know from where he had that information. Apparently the naughty ladies of what is now Ancient Corinth came out to entertain, if not Hadrian, who didn't care for ladies, certainly his men.

Water, being so precious in Greece, is the source of a great deal of friction. We were furious once, on going deep into the tunnel, to find that one of our neighbours was stealing our water. An illegal rash of little prefabricated houses on the ridge above, having no water of their own, have to buy it by tanker. One of these neighbours had gone to some considerable trouble to go down an ancient shaft, brick up the channel to pump up the water. It would have been different if he had asked. So we tied up the pipe, and waited till he arrived, furious, to ask properly.

One of the shocking, and in my opinion, immoral activities, rife in Greece, was the selling of water. Any little farm, however small, yet with a good well, could rig up a pump, hang an 'elephant's trunk' over the road, and tankers would draw up, fill up, pay, and push off. Easy money for some, a lower water table for the neighbours. Many was the time when people urged the generally destitute Stamos to sell water, and it was with pride I heard him hotly refuse.

'Water is a gift from God, we will give it, not sell it.' And give it he did. We ran a pipe under a culvert to the Petroplous, who despite being so close, had a mere trickle from their well and regularly had to buy tanker loads. The Rom sometimes came by with their rattletraps piled with barrels and cans of all sorts, and we filled them. Which brings me again to my motto, 'Goodwill is Pure Gold'. There was supposed to be legislation over the selling of water, but if there was, it was loose, and disregarded. We got to hate our several neighbours who sold their/our water, and got rich while we and others struggled.

One of our other neighbours did just this and prospered mightily. They built a smart new house. (Hideous). They bought a fine tanker and pick-up. We were considered the fools, they were smart. Could even be in the long run they were right, while we paupers were wrong.

When their daughter-in-law gave birth to her second daughter, Stamos' daughter Maria and I went across to visit. Sadly by the time we arrived, the baby, disabled in some way, had died.

'Well, thank God it was not a boy,' announced the grandmother, to my astonishment and Maria's furious indignation. They did have a son a couple of years later, and I remember watching incredulous, as the elder sister, his unwilling guardian, had her ear savagely tweaked, because the clumsy little boy had tripped and fallen.

The water in the cave is held back at the tunnel end by a low wall, a sump, a frequent pitfall to the drunken or unwary. So despite there being no barn, the cave came in useful as a place of storage and when the weather was poor, for parties.

My first winter, Stamos had his birthday, 12th December. Of course I must make him something, but what? He had no slippers,

31

so unknowing, I designed a pair for him, Pothies, from the word foot in Greek. Those first ones were awful. One long and slim, the other short and fat, but, what success! It was a hoot seeing Maria shuffling about in them, like a yeti. To this day I make Pothies, a huge success now perfected, and eventually a huge help with selling them for our survival.

My second spring, a chill Easter, there was a mean drizzle, so we carted everything to the cave, and planned to have our feast willy-nilly, but under cover.

Stamos was, as his uncle and his grandfather had been, an honorary consul for France, a position which occasionally took us to consular functions in Athens. Once, we met an extremely nice Russian couple and we invited them for the Easter weekend. Fearful that they would be shocked by our basic accommodation, I delved into my trunk, hung up some precious tapestries, and so did my best to cheer the place up.

Most of our kids were with us, including Maria, who was, like my boys, on holiday from school in England. Several other young people were there too, and we did our best to ignore the rain, and ate and drank as one does at Greek Easter. Suddenly Maria piped up, addressing our Russian guest.

'And what about Afghanistan?'

Oh, oh, oh. A stunned silence followed. I, horrified by her lack of manners, leaped to intervene. 'Have any of you seen the film on gorillas,' I blurted, 'and the way they reprimand their naughty children?'

I then proceeded to waggle my brow up and down furiously, trying to mimic the angry gorilla parents, and turned my ridiculous frowns on Maria. There was after all, an Iron Curtain at that time, quite apart from the fact that these were guests. Another astonished silence. Then the chivalrous Russian smiled in understanding, for he had two daughters.

'Ah, but we are amongst friends, Judith, are we not?'

And he and Maria proceeded happily to thrash out Afghanistan. Which brought us somehow on to Solzhenitsyn, which caused our poor guest to return to the correct path of damning him as unpatriotic. I, having just read Cancer Ward, found it was my turn to argue, for, I struggled to explain, surely it was the beauty of human nature, suffering and the literature which mattered?

'After all,' I blundered on, 'Do you suppose that Dickens was popular in his day writing about the terrible conditions of his time, in our country. Remember the poverty and hardship, children sweeping chimneys and so forth? Now, his work is classic.' Nice man, he listened, even agreed. Perhaps it made sense; anyway, it was a memorable experience.

I remember gazing through the smoke of the fire, thinking about this remarkable cave. Once, in prehistoric times, the trickle of water must have been the life source to the humans who lived here before us. They who hunted with stone, and scattered those shining flakes of obsidian everywhere. Possibly the first export/import business known to man. What did they trade I wonder? What did they give in exchange? Water? Food? The nearest source of obsidian is the island of Milos in the Cyclades, far across the sea. What boats did they travel in? Impressive.

Then who? The early Hellenes, worshippers of Demeter? The Romans, the Goths, the Franks and doubtless others. Waves upon waves of them. And then, lately, a Dark Ages, a mere five hundred years ago, the Turks. After that, my people, then the Germans, who had used our house as the officer's mess. Indeed we suspected that the occasional German tourists who drove up the drive, loo roll under arm, asking if they could use the bathroom, were showing their families where they had been billeted.

Yet here we still were, in that ancient cave, a party of many races, happily celebrating the Greek Orthodox Easter.

That first Easter, I knew little of all that. Having tidied my affairs in Athens, I moved in with Stamos and began preparing for the arrival of my three sons with a friend for the school holidays. I met his two sons and daughter who were quietly welcoming, if amused at their father's new lady friend. Despite my schoolgirl French, I remember it was the only way I could communicate with Maria, who was fifteen.

Not only was the farm a cheerless place, it was without life, for his children were living in Athens and there was not even a dog or cat. Probably I remarked on this, for one day the kindly Stamos told me to keep any scraps of food to give to a 'gentle dog' who visited sometimes.

Sure enough she eventually appeared, a very nervous young black and white bitch. Very afraid, she grovelled on her belly to the dish I set out for her. Ravenous, she gulped it down and looked at me expectantly, hoping for more. In a matter of days she had made her decision and moved in with us. I called her Brock, for her colouring and badger-like markings. She was a sweet creature, the first of many good canine friends we were to have on the farm over many years.

It was soon obvious how badly treated she had been, for one day I set about sweeping the area in front of the house and seeing me with the broom, she screamed and fell away yelping. Dropping it, I went to her, speaking gently, took her on my lap as I sat on the bare earth, and consoled her. When she had stopped shivering I quietly resumed my task, gently reassuring her all the while.

Just once more we had the same incident with a broom. Due to my shock at the state of the church, after removing the damp ikons to the house, I decided to clear it up. Hard work. First I trundled all the broken roof tiles in a barrow and dumped them in the potholes on the drive. Next I shifted the rotten old beams which Stamos cut up for the fire. Then I began sweeping. By now Brock was well established and quite obviously in pup. Content to follow me everywhere, she lay in a warm corner while I toiled. While loading up the barrow, I propped the broom up against the wall. Suddenly it fell over, as they do, but poor little sleeping dog woke screaming with such a fright, I had to do the reassurance act all over again.

Sitting on the warm uneven old paving stones I caressed her into calmness. The sun was high, the sky the deepest blue and the broken walls protected us from the chill wind. Little did I know, thank heaven, what the future would bring for me in that special place, the joys and sorrows. The baptisms, marriages and the funerals.

That first Lent, I was astonished at how very strict the people were with their dietary laws. If anyone came to the house, I was hard pressed to know what hospitality to offer them for they were permitted to eat so little. No meat or eggs. No milk or oil. Fish and vegetables, and plenty of that sustaining and delicious if fattening Halva. All this ritual stemmed from the hard times past when, end of winter, stocks were very low. Every smoky little house is turned out and well cleaned and whitewashed, destroying the hiding insects before they multiply with the spring. Minds are taken off rumbling stomachs by work and diligent church-going. So the crafty elders turned it into a religious fast, saving what little stocks were left, for the old, the weak and the children. Soon spring would come with its abundance. So, very clever.

That first Easter, the most important Orthodox feast of the year, was to me, a newcomer, a very special occasion. An early Easter that year, Stamos and I went alone to midnight service at a monastery in the hills. Tall and slim, I wore a long black coat to keep warm; definitely not a Greek peasant. We followed the throng inside where Stamos bought two candles and handed me one. He then left me, just like that. Shoved off, without a word. Not understanding, I watched, stricken, as he went to the other side of the church and left me alone. Hurting, I clutched my candle and wondered why. Could it be that he was embarrassed to be seen with a tall foreigner? Our relationship was so warm and loving, it was a real shock to find myself abandoned. Gradually, as the service began, I regained enough composure to start taking notice. Then I realised, fool that I was, that I was standing with the women. Stamos was on the right of the church with the men. Relief flooded over me as I remembered once

35

in an old church in London, doing the same thing. Segregation. No hanky-panky. Being the norm to him he simply had failed to tell me. I later found that most village churches stick to the segregation rule while the big town and city churches are more relaxed.

There was a great deal of incomprehensible chanting. Old men took turns to sing out, assisting the priests. A myriad of smells wafted over the crush of bodies. Incense, beeswax, cooking, sheep and moth balls. Everyone was smart in their best clothes, clutching candles of every size, some decorated and fancy, whispering quietly, moving around greeting friends and relatives.

Dramatically just before midnight the lights went out. A highly charged air of expectancy filled the dim church and then, an arm appeared at the altar with a single lighted candle,

'Xristos anesti!' (Christ is Risen.) Came the cry.

'Alithos anesti.' (He is risen indeed.) Everyone responded.

All new to me, it was beautiful to watch the wave of lights sweep back through the church, every hand eagerly reaching forward to light their candles. As a shining tide, it swept from the priest's hand, right through the church to the back, at last, reaching the west door and out.

It was then, and always shall be, a wondrous moment for me. As soon as my candle was alight, intent faces and gnarled, work-worn hands reached towards me. As I steadied my hand for them, not only the holy flame but a beautiful moment passed between us.

Where there had been darkness now was light. A glow of quiet satisfaction lit every face while the bells rang out with a fearful and joyful clamour.

Outside in the chill night again we extricated the van from the turmoil and set off for home. I nursed the lighted candle while Stamos drove precariously down the track between dozens of people, put-puts, donkeys and pick-ups. There seemed great joy and fellowship and we were assailed many times with shouts of 'Xristos anesti.'

So I had to quickly learn the response, 'Alithos anesti.'

We were hailed several times by figures in the middle of the road demanding we stop and hands reached through the van windows to re-light candles which had blown out in the cold wind. It was imperative they should arrive home with the Light of Christ, and make a smoky cross under the freshly white-washed door lintel. I was utterly charmed and touched by the whole experience.

Having done what I could to prepare what existed of the church for Easter, setting up candles and incense, vases of wild flowers, I was surprised to find that by the time I went to light them in the early morning, it had already been done.

In truth, I was not aware that I was being watched. Apparently they missed nothing, those excellent peasant neighbours who not only loved, but sorrowed for the lonely Stamos. Unknowingly, certainly not because I was either Greek Orthodox or actively religious, my action in cleaning up the ruined church, gave me a good press from the earliest days.

Over the coming years, it would be my happy task to get the house in order for Easter. Whitewashing everywhere, particularly about the front door so the smoky cross could be made, straight from the flame of midnight service. All alone, sadly, Stamos had done nothing. Even so, we managed a cross, the first of many we made together.

There was no need to be invited, Paska (Easter) is Open House day throughout Greece, so, first of many Easters, we walked across to our Petropolous neighbours. Here what had been a great fire was already burning low and very hot, and with beaming, pink faces, we were drawn near to take part.

I watched fascinated, and in time I too would learn, mostly from the Petropolous, how to do everything. First the small glasses of wine with much greeting. Then the red eggs, the ancient sign of re-birth, the spring festival. Metre long metal skewers were brought from the fire and curious charred morsels scraped off onto a platter. This was the first meat most had eaten in a month and they busily tucked in, with relish and much finger licking.

Kokoretsi, is made up of the offal and guts of the lamb or kid. (It seems that the idiots in Brussels, have now banned it.) Then, I gazed with typical, stupid Brit horror at the nameless bits and pieces and shuddered. Yet, on tasting, eyes closed, I found them delicious, if strange. Very tasty, burnt and crispy, it was a first time experience. Some pieces were like eating India-rubber. It never crossed my mind then that in future years I would be making kokoretsi, the whole gory, smelly works, and end up feeling very chuffed with myself for the achievement.

Quite an art, first the intestines have to be cleaned, which is really not a pleasant task. One end is fixed onto a running cold tap, and almost alive, it squirms and twists while the water pumps out the very smelly contents. Only when the water runs really clear is it done. The whole lot is then dumped into a large bowl full of vinegar-laced water.

All the offal, the lot, is cleaned and cut into bite sized pieces and mixed in a big bowl of oil, garlic and generous seasoning. The skewers having been well cleaned are finished off with a good rubbing from a whole lemon. A communal effort, using hands, a slippery, garlicky mess, the pieces are carefully threaded onto the long skewers. Liver, heart, lights, and so on, and all over again, till the skewer is full. When the skewers are tightly packed and ready, the intestines are drained and with much shouting, the next important stage is begun. While one holds each end of a skewer, it is twisted, while someone else bales out the slippery intestines. The skewers are slowly turned so the translucent tubing is wrapped round and around, up and down, crissing and crossing, till a tight, long, parcel is completed. SO much work and so clever. Nothing is wasted, and everything is delicious. I do not doubt for one moment that this traditional fare will last far longer than the ridiculous bureaucracy of Brussels.

When the fire was well down, a mere heap of very hot, grey ashes, the sacrificial lamb was ceremoniously carried out of the house where it had been kept, well draped in sheeting against flies. A long iron bar with a cross piece, called the soufla, skewered the whole lamb, and had the backbone firmly wired onto it. I would learn that stitched inside were whole lemons, lots of salt, pepper, garlic and origani. Carefully, it was set high above the ashes on two forked stakes. Then the turning began, with someone dipping a rag tied on the end of a long pole into the oil and lemon mix to dribble it over the turning carcass, to keep it moist.

Now and again the stakes would be hammered down a little to put the soufla closer to the heat. The ashes were stirred up gently. Everyone had a turn with the handle, shielding their faces from the heat with whatever. This is the time for the elders to wield their knowledge and everyone listens to them and jumps to it. What looks like a simple task is indeed quite the contrary. It is specialist work, passed down through generations with unconscious pride.

Music blared. Friends and relatives stopped by for a drink, a bite. Red eggs were happily smashed together. The traditional Easter cookies handed out, and when we left we were always the recipients of bags full. They are soft and sweet, using the spring flush of eggs and butter, and they are called Koulouria, I think. Because the word is so similar to the rag rugs, kourelou, I ever get them muddled.

Once in Athens in a taxi, I suddenly felt so hungry, I asked the driver if he could find some Kourelia. He was perplexed, but thankfully kind, and by the time we had sorted out my mistake, we were both laughing. I was lucky that time, for they were not always so nice. Once I was put out of a taxi because the driver thought I was American, as there was, for some reason or the other, strong anti-American feeling at that time. I was so shocked by his ugly aggression, and so unable to defend myself, I gladly got out. So whether kourelou or koulouria, the biscuits were delicious and, kept in a tin, lasted for ages after Easter.

The men concentrated on the roast lamb while the women rushed around attending to the guests. A long bed sheet-covered table was set out with plates and forks. Knives were barely used, but a few were laid out to be shared, otherwise fingers would do. The table, suddenly impressive, groaned with plates of fetta, bowls of olives, terrama salata and the finely sliced early spring Cos lettuces, doused in oil and lemon juice. Not least was the wonderful home-made sour dough bread, specially decorated for the day, baked with red eggs pressed into the glazed top and smothered with sesame seeds.

Finally, when the lamb was deemed so perfect it seemed ready to drop into the fire, huge tins of lemon baked potatoes came out of the little beehive oven.

What a lovely introduction to Greek Easter. With the risk of becoming boring, I have to say again how blessed we were to have such excellent neighbours.

I was once reprimanded for not knowing how to do something.

'Did your mother not teach you anything?' the indignant dame hurled at me.

'My mother is a foreigner, she does not know.' I meekly defended myself.

'Then,' she was determined I was hopeless, 'ask your mother-in-law?'

'She is a very old lady.'

'Well then, ask your sisters-in-law!' she hammered on, irate at the stupid young woman and determined to have the last word.

I wondered if in fact my city sister-in-law did know any better than I. Then I had a brainwave.

'I do have a wonderful neighbour,' I offered.

'That's it then,' she yelled, 'ask your neighbour!' Jubilant, battle won, she left me. So Angiliki Petropolou became my mentor. I did learn from her, in many matters over many years. But that first Easter I was not to know that. I was simply delighted with, and grateful to her, who had welcomed and entertained us so royally.

Chapter 4

Trip to the Mani

The children arrived, my three sons and Lucy, daughter of a friend in England. Together with Stamos's second son and daughter, an attractive pair of seventeen and fifteen, we set off, to the Mani, en famille. We had gladly accepted the offer of the charming house of my friends. A simple village house, built on a solid rock foundation, it had barest amenities and few rooms, each one reached from outside. Indeed one bedroom, which had originally housed the beasts, was dug out of solid rock, as a cave. It was wonderful. The garden, such as it was, had great bowls scooped out of the rock, presumably originally for food and water for the animals. Situated high above the sea, the views were impressive, the sunrise and sunset never forgotten. Early mornings with our cups of coffee, we watched the tiny fishing boats chug out to their secret places where they anchored and sat all day. In the evenings at sundown, nursing our glasses of wine, we watched them chug in, leaving a huge silver wake behind them. Occasionally we went down to the coast villages to buy fish, but being foreigners, found ourselves, even Stamos the Greek, last in the queue. I was intrigued with the weird and wonderful selection of strange fish which everyone happily ate. Some tavernas sported clothes lines draped with octopus drying in the sun, but they were then quite outside of my culinary skills. Despite being a grossly over-fished sea, there are fine, big octopus waiting to be speared by the patient. Most sold in taverns are imported. The traditional way to tenderise them is to beat them against a rock. Stamos assured me that many we saw being so thrashed, had only recently been thawed out. Imported from who knows where. Traditions and keeping up the pretence they had just been caught, had to be retained for the ignorant tourists.

So we happily idled away the days while the children got to know each other. Meanwhile Stamos and I worked at providing entertainment and large and regular meals for our brood.

Below us stood a few Mani towers, some fine, all too many in ruins. Evidence of the stormy past of feud and strife when stout doors were locked and barred and boulders were tumbled from the ramparts onto any would-be pillager.

In appearance large, inside the towers the rooms are small, due of course to the immensely thick stone walls. Generally there are three rooms, one above the other with a simple internal wooden stair. Usually, there is a good sized kitchen cum family room tacked on. Wonderfully romantic and wildly impractical, I dreamed how lovely it would be to own one.

Nothing had changed for centuries, and even little has changed since I first went there. A few paths are now smooth and cemented, but most, winding through the steep villages, are ankle-breaking meanders of loose stone. There is stone everywhere, and only recently has the concrete block started taking over. The old houses cling, higgle-piggle precariously to ledges, nowadays often sliding in confusion to melt back into nature.

Some of the churches are filled with exquisite Byzantine paintings, done by some long-forgotten Italian prisoners, who served their time centuries ago by going from village to village, there to be fed and leave their gifted mark.

Whole flocks of goat or sheep used to rush through the narrow lanes like the wind before a gathering storm. Astonished to see strangers, they would stop dead, stand stock-still, gawping at us. We meanwhile, equally shocked, scrambled out of their way as best we could, scratching hands and legs on the steep banks, so they tore past. Many of them went into the mountains all day without a shepherd. Instead, they had dogs, small, kindly mongrels, who simply grew up with the flock and spent the days in the hills with them acting as guides and guardians.

Intrigued, I watched a flock mustering for milking while the little dogs looked expectantly at their master for their supper. Amazed I saw them gulp down the contents of their tins. Scraps of bread were mashed up with myzithera, a fresh cream cheese and, incredibly, dried figs. No doubt they got meat scraps from the kitchen if there were any and certainly they must have foraged in the hills, for they looked very healthy.

I love myzithera, a fresh, rich, spring-time cheese, which years later I learned to make simply with boiled milk and lemon juice. Utterly delicious straight, it makes a wonderful desert served with honey. Apparently Mistras, the last Byzantine city in the Peloponese, took its name from the cheese. Not the other way around. Or so I was told.

Due to their quiet lives and lack of reading, the village people remember everything and everyone. It is a joy to greet old friends after many years, who seem not to change one jot, their weather-beaten faces wreathed with smiles of welcome. Their warmth and generosity is as well known as their shrewdness.

It was very pleasant to sit in the platea in the afternoon and watch the grandmothers making straw braid which would be made into good sun hats. All dressed in faded and patched black, scarves tied over their skimpy plaits, they enjoyed working, chatting in the late sunshine. Their work-worn hands deftly twisted the golden lengths of straw, the braid grew slowly in a long curl, to be carefully rolled and tied. A hat maker would call every month bringing new straw and after his careful measuring, under their intense scrutiny, would pay for their braid. So these old ladies, all widowed, earned a little extra money to supplement their tiny incomes. True, their needs were few, their lives being so simple. Some had a goat or sheep for milk and a few hens. A tiny area, well wired against the many four-legged opportunists about, would provide some vegetables. They might have an orange or lemon tree too, but their main income came from their share in family olive groves.

Years after that first Easter, I bought ten dusty postcards from a village shop along the coast. Thinking that they might be pleased to see what I was sending abroad, I showed them to the old ladies. For there on the colourful card they sat, braiding the straw. Oh dear, oh dear. Little did I realise what I was doing for they immediately set up a pitiful lament. Stabbing at the cards with worn fingers, kissing them, crossing themselves, pointing again at the picture and wailing afresh. Poor old things. I had ignorantly inflicted such a sudden and unexpected event in their quiet lives. It took me shocked moments to understand what it was all about.

Firstly they had never seen the card, taken years before. Secondly, obviously and alas, several of their number were now departed. It was embarrassing for me to have provoked such sorrow, and I too was sad. Of course I lost all my cards to them, clutched tragically to spare breasts, the day had lost its brightness. As one, they left, mourning as they returned to their homes, probably showing their cards to anyone by the way, with fresh lament. No doubt since then, those cards, probably the only photographs ever taken of the old ladies, are set up in their little houses in the place of honour, the corner with the ikons and lighted lamp.

It seemed an idyllic life, and we were envious of their simplicity. I do, however, have two jarring memories of that first wonderful stay in Mani.

One was outside a taverna. Wanting to learn everything, I watched a woman making tzatziki. I was surprised, seeing her hands right in the big bowl, mixing the yoghurt, cucumber and garlic. I suppose, feeling for the Greek words I must have mouthed to myself.

'With the hands.'

As if I were criticising her, she turned on me and spat.

'Well, what do you expect, that I use my feet?'

Foolishly I was shocked and hurt by her response, for I had not intended criticism. I realised that she must have been exhausted and all she was doing was having a much needed sit. For when I came years later to be working as hard as she, preparing food for tourists to earn our living, I too knew about heat and exhaustion, and that it did not take so much stirring to make tzatziki.

The other time was more shocking, and totally out of character with Maniots. We were happily, sight-seeing, just being tourists, when we saw a villager walking along and stopped to offer him a lift. Continuing our stop/start journey, he suddenly announced as we returned from inspecting yet another ancient church that he had to leave us on some pressing business, and rushed off. I soon realised that a then large sum of money had disappeared from my bag. The equivalent of half a month's salary of say, a bank clerk. Not only was it quite a loss, we were all upset. The man was a neighbour of our hosts. What, if anything should we do? When questioning another neighbour, we understood he was a card player, and a loser. Not much liked by anyone, most of his family had gone to America and I suppose, knowing his weakness, did not as was usual, send him gifts of cash. We did nothing.

Each time I see him, even now, I consider asking him for a can or two of olive oil, then thanking him for that old debt re-paid. For he owns olive groves and I love the Mani oil. But so far, of course, I have not found the courage.

Here, I first met the charming old Byzantine custom of plates being embedded in the church walls. Some wonderful, ancient plates are still in situ, the ones protected from the weather almost perfect and brilliant in their colours and design. Apparently this was to indicate to strangers that no one would be refused hospitality at that village, a sacred duty as it were.

There is a story about a young back-packer, who years ago, roamed into the interior of the Mani which has the reputation of being none too friendly to strangers. Unable to converse, the young man took out his tin plate and using mime, asked where he could find a meal. Not only did the villagers not respond, they simply went their way leaving the visitor hungry. Bewildered, he gave up but found a well and at least drank the good water. With night, he settled down near the well, and slept.

When in the early morning he woke, he found that he was surrounded by plates of food. Each plate was covered with another and a goodly stone placed on top for safety. Gratefully he ate. Yet when he tried to thank the people who came to the well, they ignored him. Bewildered but grateful, the young man washed up the plates, and leaving them neatly by the well, he went on his way.

Whether or not this story is true I know not, but it prompted me some years later, when we restored the little church at the farm, to put my best loved, if no longer perfect, very fine English Delft plate, in the apex at the east end. Younger for sure, than the original church, nonetheless, it looks very fine. It was ever my policy to offer food to anyone who came by, and never to refuse anyone hospitality. Having learned this during my first Mani visit, I felt this sealed my commitment to Greece, by adopting that beautiful old custom.

Having been brought up in the East, I had heard jackals before. Yet it was such a surprise to sit out in the evening on the vine-clad terrace and hear them howling on the slopes below. Quite eerie and frightening, although in fact, they are timid scavengers, creatures who would not normally come near or harm humans.

The clear skies and the brilliant and beautiful stars were astonishing. As clean as was the atmosphere, so too was the sea. Cold, it was crystal clear, every pebble on the white marble sand of sea bed, vivid.

Such contrasts! Clear, pollution-free heavens. Crystal clear sea. Yet all about us sadly, the human animals destroyed that lovely place with their filth and carelessness. Each home was spotless, swept daily and mopped. Yet, directly out on the stony paths lay evidence of rubbish hurled out of the windows for generations. Vegetable waste generally found takers, it was the indestructible stuff which was the problem.

A favourite way to dispose of any unwanted larger object was to find an isolated place along the road, stop the van and hurl. As bees to a honey pot, the dumping ground soon became well known, for in no time at all, it was a proper rubbish tip.

Inside the villages, domestic waste simply flew out of the window. Rusting tin cans, razor blades, plastic and glass bottles. Scraps of rusting old iron, and shards galore, off the roofs and from the tables. Occasional animal bones too large to have been eaten by anything never decayed. It was a veritable minefield waiting to cut or maim any hurrying leg or un-shod foot. To us silly Westerners, it was quite shocking. When I asked about it, shoulders would raise, hands would spread.

'What to do?' A favourite Greek expression.

Actually there was a basic rubbish collection, for I once saw a splendid fat man atop a huge mule, his wooden saddle well hung with plastic bags of refuse. Alas, it was just a small gesture toward keeping the village clean, for we later spotted him hurling his bags into a ravine from a bridge. How to explain to ignorant folk that the stream at the bottom which ran at some times in the year would also be polluted?

How can we even begin to understand these simple people and their way of life? In truth, except for those who had been abroad, they are as mystified by us and our funny ways as we are of them. They had been so wretchedly poor for so very long, rearing their children was the one important factor of their lives. Food. There had been so little waste, because there had simply been so little. Now suddenly, there was more of everything, which meant more waste, and what to do with it?

Being accustomed to running water, sanitation, built in loos and toilet paper, what could we know of isolated village life? When I asked a village woman if I could use her loo she took me outside at the back and pointed to a square of ground, that was it, she had no loo. They had none of these things until very recently, and for lack of anything else, used a stone to wipe themselves unless water was to hand. As in many poor countries of the world, the dogs did the cleaning up. Thanks to the European Union, there are now magnificent great wheely bins everywhere.

One of the lovely recycling crafts the women enjoyed was weaving the Kouleria, the rag rugs. I can well imagine how they felt, to escape the heat and back breaking toil of the fields to create something. To actually sit down for a change, no sweat, no aches and pains, what joy. The apothiki, (store-room), is usually under the house opening onto the path, and light, air and company would come in through the open door. This too is changing, the young women preferring to buy ghastly and tasteless rugs, despising the home-made. Fortunately there are still the elders who take pleasure in making something out of nothing.

It was always a delight to track down the click-clacking of a loom, peer into the open door, find her in the gloom, give and take a warm greeting, then settle down to watch. Always pleased to have company, the mothers and grandmothers still provide these colourful, hard-wearing rag rugs which adorn every peasant house. They wash and wear for years, and are so easy to make. Woven on home-made looms, which resemble a four poster bed, they need more space than the Scandinavian uprights. Almost always masterpieces of make do, they are a 'grandfather's axe' indeed.

'This is my grandmother's loom,' a woman might say. 'I believe when my mother had it, she put new combs and treadles on. Then my elder sister replaced the cross-bars and recently, my husband made new uprights for they were rotten and he made me a better seat.' I would gaze at the contraption in awe.

'Yes,' she says, with an almighty thwack, as she bangs the weave tightly, 'it is my grandmother's loom.

So I would sit and chatter, delighting to learn and perhaps wind some 'shuttles' for her. Simplicity itself, about two foot lengths of bamboo, they were twisted with lengths of rag strip, round and round tightly, up and down, not unlike the Easter kokoretsi skewers. Sorting through her pile of shuttles, she would choose her colours, press hard on the pedal, then deftly thread it through the warp before making the satisfactory bang. So at least old clothes were usefully re-cycled and not hurled out of the windows to trip the unwary.

I remember my mother telling me of her New England childhood. Sitting on the floor playing with the precious and colourful scraps while the women made patchwork quilts for a special occasion. Economy bore forth so much beauty and satisfaction the world over. The pity is that all too few of our daughters know or want to learn, so sadly, we lose it.

In the past in Greece, the women in every family would collect old clothes to prepare rugs for the dowry for a forthcoming wedding. Just as for those magnificent, North American quilts. In the villages, where so many are in constant mourning, there is a great deal of black, which in fact makes the rugs rather handsome. Certainly they don't need so much washing as the pale colourful ones now churned out by machine for tourists. Nowadays, the idle can buy strips, ready torn, rolled into big balls and sold by weight. It is one of many things sold, along with a wide selection of necessities for village life, off the back of trucks, which come around regularly. Parked in the platea, the loudspeaker noisily announces its arrival. Setting up a distinct and nasal echo in the hills, which no one in the village can fail to hear, with what is for sale today.

Later on, I had my own magnificent loom, inherited from a kind artist friend, and on which I taught many young people the rudiments of weaving.

The hygienic disposal of waste was then, and probably in outlying villages still is, a huge problem. I suppose one might say that the rats which abound, feed the many cats. It is the modern appliances which don't go back to nature which are the main problem, but, here's hoping that the EU can also solve this one eventually.

I always give lifts, being fortunate to have a vehicle. A couple who farmed a tiny plot on our borders, lived in town and came out several times a week to work. On seeing the wife, well laden with what I thought was produce being taken home, I drew up and offered her a ride. Gratefully she clambered in and we drove off. After a short distance she asked me to stop which although surprised, I did. On opening her door, she then threw out two of the plastic bags into the ditch.

'What are you doing?' I asked perplexed.

"I am throwing my rubbish.' she announced.

Horrified, I glared at her. 'Just because you live in town where you have a daily collection, you do not care about making the country filthy and unhygienic.'

Puzzled, she gazed at my indignant face.

'Neither,' I waded on, 'do you think about us, who live here.' Now it was her turn to look perplexed.

'But I always throw my rubbish there.'

So it was, incredulous and livid, I forgot myself completely and made one of the very few peasant enemies I had in Greece.

'Out!' I told her. 'Out with your rubbish, you dirty woman.' (Oh dear.)

Uneducated people cannot change their ways of a lifetime in a hurry, it is now up to educating the youth.

The Mani is a favourite tourist place for many nationalities despite the narrow roads. Indeed, whole villages in the hills have been taken over by Germans. On the one hand, they have surely saved many wonderful houses which might well now be a pile of rocks. Certainly they spend money on materials and give much work to locals. Unfortunately, some of them look like a little Tyrol, when they could have tried to preserve the best of the local architecture. With their out-of-place and fancy shutters and iron-work, their houses can only be described as 'twee'. If only everyone could follow the lead of, say Patrick Leigh Fermor, and lovingly create as he has over many years, a beautiful, gracious, mellow, and entirely fitting house, even if a bit Italian.

Stamos and I were once at a taverna above the sea, which happily still exists when, unusually for him, he drank too much, always a disaster. Casting his eye about the other diners, he noted that most of them were German. Forgetting his manners, and that indeed his own grandfather had been a German, he held forth, loud and clear, in English.

'They have to know,' he raised his voice glaring at the many young people around us. 'They think we have forgotten. We will never forget.' Crescendo.

'Stamo, Stamo,' I entreated under my breath, horribly embarrassed. 'Please lower your voice, and remember, they are only children.' Which of course, fell on deaf ears.

'Children or not children,' he carried on furiously, 'They have to understand, they must know, how much we hate them. We are only interested in their Deutschmarks, nothing else.'

I, who knew so little of the sorry past, was ashamed and even now, when at Kaliopi's, remember that awful incident.

It was, that first time, a happy little holiday for our two families staying in that idyllic place, that charming old house. It figured many times in our lives over the years, and, it was there, on that first visit, that Stamos asked me to stay with him. In that cosy kitchen, sitting at the wooden table under rough rafters and the golden, bamboo lined ceiling, I confided in my sons, asking them for their opinions. Dear boys, grinning, amused, they cheerfully gave me their blessing, for they liked Stamos and recognised our happiness. My fate was sealed.

Chapter 5

Wives and Mistresses

After the kids had returned to their various schools, we were alone again and blissfully happy, working together to restore the farm.

Now of course I had known about Stamos' wife Eleni. There was some sort of mystery there. She was rarely mentioned, and then in hushed tones and she was obviously not accepted by Stamos' family. I had in fact met her briefly in Athens some time before meeting Stamos, when we had made immediate and warm contact.

Although I was rarely alone in the house, I did sometimes answer the phone. It could after all be a call for me, from friends in Athens, or family abroad. All too often however, a dramatic sigh would drift across the line, before, with a bang, being abruptly cut off. No word was ever spoken. I told Stamos about it, wondering who on earth it was and his casual reply was, not to answer the phone. Eventually, thoroughly irritated, I asked him again who it was, and, the rat, he confessed it was – 'An old mistress, from the past'.

Well she didn't sound so 'old', or indeed 'past'. So I tackled him. It turned out that the poor woman had indeed been his mistress, right until he met me.

'But,' my beloved explained pathetically, 'I have been trying to get rid of her for a very long time.' (Oh yeah.)

Ever the feminist, I was annoyed with him, on her behalf and my own. I told him he must go to see her and break off their relationship, properly and kindly. But he could not, and I do not think his guilt ever allowed him to completely. For, poor woman, she had virtually given her life to him, never married, was always there for him. She had even gone to France to learn French, with the dream she would one day be the wife of the Honorary French Consul of the Corinthia. I felt deeply sorry for her, despite my irritation. What it came to, was that she was not good enough for him socially; that she would be unacceptable to his family, (as was his first wife, even if for different reasons). So he had used her, the old, old, story.

It came to the crux, when one day, rather nervously, Stamos announced that, 'Jenny was coming for tea.'

(Tea!) I was incredulous. Why should I entertain this unfortunate woman for tea, or indeed anything? She was nothing to do with me, indeed my little contact with her had only been unpleasant. Long dramatic sighs, and banging down of the phone. Tea indeed! I considered just going home to Britain, for really I could not cope with this silly man and all his nonsense. Then I thought,

'No.' I would pay a long overdue visit to my good friends in Athens. Then, finally with his pleadings decided that,

'Yes.' I was the mistress of the house, I would not be driven out, I would stay and entertain her.

'Please Judaki,' he appealed, another nonsense. 'Put some rose on your lips.'

Said 'Roze', of course.

The impertinence. First he expected me to entertain his (ex?) mistress, then to make up my face for her, something I very rarely did. In truth, I did not want to meet her, fearing she might be a beautiful, sophisticated and articulate woman. It was their affair, not mine. I considered making a cake, then got out a packet of biscuits. Why the hell should I go to any trouble for this ridiculous tea party?

Through no fault of her own, she arrived very late, causing Stamos to be a bundle of nerves, a pacing lion. In those days the inter-city buses were wrecks, constantly breaking down. Often if pushing by the passengers failed to get it going again, eventually they might abandon it to hitch hike to their destinations. So the poor woman arrived exhausted and frazzled and I only felt sorry for her.

I need not have worried, for, she was hardly a beauty. Small and dumpy, her black hair, streaked with white, was severely parted down the middle and fell in curtains to her shoulders. I never once saw her eyes, for she wore enormous, round, bluebottle sun glasses, all the time.

In sympathy, and true British style, I offered her a cup of tea.

'If,' she retorted in French, 'I want a cup of tea, I shall make it myself.'OH! Right.

Well, if that was going to be her attitude, it would make things a lot easier for me. I made tea and took it out to the side terrace where she and Stamos joined me. The dear dog Brock had produced puppies, and the one we had kept was a splendid fat golden roly-poly which I nursed on my lap. Very recently, my sister and I had been to see the film, The Sting, and I had Scot Jopling's jaunty music playing. To this day when I hear it, I recall that silly afternoon.

It was really very embarrassing. Gazing west at the ever fascinating mound of Akro Corinth, I steeled myself to be polite. Without coming up for breath, she launched into what a dreadful man Stamos was. She had to tell me. I had to know. Dishonest. A liar. Egoistical. Spoilt by his family. Lazy. On and on. Sin after sin. I got the gist of it, with some cheerful, occasional interpretation from Stamos. It was a hoot. Not only was my French poor, hers was, if possible worse, being heavily accented. Yet, she told me dramatically, shoulders raised, hands spread, that despite all his faults, she loved him. Well

I knew all about that, even if, in those early days, I did not yet know any of his faults. Eventually it ended, the French farce, and she went home.

It did not end there either. Now and again she would get some English speaking friend to ring me up to harangue me. Poor things, what a boring friend to have. I tried hard to be patient, for my sympathy is always with the woman. Sadly for her, and happily for me, it was me he loved, even if his guilt caused him to keep up some sort of a relationship with her right to the end. She certainly never gave up. Over the years I came to understand that very many Greeks had lovers and mistresses as an accepted fact.

If Stamos had not introduced her to his family, he did me. I met his elderly and charming parents, his sister and various other relations. Old though his father was, he recognised me as British and invited me, most courteously in perfect English, 'to be seated.'

As they had, one and all, totally disapproved of my predecessor, naturally they must have been wondering what Stamos had brought home this time. Not only did they observe me carefully, I was amused by some ill concealed, indeed blatant scrutiny, of my jewellery. Surprised to get this from reputedly educated people, I did not let on that I recognised it.

My pearls were not real, real, they were cultured and rather good. Whatever I had was real, certainly not of great value, genuine, if not top notch, but never junk. I did not jangle and flash as a Christmas tree, preferring unusual, interesting pieces rather than investment. Slightly puzzled, I suffered the obvious assessment of my standing without saying a word to Stamos.

When however, he asked me in a peculiar, rather apologetic way, if my parents owned a car, I was so astonished, I burst out laughing. Then reality hit me and I just thought it pitiful. Stamos, who didn't even own a suit, wanted to know if my parents had a car. (They had of course, and when they had been younger, owned two, which I did not mention.) It shocked me, from that lovely man, this superficial valuation of people. It was during my early days in Greece and I had much to learn.

Another relative, who on first meeting I thought lovely, questioned me carefully on my family. Well how to explain to anyone the mish-mash of a colonial background? An American mother, British father, with fascinating and diverse origins. Who would be interested in those incomprehensible and far flung blood lines, respectable, intriguing, if not particularly grand? It would take me years to understand that you must lie at all costs according to the situation. Obviously my truthful rendering of my roots were not up to scratch according to her book, for sadly, she never came up to my expectations. Really it was a disappointment, for I liked her.

So snobby Britain wasn't the only place to have a stratified society. Nonetheless I would learn soon enough, that the most worshipped god of Greece, is Mammon. I found it ugly then and even worse now.

When, much later, we did get married, the pestilential ex-mistress announced that I had married Stamos for his money. Well aware by then that he had nothing, I forgot for a moment that by his being Greek, my humour would not appeal. I foolishly put on a jolly act, rushing about the room, looking under cushions, in cupboards saying, 'Where, where is it then? Where is all that money I have married you for, quick, tell me where you hide it, show me, because I haven't seen any of it yet.'

Oh, oh, oh. How could I be so foolish? That was not a clever joke. Although I had been told that Greeks are short on humour, I was yet to understand it. My shocked, very Victorian husband made it quite clear, that he was, not amused.

Years later, it was my turn to be shocked when the tables turned and one of the sons told me that his father had married me for my money. Knowing to this day how much he loved me, I nonetheless, in retrospect, do wonder if in part, it was true.

A powerful god that. No doubt, I thought again, all the results of a harsh history.

Another time, again with differences in culture, I was really offended. I mentioned playing tennis, which we did a lot of in England. For probably the first time, Stamos was actually rude to me, very scathing. Having spent years in France, where only the wealthy played tennis, he thought I was putting on some grand act. He should have known me better, so now it was my turn to be tough.

I explained in a hard voice, that as tennis had been invented in England, playing it is available to all and anyone. Not only did we automatically play at school, most towns and even villages had courts, as well as at private homes. It was not reserved for the wealthy. Perhaps I had taken democracy for granted. I certainly had thought it existed where it was supposed to have originated.

So the early days were perplexing, there were often crossed wires. Trying to understand our different cultures was hard. There was so much I liked about Greece, yet I found the so-called educated people very complicated. I had supposed Greece civilised due to its ancient history. In fact it is so ancient, their history so harsh, that only now are they re-emerging from a chrysalis.

Spring turned to summer, and I realised I must return to Britain to tidy up my affairs. It was agreed that Maria should follow me a week later, to spend a month's holiday with us, her first visit.

Stamos and I parted with love and the promise that I would return at the end of summer. He was planning to sell his van, to pay his taxes, so I intended to bring back a Landrover and trailer with as much of my furniture as possible.

As soon as I got back to England, Antony my eldest, just seventeen, took off alone for Greece on a push bike. I was in a terror for him, feeling that if there had been two going, it would have felt safer. But no, he was determined to go solo.

Maria arrived, and to my great surprise, gave me a letter from Stamos. In it, he asked me to put her into school in England, stating the sum of money he could afford to pay. I was astonished. All this had happened in the one week since my departure and being the end of term, it would be quite a task. It did not occur to me to argue with the plan so I set about it quickly.

However, it was not to be easy, for Maria refused to go to my old boarding school in Sussex where she was offered a place. Far too independent, in her own eyes, too grown up to board with a whole lot of kids, she totally rejected the idea. True, she had been obliged to grow up very quickly by lack of parental care.

When, a couple of times we had visited the children in Athens, I had been shocked to find them very much on their own, with what was now a growing knowledge of the domestic situation in Greece.

The fifteen year old Maria was expected to cook, wash up, clean, et al, for her two elder brothers. This is how it was. No question of Maria doing the cooking while the brothers took it in turns to clean the flat and wash up the dishes.

It came to me slowly that Maria was the most clever and logical of the children, something which always so pleased Stamos when I told him. Naturally, and having her own studies to do, she refused point blank to do everything, despite much pressure and unpleasantness.

This is how, I assumed she had, in one short week, persuaded her father to let her go to England in school, to escape an intolerable situation.

She told me she ate mostly bought cheese pies and what she could scrounge from friend's homes as her allowance was so small. I told Stamos that he should arrange for large baking tins of food to be delivered from a nearby taverna to his children several times a week. Nothing happened. So Maria seized her chance and escaped to England where we celebrated her sixteenth birthday, giving her new clothes and fun. It was a happy time for her with so many new experiences and freedom from pressure.

On the one hand I wanted so much to please her, for already I was feeling some strain with being a step-mother. On the other hand I was filled with anxiety at leaving her alone in a foreign land without any close family. I wanted her to enjoy being young, worry-free, busy and as she was clever, in a scholastic situation where she would blossom. But no, she wanted to have her own-bed sit in a student house, which she had eventually, and inevitably she became desperately lonely so as I feared, it turned out a disaster. Reluctantly, I had to acknowledge that she might not fit in with the other girls in boarding school. Already at fifteen, Maria was a habitual smoker, something which horrified me and certainly would not have been acceptable in school. Also, I had been told, almost casually, that she had been in a serious relationship for 'some years'. So no, perhaps she was right, perhaps she would not fit in. Yet it was she who had wanted to leave Athens and go to finish her schooling in England. It was not at all an easy task which I had been given.

Greece seemed a country of many contradictions. The country girls had to be virgins at their weddings. Essential. If a girl lost her virginity before marriage she was black listed. (Unless, which did happen of course, to the chap she was engaged to marry.) No one wanted her. Soiled goods.

Yet I was given to understand that most of the Athenian friends of Stamos' children were sleeping around from their early teens. Added to which, instead of being sensible using contraception, they had abortions. So, I was an old fashioned body, and yes, I was deeply shocked as well as being concerned as to what they were doing to their poor bodies.

I put it all down to hard working parents always trying to satisfy the material demands of their children. They had no time, or were too exhausted, to attend to their emotional and physical needs. Stamos insisted that it was perfectly acceptable, indeed admirable. The younger, the better. In his opinion, IF, the children did NOT have relationships so young, then they, 'Had a Problem.'

My response was, that neglected and un-loved children sought what they understood was love, from wherever they could find it. Their problem was lack of parental love, now that was their real Problem. (Which led to plenty more.)

Stamos would however, hear none of it and told me that because I came from a cold country I could not understand a thing! We, all people from the North, had a problem. Ridiculous. Listening from the side-lines, my eldest son, who mixing with the young people, clearly understood the situation far better than I, piped up.

'Perhaps having problems is a hobby.'

In my book, promiscuous children often resulted from poor parenting. It was all very confusing. Someone told me it was due to the climate. Well, didn't the peasants have the same climate? Worried and baffled, I let Maria have her own way, probably to both our regrets, as things turned out.

On arrival, her entire wardrobe consisted of one dress and several pairs of jeans, so it was fun shopping together for pretty things. Kitting her out with uniform and an entire wardrobe, I carefully kept all the bills to present to Stamos on my return. But, I actually just did not know Stamos at all. A very spoilt only son of a well to do family, there had always been someone to pick up the bills. Wonderful, charming, generous, he had always been so indulged, he never learned to shoulder his responsibilities. Never, ever, which I did not know then.

Having had parents who started their married life during the Depression in the States, this was out of my experience. They had instilled in me never to borrow or owe, and to always pay bills on the nail. Having asked me to do so much for him and his daughter, Stamos now simply turned aside from paying up. I had my own children, why should I pay for his? We were not even married. It was the first of very many times, loving him, hating unpleasantness, that I made the enormous mistake of letting him get away with it. There seemed to be no alternative.

It took Antony thirty hard days to bike to Greece. He had drawn a straight line, and simply tried to adhere to it.

One day, driving through Sussex with Maria and my two younger sons, we passed a laden cyclist and I determined that we must give him hospitality. We did, somewhat to his astonishment. He climbed into the camping van and had a meal, and we explained about Antony cycling, now probably, through Yugoslavia. An American, our visitor was very pleased and tucked in. It was a happy interlude.

Later, when I told Antony about it, we worked it out to be almost the same day when he too was hailed off the road, and similarly entertained.

This next story is his, not mine, but is too good not to share. Filthy, exhausted, he rode at last into Greece, his long blonde hair blowing behind him. Seeing a kafé neon, he pulled in, parked his bike, and sat down. The usual collection of old men, were also sitting outside with their little cups of coffee or ouzos, playing backgammon.

'Is it,' queried one old fellow to the world in general, 'a boy or a girl?'

Silence, interrupted with the cer-ick-cer-ack of komboloi (worry beads), while the next move was being considered.

'Hasn't got breasts,' volunteered another.

Another silence while the dice were thrown.

'Well,' continued a third, 'that is nothing to go by nowadays.'

The garcon came out and hesitated, pad in hand, in front of the foreign object of speculation.

In passable Greek, for he was determined to learn it, Antony trotted out.

'A cold beer, please. And have you anything for me to eat?'

Total silence. When the beer arrived, the smiling Antony raised his glass to the cowering company.

'Ya mas'. (To us).

Naturally they did not allow him to pay for anything, and were genuinely impressed by his journey, warmly including him in their little party.

It was the first of many times when he received admiring hospitality along the road. Sometimes, on a homeward journey after an exploration, he put the bike on the roof of the bus. Then he would settle back and listen to the remarks flying to and fro, all unaware that he could understand. Unable to resist teasing them, he would eventually drop his bombshell and ask some silly question in good Greek. This of course, broke the ice, embarrassment over, hospitality flowed. They wanted to know everything, absolutely everything, about him and his trip. Questions flew and answers would be yelled across the bus so everyone could hear. Not only did Antony improve his Greek and grow to love Greece, it happily passed the long uncomfortable rides.

Stamos and he became fast friends, as work continued on the farm. Antony loved Stamos for his kindness, lunacy and fun. While Stamos loved Antony because firstly he was my son, and secondly, because he was so talented and interested in everything. An added bonus with Antony staying was that he could cook. It has been my principle to teach all my sons, which has been of great use to them in many situations. So Antony at seventeen became the much appreciated cook, which generally improved the bachelor existence on the farm.

By the time I flew back from England, the farm was no longer a desolate place with one man living there. His sons regularly appeared, usually with friends, stayed a day or two, emptied the fridge and departed.

Although I understood very little, I was ever shocked by the raised voices on far too many of these occasions. On an earlier visit to Crete, a Greek friend assured me that shouting is the norm there, and not to be taken much notice of. Everyone shouts, she told me, because of big families, for no one would hear, unless they shouted. An interesting view, which nonetheless appalled me. Watching the distressed Stamos trying to defend himself, I sorrowed as I did not feel it applied in this case.

In those early days, shocked by the racket, I tried to persuade the boys not to quarrel and shout at Stamos, who I truly believed to be a good and loving father, always doing his best for them.

Previously seen wild-life films on TV reminded me of the family. There is a time, when their rearing task is almost finished, when parent King Penguins are exhausted. Frantically rushing about, they try to escape being pursued and hammered by their Bobbys. Which is what those great, fluffy and irate children are apparently called, always demanding more. Not understanding it all, hardly helped, for most certainly I got the gist. Which was 'More'. Give us more, just like the young penguins.

A friend told me that they were jealous of our happiness, and our life together. Amazed, I insisted that they were always welcomed to share all we had, of course, participating in our lives, and cooperating. But no, I must make no conditions. The rows continued endlessly, it was painful, distressing for Stamos, I begged them to stop.

My appeals were ignored of course.

Chapter 6

Family Life

Nothing alas, and don't we all know it, is perfect. My growing happiness with Stamos had to have its pitfalls. In those early, halcyon days, we lived for the day, delighting in each other, working hard, and trying to understand our diverse cultures. It was inevitable I suppose, with the classic situation of step-mother, and step-children, things went from bad to worse. I would, as the years went by, understand that everything in Greece is 'over the top'. The wild flowers are more vibrant than any I had seen elsewhere. The humour is more humorous. The drama, more dramatic. Personal relation-ships are often more passionate, this way or that, than I had previously experienced. Moderation barely exists; it is all, or nothing.

The one who suffered most was poor Stamos, the pig in the middle. Indeed, it eventually made him ill. I suffered too, for I felt that I was doing my best to help all the family and could not understand the lack of appreciation.

Apparently, while his children grew up, meal times had been a pretty sketchy affair. 'Frying Pan Annie', plate in hand on one leg. Stamos delighted in my insistence that we SAT, at the table, and enjoyed our meal while being sociable. It was after all, I told him privily, the moment to check if all was well with everyone.

Lack of cooperation, downright rudeness, and the regular invasions of our peace, took its toll. There having been no one at the farm when I first arrived, the changes had proved too pleasant to ignore. Suddenly it was an attractive home, unlike before. The fridge was always full and there was always food on the table at meal times. We had removed a bed from the kitchen, and replaced it with a counter. On this stood the bread crock, margarine and jam, always available for anyone hungry between meals. The house was well kept and the general decay was being replaced with order. Being me, a tough mum to my own boys, being a foreigner, a stupid Brit. Sadly I found I had now become, The Wicked Stepmother.

I was always a good housewife although my dislike of housework had, over the years, been overcome by liking a tidy and orderly establishment. However, I really enjoy cooking. Nothing pleased me more than providing a good meal for a gang of appreciative youngsters. A phone call announcing the arrival of a group of kids was a rarity. They generally simply arrived, without warning, in a swirl of dust. The motorbike brigade I called them.

At night, smelling burning, I might go downstairs to find the kitchen blue with burnt fat and cigarette smoke. The remains of what was to have been tomorrow's lunch was strewn all over the table.

'Whatever are you doing?'

'We were hungry.'

'Did you not have supper?'

'We wanted meat.'

'But you had meat for lunch, and you had a good vegetarian supper.'

'We wanted meat, and this is our house.'

'And those are my chops you are eating, paid for with my money and they were marinating in the fridge for lunch tomorrow,' I unwisely replied.

In all innocence, another mistake I made, was to gather together a pile of broken and useless old bikes, to have them repaired, at my own expense of course. Summoned, taken to task, I was firmly told not to interfere with their possessions. Astonished, I did not, and years later, they all ended up at the tip.

There was the occasion, later on, when I drove to Athens to clear my sister's flat after she left Greece. There were things to sort, to take home, to dispose of, and to sell. I was offered 10% of any sales. There were not many Landrovers in Greece at that time, so I offered to allow a step-son who hitched a ride with me, the use of it for the evening. Away, off he went, happy to show it off to his chums, with the promise that he bring it back by ten next morning.

By eleven I was getting annoyed as I had a lot to do and it was getting hot. At noon I rang Stamos and asked him if he knew where the boy was.

'Oh, he's here,' he replied. 'He arrived two hours ago.'

'Well where is my Landrover then, because I am running late, and I need it.'

'Oh, that is here too, he came in it of course.'

Of course! What of course? I was stunned. I had lent my car, (illegally as it happened, with foreign number plates which Greeks were not allowed to drive) and here I was stranded in the city, with a job to do, my Landrover being eighty kilometres away.

'Tell him to bring it right back,' I said coldly. 'Immediately. How dare he go back to Corinth with my vehicle without my permission.'

Now it was Stamos' turn to be angry, but, not with his son, oh no. With me. He demanded I return by bus. I was incredulous, and as it happened, although of course I could have borrowed the fare, I had practically no money.

Pointing out that I had a task to do, a landlady to meet, things to settle, I was in Athens to do them and would not leave until the job was done. As for returning on the bus, no. I came in my own car and I intended to return in it. This time I was really annoyed.

All this was totally out of my previous experience. No doubt, also completely old fashioned, I believed that elders were betters. In my day, children obeyed their parents without question. They were not rude to them, they cooperated for the family good, they helped. All this now, seemed from another world.

So I remained with my friends, miserable, and astonished at the turn of events. Unexpectedly, without forethought or plan, it was the cause of a strange, totally new experience, a one-off, never to be repeated. Seeing my sorrow, my friends offered me 'a trip'. Old fashioned? Indeed I was. Ignorant? That too. Drugs were an unknown and fearful area, quite outside of my experience. Then I considered how short-sighted I was, ever hammering my sons to never, ever, have anything to do with them. If I knew nothing, I truly was in no position to advise anyone.

I accepted, no doubt through my desperate emotional state, and swallowed a quarter of what looked like a tiny lentil. The day which followed was memorable. My friends watched over me with great care. Afterwards, they told me how very fortunate I was having a 'good trip'. One thing I soon realised, and compared with my dislike of flying. I wished to GET OFF, as with a plane, I could not; I was stuck with it until the trip was ended. It seemed to go on forever, I was glad when it ended.

Stamos came for me, poker-faced, two days later. No explanation, no apology. Much later, when life was calm again, I told him about the experience I had had. He was furious. How dared I do something like that without his permission, his knowledge. I had to remind him very firmly that as I was an independent woman, I would do exactly what I wanted to with my own body. There would be a few more such comical, heavy-handed husband instructions over the years, usually, after the horse had bolted.

Once again I got on with the task in hand. Amongst my sister's things, was a small fridge, and Stamos' children asked if I would sell it to Eleni for her tiny flat. Muggins me, of course I would and, being family, naturally forego the 10%. Anything electrical was hideously expensive at that time, and with that climate and food going off quickly, a fridge was really an essential. The fridge was removed and payment was promised. Although it was a very long time a coming, knowing the family situation, I did not press for payment. Eventually, the kids told me that their mother did not, after all, want it. Exasperated, back to square one, I began to ring around and advertise it again, till finally, I found a real buyer.

BUT, still not the end of the story, for guess what? Their mother had sold it. I received this news astonished. There were no apologies whatsoever, from anyone. Neither any offer to compensate. So not only did I forego the 10%, I had to pay my sister for the fridge!

Stamos consulted me during the summer holidays as to whether he should buy his younger son a guitar. He wanted one so very desperately, and, there was one going cheap, just one month's salary. Etcetera. I considered his query. The boy was supposed to be studying for his exams. He should not waste time messing about with a guitar. So I gave my views to Stamos. To promise to give it to him, THE day of his last exam and not before. Which were naturally disregarded, and in no time at all, we were all suffering agonies, being obliged to listen to an insensitive learner, directly outside the window. Day after day, the same piece over and over again, till we were almost mad.

Not unexpectedly, the son failed his exams. He was terribly angry and naturally someone had to be blamed. Unbelievably, that someone was me. With childish fury, I was told it was because I had wanted him to fail. He then sold the guitar, and went off on holiday on the proceeds. Peace.

A little time later, an embarrassed Stamos asked me for money. When I asked what for, he told me quietly, to pay for the guitar. Apparently he had been bullied into buying it, silly man, merely paying a deposit of one sixth, the rest to be paid later.

'But, why wasn't it paid off, when it was sold?'

Silence. A fridge and a guitar were, as it turned out over the years, just the smallest tip of the iceberg. If I had been wiser, more aware, perhaps I might have avoided many similar situations, then and in the future.

There is an excellent Muslim saying which goes –

'Take what you want,' said God. 'Take it, and pay for it.'

It was all very distressing and boring, as indeed it must be for the reader. It had not dawned on me yet, that, as I have to assume, being a mere woman, my rights, feelings or possessions were never considered important. Would the abandoned mistress, Jenny, have done any better? Could she, with her Greek upbringing, have managed the situation better than I did? I suspect so, and have been more acceptable even if she could not offer them the advantages I did. Certainly she might have turned the other cheek, and always, for the sake of peace, let them have their own way. A door mat.

Distressed, astonished, perplexed, I approached good friend Emilios, who tried to explain to me the Greek male psyche. I listened carefully, taking it all in, unbelieving.

'When,' Emilios told me, 'a child is born, it is warmly welcomed, boy or girl, for with the high infant mortality of the past, any child is welcomed. Of course, a son, or several sons, are what is wanted. A girl, or even two, would be welcomed to care for the elders in time. But as girls are costly to marry, their dowries, often beggaring the whole family, sons are definitely favoured.

The little girl is greatly loved, fondled and made much of as a baby. By the time she is three, she is taking her grandfather his slippers. Or father, his cigarettes. Or her brother his book. It starts quietly, kindly, the service and toil which will be her life till she dies.

When she becomes a woman, a family gathering is called and she finds herself, unusually, the centre of attention. The relatives scrutinise her carefully. Is she tall? Fair? Beautiful? Clever? Or is she short? Dark? Ugly? Stupid? Accordingly, they make their plans for her dowry. A field? An olive grove? Gold? A taxi? All or any of these things must be accompanied with a house, or the cash to build one, or onto the in-law's house. At least, an abode. Fully equipped and furnished too.'

I listened, amazed and horrified at the pressures put on families and recalled my years in the East, where the system is exactly the same. The more attributes the girl has, the less dowry is given. And sadly, vice-versa.

'Now,' continued Emilios, 'if the babe is a boy, there is unrestrained rejoicing. In the past, in the dark days, this would mean there was another man to carry a gun. From the day of his birth, the boy would be pampered, usually over-fed and to his detriment, over-indulged in every whim.'

These words bring memories of my watching a ten year old boy being dressed by his three year old sister. Indeed I saw he could not even do up his buttons himself. Another time, on an island, I saw a woman with a normal, healthy five year old boy draped on her lap, taking his milk from a feeding bottle.

'As the girl grows, she is at the beck and call of all the family. If it is a peasant family, she labours in the fields after, what is now, compulsory school. In the evenings she helps her mother, cleaning, cooking, and care of the livestock. In school holidays she works alongside the rest of the family. Being on show as it were, she is observed by those around about, who are on the lookout for a bride, for family or friends with sons. So eventually, a match is made and, poor girl, she dreams of ending her drudgery, to be mistress of her own house with her own man.'

He stopped and mused for a while, that honest Greek, trying to give me the true picture of his much loved country.'After the fun and games of the marriage, the young bride soon finds out that she is still in an endless trap. The very first problem, and every subsequent problem, which hits the young man, takes him scurrying back to his mother, who will solve it. Even till her death, when he might grow up at last. That is if he has no sisters. If he has, they may well step in, and take over supporting their boy, whatever the crisis.

When the young wife has a son, which is her duty, all the love she should have for her useless husband is now passed on to him. She will now follow the pattern of centuries, little changed, even now. It is very hard for many young men to enter into the reality of the harsh world. They do not understand discipline. They might not know about real work. They suffer greatly from it, because they understood that they were gods. Everyone told them so, all their lives, for years and years.'

Why not believe that they are the gods of creation? Who to believe but your own mother? I freely admit that it is all the fault of my sisters, the women, who cripple their sons with love. So it is, poor things, growing up is very painful. Real life, the big wide world proves so hard, it isn't fair. Often, their solution is to marry a good wife with a decent dowry. This will cushion adulthood, there will be someone to tidy up for them, provide in every way, remind them how special they are. If they marry an old fashioned girl, they will be cared for as before. If they don't, be absolutely sure, any problem can be taken home to mother.

We talked of it well into the night for it was all new to me. It seemed to be general in the Mediterranean, the Middle East.

'Is it really true then, generation after generation,' I asked, 'This terrible spoiling of sons?' He just nodded and looked at me to see if I really understood. This endless and vicious circle. I did.

'Ouch.'

That conversation took place in the early seventies. Now, with the new millennium, I am glad to see the worm is turning

Chapter 7

Work Force

Young friends from Scotland valiantly drove my Landrover and trailer loaded with my chattels and furniture to Greece. We drove north in the van with Antony and Emilie, my two year old Goddaughter, to meet them at the Yugoslav border.

My first trip north, I found it fascinating as we went through the different areas. At that time the road was generally terrible, so the journey took far longer than I had supposed it would. Some stretches showed lovely hills and dales, with familiar farmsteads and grazing flocks. Later, we drove through great plains where cotton grew, with ample evidence of the recent harvest spread far and wide. White shreds of straggly snow, possibly hundreds of kilos of raw cotton which had escaped the machinery, were strung everywhere along the verges.

Sea glinting to the East, with towns, big and small supporting fishing fleets as well as one quite important port. Eventually, we drove through wondrous and mysterious mountains, the highest ranges to the West. Myth and history was all about us, far more impressive than any travel book or film.

We booked into a small hotel, all rather suspicious, my being a foreigner, the border and all that. In the evening we had a meal in rather a big taverna which seemed full of soldiers from the local garrison. It was perhaps the second time I had seen Stamos drink too much, and I quickly realised that it didn't take much for him to get silly. He was quite obviously still dwelling on my total lack of interest in politics. Attack! To his irritation, I would not be drawn into an argument. He waved the thick moulded tavern glass in my face, then a plate, assuring me that even these mundane things, depended on – you've guessed it – Politics. I was not impressed, and probably noticing I was becoming tired with his nonsense, he inevitably became rude.

'What a boring woman you are,' he said in English and too loudly, for not surprisingly, we were being well observed. His one eye glared at me menacingly.

'All you think about is cooking and babies.'

I was offended. What an oaf. But, I refused to have a row and in a public place.

In bed at the hotel, he fell to sleep instantly while I lay and sorrowed and worried. Not for the last time I wondered whether I had been wise to throw in my lot with such an idiot?

I woke in the very early hours from a beautiful dream. Listening to carts rattle by over the cobbles outside, I lay savouring it, so innocent and gentle, wishing it would come true.

Sober and sweet again, Stamos enquired of my night, but I told him my dream was too lovely to share with him, he would not appreciate it, rude man. Of course, and happily, I was persuaded to tell it, and here it is.

We had a beautiful little daughter, prompted no doubt by having Emilie to stay although they were nothing alike. Our daughter was leggy, like my sons, not like the robust Emilie. She had curls, lots of them, unlike my sons and Emilie, and she looked just like Stamos' mother.

The scene was in the centre of Athens, where Stamos was taking our daughter to the children's fancy dress party at the French Embassy. Tenderly, he carried her across the busy road. Dressed in deep purple satin pantaloons, soft green cuffs and trim and yellow tights, she lay in his proud arms. A purple hat with a green stalk sat on her curls. For, she was going to the party dressed as an aubergine!

How we laughed. All unpleasantness from the night before evaporated. I felt it was a very telling, amusing dream. Cooking and babies, yes.

We met up with our young friends and drove in convoy south and home again. Their two very blonde little children and Emilie became fast friends. I have a marvellous memory of them with Stamos. A nature's child, he was the most self-confident and un-shy person I knew. The three little people needed to go to the bathroom, where Stamos was taking a shower. There being only one bathroom, I went in and asked him if they might. Of course, no problem and in they all went.

There was a curious silence, time passed, so I peeped around the door. First I saw Stamos standing under the shower in the bath, soaped all over, from head to foot, literally lathered. Then I noticed, their backs to me, the three little figures, watching intently, stock-still, fascinated. The soapy figure waggled a diligent finger first in one ear, then the other. He then blew his nose loudly, soap and water everywhere. One finger in one nostril, wiggle, waggle, then the next.

Then, he removed his eye. Diligently washing it with soap, he rinsed it well under clear water, and carefully put it back in. I watched as their glance moved to the other eye, waiting for that one to come out too. Back in the kitchen, unable to conceal my mirth, I told them what was going on. We all had a good laugh.

When we returned to the farm, the family resentment against Stamos and me reached a crescendo. We then decided to move out and searched the neighbourhood for a small house to rent. As there was nothing, we planned instead to move into the spitaki. A dear little long, old house on one level. If the Petropolous family had lived there, I was quite prepared to move in, feeling it would be sufficient for the two of us after a little work was done.

Stamos, always with ideas of grandeur, decided it was not good enough, as it was, and, or, it would fall down at the next earthquake as had the church near by. Certainly the latter was a possibility, for the roof beams were slender and wormy. The plan, which somehow never came about, was that the very able young carpenter friend from Scotland, would make it safe and habitable.

Stamos then cheerfully decided that we could restore the little house ourselves with outside helpers, so he sent Antony to Athens to recruit two lads to help with the re-building. For inevitably, he had rushed, with his usual optimism, into ripping off the roof, thus laying bare, the stone and earth walls to the elements.

Sitting at one of the smartest cafés in Syntagma Square, Antony concentrated on reading Kathimerini, a good Greek newspaper. Tied around his long blonde hair was a head band, tucked into which was a notice saying,

WANTED. 2 WORKERS.

So we gained our first two, Martin and Pat. Pat, the mad Irishman, who still writes and rings, from Australia no less, and warms my heart.

Alas, the spitaki was not to be re-built for many a year, although there were bursts of work done on it. With time, it crumbled to such a degree, it was only fit for a pigsty; but that is another story.

The boys fitted in to our little family as our own and roared happily around the area in the old Landrover, leaving their mark wherever they went. There was Pat's Leap, Pat's bump, and Pat's Skid, and so forth.

'You will go straight back,' I raged at him. 'And fix that fence before the neighbours come to complain and demand huge sums of money for repairs.'

So off he went and did some artistic repairs with wire and whatever, one existing to this day, with 'PAT' carefully worked into it.

We did not learn till his third or fourth stay, that, in fact Pat, (the rat) hadn't even got a driving licence.

A recurrent situation with Stamos' children was that they would arrive, furiously tell us how useless we were, hound us out and take over. In no time at all, they got thoroughly sick of the responsibilities and of each other, so left. So the pressure to move out of the big house was off and Pat and Martin were the first of many to stay with us happily, for the equivalent of two pence ha'penny and their meals, joining in with whatever was happening on the farm. They were free to go and come as they wished, and many of, as I still call them, our young people did just that. Sometimes there were too many and we packed them off. Other times there were none, and we struggled on alone till Stamos either sent me out to find more, or they arrived by themselves.

Often, children of friends of mine came by invitation, not always successfully as they thought they were coming on holiday. Work was sometimes new to them, so they quickly learnt, no work, no food. We assumed the rest came by word of mouth which got about in the hostels of the world. Little money, good food, and a lot of fun.

Ours was not proper work although it was often very hard work particularly in the heat. It was as in a family. They had a bed, even if in a tent, and good and plentiful food. I did their laundry in the machine. It was often quite grey by now from their inadequate, on-the-road hand-washing. I doctored their ills, mended their clothes and got very sick of patching jeans. Those who did not need to earn much money were glad to feel safe, in good company, with parent figures and many have remained loyal and loving friends to this day. Those who needed cash badly we passed on, often with foreboding, to local farmers. All too often, taking back the solvent but miserable and exhausted youngsters, we kept them for awhile, so that they could recover their equilibrium before going on their way.

We were a substitute family to many. They appreciated and toiled for us, while we cared for and appreciated 99% of them. Of course there were dismal failures, even thieves. But on the whole we felt privileged to have their ever-willing and cheerful assistance and company. We were often likened to a Kibbutz, but some Israeli kids, themselves kibbutzniks, laughed heartily when they heard that, assuring us it was very different, for here, they really had to work.

We had our first apricot harvest from the neglected trees which I had pruned and from which we actually got a decent crop. They were so delicious. Having never liked those ghastly, stringy tinned apricots, this was a revelation. It was also my first experience as to how badly the farmers in Greece were treated. We were not paid for that crop for two and a half years. Imagine? You have to irrigate and spray. You plough and fertilise. You have to pay your pickers and you have to eat. It would not be the first time I would be shocked by such treatment. Farmers were considered savages, below contempt and not to be considered at all. Indeed the word for farmer in Ancient Greek, Agrios, also meant Savage. It is the root of aggressive. (Also agriculture etc.) We often certainly felt pretty aggressive with the nonchalant attitude of the big factories.

At last, we moved forward. We planted a small orchard of one hundred apricot trees. It was very exciting, I was inordinately pleased with our progress. As the irrigation system was broken, it was a constant labour having to take a tank on the trailer down to the end of the land, and bucket water every tree. Little Emilie had her own tiny plastic bucket, an empty jam container. While re-filling our own buckets, we would fill hers, and off she would stagger, determined to help.

Having paid for the trees, I obviously had taken a greater than usual interest in them and was determined that they would not die from neglect. Alas. My enthusiasm was to have repercussions, for unthinkingly, I referred to them as, 'My little trees.' A very foolish mistake. For incredibly, this threw Stamos into the most enormous sulk. It was then I learned about his black moods. They were the blackest I had ever experienced in my life. Not being a sulker myself, I was devastated.

I would learn over the years that his black moods took over completely, like noxious thick clouds, which smothered us all and had to be suffered until they evaporated. Many years later, when he was in his normal, lovely mood, I questioned him gently about his dark days. He thought deeply, not offended at all by my question, then told me sadly, that he just didn't know. That first time, while we had Emilie staying with us for weeks, it was she, the little love, who broke that particular wicked spell. Approaching Stamos at the end of siesta, 'out of the mouths of babes', she asked Stamos in her childish wisdom.

'Are you still in a bad mood?'

He looked at her fondly, surprised perhaps that so small a person had even noticed. The air cleared immediately, for he could not help but laugh and swept her into his arms for a cuddle.

How we loved that super little girl. Chunky, with legs like trees, she would valiantly stagger after us in the fields, always trying to help. But oh, how she missed her mother. Sadly, at the beginning, she was desperately weepy. Our being under the main flight path proved a distraction, for I used to encourage her to wave to passing planes, to Mummy, which somehow made her happier. Some idiot had given Stamos several 'naughty' magazines, and at siesta times Emilie and I would go through them regularly.

'Mummy!' she would point a fat finger to a lovely, slim and naked damsel. 'Naughty mummy, no knickers.'

Which to this day is an expression we use; thus are born family jokes. So too was born our mutual desire to have a child together. I do believe that truly loving people always feel thus. For sure we were both getting on. Certainly our other children were growing up. But the deep wish to have a child persisted. We independently wished on every sliver of a new moon, and cast caution to the winds. Wise or not, it was now in the hands of the gods.

As my English money was running low, I was grateful to be offered a job drawing for the American School of Archaeology. It was just a small job for a few months, but through it I met some excellent people, some of whom I still am in touch with. At the time it opened a door for us, for Stamos appeared to have few friends in the neighbourhood. He considered Corinthians as Hill Billies, so went, and usually alone, to see his old friends in Athens for company.

It was therefore wonderful for me to meet and speak with interesting people. The boss, the late Dr Paul Clement of Atlanta, became a good friend to us. We had an amusing reciprocal relationship. He would call occasionally and announce in his slow Georgian drawl.

'Judith, I have some guests arriving from the States.'

A pregnant silence.

An announcement I knew meant he would like some help with entertaining them and I immediately arranged which evening would suit everyone. Certainly our hospitality was never lavish, but it was interesting, hearty and fun. One occasion I remember with a smile was an evening when we might have been twenty about the long table. Cool under the walnut trees, it was a pleasant way to spend some hours with company, our menagerie all about, being part of it.

Suddenly, twin kids, attractive little black and white devils, leapt up on to one end of the table. Obviously surprised by what they had done, for a second they surveyed our amazed faces. Then, with a wild, springbok boing, boing, boing, they bounced the whole length of the table, sending glasses and cutlery flying, before taking off the other end, with a huge jump and twist. Quickly recovering from our astonishment, how we laughed. How too did our guests enjoy that impromptu floor show, a charming interlude to recount when back home.

In return, Paul used to invite us to join them at the best tavernas. A rare luxury, good and different food in new surroundings, it was much appreciated. In times of stress, and there were quite a few, those bright, kindly people lifted me up and firmly made me aware of my own value.

Stamos used to drop me off at the excavation house in the morning and collect me in the afternoon. One might think that sitting drawing all day at a desk was restful, but by evening, I was certainly quite tired. It amused me at first, how when we entered the front door, Stamos and son, who happened to be staying, turned left into the living room, while I turned right to the kitchen to make supper. There was never any offer of help. For sure it was my own silly fault not to have left a list of things to be done, peel potatoes and onions and so forth. Stamos was in fact good in the house, how I can't imagine, yet when I was about, he left me to do it all. So there I was, the only one earning in the family, and still having to do all the cooking and housework. Apparently in some small way, ever hotly refuted, I was becoming Greek.

The Landrover joyfully opened up Greece for me. In the early, occasional work-free days, we went off, even for a couple of days, high into the mountains, down, through wildly inaccessible ravines, to the sea. We were happy, we were optimistic. Somehow we were sure, our love would solve all problems.

Once we drove into the high mountains due west of Corinth, our bed made up in the back of the Landrover. Pure and fresh air, magnificent views, for me, this was the real Greece. I could not understand those tourists who chose to lie on a stony beach strewn with cigarette ends and bottle tops. The mountains in Greece are truly glorious, the people who somehow survive well up there, are very special. We drove through tiny villages, stopping for drinks or to buy local cheese, Stamos often known, happy to chat with anyone. We just drove, without plan, eventually following a track which resembled a dry, rock strewn river bed, till at last we came to a river and a mill.

Shortly after we arrived, so too did two huge mules with two rotund ladies perched on top. Another meeting, with Sarakatzani. It was with much effort and laughter we helped them dismount. I found myself hanging on for dear life to the mule's heads while Stamos and the miller hauled both women down. After much brushing of skirts, and tidying of headscarves, giggling and catching of breath, we were next requested to somehow undo the huge bundles tied behind the mule saddles. Another cheerful task with plenty of the usual shouting and advice, being thrown about.

I was incredulous and thrilled to have another first time experience. They, like the shepherds at Argos from whom we had bought Comealong, had made flokatis. Fingering the shaggy blankets, I was awed by the amount of work, the hours of labour, which had gone into each one. First the fleeces had to be washed, then, after picking off the burrs, carded, itself a long job before hand spinning and weaving. I could not begin to work out how many hours each one had taken. Stamos happily passed on my words, but surely, they could see from my face, how impressed I was. They were as delighted with my praise as I was with them.

For a small fee, the miller was to leave the blankets in the millrace to thrash and tumble for awhile, into silky softness. Uplifted by this new knowledge, I observed the two ladies clothes, which were all home-spun. Probably due to the bulk of the cloth, necessary for the chill dawn and dusk of the mountains, I suspect they appeared more rotund than they really were.

Happily, we bought a bag of yellow flour before we left. We wondered, as we drove off, how on earth the ladies would get back onto the mules. Obviously they had come some way, but were not yet ready to go home, needing to linger and gossip before returning to their busy lives.

That time, our happy trip was thoroughly ruined on our home-coming. A taxi had just arrived and dropped off a girl, friend of the children. We found one of Stamos' sons and a friend in the house, obviously having a good time.

I was really distressed to find all my long playing records scattered, out of their sleeves, in the dust on the floor. Indeed they had obviously been walked on, for one, a favourite classical guitar, a Segovia was actually broken. My most precious antique walnut commode had a cigarette burn right on the front. No one ever confessed and no one apologised.

Going into the kitchen I found the place in turmoil, there not being one single clean plate or glass. Cross, I turned on the girl, foolishly forgetting that she, like us, had just arrived.

'What is all this mess?'

I did get to know her later, a good girl, but that day, she was as angry as I was.

'You saw I have just arrived.' she replied angrily, surveying the scene. 'I had nothing to do with it. They phoned and asked me to come for a few days.'

Sadly, it must have dawned on both of us at the same moment, the reason why she had been invited. Merely to clear up. Poor girl. Poor us.

It took ages for me to understand that many of these young men actually never succeeded in anything in their lives without the very real assistance of women. Be it grandmothers, mothers, sisters, girlfriends or wives. I will not be popular in saying it, but that's how it is. The sad thing is that their women folk, who ever sacrificed their all, are never appreciated. By being born male (Simone de Beauvoir would agree, being earthy and explicit), they consider, by their appendage, everything is naturally their due.

During the summer holidays when Maria was home from England with some of her friends, we had again taken courage and gone off the road precariously exploring. As my first Landrover was old, there was always the fear we would break something, and then, far from everywhere, what?

We called the place we went to Obsidian Beach, because of the flakes of obsidian we found there, obviously another ancient site.

Stamos took us, and left me with about five kids. We had a plastic wine barrel of water. A demijohn of wine. A crate of tomatoes. Several salamis. Two trays of eggs, a lump of fetta and lots of bread. Such an adventure.

It was wonderful. Alone, totally out of touch with the world, we swam, we ate, we slept, and I, as usual, hunted for ancient artefacts. We had to swim with T shirts on to avoid getting our backs burnt. We would lie on our bellies, snorkels aloft, and gaze down at the rocks and occasional fish. We had difficulty escaping the heat of the sun during the afternoon siesta so collected driftwood and erected flimsy shades. At night we made huge fires, clearing all the flotsam on the beach systematically, for sadly, the Mediterranean is a dump.

One of Maria's English school friends, who for some reason had made herself unpopular, suddenly came to life when I taught her to spin. I carved a spindle for her, first a long sliver of bamboo, then a very soft pottery shard into a circle. Using the point of my penknife, I carefully drilled a hole, and hey presto, a spindle and whorl. Off she went happily to scour the hills above, for the shreds of wool left on the thorn bushes by the scrub sheep. It was awfully coarse, but still, she learnt with huge pride, and thereafter, we did not have any more trouble with her. She was the first of many I taught to spin by hand. Having, years before I went to live in Greece, been taught by a Greek islander, when storms prevented the ferry boat from leaving, it was a joy to pass on that ancient craft. I used to send the girls off with spindle, whorl and wool, assuring them that they would make many friends in the old ladies along their way. A great ice breaker that, and fun being told how NOT, to do it, at full decibel.

Stamos and gang arrived the third evening to collect us, so we all swam again in the beautiful evening, as the great red sun, fell into the sea. I am sure all those young people will still remember it, which is as well, for I fear it is a paradise lost. The last time I went to Obsidian Beach, it was all fenced off in building plots.

Chapter 8

The Staff of Life

That first sack of flour from the mill in the mountains started me off again with bread-making. The young people joined me with enthusiasm, happy to learn something new. It was not a flour I had used before, being quite yellow. Unfortunately, it came alive, all too quickly, little moths taking off each time I opened the sack. Being of a frugal nature, this certainly did not stop me from using the flour. So, before baking, we had a long, drawn out sieving session to remove unwanted 'animal' ingredients.

Amongst our small group of workers, was an American couple. They were travelling prior to getting involved in their studies, and were in Greece en-route to the East. All too often, the girl, whose name I do not remember, would cry out in alarm at some harmless creeping or crawling creature. None of us was impressed. I told her firmly that if she couldn't cope here, she should certainly think twice before travelling any further East. I guessed they would have a horrible time there with her aversion.

However, I was pleased when she, being impressed with our bread-making, asked to learn. Happily I agreed, giving a big wink to a couple of experienced bakers, to 'make ready'. Understanding just what I meant, off they quietly went to sieve the flour. We were well aware that if she had seen the moths emerge, not only would she not have made the bread, she would never have eaten it again. We joked about it privately later, congratulating ourselves for preparing her stomach for worse to come.

During my first months in Greece I constantly sought out good bread. It was hard to find and brown bread was rarely obtainable. The bread from the bakeries was somehow unexciting and didn't taste of anything. The brown bread I did find was quite strange, being soft and very sweet. None of it was crispy or solid and it became stale the moment you took a cut from it in that dry climate.

All our neighbours made their own bread, of course. Friday was the day. Clouds of smoke rose from every little steading, the fournos (beehive oven), once lit, would be well used, as fuel was precious. Usually the only oven in the establishment, it was built a little distance from the house in case of fire. Inside the house, generally two small gas rings served for other cooking. It was the women's big work-day of the week. Life revolved around it.

Every couple of months or so, a huge truck would come around the villages. Parking in regular places, he would blow the horn for some moments to alert the ladies. On board he carried every kind of flour (except brown.) White, for the church bread, off white and yellow for everyday. He also carried every kind of animal feed there was. Heavy, it was a great convenience for the country people not to have to carry sacks from the mill or wherever, as, at that time, few had cars or indeed time. So it was an event, a small interlude in the daily toil to go to the back of the truck to order and buy. Word would fly about the immediate area, and the housewives would arrive, happily exchanging gossip and making sure all mouths would be kept fed.

On Thursday night, the dough would be well mixed in a great bowl or the huge, wooden washing trough. Simple bread, it was made with flour, water, salt and a little olive oil, with a small lump of sour dough as starter from the previous batch. The dough would be left in a warm place, well covered with a damp sheet, then loaded over with home spun and woven blankets, and left to rise over night.

The tradition amongst the country women in the past is so lovely, I must diversify to tell of it. Every woman kept a lump of starter in a small, usually pottery jar. To keep it good, the surface was scattered with course salt, then a good layer of olive oil. Then it was well sealed, firmly tied down and kept in a cool place till next bake day. They call it, 'maya', the word for yeast. When a bride moved, as inevitably she did, to her mother-in-law's house, she took her own starter, which would have been going for years. From her mother's house, and her grandmother's, and so on. A sort of magic brew of ages, house to house, a blending together, a sort of witchcraft. In turn, she then added hers to the dough of her new home, so continued the tradition.

While the bread was rising, there was much activity. Sitting outside in the yard, weather permitting, there would be much chopping and scooping out of vegetables. Huge round tins would be made ready, filled with delectable stuffed vegetables. Their thrifty use of minced meat would spread a long way. In time, I too became an expert at stretching minced meat. Indeed I reached a stage that when anyone came to the farm bearing a gift, I translated, usually sorrowfully too, as to how much minced meat it would have bought. The Greek women are experts at making wonderful, diverse and tasty dishes with it. If they had none, rice and herbs, nuts and currants, would be equally delicious. Colourful, highly economical and wondrously tasty, these tins went in after the bread, to cook slowly for ages. It is rare for country women to have electric or gas ovens, they cost too much to buy and to run. Wood gathered from here and there, fruit tree prunings, whatever is to hand, is quite adequate and a wood-fired oven is far superior to the modern ones, which seem to have no soul. So they roasted and baked as much as possible in the residual heat of the beehive oven which gave a couple of days off from cooking, when other time-consuming jobs could be done.

I used to watch with envy as the wood-smoke rose from the Petropolous steading, and hear her dear voice raised as ever, chiding her poor daughters-in-law. Theirs was a small and quite wonky fournos, well-used and uncovered, it suffered from the weather. Although the mud was thoroughly cracked, in all the years I knew them, it provided excellent weekly feasts, standing in the corner of their yard. Battered by sun, wind and rain, now and then, with her usual noisy enthusiasm, Mrs Petropolous would slosh a daub of mud over the cracks and when dry, a lick of white wash. Very often she came across, hurling stones at our zealous pack of dogs, to present us with a small, triangular loaf, hot and smelling wonderful.

'Another story.' announced Stamos tearing at it happily. (A favourite saying of his, in English I suppose it means, now this, is the real thing.)

Quietly, I dreamed of joining my peasant sisters in this most basic and endearing task. It was to happen eventually, all of it. A fine, big beehive oven, joyfully made from our own hands. Weekly baking. The piece de resistance, our own flour. But till then I managed to bake with what I could find. It wasn't always satisfactory.

At last I found a baker on the outskirts of town who had brown bread twice a week. The loaves were long and slim and not at all like the solid, tasty brown bread I was used to. Plucking up courage, my Greek by then just about sufficient, I asked the baker if he would sell me some brown flour. It was illegal, but that meant nothing.

'No!' he replied brusquely, turning away. He hadn't any, soon, maybe next week.

Not knowing quite what to believe, despondent, I left, to return the next week, and the next. It was a newly built, cement-block box of a shop, with huge windows on to the street. Great baskets of various hard tack type of biscuit lay under flimsy sheets of net against the flies. Shelves were stacked with all kinds of bread. Closed sacks lined the walls. Generally, it had a good feel. Except himself, the baker. Grumpy.

Once again he glared ferociously at me, indignant at my persistence when yet again, I asked for brown flour. Obviously, I was heartily unwelcome, for he turned away yet again to continue his chores, his surly face set.

Bewildered and sad once more to fail, I stood and gazed into the middle distance.

'You know,' I began, by now desperate, 'in my country, in England,' I spoke to the myriad flies on the shop window, 'we have such good brown bread. And I so much want to make some for my husband.'

There was a stunned silence as he stopped in his tracks. Staring at me, intent on my hopeless Greek he yelled,

'What did you say?'

Slowly, I began again, trying to get it right and clear.

'In my country, in England,' I repeated, to be roughly interrupted.

'Are you British?' he shouted, floury face transformed and thrust close.

'Indeed!' I replied startled.

'Well then,' he roared happily, making his way to the line of sacks, 'Why didn't you say so?' and proceeded to brandish a large scoop at me. 'How much do you want, I thought you were German!' All in one breath.

Oh dear, oh dear. After so many years, bitter memories still remained.

From then on, we have been fast friends, yet I never had the courage to ask him if he he'd had bad experiences during the war. I even used to take him some of my English brown bread which appeared to interest him and of which, he seemed to approve. Sometimes I took him some of our fruit, which he loved, straight from the trees. We became, despite our early days, good chums, and until we had our own flour, I was a good customer. To this day, when we meet in the town, for he is retired now, we greet each other as long lost friends.

The Corinthia was mostly a fruit growing area, with very occasional, tatty little fields of wheat grown 'because they couldn't think what else to do with it!' The straw rose to a pathetic height and the ears only grew half full of grain but at least it was something. The combine always cut very high because those fields were such a mess, full of rocks and often as a minefield, with years worth of village rubbish.

Not so ours. It was a big field, level and clean. When the wheat came up, velvet green, then gold, with not one weed, it was really a field to be proud of. People seeing it even asked us what it was! Stamos was justifiably puffed up with pride. It was in all truth, particularly in Greece, a triumph. The day the combine first came to our farm was history. Taking our little boy up with him, Stamos sat beside the driver, in seventh heaven. Not to miss out on the event, I packed up a picnic lunch for us all. So we congregated happily in the bright sunshine, watching the great machine cutting swathes, it was magnificent.

At first I took a sack at a time to an old mill inland in a lovely old hill village, left behind because of a new road. It was a peaceful backwater and it was always a joy going there. High above the Gulf of Corinth, with amazing views of the sea and mountains, the old houses border narrow and steep lanes. Pure water still runs from the well, far from urban pollution. The women still go there to the great stone basins to wash their rag rugs and blankets. Night and morning, flocks of sheep and goats go to drink from the huge stone troughs.

High above the village are the remains of an even earlier walled town. Quite crumbled now, the streets can still just be picked out. Great towers stand like sentinels. It is beautiful. We often used the milling of the wheat as an excuse to go there for a picnic. Far away from the kitchen and endless farm chores, we lay on the scrubby, herb filled grass and drank in the view. Happy memories.

Unfortunately, the two old boys who ran the mill were as dilapidated as their machinery. Everything was magnificent, mostly made of wood, but fit for a museum and quite filthy. Our flour was always 'alive' in a matter of weeks. At last I decided this would not do. I must be independent, have a small mill, an electric table model.

Eventually, on a trip north to collect a calf, we went to a big agricultural fair in Salonica. Stamos was in his element. At that time I was solvent, which as time went on, became a rare experience. He felt very secure. He adored machinery and was extremely gifted with it.

I diversify to my early days once more. That first spring, when the glorious growth of green erupted with the warmth, the house seemed to be sinking in a sea of weeds. I scouted around for a scythe to cut the odd path. As with most things, there was none. When I asked him, he cheerfully said he'd buy one for me. Off he went, to return a full day later, pent up with excitement, a load of 'parts' filling his van. He had 'found' a little mower, in a thousand pieces, without a manual. He had been offered it VERY cheaply. He could pay when he could. I am ashamed to say that to this day I don't know if he did in fact, ever pay it off.

I watched incredulously as he unloaded the whole lot and scattered it on the bare earth in front of the house. As there was no barn, this was his regular work station. Totally engrossed, he worked it all out. Three times he put it together, and three times he tore it apart once more. At last, it was born, whole and healthy. As I said, he really was a very talented engineer. It fixed on the back of his little blue tractor, and he loved it. I never got the scythe. Later I bought one for myself. Still, we were lucky for his was a natural gift with machinery which happily he seems to have passed on to his sons.

Back to Salonica and my little flour mill. Imported, it was of course expensive. All machinery seems more so in Greece than anywhere else, maybe because it is not a rich or industrial country and the exchange rate is often poor. I wanted a handy table model for the house, for flour, for bread. He totally disapproved. The big one would be of more use. He didn't think much of the small one. He whinged, he wheedled. The bigger one was hardly more money, AND would be useful for other grains. As ever, he got his way while I paid the bill.

On that same trip, he took to disappearing for hours, returning with his face aglow like a woman who has seen a treasure she wants. He began telling me about a baler. It was an old Italian model, utterly shabby but on opening it up, he had found it shining and perfect. That it was sitting under a railway arch and somewhat sheltered from most of the elements was a huge advantage.

It was love at first sight. His passion could only be satisfied by buying it. He pleaded with me, the banker, to let him buy it. It was always very, very difficult to refuse Stamos anything. Getting it home, from the north to the south of Greece, was the problem. Nothing daunted, he made the arrangements. It would travel south by train, (adding substantially to the cost of course).

The problem was, once it had arrived at Athens, how were we to get it home? The railway gauge changed for the Peloponnesus. Once again the cheerful Makis was summoned with his truck. I didn't witness all this palaver at the Athens terminal, but heard about it later.

Apparently, it lay on its flat bed in a siding waiting to be lifted off. There was a small crane parked nearby. When Stamos asked if it could be used he got pretty short shift. A great deal of shouting, gesticulating, threats, the usual. The group of boys there to help him recounted all this very merrily. Losing patience, Stamos took the law into his own hands. Not an unusual occurrence. Determinedly, he mounted the crane. The station master was summoned by the objectors and, to everyone's surprise, announced it to be quite the best and only solution. One sane person in that mad house, what a miracle.

While all this was going on, I was at home. To my surprise, a crane trundled up the drive and informed me that Makis had phoned for

91

him from Athens. Not long afterwards, Makis arrived with the bailer on his truck, and some of the boys on board with him. A new wave of shouting and gesticulating. I watched as the object of Stamos' love was hoisted high into the air. Terrifying. Slowly it was lowered, until, it was about a foot off the ground. Then BANG! He dropped it with a ghastly crunch.

That baler! Oh but what loving care was showered on it. Bas, the gentle Dutchman, lovingly worked on it for months. Laboriously and carefully he sanded, oiled, and painted every single part. At least and unlike the early days of the mower, we now had a barn in which to do it. It worked, hurray. Another success. (Another toy.)

Now we had our own mill. It was not entirely suitable for my use as I had to commandeer Stamos to tack it onto the back of the tractor whenever I needed flour. However, it did prove useful and we also ground our maize for meal and did jobs for other people as well earning either welcome cash or goodwill.

After that, we grew a small field of wheat every year for the house, usually in some small and unwanted corner. When the time came, we just 'high-jacked' a passing combine to harvest it for us. Always ready to make an occasion of the most simple event, I heard that wheat likes flute music! More than once, the girls and I took the little gramophone out with a long, long lead. Happily doing our chores, pealing, slicing, we sat listening, along with the tender young wheat, to baroque flute music. It must have enjoyed it as much as we did, for it grew wonderfully.

It was great having our own flour, from our own wheat. Nothing tasted so good before, or has done since. Stamos loved the bread, so it didn't take long to persuade him that it might be fun as well as economical to build our own fournos.

Always loving to be creating new things, Stamos took to this project with his usual enthusiasm. First, we had to track down a fournos 'specialist'. This was easy. The local expert was a fine old man, the father-in-law of the eldest Petropoulos daughter, who lived in Examilia just up the road. Delighted with the idea, he told us what to do, step by step, blow by blow, and what to gather and from where.

These peasant ovens come in many different styles and sizes. Made of whatever lies around, they are economical to make, often costing nothing. Basically they are like a beehive. In the mountains and wetter areas, the earth and tile dome is encased with stones as protection from the elements. They are so dark and cosy inside, it isn't unusual for funny little hens to insist on laying their eggs inside them. Above ground, safely out of the way of four-legged thieves, it is the wise owner who allows them access. Except on bake day, of course.

At that time, we were a thriving and happy farm. Full, often too full, of young workers of every nationality, this was a new project, an adventure. Here was something real, unusual, productive and wholly Greek to learn. Everyone on the farm, young and old, threw themselves into the making of Our Fournos, with enthusiasm. British Brian and Kiwi Dave, were the 'maestoras'. They led operations and did the bulk of the work while the rest of us happily supported them by collecting materials. It really was fun! It was also quite a major operation, which grew in fits and starts and took many months to complete.

Stamos marked out the base, enormous of course (years later, its large size was to be a boon to me when earning our living, catering for tourists). A solid concrete and stone platform went up, leaving a fine arch underneath. Supposedly for storing wood, endless kittens and puppies would eventually be born there. Suddenly, pleased that we should be doing something so very and typically Greek, the neighbourhood came to life on hearing of our enterprise. Considered rich, (oh if only they knew), they were pleased that we were undertaking such a traditional task. Surprised at first by their enthusiasm, we were grateful when messages came, or locals called by and pointed to fallen barns and old houses. There we took to gathering huge quantities of broken roof tiles, always on the lookout for sleeping snakes, we made many journeys with the pickup laden down. It was surprising just how much was needed.

As part of the enterprise and whenever possible, we took to stopping off on the way home at the little shop in Examilia. While we enjoyed powerful little ouzos, 'the specialist', Pappou (grandfather) gave new instructions. It really wasn't all that simple. Indeed, it was a heap of dirty toil, plus a work of art and love. The tiles had to be put to soak in an old bathtub for a start, then scrubbed.

Next came the collection of white clay. Nothing else would do. Every area has its traditional source. The owners of the land are unofficially obliged to allow fournos makers to help themselves. It is useless for anything else anyway. Ours was just beyond Examilia, a low bank in the middle of a very scruffy wheat field. Armed with a fine assortment of tools, carrying large plastic barrels, we descended on it en masse, like bees.

Back at home, the barrels of white clay were filled with water. Any passer-by with time and energy would grab the pole in it and thump away, to break up the lumps. At last, the sloppy mess had straw worked into it, as a fixative. Very Biblical.

The last collecting excursion set off to the beach. There, illegally and carefully, we scraped up the fine sand into sacks. After they had drained awhile, still very heavy, they were loaded up and taken home. Pappou told us that this was the finest insulation for UNDER the floor. Anything Stamos did had to be the biggest and the best. To hell with the law!

The platform complete, a nail and string made the circle diameter. Stamos drew up the door and frame which were beautifully made by our blacksmith friend. That and the fire bricks were the only expenditure of the whole operation. The sea sand spread first, the iron door and frame in position, next the fire bricks were laid. Rarely used by peasants, himself insisted we must have them. The dome rose, like an igloo. It was very exciting. With the clay/straw mix used as cement, the broken roof tiles became walls.

During these operations, a dotty event happened which is worth recounting. Dave suggested that he should make his speciality, pumpkin soup, for supper. Unfortunately he was very heavy-handed with the pepper and it was inedible for most of us. So, with merry enthusiasm, the contents of the pot were flung into the clay mess, to add – heat!

Work went on in fits and starts and the walls rose. Two little holes halfway up were like ears. These ventilation holes, I would soon learn, must be blocked up with damp rags to keep the heat in. When complete, as a mini igloo, two final coats of slip were smoothed over the rough tiled surface to make a neat, bald dome.

At last it was time to summon the specialist. We all gathered to greet Pappou who arrived with his wife, perched on top of a tiny cart pulled by a much-loved donkey. He was enjoying himself immensely. No doubt at all, the entire neighbourhood knew where he was going and why. Strutting around the new fournos, full of importance, he tapped, stroked, walked all around and peered carefully inside while we, the crowd of builders waited for his verdict. Finally he proclaimed –

'Alpha Ena!' (A1)

Brian and Dave, the maesteras, were warmly congratulated. We, the humble labourers, got our share of the praise. Stamos beamed. We were a very proud and happy bunch. (I do wonder if, as a result, any fournos have sprouted up in odd corners of the world?)

Aha, but now it was time to learn HOW to use it. No easy knobs and dials here. Common sense. Trial and effort. Lots of mistakes. Ouch. Before anything could be cooked in it however, we had to fix the clay by lighting a small fire. When we deemed the fournos to be really dry, a small fire was followed daily by increasingly larger fires. This so that the dome wouldn't crack, the clay baked hard as brick. At last it was ready for use.

And where but to the neighbours Petropolou went I to learn? First what wood to use, and not to use. Being clever people, they never used pine. It is full of tar and would be carcinogenic. Fig wood smelt bad, apricot roots too, tainting the food.

I really learned the hard way. I made lots of mistakes. Too hot a fire burnt things, too low didn't cook it at all. Before long we had constructed a roof over the whole fournos to protect it from the weather and to keep the wood dry. Completed, it was a magnificent fournos which stands to this day.

Like most Greek wives, I baked once a week. As it was quite an operation, I made sure there was to be no other big thing on the agenda. Usually taking a short cut, killing two birds with one stone, we generally had pizza for lunch. The bread dough topped with a rich tomato sauce, thick with onions, garlic, green celery and maybe peppers, made an excellent meal. Huge and rustic round tins, we topped them with all sorts of tasty things. It was a self service affair, but necessarily carefully timed to fit in with the rising bread. We set out little bowls full of sliced salamis, anchovies, capers, olives and of course cheese. Everyone did his own speciality. Delicious.

Our bread was generally quite simple. Flour and water, and risen with fresh yeast creamed with a little sugar. Having no Greek foremothers, I had no sour dough starter, so baked our bread my way. I added olive oil, salt, maybe oregano, basil or cinnamon. For occasions I threw in a couple of eggs, some sugar and perhaps some cut up dried apricots (my own of course). The big round loaves, stacked up like long-playing records, lasted the whole week. In winter they sat on a marble slab covered with a clean sheet. In summer they went into a cool fridge.

The locals were really amazed. They didn't quite know what to make of this strange foreign woman. On the one hand, country women were slightly despised for their primitive way of life. On the other hand, they were much admired. Stamos, a happy and proud man, often and to my irritation, gave away the bread to visitors. Praising it, they spoke of it with nostalgia and of the past. This was how the bread tasted in those past black days of strife and hunger. Good and wholesome.

From observation together with noisy enthusiasm from Mrs Petropolous, I soon learned how to prepare the special breads.

Church bread, which is taken to be blessed before being cut up and distributed at home, is of the finest white flour. I never liked it, but I loved the beauty of the neat, small, flat round loaves. For they looked lovely, with the holy symbols pressed into them, from a wooden mould. Some families had ancient moulds, worn and blackened from use and age, very precious. To this day they are sold, even if ever fewer women home bake. The mould has to be well soaked in water before being firmly pressed into the round, risen loaf. Then it gets a quick glaze before being slipped off the wooden shovel into the fournos. Inevitably, plastic moulds are on the market now, which will no doubt and sadly, eventually usurp the wooden works of art.

Easter bread, being for the family, is made with good flour, but the robust every day kind. Added to the dough is a little sugar, salt, oil, maybe some oregano or cinnamon, entirely due to preference. Usually a dough cross is draped over the huge round loaf. Well glazed, it is liberally sprinkled with sesame seeds before the strongest shelled, red dyed eggs are pushed well in. Perhaps one in the centre, and four in each quarter of the cross. They are usually so handsome, I feel foolish but real regret when they are demolished.

Christmas bread is very similar except it might be more spicy, with perhaps raisins, lots of spices and even nuts in. Whole walnuts in their shells replace the red eggs as decoration, and again the surface is well covered with a sugar glaze and sesame seeds.

It is so interesting to see the imagination and care used, and the different loaves which are produced. Apart from Easter, I was to learn and much enjoy the two other big days in the Greek calendar.

The National Day, 23rd of March is when Greece got independence from four hundred years of being ruled by Turkey.

Oxi Day, (No Day) reputedly comes from when Metaxa, the benign dictator of the time, replied 'NO', to Mussolini's request, that Greece join Italy and Germany against the Alies. 'No!' Greece would not join them, brought about another happy holiday.

Both days are national holidays and bring forth all the populace, the services, schools and almost anyone else who has the inclination, to parade.

We had the misfortune to live a mere two kilometres from a large garrison. Before these Do's, they practised marching, and we got it, full blast, for days on end, on the loudspeakers. Of course, as a regular thing, we had Reveille, Come to the Cook House Door Boys, or whatever. I was told that due to national pride, they would not play the spanking military marches of say, De Souza, or from any other country, so we suffered utterly dull, home made-music. It could have been joyful if they had used the traditional Greek music and adapted it. Sadly, they churned out the dullest stuff, not uplifting in the least. By chance I made friends with some charming young officers all from the north of Greece. Their vintage ex US truck died in town and spotting me with the Landrover, whose bumper was the same height as theirs, they asked me to push start them. Hence we became friends, so I had a little moan to them about the music. I even lent them a splendid LP of military music from Britain, and hoped they might be able to slip it on the turn table and cheer us all up. Regretfully they explained it would be the firing squad if they did, but, they kept the record for some weeks and told me that they enjoyed it in private. An interesting way to make friends, particularly as the army was not encouraged to fraternise with the locals.

On these holidays we would drive into town, park and walk into the centre, admiring the bunting on lamp posts and very nearly every house sporting its attractive, blue and white flag. Milling amongst the crowds, we always met people we knew and it was all very jolly.

The town band, as many small town bands, was quite dreadful, knowing perhaps three tunes, but producing them with gusto. They led the parade while we were herded onto the pavement behind a cord by the local constabulary. Then they took up position in the square with the mayor and town dignitaries to play and watch the march past.

First would come the nurseries, the tiniest children you could imagine marching. Arms swinging with serious exaggeration, family and friends would smile on proudly. Quite adorable, they were all dressed up, as say Cretans, or rabbits, or whatever the proprietor thought up for that year. They came in erratic waves, each group marginally taller than the ones before. Diminutive Boy Scouts, Sea Scouts, taller and taller Scouts, or as Stamos innocently miscalled them, 'Scoots'. Then the junior schools smart in proper uniform, all matching up, for a change. To my constant delight, amongst the school children were many in their national dress.

Topped with a sort of red felt beret, black tassel dangling, they all wore the pleated, white fustanella, which Byron once referred to as 'ballet skirts'. Their jackets were usually red, sometimes blue. Often splendid, richly embroidered, they were more a symbolic waistcoat, with curious shoulder flaps, than jackets. Some were from fathers or even grandfathers and were for me, a rare feast for the eyes. Long, white tights ended with the traditional red shoes on which sat handsome black pom-poms.

Separately of course, came the girls, the little ones first, again either in uniform or in their Amalia costumes, or better still, original clothes from weddings, handed down from grandmothers. The embroidery on some of them was exquisite, and many were from other areas, each region having their own style.

It was remarkable to see the plainest girl swing by in her fantastic outfit. Thickly pleated skirts of hand-spun and woven cloth, stiff enough to almost stand alone. Beautifully patterned, multi-coloured knitted stockings peeped below. Gold or silver, many coloured silk embroidered jackets or waistcoats over fine, pure white, hand-made lace blouses. Generally their heads would be covered, as of old, with a kerchief. Usually silk, they might be adorned with golden coins, their dowry. Eyes demurely down, a goose would blossom into a swan, looking for all the world, mysterious, a beauty. Apparently the clever photographers sought out these costumes to hire out, then took splendid portraits of the girls, which would thereafter, sit in pride of place in family parlours.

Over the years, local friends with daughters often approached me, knowing I had a box of treasures, to borrow something to complete their outfit. I did have a couple of fine, hand made aprons which went first. Then, out would come, my precious collection of lace runners, which would be pressed into service, firmly tucked into a skirt, making another lovely apron.

The marchers grew larger with every wave, till the theological college paced by seriously, to be followed by the well-polished police and then, the fire brigade.

Impressive, the latter drove slowly past in their gleaming, bright red, beat-up wagons, some unfortunate fellow on top, in full fire fighting regalia, no doubt melting in the spring sunshine. Fire being a constant hazard in Greece, these men were much valued and admired.

And at last, the Army. The chosen few, burnished and starched into smartness, it was they who brought up the rear of the entire parade. Only now did Stamos perk up and take notice, having viewed their predecessors very casually. He was the most realistic and loyal Greek, knowing every shortcoming of his people and admitting to them with humour. But, as he explained to me, the army was our hope and our pride. This is when he began clapping. Which, like whatever else he did, he did heartily.

Well, they were really just a bunch of scallywags having the day off and they were out to enjoy themselves as best they could. Eyeing the girls, hop, skip and jumping to get back into step, they tramped along, with their irritated officers obviously in despair at their nonsense.

When a Greek shepherd wants his flock to stop he utters a long drawn out, 'BBBbbbrrrrrrrrrrrrrrrrrrrrrruuuP!' Knowing what it means, his sheep might hear and stop.

I was delighted when right in front of us, a platoon was thus brought to a ragged halt, sung out by a naughty soldier.

'BBBbbbrrrrrrrrrrrrrrrrrrruuuP!'

They shuffled and crashed to a stop, deliberately looking daft. Recognising it, unable to contain myself, I burst out laughing, which brought me some barely concealed and appreciative grins.

If we were lucky, some planes would screech overhead at the right moment, and add to the excitement and racket for a few seconds.

So Easter is the big day, when friends and families come home to celebrate. The airlines are fully booked way ahead, for no matter where Greeks are at Easter, they will do their level best to get home. Not just to the smart flat in Athens or Salonika, but to the village, the island, the real home. Their roots.

The bus and train services are horribly overloaded. Every passenger takes along his own weight of luggage, gifts and chattels.

The roads! Well perhaps we should not go into the roads. If possible, we just stayed at home, or at least tried to keep off the major highways and steer clear of the lunatic egoists. The national news dwells heavily on the accidents on the roads each holiday. Every day, for the long weekend, lurid reports on numbers injured and killed are trotted out religiously. A carnage. Sadly, and inevitably, the hospitals are always full.

Even so, open-house and unstinting hospitality to all comers, is the rule, however rich or poor the family. Hard work, mostly by the women, happy that winter is over, results in a great feast.

The National and Oxi days are occasions out of the home, but just local. Fun, but quite different from Easter, which is really a religious feast together with being a family affair.

The parade over for the year, the crowds slowly disperse. We might call in at Marxos bar, or at Steffis, adding liquid spirit to the

101

occasion, then battle our way through the stragglers and countless vehicles. Hurrying home on the straight, we would hope that we hadn't been burgled, always a real possibility on such days, on feast days, when people are out.

The beautiful costumes, bunting and flags would be packed carefully away in camphor till the next occasion. The town would once more regress into dullness.

My sister-in-law gave us a magnificent, nun's-veiling flag, originally from, I think, a battleship. Not the usual attractive flag with blue and white stripes, a cross in one corner, but the simple white cross on a blue back ground. I proudly hung it up each time of celebration and I have it yet, safely stashed away.

The various feast days, were the usual time for entertaining family and friends. We were usually also invited to weddings, baptisms and funerals, when a meal would probably be laid on. Otherwise, there was little entertaining done by the average local. When you called, for whatever reason, you would always be pressed to accept a tiny saucer of some sweet meat with a glass of water. If there were men around, it would more likely be a glass of retsina, and the woman of the house would quickly produce some small eats. Even the few foreigners married to Greeks whom I did see occasionally, never invited us to a meal in their homes. We must have entertained them at least twice a year for years. Our hospitality became famous in the area. We entertained friends and neighbours on a grand scale, generally using our own produce.

There was one close neighbour, obviously a clever chap as his tiny farm brought him a good income, disgracing us with our acres, who barely survived. He had been abroad for a while, hence he rather fancied himself. I struggled then, as I do now, to speak Greek and without a doubt with frequent and silly mistakes.

The big traveller, who spoke at least ten words of English as well as having no manners, asked me rudely, why my Greek was so bad. My admiration of him evaporated instantly. 'How many times have you been for a meal to our house? How can I learn to speak Greek if you do not invite us?'

Silence. Followed very shortly by an invitation which sadly, having a full programme, I was unable to accept.

Chapter 9

Matchmaking, Dowries and Weddings

The first months in Athens, before I met Stamos, gave me my introduction to Greek Orthodox weddings. Or at least, city weddings. Delighted to be invited, dolled up, present under the arm, off I set in anticipation of a happy time.

Oh dear, but what a disappointment. Being reticent to shove forward to see, I didn't really get a good view of the goings on. Having shared and hurled my rice, which I enjoyed, I went with the tide towards the door. Handshakes, greetings and congratulations, a dainty net screw of sugared almonds in my hand, I left. And that was that. No reception. No fun. The End. Quite deflating altogether. So much for city weddings. However, having moved in with Stamos, country weddings were to soon become a regular pleasure to me.

One day, the gentle Kostas, a Sarakatzani from Zyria, came to call at the farm. I grew to really like him and was to be grateful to him in the future for he helped us buy our Mountain House. This visit was an elaborate and crafty move to involve us in the wedding of his wife's sister. Kostas was a small shepherd and at that time, had no vehicle, so we were to provide the transport. Being the proud owners of a large Land Rover had its uses. At the allotted hour, we collected Kostas and Eleni and loaded up the car with vast quantities of goodies of all kinds. It was a cold and windy day, and had rained heavily in the night. Cloud hung low on the mountains as we drove towards Epidavros, the sea, grey and forbidding, spread far below us. Now and again Kostas ordered us to stop, and there, sure enough, waiting patiently, more passengers stood on the side of the road, waiting to be collected. Naturally every one was loaded down with baskets of gifts and donations for the feast.

Eventually we left the Tarmac road and leapt and bounded up a fearful track to a small village perched on the mountain side. Doors opened at our arrival, wind burnt, finely wrinkled faces peered out and smiled at us. We were strangers, and I, a real foreigner, so we got a terrific welcome.

'Come with joy! Are you well?'

'We come with joy. Yes we are well. Your family, your children, are they well also?'

'Yes well, and how are you?'

'We are well.'

'And your family and children?'

'We are all well, thanks be to God!'

Formalities over, several times, we were led through the mud to the house of the bride. The front door was in the centre and reached by stone steps to the upper floor as underneath the whole house were the usual stables. Directly inside the front door was a tiny hall off which led three rooms. Directly in front was a tiny bedroom which appeared to be packed with young women assisting the bride to dress. To the left was a larger room, the parents' room and general store. We bundled in with our donations for the feast, a sack of oranges and a demijohn of wine. There seemed little space to put them as it was already full of gifts. Then we were ushered into the parlour, where the feast would be held. There were so many chairs and tables in there, it really was difficult to move.

A kerfuffle caused everyone to shout and strain to see, for a single taxi was lurching up the track, a veritable morass. There were 'Oohs and Aahs' as the poor vehicle seemed to bound from one slippery boulder to the next. But Greek taxis are made of stern stuff. And Greek taxi drivers are remarkably good at getting the most out of their unfortunate yet trusty steeds. With a flourish, it pulled up perilously close to the front steps and rather gingerly, out stepped a very smart young man. Intrigued, I asked Stamos if he was the groom. But no. This was a cousin of the groom who had come to accompany the bride to church.

A light clapping of hands, and out she came, looking glorious in white, but wearing a hat, not the usual headdress, which I felt incongruous. Then the new arrival went forward, and gallantly on one knee, put on her shoes, apparently a custom. More applause and down the steps she went, hanging on to her hat, her dress being whipped up by the wind.

An awful lot of people seemed to get into the taxi, but as it was all downhill, no doubt it would get there. Next, every man, including Stamos, made a dash for a farm pick up, piled into the back, and off they went, rattling in hot pursuit.

Which left me, all the women, and my Land Rover. They all looked at me, bright eyes smiling in anticipation. I pointed to the Land Rover, shoulders raised with enquiry. Without hesitation, in they went, sixteen souls of all sizes, good naturedly packing in. What a squash. Slowly sliding into gear, I eased forward, but was alarmed when I felt the whole car buck and quiver. For a moment, fearing disaster, I glanced into the rear mirror. The reason for the rocking became clear. Each and every one of my passengers was 'crossing' herself. THREE times. For we were about to go on a journey. God and the saints must be called upon to protect us, with that road and that load, we needed them. Having passed the church on our way, I knew that the journey was all of two kilometres.

'Hurry, hurry,' they begged me, 'we must catch up, we must arrive all together.'

I hurried. We, as the previous two vehicles, hurtled and slid down the steep track and gratefully on to the small road. Then, just as we neared the little church, a small girl kept demanding something of me which was unintelligible. At last, very determined, somehow, she managed to slide her skinny little arm through the crush, under my arms and clamped her hand on the horn. We arrived safely and in correct style, horn blaring as custom decreed.

It was a little old church, not ancient. Rather like a village hall, or scout's hut. The groom stood waiting on the steps, very smart and handsome in his new suit. When the bride approached, he took her hands and decorously kissed her on both cheeks. We shuffled inside after them, a large congregation and the little church was packed.

The lack of music was new to me. I missed it. Instead, the priest and helper intoned and chanted, really not very musically either. The service waxed and waned, and intrigued, in a whisper, I asked Stamos to explain it to me, which brought forth ferocious hisses from all sides. This was my first experience of the Sarakatzani hiss, the ear-piercing whistles were yet to come.

The only real foreigner there, I felt very conspicuous and wished I were a foot shorter. An old man sidled up to us and whispered loudly to Stamos.

'Now, if you had come to MY wedding. Now THAT was a wedding.' Which brought forth more hisses, if possible more ferocious.

Joined by the flimsy ribbon attached to the 'steffania', the floral crowns, on their heads, the happy couple walked three times around the small altar. Enthusiastically, we all pelted them with rice, while the poor old priest walking in front, held up the large and elaborate bible to protect his face.

'Let us live, let us live ' he cried

At last it was over and we tumbled outside, I happily with my small camera, the best contribution, and did my bit for posterity. A ray of sunshine flashed through the dark clouds for a precious moment.

'See, see,' someone called out, 'The sun shines for Dina.'

Once again, everyone piled back into the cars and we careered wildly up to the village again where the smell of roasting lamb wafted out to greet us. Now everyone ran hither and thither helping till at last, at least fifty people were packed into the small parlour. The mood was light, with everyone laughing at the discomfort, squeezing to find a seat. Then, oh dear, to my horror, some tsingania musicians arrived. Unbelievably, room was found for them to put their equipment and instruments. They began to play with loud speakers too. So much noise, the decibels, oh!

At one moment, realising that I was the only woman seated, I struggled to get up to help, to be firmly pushed down and wedged in so tightly, there was no escape. The din was fearful. The party warmed up. It was not possible to speak or hear. Sitting with the women I glanced across at Stamos through the now thick pall of cigarette smoke.

Over the years, while loving these gatherings, I learned to try to sit by a door or window. Smoking is the norm. There is no consideration for others. Even so called educated people don't bother to ask, 'if they may?' It would be interesting to know the statistics on lung cancer in Greece.

Years later, I picked up a gang of lads hitchhiking on the National road. They were so pleased, and pleasant. Until one of them lit up. I stopped the car.

'Out' I said.

'Why?' they asked astonished.

'Because this is my vehicle, and you are smoking. I do not smoke. Why should I suffer when I am kind enough to give you a lift?'

Quick extinguishing of fags! Peace restored. On we went. I hope they learned something.

The feast began. The women arrived carrying plates of black and green olives. Fetta sprinkled with oil and oregano. Saucers of tzatziki, that delicious thick yoghurt, cucumber and garlic dip. Pink taramasalata. Finely-sliced cabbage salad. Roasted potatoes swimming in lemon. Great chunks of still warm sour dough bread and the inevitable roast lamb. Everything was home made and home grown.

In those days, in the mid-seventies, life was hard and primitive in the villages. There was little refrigeration, and the animals were often slaughtered just the day before a feast, for lack of safe storage. Hence the meat was all too often dreadful, being un-hung, it was tough and stringy. Well I suppose one can get used to anything, and many of the older people have remarkably good teeth.

Little glasses were constantly topped up and raised with the pleasant pink retsina of the area. Toasts made, much laughter. Nothing could be heard for the music, for even in that tiny room they had to have their electrics.

At the beginning, I frequently suffered from a very different upbringing.

'Clean your plate and empty your glass.'

So it was that I learned the hard way, that it is quite the opposite in Greece. An empty plate means you have room for more – and more you get. An empty glass likewise. If you do not want any more, just a little in the glass signifies it. We foreigners drink too much anyway, and it is a rare Greek who over indulges. It is my firm belief that despite the fearful, egotistical and dangerous driving in Greece, they are usually sober.

When the room began to clear, I noticed a tall and colourful bank of cloths displayed, stacked up against a wall. Going over to it, I found that there were many and varied hand-woven pieces. Everything from the familiar cotton rag rugs, through to goat hair mats, to cotton bed sheets and woollen blankets. They were excellent, colourful and wonderful. The stack was about five feet tall. Every cloth was skilfully folded to advantage, and sat upon a sturdy plank resting on two good, smooth flat stones. Immensely impressed, I asked the bride how long they had taken her to make. With a wry smile, she told me.

'Oh, very many years!'

This middle daughter had apparently been a rebel. Refusing many prospective husbands, she had spun and woven, creating this magnificent dowry, taking her time, till at last she made her choice. At twenty eight, she was considered old.

As the day began to wane, farewells were called across the smoke-filled room. There were flocks to milk, jobs to be done. The weather being so grey, it would be dark soon. One after the other, the beautiful shepherds' crooks, called glitsas, were taken from where they leaned in a row against a wall outside. Polished smooth from handling, some were plain, the wood beautiful and gleaming, while others were intricately carved, depicting perhaps the heads of maidens, horses, or snakes. Generally home-made, these are not like ours, they are the small crooks, for hooking ankles rather than the big crooks which we know, for the neck.

Somehow I was reminded of other weddings in another land. There it was the smart cars which were collected on departure. Here, the old men set off home, crook in hand, heads bent against the wind, replete, happy and no doubt with their memories.

Once more in the Land Rover, somehow with even more passengers to drop off along the way, we set off through the mist. I shall never forget that first of many country weddings.

There were many more of them over the years. Our neighbours married three children while I was there. Real country style, they put on a grand feast for friends and relations, before the ceremony. In that patched little yard, long tables covered with snow white sheets were spread. Later, when I was earning our living by catering for tourists, I was glad to be able to lend them all sorts of equipment. Otherwise there were places in town where one could hire almost everything. The women worked like troopers. Everybody helped in some way. Once during a summer reception, great olive sheets were put up higgelty piggelty to protect the guests from the heat of the sun. Although stained and ragged, they did in fact provide a curious half shade. I remember being quietly amused at the wedding feast, when the bride helped serving, wearing her curlers. When at last they were taken out and she was dressed in her, hired for the day, gown, she looked lovely.

It is the usual custom, in the country anyway, for the couple to go together to the special bridal hire shop a short while before the big day. There, the shy bride parades in her finery, until himself chooses. It is then his duty to pay (and very handsomely too) the bill.

Whatever anyone says to the contrary, the dowry system still prevails, in one way or the other. It is a lifelong task, and one that is often very heavy on simple folk. If it is a love match, and the bride has nothing, if the gilt fades, there might well develop quite severe unpleasantness with the passing of time. Without a doubt, a bride gains status if she does have a dowry.

I do actually know a nice woman who was married at thirteen, and to a priest. Quite apart from her youth, he apparently was not a very nice man, so it was a disaster. This is now against the law, thank heavens, and marriage before the age of eighteen is only permitted if there is a shotgun situation.

The family men get together the dowry. The women, in the past, spun and wove and each village had several women whose life's work was to assist with the making of all the bride would need for her new home. Spinning, weaving and embroidering, their days were joyful creating serviceable and beautiful house linen. Now they buy it. Few young women know or care to know how to spin or weave. Sadly so much is lost, the alternative is generally of poor quality, and certainly won't last even half a life time.

Progress marches on. Instead of spinning and weaving, many hours of intense concentration are spent on producing lurid embroidered pictures. Taking pride of place, they cost a fortune to buy and a fortune to frame. A lot of tatting, or fine crochetting of doilies, anti-macassars, sometimes, thank goodness, even fine traditional patterns are copied. Whatever the subject, or the end product, the work itself is generally of the highest standard.

However, the bride goes to her marriage well equipped, and technically speaking, what she takes is hers. If the marriage fails, or, she is widowed, she is entitled to take it with her. Of course this often causes bitter feuds. No one likes to lose out. It can be very many years of expensive legal wrangling before, if ever, there is a solution. It is all too easy, in the early flush of love and optimism, not to tie up legalities with 'wire'. (Which is something I learned years later, to my cost.)

The arranged marriage still does, despite indignant denials, take place. Town girls generally choose for themselves. Country girls even now, are guided by their parents. The divorce rate in towns is high, in the country is low. A young friend put it like this:

Modern girls like the excitement of rebelling against their old-fashioned parents. They thrive on the illicit meetings. They enjoy the battle to get their own way, which they usually do. Then there is the glory of being – The Bride. The centre of all the attention. They revel in the arrangements, the rich romantic affair. After the wedding, they settle down to married life. Very soon, especially if they don't have the prompt arrival of a baby (with all the attention that that brings), they get bored. On to the next drama, the divorce. More excitement and theatre.

This is a word much used. I listened, impressed by that wise country girl. She went on, using the word 'peasant', without shame.

The peasant girls know that their parents love them and want only the best for them. We know that our parents will choose wisely for us. We don't look for trouble. Of course we can refuse. The first, second, maybe the third choice. But we are busy people. There is little time to waste.

She explained to me the organisation it took for them to go down for a meeting. Her family were Sarakatsani from the mountains. A relative or neighbour would have to be persuaded to come and stay to look after the flock. Either for payment, or in kind, it was nonetheless never ideal.

'They told me about the young man. He was a few years older than I, his parents were shepherds also. They were a good, hard working Christian family and my parents asked me to see him.' She stopped and smiled shyly. 'I was very nervous. We met in a tea shop together with the four parents and the matchmaker. I kept my eyes down, but I badly wanted to look at him, so I peeked.' She gave a little demonstration and laughed. 'He did the same thing at the same moment! I quickly looked down and tried not to giggle!'

The matchmaker is generally non professional. A family friend with time on their hands. Often a widow, lonely and bored. They cast around, far and wide, and try to get people together. There might be a payment for the service, otherwise a handsome gift. They are the master of ceremonies at each meeting, the intermediary and an honoured guest at the wedding. It must liven up an otherwise lonely existence for many. There are newspapers specifically for matchmaking.

'I was very nervous.' she repeated.'

'But you liked the look of him?' I pressed.'

'Oh yes, he seemed nice.'

'And how many times did you meet him before the wedding?' She thought for a moment.

'We came down once more to make arrangements. Then once again to hire the wedding dress. Then at the church on the wedding day.' (Four times.)

In this case, they were both lucky, for they are well matched.

'We grew to love each other, although at first it wasn't easy. He was always kind to me but my mother-in-law had me running around all day. It was a relief when he came in at night, I used to look

113

forward to seeing him. Then when the children were born, he was pleased, and our love was good and strong.'

One thing that really impressed me, was that there was no stigma about physical defects. A pretty girl who had toppled into the fire as a baby, scarring her face, had little trouble in finding a husband. Her good qualities overrode the scar. What is always sought is a good strong girl. If she is easy on the eye, so much the better. If she did well at school, fine. Of course if her dowry is handsome, well, a burnt face can't be passed down to future generations. It is literally skin deep.

If a man is very short, he usually wishes to marry a taller girl. Why to bring more small statured people into the world? So a discreet box is set for him to stand on when the studio photograph is taken. No one seems to notice. Inevitably he gets his wish and their children all end up taller than himself.

The country folk are wise. Theirs has been a hard past, and they have survived so many privations by using sound common sense.

Another friend was promised when she was sixteen. The man, it gradually became known, was no good for he chose to run about in bars and music halls. At last, when she was twenty six, it seemed she had become a problem. I can't think why, for she is a lovely woman, intelligent and pretty. Always with a smiling face, she has large grey eyes and healthy wavy hair, a catch indeed. At last, an old man in the next village who had been watching her, demanded her for his only son. It is a very good marriage with lovely, clever and handsome children. So it was a fortunate wait in the end.

Another one told me:

The first time we all met in a taverna. I with my parents, he with his, and the matchmaker. I was so afraid that I didn't look at him once. Then they suggested we meet the next time in a modern coffee shop but as I couldn't recognise him, my father came and introduced us. I was still very shy, but after my father left, I could look up. He was so nice, always trying to make me laugh!' She smiled merrily at the memory. 'It was the same at our wedding. He was very gay. He kept joking. All the same, that night I was very silly and cried like a child. He was very gentle and patient. He told me not to be afraid, that we were married now.' A quiet moment of reflection and then she smiled radiantly at me. 'Then, it was all right!'

Hers too is a good marriage.

In the past, if a boy 'stole' a girl, they were more or less obliged to marry. If for any reason they did not, the girl was considered 'spoilt'. I know an excellent young woman who is 'un-marriageable' for this reason. Her mother died when she was young, leaving her without sufficient loving care and she was 'stolen'. They did not marry. Her life was literally destroyed. It reminds me of a book I read about the seventeenth century Dutch East Indies. A young maid servant was found to be pregnant. The report read: 'After the girl was beheaded, the young man also got his punishment of a good flogging.'

Something about sauce for the goose and the gander here.

There used to be feuds and violence between families if the boy didn't do the honourable thing. Nowadays, as abortion is rife, foolish young people are not absolutely obliged to marry.

Country brides of today are expected, as of old, to have 'stained sheets'. It is usually the mother-in-law, discreetly or otherwise, who examines the laundry on the clothes line. I was told, with some hilarity, that if there was no stain in the past, the bride would be expected to – 'leave by the window'!

There are still many lovely customs in the country. The day before the wedding everyone meets in the couple's future bedroom, the priest is invited. There may be some prayers. Sweet edibles are handed around. Someone's baby son would be bodily thrown, three times, onto the marital bed. Generally he didn't like that at all. I once experienced this custom, poor little Fredo, thrown like a doll. And it is a marvellous coincidence I know, but that couple now have three sons.

115

When the festivities are over, an elder woman in the family takes up a large white scarf or stole. Looping it around the necks of bride and groom, she draws the young couple in through the door together. Then she gives them a spoon of honey to share.

'So that their lives may be sweet together.'

There are very strict rules about intermarriage. Relatives are not allowed to marry, even cousins. This extends to relatives by God. A son of the family may not marry a goddaughter of the family, etcetera. Generally any blood relationship is forbidden, a wise precaution against the build-up of genetic disorders in far flung villages. This must have helped in the survival of a hard-pressed people through a turbulent history.

Chapter 10

Migration

One morning, having as usual, done my shopping early to avoid the crowds and heat, I started for home when I become aware of a hold up. Unable to change course, I soon found myself well embroiled in a fearful traffic jam.

My first thought was that it must be a funeral, for the cemetery is at the west end of town, on our side. Greeks, ever respectful of death, for once forget their hurry and generally trail behind slowly and quietly. It is of course quite a regular occurrence, one to be tolerated with sympathy, for who knows who will be next. Many was the time I crawled behind a funeral procession. The priest and attendants, leading the solemn mourners on foot behind the hearse. Perhaps too, if the family were rich enough, with the town band, bringing up the rear with noisy dirges.

So this wasn't a funeral. If the hold up wasn't a funeral, it must be the railway crossing. For the little Patras/Athens train went right through the town at east and west ends, always irritating us with unnecessary long waits while the bell rang with infuriating regularity. Perhaps I thought, the wretched thing had got stuck again, except that cars were appearing from the other end.

Yet today it was obviously something different, for there was no respect and traffic was running freely albeit slowly. There was plenty of noisy jostling as pick-ups mounted the pavement to get past, with much ill mannered hooting.

Puzzled, I crawled along behind the tail back, not understanding a thing until I noticed that on the road, good gracious, there was masses of muck. Millions of little, shining black pearls; sheep dung, scattered far and wide, all over the street.

A flock in town? Why? Just being moved? Why? Then, like a ray of sunshine on a dull day it hit me. Early summer, it could be only one thing.

A Migration.

Oh joy, to see close to, a proper, traditional migration. They were on their way, by foot, from winter quarters on the low lands to the summer pastures in the mountains, wow! I knew they had their traditional routes, but here in Corinth, ever a hopeless bottleneck, they just had to go through the town.

Eyes alight I crept forward, trying to ignore the rowdy impatience of the other motorists. Eventually we caught up with the tail end of it. Happily I hung back while my fellows jostled and shoved to pass and speed away, desperate to make up for the few precious moments they had lost.

Walking tall, the older men brought up the rear. Glitsas in one hand, the other wielding long thin wands, they walked slowly, their dogs slinking close behind them. From what I could see, it was a huge flock of sheep and amongst them, splendid, tall mules, laden high. Some were carrying huge rolls of a dark, red/black cloth which were at that time, a mystery to me. I crawled along, ignoring the angry hoots from behind, until eventually, a widening of the road obliged me to creep past.

From the corner of my eye I noted that as well as the enormous rolls, there were several equally impressive two handled copper pans. Small, low tables and stools, a cradle, and all manner of nomadic furniture were strapped on the huge wooden saddles. Other mules carried great basket panniers on either flank from which arose a fearful din. I gawped as best I could, desperate not to miss a thing and grateful for my high car. Each pannier appeared to be stuffed with lambs. All I could see was their little heads and wide open mouths all yelling blue murder for their mums. Naturally the mothers were running alongside answering as desperately, but in falsetto. Poor mules, totally surrounded with that awful noise and for some days too, they just plodded along with resignation. Eyes glazed, they seemed to follow my leader, looking utterly fed up, their ears flopped down sideways. I would later learn that the lambs in the panniers were individually tied in a draw string bag up to its neck, so they would not be trodden down by their fellows. Clever.

Next, skittering on dainty hooves, went the donkeys, being buffeted about by their neighbours. As far as I could see, they too were equally well laden, but mostly with bundles, sacks and domestic ware. One carried a big square basket full of bantams, suffering a gale force eight. Poor things hung on to their temporary perches as they were being rocked about with the swing and stride of their carrier. On the fringes of this gaggle walked the full skirted women, headscarves tight about their heads, their faces stern. Also wielding long wands and obviously hot, they appeared to be wearing as much of their heavy clothing as possible.

In front of the main flock went the rams lead by the young men, again, with dogs at heel. Handsome, looking straight ahead, they strode along ignoring the insults which showered from all around upon them.

The road, well scattered with dung, the air filled with the rich, homey stink of sheep, the noise of the beasts and the irate population of Corinth, it was quite an experience.

Free of town and the tangle, I rushed home to find Antony, hastily picked a bag of good oranges and made up two big jugs of hot sweet coffee. Then, judging approximately how far they would have gone, we did a circuit, in order to meet them head on from the west. Baffled, I could not find them. They seemed to have vanished. Desperate that Antony share in this joyful experience, I searched every small lane in the vicinity until at last, there they were, resting.

Relieved, we pulled up, and obviously to their surprise, offered them coffee in little plastic mugs and handed out the oranges for later. They eyed us curiously, not at all sure what we were about. Then we understood the reason for the stop. For there, on the side of the road, lay a sheep giving birth, an old shepherd on his knees beside her. Awed we clustered around, sharing the beautiful moment, watching as he gently helped by pulling on the wet legs of the lamb. Thrilled as was I, Antony joined him and took photos. While the lamb suckled and bonded with its mother, we talked, eager to know about each other. It was a strange encounter, nomadic Sarakatzani shepherds and us. The young men, amused by our interest, spoke happily with Antony, firing questions at each other, dark haired gods with a fair one.

Then came a disturbance. I watched intrigued as some noisy sheep arrived, accompanying a patient donkey. As she was brought forward, I realised that I had not noticed her before in the scrum. Over her back was draped a beautifully made, strong cloth saddle bag affair. Full of pockets, it was packed with tiny lambs all crying pitifully while the new mothers rushed about calling back. The old shepherd, locating an empty pocket, stuffed the new born securely in, with just its head out. Once again I was impressed with this simple and clever system. A snug hot water bottle taxi service, would keep the flock moving. Frantic at the loss of her child, the new mother joined the other bereaved sheep, rushing about under foot causing the whole lot to start up again. Poor donkey. What a racket.

Reluctantly, we waved as they moved off, still with many miles to do; it was a warm leave taking. Almost stunned with the experience of meeting them and of learning something new, we went home, heads full of impressions.

We were sad though, that those fine people should have to suffer so much agro from the stupid town folk. For they themselves were a mere step from such an existence, if they could but admit it. Also we realised that this had been a very special experience, for the migrations on foot are almost over, the modern world has caught up, and nowadays they migrate by truck.

On a high, I excitedly told my neighbours all about it while, knowing about it all too well, they listened to my enthusiasm with smiles. It did however, through a new daughter-in-law, bring us another similar experience, when we learnt more of what we had just seen, not all of which we had understood.

Anastasia was the eldest of three daughters of shepherds. An intelligent girl, she had married the elder Petropolous boy and moved in with the in-laws. I frequently pitied her as the raised voice of her mother-in-law drifted across to us. It seemed, despite being efficient and hard working, she could do nothing right. The main cause for the friction was that she had not become, as was expected, pregnant immediately. This had, by the way, brought us closer together, as every month, Anastasia would saunter, empty handed, up our drive to see me. Tucked in her blouse was a syringe and ampoule for me to give her, a doctor-prescribed shot. Happily she soon had two fine sons, but at that time she was miserable and often lonely. Remembering our funny enthusiasm for the migrating shepherds, she came over one day with a suggestion.

'Tzoudy' she smiled hopefully, (there is no J in Greek, so I was called many odd names.) 'Shall we go for a volta (trip) to visit my home in the hills?'

What a lovely idea! As soon as a free day presented itself, Antony and I made ready and collected her, not unexpectedly, laden down with the inevitable bags of goodies to take to her isolated parents.

A nice looking, tall girl, I couldn't help noticing her extremely large hands. I wondered if it had been due to her milking sheep all her life, or as she told me, from the age of about six.

It was not a good day, with low cloud, wind and occasional heavy showers. With anything other than a Landrover, I would have been hesitant going off the roads on to the muddy mountain tracks. We seemed to go on for ever, the Bay of Corinth sullen below us, winding far and up, often forging through veritable lakes of puddles.

Well off the road, her eyes brightened and she leant forward as we approached a clearing in the dripping pine forest. Such a sight! Set in a thorn-fenced enclosure, were two 'humps', as early burial mounds, a gentle smoke rising from all over one of them. Impressed, we worked out that the larger must have been up to thirty feet long, ten wide, and perhaps seven foot high. As we parked, a small door opened and her mother came out. Antony and I gazed spell-bound, soaking it up, while the two women greeted each other.

Now we understood the huge red/black rolls of cloth. These homes which looked so like ancient barrows, were mammoth 'benders', totally covered with long rolls of home-spun, coarse, goat wool fabric. We examined them, seeing that the narrow strips were dictated by the width of the loom. Ropes, anchored with rocks, were slung over at regular intervals to keep the cloth in place. Courteously, the narrow door held open, we were ushered in. Ducking under the low lintel, we entered the gloom and more surprises in store for us inside.

When our eyes grew accustomed to the dimness, we were sat down on low beds and stools beside a small fire. Our hostess quickly took out a brique, a small coffee pot, and blew up the flame. While this ceremony was taking place, I gazed about, determined to absorb everything.

It was a large, oblong room, the roof supported in two places each end, by sturdy posts firmly set in the earth. Well studded with big nails, they were suspended with all and sundry. The frame of the house was saplings, which the father told us, when he came in later, were left as a skeleton, being repaired annually if necessary. Bound well with fine ropes, it had to be really secure before unwinding the cloth over the whole structure to make the roof. Later outside, I noticed a storm drain dug all around going off down a slope. These people obviously knew a thing or two.

The kitchen end, by the door, was lined with quite substantial wooden crates stacked up as cupboards for storing food, pots and pans. Everything was very neat. A quarter into the room stood the first support post, this one well suspended with kitchen equipment. The hearth stood in front of it on a small raised earth platform. A low stone wall, as an U, backed it, protecting the fire from the draughty door. With all the wood about, a small fire burned around the clock in their neat fou-fou (fireplace) to keep out the damp and insects as well as for cooking.

A little into the room, the walls were lined with simple, low, wood and cord beds. Although there were now only three people sleeping there, two daughters being already married, they remained for occasional visitors. The area along the walls above the beds, were hung with beautiful, brightly coloured woven cloths, obviously done by the women. This lining she told us, added extra protection to the sleepers. Pleased with our interest, they earnestly assured us that their home was weather, wind and rain proof as well as being very warm.

At the far end, the second, well studded post was obviously the wardrobe for it was piled with hanging clothing and many draw-string bags. Along the end wall, neatly, as with the kitchen, wooden trunks called 'bowla', containing all their possessions, were stacked high and draped with more fine woven cloths.

Sipping our tiny cups of scalding sweet coffee, we badgered our hostess with questions. They were very amused, but I suspect quietly pleased with our enthusiasm. As the smoke struggled to seep out through the woven ceiling, a dense layer seemed to press ever lower on our heads. Gradually, eyes smarting, we were so engulfed, we ended by sliding down to sit on the rugs on the beaten earth floor.

One thing I noticed over the years, was that some of the older shepherds had cancers on their faces, particularly on their mouths.

Whether this was from their endless cigarette smoking I don't know. Most of the fire wood they use for all purposes is pine. High in tar, this also could contribute.

Amongst all the clutter, the lady of the house had her spindle handy, hanging on the post above the hearth. I noted, as seems the habit wherever in the world, women spin, the end of it was quite charred and black from prodding the fire. Her dismountable loom caught my eye. Strongly made of boughs, it was very simple, four strong posts well set in the earth. She was obviously a fine weaver and her loom par excellence, judging from her magnificent colourful rugs.

I was very impressed with this practical abode. Clever, safe, economical, how sensible of them to live like this, using what was available. Of course they did have three daughters to find dowries for, so obviously all their earnings from lambs, meat and cheese went into the kitty for that purpose while they lived in utter simplicity.

Before we left they showed us the other 'barrow' a little way off. Smaller, it was in fact the cheese factory. I was again incredulous of the simple yet clever innovations. They had built the frame around an old pine tree, and used the regular radiating branches to hang things on. It was a sight, festooned with very round, skull like white cheeses suspended, well tied with string. Simple, tilted plank tables were all laden with more cheeses, big flat stones weighing them down so that the whey could freely drip into the vast pans below. Barrels full of fetta were stored on one side waiting to be sold, while the empties sat upside down to keep clean.

There were two kinds of cheese being made. Fetta, the full fat, rich and usually wonderful traditional cheese, and the hard mizithera, the Greek equivalent of hard Parmesan. All from sheep's milk, of course. The home-made fetta comes in thick slabs, which keeps indefinitely, stored in barrels in briney whey.

Perhaps fetta is as xorta and indeed olives, an acquired taste. At first I found it very salty, not knowing then that all it needed was a night in fresh water, to leech it less so. Like all cheeses, there is fetta, and fetta.

The round mizithera are hung up and dried, and also last for ages. It is made only from the whey, for nothing is wasted. When semi-dry, the round cheeses are buried in wooden troughs of coarse sea salt which it absorbs and which acts as a preservative before being hung up to dry again. High in calcium, low in fat, it is often an ugly grey-white grating cheese, which is used with pasta. It often looks awful, most unappetising, and I was put off by the colour of the nomadic mizithera until I realised that it was just from smoke. However, the factory mizithera generally sold in shops is usually pristine white and if more hygienic, is probably not as interesting. Whatever, it is surprisingly tasty and with pasta, that great standby, a very nutritious addition to limited diets.

Presumably, unless a little for themselves, they did not make the fresh myzithera I love so. For being a fresh cheese, it would need immediate transport to get it to the shops, and they had no vehicle.

Also hanging up to dry here and there in the tree, were the very strong, cream coloured cheese cloths. Many of the women express their artistry by using splendid and different colours in the thick plaited wool cord loops. Hand spun and home dyed, they are strongly attached to the corners for hanging up the heavy, dripping cheese. They must be strong to withstand tight winding and suspending the fetta to drain.

Outside, close by the 'factory', was a broad hearth on the ground, made up of huge flat stones. This was where they made a good fire in all weathers to boil up the twice-a-day sheep's milk in huge, ancient-looking copper pots, before adding the starter. Beside it was a stack of wood, more or less protected from the rain with a ragged piece of corrugated iron.

I was not to know then, that eventually I too would one day be toiling with cheese making as were these people. Thank goodness, unconsciously I must have been stacking away so much in my head, learning from them.

Years later, when the third and last daughter was married, the parents were able to give up their life's toil of collecting together dowries. Ending too their life in the pine forests in the mountains, they moved in with her, abandoning their traditional way of life.

Anastasia and I went to visit them again. The contrast was total.

It was as much as I could do, not to cry out in horror at their cement box of a house, which they showed me so proudly. The walls were hung with garish, surreal pictures, while the ceilings had plaster decoration all around. The furniture was stiff, shiny and uncomfortable. Knick-knacks abounded, not one lovely rug was to be seen, on the fearfully expensive marble tiles. Of course, beside the telephone, a huge TV stood in pride of place.

It was the kind of modern Greek house you see everywhere, thrown up with concrete blocks, it is freezing cold in winter and very hot in summer. Did they ever, I wonder, remember and yearn for the peace and simplicity of their mountain home?

I did understand the many disadvantages of their previous life-style. The third and prettiest daughter, had, as a little child tripped and fallen into the fire, burning one side of her face badly. Anastasia told me that just she, aged ten, was there, her parents being out with the sheep. Miles from everywhere, with no car or phone, I could understand how desperate they had been, trying to get the little girl to hospital.

Even so, I did in many ways admire and envy them their uncomplicated lives of old, and now realise with such gratitude, just how lucky I was to experience those days, now lost for ever.

Chapter 11

Rom

Apart from our few peasant neighbours, the other locals I became involved with were the Rom, generally known as tzingania. The average Greek knows absolutely nothing about Rom or Romanies. They just dislike and distrust them. Most of the Rom are dark like Indians, partly due to heredity and partly due to the sun. Having spoken Hindustani as a small child, and still retaining some 'kitchen Hindi' in the mists of my memory, I recognised a few of their words, which somehow, over the centuries, they have retained.

When insulting each other, as they often do, they use 'Gyfti' (gypsy) or, (to my amusement) 'Ellinas' (Greek).

Stamos was always a man for the underdog. He had employed the Rom, and grew to really care for many of them. I have to say, to my knowledge, though charming, a lot of them are thieves. I would like to think that one or two are honest but really, I don't know. Anyway, they were Stamos' friends, and became friends of mine and I hope always will be.

My first meeting with Xrysoula, which translated means, 'the Golden One', came very early in my life with Stamos. Anything but golden, she is a slight, dark woman. Stamos called her because I wanted to learn how to pick horta. This is basically mixed wild weeds, almost a staple indeed, searched for and cut by every good Greek wife. Stamos told me that Greece would never have survived the privations of war without it. Firstly, it was free, there for the taking. Secondly, it grew mainly in Spring, before any other vegetable was up, nature's bonus at the end of winter. As with most things, the women used skill and imagination when preparing horta. Apart from straight boiled and served with oil and lemon juice, they made the most excellent pittas, (pies). Similar to the usual spinach pie, it tasted, and no doubt was better than the cultivated spinach. 'Hort-o-pitta' except during Lent, might have fetta crumbled in it, a few chopped green spring onions. Sometimes, they use anitho or maritho, feathery, bright green fronds of the anise family, which add a special taste. There might also be a mere spoon of rice to give it a little body, and encased in fillo (leaf) pastry, it was a feast. Although there is a fillo maker in every town, the village women, despite their efforts to make it thin, produce a thicker leaf pastry, which is crispy and much more tasty, than the bought stuff.

Again, being an ignorant foreigner, I was, in my early days, amazed by the mess of greenery which was lavishly doused with olive oil, lemon juice, salt and pepper and served up at table. Although not unlike spinach, it took me a little while to get to like it, probably not until I started gathering it myself. Most of these weeds are long-rooted, thus full of minerals. They are delicious and very healthy, and the younger the weed, generally the sweeter. Old horta can be very bitter and is valued medicinally, I can only suppose for the eradication of worms.

Another diversion. As with the sound of cymbals, when I learnt about the word HORTA. As the sound we use for H does not fit with the Greek alphabet, it is always spelt there with an X, Xorta. So, suddenly, the dawn of understanding, HORTICULTURE meant growing green things. Another root from Greek.

Unfortunately Xrysoula did not know many varieties. I went along with her and learned the few. Stamos paid her well. Later I had lessons from the other women, my neighbours, and gradually gained experience.

Xrysoula was and still is, the poorest of the poor. Her man, Yannis, a useless drunkard, had one virtue, he stayed with her. They weren't legally married, till at last, after perhaps thirty years of being together, they tied the knot in church. There stood the groom Yannis, clean and for once, sober. The happy bride Xrysoula, all in white, gap toothed, smiling for the camera, while we, and half their children, looked on approvingly. It was a happy affair.

The Rom are the fruit pickers of Greece. They drive huge trucks, small trucks, and an assortment of pick-ups. Each and every one is a total wreck. Wherever they go, whenever they go, they are wildly overloaded. Everything and the kitchen sink, plus a lot of children, and the odd dog, are perched on top.

We used to refer to the Rom village at Examilia as 'the gypsy camp'. There are an assortment of dwellings, ranging from houses, old buses, benders to tents. The houses would be better described as shacks which are thrown up with concrete blocks, any old how, and roofed with corrugated iron or asbestos. Generally there is a small entrance hall and a room on either side. That is it.

Then, there are their travelling homes, beautiful hand-made bell tents which go with them to their harvesting. In the heat of summer, the sides are hitched up and what breeze there is moves freely through. There is one central post and the canvas sweeps almost to the ground. According to the size of the family, the tents are either huge or medium. As in the houses, they neatly stack against one wall, what is virtually their furniture, the night time pile of quilts, rugs and blankets.

One other abode worth mentioning is the temporary shack. These appear and disappear, no doubt being cannibalised many times over. Often put up by daughters, who with hordes of children have, 'come home to mother', they are made of whatever comes to hand. A wooden frame is filled in with heavy duty plastic, cardboard, sacks, old carpeting. In fact anything to keep out wind and rain. This is tacked up nearby her parents, thus getting basic support while still being independent, and without causing even greater overcrowding and friction within the family home.

All Rom homes are kept swept and clean. In winter, the floor is laid as thickly as possible with old carpets and rugs, according to the wealth of the whole family. At night, children collapse on the floor like puppies in a heap, and are covered by their parents. Sometimes the parents have a proper, albeit ancient, bed. In winter, every house has a stove of some kind. These are often battered and dangerous and there are many dreadful accidents. The tents sport a stovepipe too and can be made quite snug. As however, the Rom camps are generally situated on desolate waste ground which no one else wants, they usually get the full force of the cold wind in winter and the hot sun in summer.

There are no mod cons whatsoever, and only very rarely is there a communal standpipe outside. Water usually has to be fetched from near or far. This often causes bitter feuds with the villagers who savagely hate the Rom, saying, rightly as it happens, that they pay no taxes. (So are not entitled to anything.) An important part of Rom life, always loaded on their wrecks of vehicles, are their varied and great water containers. Many was the time they rattled up our bumpy drive for Stamos to fill them up, and gratefully sloshed away.

Despite the filth and junk strewn everywhere, there is little stench. Their dogs, whom they generally love, albeit roughly, clean up human faeces, their main diet. The women, always having plenty of time when not fruit picking, sweep their tiny front yards, and, if they can, often grow little plants, watering with household waste water. It is touching to see a few straggly marigolds, or perhaps some peppers or tomatoes.

They always remove their shoes, as do many wise and simple people the world over, on entering a house. A courtesy and a sanitary rule (if indeed they were wearing shoes at all) so I was approved of when I did the same.

Everything depends upon whether the family has sons or daughters. A mother of sons becomes a ferocious, strident-voiced matriarch. Often huge, for she shows her families' success by her bulk, she controls the purse strings. Her sons work, and she takes the money. Their home, whatever and wherever, has the tallest pile of the best rugs and blankets. Bought up and down the country on their fruit-picking sorties, they are displayed to show their owner's wealth. The Rom do not spin or weave at all although they do prize those woven by others. They also often have many fine copper and brass decorated pots, some of which are made, or perhaps repaired, by the metal-working Rom men.

If the family has mostly daughters, as did Xrysoula, the situation is grave. For the girls do work and very hard whenever possible, but stash away their money for their dowries.

Of course, every gypsy camp is overrun with children. Oh dear, but so many of them. Noses running, filthy, half (if not entirely) naked, they abound. On arrival, I am greeted like the Pied Piper. I have to make sure that anything movable is hidden away or locked up, for otherwise it will surely disappear in the twinkling of an eye.

They are entitled to go to school and some, though extremely few, do so. Inevitably they have a very rough time from the bullying. Occasionally I have seen a valiant teacher try to start a school in the camp. Always on the move, their lives are bound by season and poverty. Very few can even write their names let alone read. But simple maths! They are as sharp as a needle. One family with sons, arranged that their ten year old learned the rudiments of keeping a bank account. It was he, to general astonishment, who deposited their earnings every week.

The babies are glorious. Chubby, with huge black eyes, looking like serious dolls, they are usually stark naked but for a few blue beads stitched into their tatty hair (against the evil eye). Tiny babies are bound tightly like mummies, as the Christ child, in swaddling clothes and for far longer than Greek babies. With their arms hanging out, the poor little things are as stiff as boards and I have seen some pathetically burnt little bottoms from lack of washing and changing. The cloth bindings are also hung with blue beads, an assortment of medals, and possibly a gold coin (jealously watched, for there is no compunction not to steal from each other). Being more or less Christian, there might also be a religious talisman. But generally all deities are taken care of, just in case.

Mothers usually carry their babies in a beautiful shoulder cradle. It is a clever design, with two rods, sometimes with carved ends, and a bright and strong cloth between them. The baby is snugly buried inside its folds, slung over the shoulder and sleeps easily with the walking movement of its mother.

It has been my privilege to be entertained many times in their homes. Always careful not to take much, I am usually offered a rickety chair, and suddenly a huge crowd gathers to look see. One nice memory was having coffee with a rich family in their huge bell tent. The mother, a comfortable and handsome woman, sat cross-legged in front of the central pole. Before her, on a small area of clear earth not covered by rugs, an opened-out five gallon tin served as the hearth. I was impressed with the tiny fire of twigs she blew up to brew the little brass pot of coffee. It was summer, and the tent sides were up. I removed my shoes on entering and sat cross-legged too. It might have been India or South America with all these brown-skinned people, their jewellery, eyes and strong teeth flashing, smiling in greeting. It was good to sit and sing for my supper, by telling them a little about their people who I had met all over the world. I have even taken them books with photographs of northern Romanies, with their benders and caravans. They are utterly fascinated and thrilled and the books are well pored over, the photographs causing great excitement. It seemed almost right that by the time the books were returned, they smelt of wood smoke, and were very grubby.

Apparently, Xrysoula had the misfortune to 'marry' for love. Unusually for Rom, she and the useless Yannis have stayed together and all of her children are his. Seven are girls, lovely sloe-eyed, elegant young women, and two boys, while two died in infancy. The elder son is a horror, a thief and a liar but the younger is made of softer stuff, shy and basically a good person like his mother.

How they have survived is a mystery. Yannis drinks and Xrysoula works. He doesn't even bother to fruit pick, but keeps busy scrounging or stealing, which results in his spending quite a lot of time in jail. Theirs is the poorest, scruffiest house on the site. How many times I paid to have their one window mended, even with wire reinforced heavy-duty glass. It is forever being broken, so they just board it up and cope somehow. Yannis can make lovely baskets, but being hopeless, always has an excuse that he can't find the cane or the willow. The fact is that when he has the money to buy it, he drinks it. It is a vicious circle. Poor Xrysoula. How many times have I found her stealing from us. How furious I got when I felt I was as good to her as I could be. Yet, when I looked closely at the situation, I knew that if my children were hungry, as hers always were, I would, if I were desperate enough, steal too. And what is more I would steal from good people like the Tripos, who wouldn't report me to the police.

Xrysoula only came to see us when she was desperate. If there was any fruit picking to be done, she was at the fore, a true and fast expert who set the pace. Otherwise, she tried to do little jobs such as sweeping, in order I learnt, not only to get paid by me, but if possible to lift what she could. I have seen her several times peep into my store cupboard and pop a bag of lentils or beans, whatever she could find, into her 'Turkish' pantaloons, the favourite place for Rom women to put their gleanings. A ninny I might well be thought, but now, years on, I am glad I didn't make a fuss. Goodwill is far more valuable than a few drax, and for sure, her need was greater than mine.

The Rom women have their own colourful costumes which happily they don't seem to be discarding. I once witnessed one being made, and was impressed with the practical pattern. It is always two-piece, skirt and top and they interchange them. The skirts are heavily-gathered and flounced, and they generally wear as many as they can as petticoats underneath. They all wear the pantaloon, or bloomer, with elastic around the knee. A really safe place to carry loot. Their blouse has one interesting feature, which acts as a breast support. On the side seams, an inch or so under the arm, there are two cords, of the same cloth, strongly stitched in. These tie around the front under the bust. They never wear bras.

It is an impressive sight seeing Rom women walking into town, usually in a group. They love high heels if they can get them. Sometimes they go barefoot. They swing along, as if on a catwalk, elegant and upright. Some of our young women could learn posture from them. We always knew when they were going to town, for our pack of dogs escorted them loudly till well past our borders. Any vehicle who passes is brazenly flagged down, usually to no avail. Stamos told me that once in our lane, one of the women was accidently knocked down and killed. Within seconds the whole furious coven, as one, were onto the truck, dragging the driver out. After they had quickly dispatched him, they picked up their dead and went home. No one knew who the murderess was, and no one was charged. A rough justice.

Knowing them well, whenever I drove to town and spotted the flock of bright parrots ahead, I stopped. In they piled, shoving the elder or fatties before them, pleased as Punch to get to the market early. They adore bright colours, lace, and jewellery. The rich ones wear the real thing, lots of it, and the fortunes of a family are reflected by the amount of gold which flashes. Their gold is their insurance policy. Rom girls will attack and destroy a beautiful front tooth, in order to have it gold-capped. Very much the fashion, a gold tooth is a sign of beauty and wealth combined, which is not easily stolen. However poor Xrysoula was, she always wore some jewellery. It was usually remarkable in being tatty and thoroughly odd. For a long time she wore one of those old brass loo chains. I make it my duty, whenever I go to see her now, to take her something, usually necklaces and bangles, and foolishly sternly admonish her not to give them away. I fear it isn't because she wants to, for she loves bright, pretty things. The next time I see her they have gone. No doubt either because she owes, or is pressured.

One day she came to the house looking more than usually dejected. To our surprise, she quietly asked Stamos for money. It had to be a great emergency for her to lower her pride to actually ask. Surprised by the unexpected, Stamos questioned her closely, to learn it was for Yannis. He had just done a short stint in prison, a not unfamiliar situation. Poor Xrysoula, what a burden, for while inside, the prisoners had to pay for their food, quite heavy for most families. (The Rom probably eat much better when inside than their families do outside.)

Incredulous, we understood that Yannis, the rat, had run up a bill in the prison café. He could not leave prison until it was settled. Knowing her, he had sent poor Xrysoula off to find it. So here she was, hang-dog and pleading.

Highly indignant, Stamos coughed up.

Another time, when we were particularly broke, I had put two cockerels in a pen to fatten for the weekend. Xrysoula arrived, once more looking down. This time her eldest son was about to come out of prison. As I have said, he was a real villain and I groaned at the news. I believe it was he who stole my beloved first piglet Papaligura, and one of my dear lambs. Without enthusiasm I delved into my Mother Hubbard cupboard and gave her a few things. That evening when I went to feed the fowl, one cockerel had gone. The door had been carefully shut.

Now I really WAS cross. Next day we drove up to see Xrysoula and, sure enough, there were white feathers everywhere. She knew that I knew, and I noted a hint of fear in her eyes, but she must have known we wouldn't report her so that vile son got his welcome home, chicken dinner and we managed well enough with one.

Despite Xrysoula and Yannis being dark, there was somewhere in their genes, blonde hair and blue eyes. Now and again one of their brood produced a lovely fair child, quite different from parents and grandparents. At the birth of one of the elder sons many children (a girl of course, apparently one of the blonde, blue eyed variety), they sold it. He then bought a fine jalopy which he thrashed about till money ran short again, and he had to sell that.

At that time, probably even now, although strictly against the law, gypsies did sell their babies, and why not? It's easy money, and girls are not welcome. They always have too many children. What is more important, it surely might give the little thing a far better life and make some childless couple happy.

Why I called at the camp that day, I don't remember. As I pulled up close to Xrysoula's shack, I saw that something special was going on. A goodly fire was burning, being supervised by Yannis and hordes of children. Xrysoula approached, wiping her hands and unusually smiling broadly, showing her lack of teeth. I often wondered if she had lost them from too much child bearing on a poor diet or a swipe from the drunken Yannis.

It quickly transpired what was the reason for the crowd, a meal was being prepared. Stunned, I noticed a small soufla leaning against the wall. Threaded on it, nose to tail, were about ten naked hedgehogs.

My foolish, sentimental heart recoiled. Of course I knew that Romanies, and indeed other poor people the world over, savoured hedgehog. It was nevertheless quite a shock seeing it for the first time.

Our dogs used to alert us to the hunt on the farm. Feeling that hedgehogs are goodly creatures, I always drove them away.

Hungry children are a misery as everyone knows and Rom children are always hungry. They have developed their own, and very skilful way of goading their elders into providing for them. They set up a low, growling moan, which rises and falls and is calculated into driving their parents mad.

Punctuated with words such as 'food' or 'bread', it is an insistent yammering, a running and sickening grizzle. There being always many children, the continued noise, threatening as an angry swarm of bees, drives the parents into doing anything, including stealing, to quieten them. Now they were hopping about happily in anticipation.

An older boy was squatting near the fire and preparing another poor little carcass for the fire. I watched with dismay and fascination. The little thing appeared to be blown up like a small balloon, and the boy was carefully scraping off the needles with a sharp knife. When I volunteered what I understood the British Rom used to do, they listened amazed. Having told them the story about rolling them in mud and baking them in the fire, they laughed most heartily. They did it quite differently. Pulling forth yet another carcass, the boy showed me.

First he made a tiny nick in the lip of the beast, then put his mouth to it and blew it up. Yes really. They explained that they killed them with a quick blow at the back of the neck, and tried not to damage the head. If however it was damaged, a nick at the hock would do, they blew it up from there instead. Once puffed up, it was a simple matter scraping off the needles.

Rubbing the little naked body with oil and salt, they were threaded together with their brethren, mouth through to tail, till the spit was full.

Deeming the fire was low enough, Yannis and Xrysoula carefully set the soufla in place and the turning began. Everyone had a go. An apology of a chair was brought for me. Yannis went off, and obviously using me as the excuse, begged a bottle of evil tasting retsina from a neighbour.

Slowly, an excellent smell surrounded us. The hovering children, frantic with hunger, began to growl again. An elder daughter arrived with a huge wheel of bread. Setting out a big roasting dish, Xrysoula carefully laid slices in it. In less than an hour the meal was ready.

At last, amidst much shouting, the soufla was lifted off the embers. With the point sat in the tin, Xrysoula carefully tore off the melting morsels and draped each piece on a chunk of bread. The children, nervous with hunger, clustered closely around, causing Yannis to feint a few half-hearted blows at them.

Finally sitting down in a circle, each child was handed his little trencher, and heavenly peace reigned. The silence was broken only with sounds of eating and pleasure. Sucking the juice, stuffing bits of bread into their mouths, licking fingers, bliss.

All the while, I, stupid Brit, sat on my wobbly chair with a tiny glass of the fiery local retsina and a piece of bread. It had been easy to refuse the meat, for it would have meant less for the children. Yet at the same time, I realised I was missing an experience. If I had been a more sensible person I should have taken a tiny piece. But I was not hungry as were those people and habit dies hard.

The daughter who had brought the bread sat with her baby in her lap. Naked and as fat as butter, he never took his eyes off her while she ate. Every time she opened her mouth, so too did he. With satisfied bellies, everybody laughed.

It is always a delight going to market, wherever it is, near or far. Inevitably Rom will be there. Inevitably, I will know some of them. A truck, colourful and over flowing as ever, rattles past and perhaps some bright eye spots me. Arms flaying, a cry goes up.

'Yassou Koumbara! Yassou!' (Hello Godmother! Hello!)

Joyfully I wave back. By being Godmother to a Rom child, I am 'koumbara', related by God, to the whole clan, hundreds of them.

'Yassas' (Hello to you all) I yell back, glowing, pleased as Punch. The thrown greetings, hand raised questions and answers fade as the truck trundles on leaving me feeling warm inside. (They are quite proud of me you know.)

And, it is very difficult not to laugh at the astonished and deep disapproval which always shows on the faces of the Greek passers-by.

Chapter 12

Menagerie

Greeks are not cruel to animals. That is, not deliberately cruel, apart from the inevitable monster who exists the world over. They use them certainly, but then who doesn't? They do often neglect them, but on the whole they are simply treated as a lower member of the family, and accordingly.

Brought up in the East where, despite a religion which decreed otherwise, I saw real and savage cruelty, so I do know about it. Skin and bone ponies or bullocks, fed on food so poor, itself from the starved earth, (religion again) could not labour hard and long. Beaten till on their knees, trembling, afraid, bleeding, panting, lying on the hard earth and unable to rise. Being savagely jabbed in the genitals to make it run faster. Now that is cruelty.

I defy anyone who says Greeks are naturally cruel. They are not, they are kind, though possibly ignorant. Just standards are different, which means all standards.

But careless? Yes. Under-feeding because they cannot afford to feed them? Yes again. Cruel from ignorance? Certainly all those.

I, who because of my love for creatures became the county rep for the Animal Welfare, was considered cruel. Why? Because when a cat or dog gave birth, I slipped a needle into the newborn so they died quickly, leaving one for the mother which she could cope with and one which we just might be able to find a home for.

The usual Greek way of disposing of unwanted pups and kittens was to drive out of town with a carrier bag and fling them, with the rubbish, into the ditch. There were many times when I waylaid worried looking children cycling along our road. On investigation, always fearing the worst, I would hear that yes, it was a bag of kits, mother said to throw them away

'But,' I entreated, 'how can you do that? Do you not love them?' 'Yes.' Eyes downcast.

'Do you know how it must be to die like this? Hot, thirsty, big flies laying eggs all over you in anticipation of your death. Would you like it?'

No reply. And from me, utter desperation, more work, more animals. How to cope with such ignorance. I gently told the sorrowing child to remember who I was, where I was, and if it happened again, to bring the new-borns to me to put down. They rarely did.

Some we saved, some we lost, all depending on how soon we found them, how long the poor things had lain abandoned. My young helpers on the farm were valiant, adopting some as their own so easing my work load. Maybe out of a litter of six pups we would save one. Bottle feeding, we took it in turns with tiny feeding bottles sent by the mother of one of our Dutch boys. Pinching off the maggots crawling in wounds, mouth and ears with tweezers. Giving the little thing an enema with a plastic syringe to get the maggots out of its behind. Oh dear, oh dear. And for what?

Having said the Greeks are not cruel, on to the next horror. Shooting. Stupid, puffed up idiots, all too often would come on to our land dressed to kill in all their hunters' finery, quite laughable really. Anything that moved, be it a sparrow, a cat, a dog and once a baby owl. Bang! So manly, so clever. They had no interests, no enemy to kill, no war to wage, yet the cult of the gun still remained strong and shoot they must. The hunting laws, like many other laws in Greece are ineffectual. If they had a permit, they considered it was their God-given right to roam on anyone's land, without permission, and they did. Furious that their leisure was being interrupted they would brandish their silly paper at me. Even more furious, I would rage back and tell them to push off, permit or no, they did NOT have permission to shoot on our land.

So who was I to complain when I lost my dogs and cats? Every year, the length and breadth of Greece, children are shot by idiot hunters. So it goes on. I developed a system which happily worked every time. The moment the shooting began, maybe I was up a tree pruning, or seeing to an animal, I screamed, blue murder, long and loud. Many years previously, I had even won a prize for screaming! It was at a Harvest Home in East Anglia. I remember I wore a deep purple Victorian style dress and rather fancied myself. I got a good laugh, for my fellow contestants just did not have the same lung power. When the judge gave me my prize he asked with a big grin,

'Madam, how did you learn to scream like that?

'Sir,' I replied, 'I am the mother of sons.'

It was always a good feeling to let the rage pour out at top decibel. Cowards, they fled, yes, it was a good feeling. But even if we did not actually receive any lead in us, I frequently felt shot scatter all about me when I was in the orchards.

How many really good four legged friends we lost, on our land, or who died of their wounds and we never found them. How we searched, calling fruitlessly, how we sorrowed and raged. I dreamed of setting up a small cannon on the roof, and popping off at the cowboys as they slunk onto our land, those empty headed gods of destruction. At the same time I did feel pity for them, ignorant, arrogant and mindless morons that they were.

It obviously was common knowledge in Stamos' day, that the farm was abandoned. Early one morning, my second spring, the dogs set up a great fuss. About six cars, five with Athens number plates, drove up and parked near the house. At first, Stamos ignored my pleas to send them away. When the Wild West shooting began, he called the police. The noise of gun fire and frantic dogs was terrific as they worked their way through the tangle of orchards.

Spluttering with indignation, I did refrain from putting a rock through each windscreen. Instead, in my dressing gown, I quietly went to each car, and carefully let down one front tyre on each. They strolled along, collecting up their bag, pitiful, tiny birds. I cannot believe that they would eat them. When the police finally arrived, our uninvited guests were furious. How dare we report them? They all had their license. This was a free country. And so on. Unbelievable and of course, nothing was done so they limped away.

Over the years, we adopted very many animals. What with the shooting, the poisoning and the road, there were vacancies all too often. I found it very hard to say no. Some of them were wished upon us, while others chose to join us on their own. Sadly many people thought that my being the county rep it was a free dogs' home which it was not, for I had no financial help whatsoever from head office or indeed anyone. First they'd phone begging to give us another animal, then they'd arrive, possibly armed with the inevitable, useless box of sticky cakes. After enjoying a meal in the country, they'd clear off, burden unloaded. Without exception, they never donated anything, a sack of broken rice, or a bag of dog biscuits let alone a note. Out of sight, out of mind. So it was a constant, heavy burden, feeding them, and trying to feed them well. Loving them made it easier of course, and I became a pest at every taverna we went to, every butcher, even the smelly slaughter house, begging the scraps. I had a huge pressure cooker in which I steamed down bones so they were soft and the soup full of goodness. Then I boiled up huge pots of kitchen vegetable peelings, mixed in broken rice and finally, a large scoop of powdered milk. Bay leaves and loads of garlic made it tasty and helped protect them against ticks and worms. Finally, all mixed well together, it can't have been that bad, for it kept them all well and happy. Certainly they looked the best fed critters in the area.

Meal times really were as a zoo. I told them, very firmly, that they must wait. Quivering in anticipation, every eye watched my every move. First the collection of battered tin plates was set out round the yard, and then I ladled a dollop onto each dish according to the size of animal. In turn, each dog was told to go to its place while I stood, broom in hand, to oversee. They flung themselves into it; for most of them, who had known starvation, this was the big moment of the day. The tougher ones often did try to see if anyone else had something nicer but quickly returned to their plates at my raised voice. When I was sure the smaller and weaker ones had had their fill, I went into the house.

Instant free-for-all.

Our pack of dogs was exceptional. There were so many of them, all special, but I could not begin to tell of all of them.

Morag was brought by a young relative who was training to be a doctor. Apparently he spotted a bitch with a big litter of pups on some waste ground near his home in the suburbs of Athens. Unable to cope with nine pups, she had pushed away five of them, and concentrated on the remaining four. Being an unusually kindly young man, he began to feed her, and understanding that this was a good human, she took back the rejected puppies. He did find homes for the pups, a valiant effort, so we took the mother, a sort of pointer/ hound dog. As she reminded me of a past horse-faced and aristocratic Scottish friend, I called her Morag. It suited her, she was a fine soul.

Something which amazed me over the years, was how the creatures we took in, quickly grew to know the names we gave them. Apart from their names, they answered to my high pitched yell at meal times. Either, 'Cats, cats, cats,' or 'Dogs, dogs, dogs.' They generally all arrived, dogs and cats, having an idea, rightly, it might mean a meal. When, years later we had several enchanting piglet families, the top-of-my-voice cry was,

'Bay-bees.' Well drawn out, for goodness knows where they got to. Whatever, they knew their names, their call, and came very promptly.

Morag arrived, a bag of bones but had obviously once upon a time had a good home. We wondered if she had belonged to an American service family, many of whom lived in that area. Maybe when they had left Greece, whoever had taken her on, a maid, a gardener, had abandoned care of her. If she heard a chain rattle, she came running, memories reminding her that it was 'walkies'. She loved sweets, and scoured the ground if there were children about. But alas I guessed that she had been tormented for she did not like children, and I had to be very tough on her not to snap. Cats were another bete noir. Once spotted, she was after them, like streaked lightning. It took a week of ferocious and wild threats to make her understand this was simply unacceptable. In no time at all, I had to hide my laughter to see a half grown kitten, actually sitting ON her, presumably for warmth. Her eyes slewed around in disbelief, incredulous at the impudence, but well aware of me in the distance, she suffered silently and maybe even began to like the company.

A call came from the archaeologists. They had a surprise for Judith. Oh! How lovely.

Now everyone knows that the mother of the house is the last to get presents. And if she gets them at all, they are often not really for her, but for the house, generally edibles for kitchen and for the family. So I waited happily, anticipating the gift, which arrived in a big box but with so much noise coming from inside it, my heart fell; another beastie.

It was the tiniest kitten, more voice than cat. One of the awful things in Greece, but, I suppose being nature's way of keeping the population down, is that the tom cats, eat kittens. I have once in the night even heard the death cries of a kit, the mother's frantic attempts to save it, and the gluttonous Tom growling in defence and pleasure with its cannibalistic meal.

We presumed therefore that this one had been dropped by a tom by accident. The archaeologists had heard the cries all day and finally located it in a deep fissure. So who to off load it to? Judith of course. But, happily for everyone, Morag came to the rescue. The poor old girl had just had a false pregnancy because I had firmly locked her in during her last season, feeling she needed to have a rest from breeding.

We called the kitten Cuckoo, for Morag took her tenderly in her mouth and ran to hide under the honeysuckle. I had a theory that there must be a spring below that area, for it is where everything, despite being quite noisy and public, went to nest.

Never have I seen such a fat cat. Her belly was so full and round, she had the gravest difficulty in walking for ages. Her most comfortable position for weeks was to lie on her back, belly up, tiny legs out-stretched. Morag adored her adopted child, constantly feeding and cleaning it, so her hatred of cats was over for ever.

Another wretched habit many of our dogs arrived with, was car chasing. That one was hard to break, and I had to be specially ferocious with them, even to the point of landing them one with the broom, if they didn't move off too fast. They learned, but with deep reluctance, that a fun occupation had to be sacrificed in exchange for love, food and security.

The locals were very impressed. Many was the time they would sit in their cars, on their way, and just sit, amazed that the whole pack was watching my raised finger in the 'No' signal. So in the end I had to tell them to 'move', for I really could not stand there for ever.

My very first real customer from the animal welfare was a young badger. I knew we had them, because I had been thrilled to see one in the very early hours on the farm, and was astonished at how pale was its coat, how slender and long-legged it appeared, probably because of the heat.

He/she, arrived in a cage, having been picked up trailing a string, in Omonia Square, right in the centre of Athens, imagine! We put the cage in a lovely quiet wooded slope on the south border, opened the door and crept away. Early next morning I went to see if it had gone, but there it still was poor thing, sitting in a lake of wee. Going up behind it, I gently tipped the cage so it slid to the open door. It sniffed the grass, looked about, then suddenly realisation hit it, freedom, and it was off. It was good having seen one, so I was hopeful it might find a mate. There were plenty of snails about, so I am sure it would survive although I never saw it again.

On one of her early visits to us little Emilie came to me with,

'Judy, there's a donkey in the field.'

'Oh yes darling,' not really believing her. Some time later again,

'Judy, the donkey is still in the field.'

'Is it darling?' Getting on with my work.Eventually, rather more determined,

'Judy, shall we go and see it?'

We did. Which is how we came to own a Jenny.

We approached her with caution, for who knows what sort of creature this was. I soon realised she was old, exhausted, hungry and thirsty, and that she had a tight piece of wire around her neck. Gently, we led her to the house, where I offered her a half bucket of water, before risking cutting off the wire. She stood, hanging her head, utterly done for and gave no trouble. I anointed the wound on her neck, gave her a quick antibiotic jab and offered her some food which she gladly accepted.

We called her Jenny, because, as everybody knows, all lady donkeys are called Jenny. (As males are called Jack.) Stamos was not impressed, thinking I was being unkind to his (ex?) mistress and began to glower. (Grief!)

At some time he had told me that in Greece all male mules are called Kitsos. Reminding him of this, I gave him our version of it, and Jenny she remained.

No doubt at all she had been abandoned by tzingania/gypsies. Old and useless, just needing care and even food, she had been turned loose. It wasn't the last time we took on an animal who had just been discarded. Indeed I am sure with the passing years, our farm (that silly foreign woman) got a name for itself. Over the years, quite a few more rejects joined the menagerie.

Always creating things with my hands, I had just made a thick rag rug bath mat, a colourful crochet rectangle which lasted all my years on the farm. Its first use was however, not in the bathroom, but as a saddle for Jenny. She accepted Emilie, a light weight, most happily, pottering about the farm but was off and away if anyone larger even tried to mount her. Of course they did, those young devils, always larking about. But it had to be a surprise mounting, for she was very smart, having learnt the hard way no doubt.

One of the best cats we ever had, we picked up crossing the road in town, more flea than kitten. Maria leapt off the Landrover and scooped it up. After several baths and flea powderings, TC, as he was called, became a favourite pet.

Stamos particularly loved him, and frequently took his turn as 'mother'. In a pocket of his shirt, the little lump would lie, close to the warm, beating heart, utterly content. I watched a visitor once, observing this odd breast with fascination. Only when the breast moved, did he understand with a slight smile, what it was.

All that love and attention caused him to grow a pace. His one need in life was to eat, if possible all day, and certainly when we were eating. He wailed and jumped up on the table and would not learn, infuriating everyone. So he was banished, to a magnificent playpen.

In front of the house stood an enormous 'Kupie'. Or could it be 'Queue-py'? A huge earthen-ware urn, a sort of fat Ali Baba pot, in which they must have, in the not so distant past, kept olive oil. In he went, yowled a little, then settled down to sleep, only to wake and remind us of his incarceration at the top of his echoing voice. He was the first of many charming cats, who disappeared, shot or poisoned, harmless, dear creatures who made the place a home.

147

Diamando, our lovely mare, had also finished her life's work and now her farmer had a tractor was honourably retired. She was a big black Spanish type horse with a white diamond on her brow. By chance the farmer's wife was called Diamando, so it fitted perfectly.

There are some regrets about her, small ones, but niggling. I had brought a small TV from England on my last trip, and Stamos loved it. We were in a trough at the time, having finished what money I had, and before I sold my house in Somerset. The TV held little joy for me and I had quickly given up all idea of learning Greek from it. Quite apart from being totally unintelligible, in those days, there were few programs worth watching. So not having the money to buy her, I exchanged my TV for a horse. Sadly, it was some time later when I realised how Stamos missed it. Fortunately, not long after, his sister gave us one.

Diamando was a lovely, kind and willing mare not in her first youth. She and Jenny struck up a devoted friendship, and pottered about together for years.

A friend from home gave me a nice old bridle and I set to with ignorance and enthusiasm, to make a felt saddle. It was hard work, really almost impossible, a masterpiece of invention. The blacksmith made up some archaic looking stirrup irons from a sketch I gave him. Efforts with the saddle were eventually beyond me, so I approached a shoe maker in town called Yorgos. What an inspiration! Eyes watering with emotion, he told me how as a small boy he used to visit the farm with his father, who had been a saddler.

Apparently they had made and repaired all the harnesses for bullocks and ponies for Uncle Frederikos for years. So he stitched my awful saddle on his machine, saving my hands, and we had kit, of sorts.

Before long a relative of mine arrived by air, with a fine old saddle on his arm, much to the amusement of the customs. Likewise all our neighbours, who obviously accepted that here was just another mad foreigner who spoke to them in Ancient Greek while riding around the country on the big black mare.

Then foolishly, for she really was getting on, I got it into my head it would be fun to get her in foal. Enquiries soon brought a nice man from some racing stables in the hills above Loutraki. True, she was old, but, it was worth a try.

I set off at five in the morning and took the shortest route to the canal. On my way, skirting the high walls of the Army Camp, I was amused to see several young men swinging, Tarzan style, up and over on the eucalyptus trees. Astonished, they gazed at us from mid flight, then scuttled into camp after their illegal night out.

All the early-bird farmers warmed my heart as they shouted their greetings to me, and hearing our intentions, good luck with the mare. Eventually I arrived at the Isthmus, there to cope with the first obstacle of our venture.

The Corinth Canal is deep and impressive, built in the early 1800s, Stamos' grandfather, also Stamos, (or correctly, Stamatis) had been involved in some way. Being a cultured young man, he had become interpreter to the French engineers, and so ultimately became the first French Consul of the family.

Dramatic and high in the middle, at each end the land is low. In the old days there were two war-time landing craft ferrying those who wanted to take a short cut. Well that is what I suppose they were, elderly and battered floating iron platforms. Attached each side by chains which hung in the water, a little motor dragged them to and fro with a splendid racket. One, maximum two, (small) cars and the odd motorbike plus some foot passengers travelled across each time. The alternative going over the big bridge on the main Athens/Patras road, was tiresome. So we had to board this unsteady craft with the mare, to get across,

Except that she had other ideas. She took immediate and total exception to the whole operation, she a quiet farm horse who had never even seen the sea before, expected to cross a few metres of it. No.

Desperate not to fail, I remembered that I was wearing a navy blue slip under my blouse, which might just pass as decent. So off with the blouse from my back and on to Diamando's head, and somehow, we managed to back her on to the ferry, and safely to the other side.

Alas, it was a total failure. The kindly manager put her in a stable between two handsome stallions, who dutifully chatted her up for weeks, but no, she would have none of them.

When I went back for her, having arranged a day and time, I found not one soul was there. Obviously we had been forgotten so I wondered about in search of her. Worried that I would have to do the trip all over again, I sang out the usual farm call. Dear girl, recognising it, she replied long and loud with such delight, so I soon found her. Poor thing, she must have been bored to sobs. Her ears were worn hairless from putting her head in and out of the door, brushing them on the lintel. Sadly we noticed that all her stable companions were weaving in boredom, so I was glad to get her away despite our total lack of success.

Unlike our optimistic early morning journey, the return ride was sad. We had no trouble with crossing the canal this time as perhaps she remembered the outward journey, and realised that she was going home, clever girl. Those who had straightened their backs from their labours in the fields to wish us luck, now offered comfort and shared my disappointment. Tail between legs, we went home and resumed life without the joy and extra work a foal would have given.

Chapter 13

Hospitals

In 1969, I went to Greece as 'big sister' to Ruth, who was due her first child. We had been extraordinarily close friends ever since she was a batty teenager. We are still close friends. She is still charmingly youthful. As with many first babies, this one was tardy, which gave me the wonderful opportunity, to spend a few days on Crete.

Emilios' relations took me as their own, and I was especially thrilled to visit that mythological and courageous island. I flew to Iraklion, and at one moment during the short flight I chanced to look down as we passed over a crescent shaped island. To the west of it, dimly through fathoms of water, I saw an astonishing sight. Streets and colonnades, perfectly laid out, dim, magical and mysterious. I even asked the hostess what island it was, so amazed was I by that tantalising glimpse of a lost city.

'Thira,' she said, 'otherwise known as Santorini.'

I have heard of other people seeing it. The plane at the right height, the right angle, the sea calm, the light clear enough to disclose its secrets. Amazing. Could it be the lost Atlantis?

My stay was a delight. Having friends there naturally eased my every move for with the usual Cretan hospitality, they entertained me royally.

Then, I became aware of some trouble. My hosts were distracted. The phone seemed not to cease, there was much discussion and whispering. Finally, unable to conceal my curiosity, I asked what the trouble was.

My host, a Cretan, was the most gentle Greek I have ever met. Indeed he was an inspiration, because he was so unusual. He did not shout. He seemed only to whisper, and I observed that everyone paid attention to him, avidly, carefully. As George began to speak, silence fell. I was to use this example many years later when Stamos stood up in court, and to his amazement, it worked for him too.

'We have a problem with one of our men,' George told me, his face a study of anxiety. 'One of our drivers, (his business was in tourism) although not on duty, he has had a bad car accident. Olympic is on strike, there is no blood. Simos is dying.'

My mind began to race. A regular blood donor, I am – Positively Ordinary. (A good way to remember.) In other words, OP. I asked and yes, hurray, I was the same as desperately ill Simos.

'Take!' I offered, sticking out my arm. 'I do it at home regularly and it is five months since I did, so it will be fine.'

It was then I had my first lesson in the general terror most Greeks have of hospital, and blood donning. (Later verified by Mrs Petropolis.) So acute is the situation, a law decreed that every person having an operation had to provide three donors, whether or not blood was needed. Very clever, very sensible. Many was the time in later years, friends knowing that I did not mind at all, I donated for their relatives.

'Are you sure? Are you quite sure?' Asked the anxious George somewhat to my surprise. I had much to learn, for I considered this was no great deal.

'Of course.' and really happily to do something for these kindly people. Also, and no mean thing, it would be the first time I would actually give blood to a known person. It was a good feeling, better than donating just to a blood bank.

I was taken to a hospital. As I remember, a military hospital, but I may have got it wrong. It was early October and still very warm. Knowing myself, I ate a bar of chocolate before belting around the hospital a couple of times. There were some amazed and amused faces peering at me from the windows.

Simos was taken by ferry to Athens, primed with my and another friend's blood, and he lived. George's doctor brother Nikos in Athens, called for me one day and we went to see Simos in hospital in the hills of the northern suburbs, where he was slowly healing.

So happy was I to see the smiling patient, I produced a hanky (which I happened to have in my bag!), in the form of a Union Jack.

'If anyone runs down the British (there was plenty of that going on in Greece at the time) you can tell them to be quiet, because you have British blood.'

Nikos translated to the surprised Simos. Spreading it out on his battered and bandaged chest, he peered at it, seemingly bemused, a huge smile forming on his face. Then the barber arrived to shave him.

'What?' he flipped the hanky in contempt, waving a cut-throat about with the other hand, 'is this for?'

Poor Simos, desperately trying not to laugh, told him. Indicating me, obviously the donor, I got a mock grimace. It was a merry scene. For me, a very good feeling, for despite not having a brother at all, now I did have one. A Cretan blood brother.

By the time I returned to Athens, the baby had arrived, a serene little girl. A trolley rolled past us as we went to find Ruth, a trolley loaded with about twenty Baby Jesus, bound in swaddling cloths.

Those were the blessed days before disposable napkins, when they were still using the traditional swaddling bands. Beaches, road sides, everywhere, might have been strewn with rubbish, but no disposable nappies. The babies were lined up as sausages, tightly bound as the Christchild. Little arms dangling and heads wobbling, I had never seen such before except in Biblical pictures. Another thing I learnt which equally astonished me, was that the babies'

153

first feeds, were always camomile tea. The original tranquilliser, interesting.

Years later, when I was still living in Athens, Stamos took me to a consular dinner, where I met a charming woman who asked me if I could spare any time. As the nurses were on strike, the situation so desperate, they were asking around the foreign community for anyone who could help. Always with a caring bent, I readily agreed and went whenever I could.

Barely speaking Greek, I asked if I might work in the Premature Baby Unit. My sister joined me when she could and we both loved the work with the infants although we found the standards frighteningly low. It was the biggest and best unit in Greece. Babies were flown in from all over, many of them with their tummy buttons tied with a shoe lace. It was cruelly hot to work in there, and frantically busy being so short staffed, but very satisfying.

On entry we were given an overall, a cap and bags for our feet. We left our possessions in lockers and showered before going to work. It was basically non-stop feed, change and wash. The racket was amazing. When Stamos and children wanted to go to the cinema one night, a film which did not appeal to me, I went to do a short stint in the ward.

'Delfi,' I called, (Sister.) And oh, the sister's face! Standing at the end of the corridor, she sighed with relief, and crossed herself, for there were seventy six babies and just she and one untrained girl on duty. Later, approached by the matron, a fine, old-school nurse who had trained in Britain, she asked me to work there, which I gladly did during the strikes.

The reason for the strikes was of course, in part, money. These girls were generally from the poorest families, they had no dowries, and little future without one. By being trained to nurse, they at least did gain some kudos in their villages. They might indeed become the village nurse in a small first aid station. Not least, it might give them the opportunity to make a good marriage. So all too few of them were in it for love or dedication. They had never been well treated, now they were treated worse than slaves. So they became hard, angry, greedy, and altogether it was a truly sad situation. Because at that time I was a foreigner, (after marrying Stamos I took Greek nationality believing it might be a good thing) I was paid less than the local girls. It was a vicious circle and the girls were treated so badly, quite different from the loving admiration we see in Britain. The first time I was offered money by anxious parents, I was taken unawares.

'But I am paid.' I spluttered. Desperate that I should give special care to their baby, they tried to persist, and were flummoxed when I steadfastly refused the proffered note.

Then something unpleasant began to happen. Money was missing from our lockers, several others had complained, a mystery. Until I went, silently in my soft cloth bags, to the changing room at the end of a shift. A girl was there, and thinking she was coming on duty, I greeted her. She looked uncomfortable, said nothing and instead of changing, went out. When I told the sister about it, I was asked to give a description. A young maid in the hospital was suspected so I was asked to tea when she served, very diligently, unaware she was being observed. It was not her.

Next, I was taken all around the building, to all offices and labs, and introduced to the various staff working there. At last I saw her, through a glass window in a door. For seconds we gazed at each other. She knew, and I knew. Her face blazed red, which even the shocked sister noticed.

'It was that girl.'

Which threw the sister into a flurry of anxiety. The girl had no business to go into our changing rooms, was I sure, and so on. Then it transpired that nothing could be done or said, because she was the daughter of one of the directors. A poor little innocent village maid servant could easily be accused, but a well-to-do director's dishonest daughter, could not. This was Greece, it was sickening, and there seemed nothing could be done. I heard no more. We were never recompensed for our losses.

Back at the farm the family again made our lives a misery, so I decided to take my children off and give them a happy holiday. I was rebuked for taking my Landrover, for despite being glad to see the back of me, my vehicle would be missed.

We went north to Bulgaria, a wonderful, green and fertile country. Sadly at that time the greedy yoke of Russia was milking her of all good things. In ignorance I had not as usual, packed loads of stores, thinking everything would be available. It wasn't. What we lacked in food, we gained in friendship. We met some excellent people, some who I am in touch with to this day. We were saddened by the rules and regulations, and the veil of fear which seemed to effect everyone. I was shocked to find, particularly in comparison with Greece, that drunkenness was rife.

We were given a young rooster who we called 'Ivan' after his donor. All his flock was well daubed with blue paint to identify them and it took months before Ivan lost his. I refused the offer to wring his neck, miming that I would like to fatten him. So Ivan became the first fowl I ever got to know, and indeed to like.

Wherever we went he came, and if we went off, he was tied by the leg to the underneath of the Landrover so as not to expire from heat inside. Miraculously, he was never stolen. He came when called, accepted us as his family, sat and ate with us. A real oddball.

At a cross-road on our return journey I asked my boys to make a decision, 'Greece or Turkey?'

'Turkey!' they announced unanimously. So we turned left and trundled into Turkey, looked up friends, swam, went sight-seeing, loved the food, and came home safely despite the crazy traffic. Ivan too.

Holiday over, Stamos met us at Alexandranopolous and the boys went back to the farm to give us time on our own. The days which followed were as in Eden.

We stayed on Samos, most lovely island, there to charge down to the sea, the Landrover rattling like a tank. We camped, blissfully happy, bathed as Adam and Eve, and our only company, was the rooster.

Next we took the ferry to Mykonos, a journey with quaint memories of how our fellow travellers responded to Ivan. He was without fear, humans were his flock, so he blatantly went about the decks begging for food. Some were so amused they generously gave him hand-outs. Alas, others, presumably city dwellers, drew back in pained surprise, squealed, shoving a foot out to protect themselves from the creature.

Sitting at a table outside a café one day, two incredibly beautiful children approached us and asked if they might pet Ivan. They were enchanted, their wonderful dark Byzantine eyes glowing, they squatted beside him and caressed him, utterly fascinated. Until a plump acquaintance appeared, stuffing himself with bread.

'Give us some bread to give the cockeraki,' our two implored.

'No,' said the fatty, still gorging himself.

'Oh, go on, give us just a little to give the little cockerel.' Charm oozing from every pore, hands out in hope for some crumbs.

'No!' said the glutton with even more determination, still stuffing his face. Which suddenly brought about a complete change in mood. It was such a shock to us, peacefully sitting there, being charmed by these lovely children. Yet just below the surface, lurked the devil.

With an eruption of fury, united, the two angels assaulted the meany. Wild and bitter abuse was accompanied with copious spittle. We were utterly amazed, shocked and amused by the fantastic and theatrical show which ensued. The cockerel forgotten, still spitting with vigour, they gave chase and were gone.

On the next ferry, a young French woman who we had met on Samos, was lying on the deck, obviously ill. With well meant kindness, I tried to shelter her from the sun when the boat changed

157

course. I gave her water, for she obviously had a raging fever, and in surprisingly short a time, I became ill too.

I am rarely ill, a robust soul. So when I am ill, I know it. I knew it, and tried to tell Stamos, begging him to call a doctor. But no, he cradled me in his arms all night, and the only way I could get the fever down was to stagger into the cool sea.

Somehow, we got home. It is a blur. Stamos' children were there, and as usual, there began endless discussions. Problems no doubt. Maria brought trays to our room, but I could not eat or drink for it all came back. My pleas for a doctor were ignored, and the discussions continued.

In between all this, poor Ivan was suffering too. Ignorant that the poor fowl still considered the Landrover his home, Antony had driven off to town. Roosting as was his habit on the axle, he must have been thrown off, for his leg was broken.

No doubt due to my weakness, this overwhelmed me, I was devastated. He had travelled so many miles in three countries, always safe. Home now, and what happens? I crawled out of bed, got out plaster of Paris and set the leg. He lay in a basket beside the front door like an eighteenth century caricature of a gouty old gent, his leg sticking out before him. At least, as he was used, he could be in on everything. A dear thing, happy for attention, he chittered away to anyone who stopped, always ready to be helped to drink from a glass of water or to be fed.

The light sliced into my head. My head, neck and back hurt. I began to feel unreal. Finally Stamos agreed to take me to a doctor that evening. At five to six I went down and got into the Landrover. Discussions continued around the table under the walnut trees and I was ignored. Finally, I rested my head on the horn till he came to stop it. We went to town, to, of all places, a paediatrician. When I think of it, I cower. There I was, so very ill, in a waiting room full of little children, incredible. Later, when my senses fully returned, I just hoped and prayed no child caught my illness. Remembering such times I have to admit that Stamos was often quite irrational and thoughtless.

'Grippy.' (Flu) That favourite Greek ailment. Any little sniffle is grippy. Any thing unidentifiable, is also grippy. The diagnosis after scanty examination. Massive antibiotic capsules were prescribed which I promptly brought up.

The dreadful thing was that I knew I was really ill. No one else knew or cared. Stamos was with his children talking, talking, all day and half the night. The usual, thrashing over their 'problems'. I began to feel reality leaving me. Pain, oh the pain. A steel band tightened around my head.

On the fifth day, a young doctor who obviously knew his job, came to see me. The examination was speedy yet thorough and he was off in double quick time. Suspected meningitis. Athens. A nightmare journey, mercifully a blur, lying on a mattress in the back of the Landrover.

A huge hospital, all white and echoing. Then coolness, which changed to terrible cold so I shivered violently and tried to draw the sheet over me for warmth. I was on a trolley on a corridor for what seemed ages. I saw my sons watching me. Where had they come from? Or was I dreaming? Being manhandled onto a bed. Begging for water. Being sick. And again, and again. Then a hard faced little nurse refusing to give me water any more. I wanted to die, for living was so very painful.

A young doctor spoke to me in Greek. Through parched lips I told him in English, I did not understand.

'All right pet,' said the Angel Gabriel, in perfect English, 'you will be all right now.' Suddenly I felt safe. Someone understood and was going to help me.

A needle in my spine, comforting words, a mist of pain.

Back into the Landrover, and being jostled and bumped away, eventually to the infectious diseases hospital, far to the west of the city, which we had passed on our way in.

This time there was no gentle Gabriel, it was a butcher. Another lumbar puncture within two hours. Rough, cruel and clumsy. A criminal practising on the helpless. A nightmare. Then at last, put to bed, both hands wired up, fluids and antibiotics coursed, the healing process began. With it, my completely dehydrated body began to function again. I asked three times for a bedpan which were brought and removed. The fourth time I asked, I was roughly refused by a hard-faced nurse.

'Please just leave it under me.' I implored. Which thankfully they did and I flowed, just poured, my poor organs grasping for life, at last working.

The room was set up for two beds but had four, so there was barely space to move. On my left was a young woman also with meningitis, and it was she on the third day who told me to ask for pain killers. None had been offered. On my right was an aged crone, and beyond her another. They did not have an infectious disease, but there they were. The yaya, (grandmother) on my right came in just after I did. The noise and lamenting were deafening and my poor head hurt ever more. It was impossible to get away from it. Her entire family seemed to arrive, and they kept up a running petition to God to spare her life. I learned when I was better that she had a severe skin rash, probably an allergy and hardly life threatening.

Her youngest son, Nikos, watched me under his bushy eyebrows. He was a sailor, dressed in his whites, a robust looking lad. Covertly he didn't take his eyes off me while I struggled to find a pot of cream to put on my burning face. Feeling that my whole body was on fire, I groped under my bed painfully, trying not to undo the drips, searching for my small night bag.

Nikos to the rescue. I was almost past speaking English let alone Greek, so mime again. He got it at last, the pot of cream and handed it to me. No way could I undo the lid. He did. In tears by now, the whole effort too much, I mimed to him to anoint my face.

Dear and gentle boy, he did. With great tenderness he sploshed it on, and days later, when I shed all the skin from my whole body like a snake, my face remained intact. Nikos has always been a good name for me, every Nikos I ever knew was as that lad, kind and good.

My sons appeared again, and to my horror took turns to care for me, sleeping on the end of my bed. On the one hand I wanted them, on the other I wanted them gone, far away. Finally they had to leave to return to England and thankfully they never caught anything. At least they had assured me that Ivan was well, and that Geoffrey had removed the plaster so Ivan was walking around again, if with a limp.

The yaya beside me continued her high pitched entreaties to God and the saints non-stop. Occasionally she sang, far more pleasing, so I learned the word 'Sing', to implore her instead to do so, which she did rather beautifully. Far more kind to a splitting head, than loud prayers.

However dreadful the nursing, the doctors were good, prescribed the right medicines and I recovered. Getting up, trailing my stand with me, I found the bathroom, desperate for some sort of wash. The building was three stories, and each floor had one bathroom which served for male and female patients. There were four loos, two 'Western' and two 'Eastern'. One of each did not function. There were four hand basins, two of which also did not work, the third ran water all the time. The floor was awash always and I never found a shower or bath. Later, I explored the other floors in the hope of finding more sanitary arrangements, but they were just as bad.

It was quite pitiful to see old ladies squatting or sitting, the loo wide open for all to see, their drip stands wedged in the open doorway. Being the mid-seventies, Greece was just recovering from colonels. Thus I suppose, few repairs were done, and the conditions were awful from lack of funds.

The hospital was a collection of buildings in a large pine-wooded compound. Apparently each illness had its own house, although

161

mine seemed to have all sorts. Apart from meningitis, there was hepatitis and goodness knows what else. I was surprised that there were buildings too for all the children's common ailments. Concrete paths connected the buildings, and we could hear the huge trolleys rattling along bringing our boring and unappetising meals. Everyone had the same whatever their illness. The only thing worth eating was the yogurt, and that was so thin it barely kept together. We had stainless steel trays with dollops of pale food dropped into compartments. Boredom prompted me to write a poem, so short I still remember it.

> The trolley gongs the meal,
> All white
> Yogurt and rice soup
> On dimpled stainless steel.
> Cold,
> Glimmering moonscape.

Hardly prize-winning material, but illustrative.

Another incident worth recounting was when I could not see, everything being a blur. So I gazed out of the window at a palm tree, and wondered, incredulous, at the magnificent, multi-coloured blooms which adorned it. Later, when my eyes were back to normal, I realised I must have been quite batty, for of course I knew that palm trees just do not have multi-coloured flowers. Yet I lay there, entranced, feeling that this was one thing good resulting from the illness, the privilege of seeing a palm tree, magnificent, in full blossom.

When my sight returned, I saw to my amusement, that alas, the 'flowers' were just pieces of waste paper. Having been thrown out of the upper windows, they had lodged in the fronds.

Stamos came to visit me after my sons had gone and presumably after he had sorted out his children. I quickly noticed that he was depressed, and put it down to the recent family squabbles. Before long, I realised it was more than that, for he was really off colour and just lay on the end of my bed. Remembering how, when at the height of my initial fever he had cradled me, I feared the worst. When I spoke to the very gentle head doctor, suspecting meningitis, he quietly suggested that it may merely be an attention-seeking ploy. I disagreed, and knowing Stamos well enough by then, I persisted until he was examined.

Poor thing. The doctor who had given me my second lumbar puncture attacked him. I heard, horrified through the open doors, Stamos groaning in pain. Apparently on the third dig, the Butcher succeeded. Stamos also had meningitis.

At least he was in the right place already. At least he didn't have to suffer for days and days before getting treatment. Being next door made it easy for me to care for him, and ill though we were, it was undoubtedly a comfort.

As I got better, I took to wandering about the grounds, anything to escape the noise and mess of the wards. Being late summer, the gardens, such as they were, were parched brown. Thankfully, the straggly great pine trees gave cool shade so healing patients enjoyed being outside, sometimes with visitors. Approaching a small isolated building in one corner I saw sudden activity as faces pressed to the bars.

'Hello,' I said.

'Hello!' they responded as one.

We talked as best we could, mostly in French. They were typhoid suspects. Locked in, food passed in through a grille, I saw their lot was far worse than ours. They begged me for reading matter, so I returned to the main building where I knew a pile of foreign magazines lay. Those poor youngsters were very grateful for them.

Apart from being ill, Stamos was deeply miserable. For no one, friend or family, visited, or wrote, or sent any token of sympathy. I later learned that some things had been sent but had obviously been waylaid. At last we had a visitor. A girl friend of the children came. Galatia, a dear, big-hearted girl, with a smile like the rising sun, she was sensible and kind enough to ignore all the dire warnings for her own health. We both felt cheered and touched by her visit. Someone cared.

We got better and eventually went home. It was a grim experience from start to finish, with such pain it is impossible to describe. I felt my memory went quite haywire for awhile. Since then, anyone I hear of with meningitis has my deepest sympathy, it is a terrible illness, but despite all, we did survive.

Chapter 14

Potatoes and Figs

Weak and wobbly, we settled in back at the farm. It was deserted, there being no young workers and the children having returned to Athens, so we gradually tackled an accumulation of mess, laundry and bills.

Someone gave us some chickens, poor ex-battery-house things, and it was lovely to see Ivan, the little Bulgarian, teaming up with a very nondescript little hen. They were always together, pottering far and wide in search of seeds and bugs. Ivan was finding his voice. Alas, like him, it was hardly impressive.

Some young people arrived looking for work, and agreed to stay, as usual, as family, for food and pocket money.

It was quite obvious that Stamos' brood had worked very hard in their bid to grow vegetables and earn money. The field behind the house had been well planted with tomatoes, courgettes and runner beans.

The lack of a vehicle obviously did pose problems. However, the situation was temporarily saved by a friendly, neighbouring small farmer. Having no license, he did have a little car which he offered to lend so that they and he could market their produce together. Being young, they unwisely used the little car more for jaunts than for business. Inevitably tongues wagged and all too soon, the car was removed.

There were of course ways to sell vegetables even without a van. Wholesalers would surely have collected if the produce was good. It was probable anyway, that the experiment was all too hard for the kids without parental help. Therefore they abandoned ship, and one by one, departed.

This left us with vegetables galore. Sadly, most were past redemption, too old, too big, or just dried out. The courgettes were now giant marrows, which were warmly received by many shepherd friends, a most welcome help in feeding hungry flocks. The tomatoes likewise had spread all over the place so we used what we could in the house till they seemed to come out of our ears. The beans however, beautifully trained on bamboos, were, despite little attention and water, excellent.

Paul, the archaeologist, had often taken us to a nice restaurant in town. Airy and light, it was quite the best although it had few pretensions. Spotlessly clean, it was rather bare, high ceilinged, and the food was good. The staff were courteous and smartly dressed. It occurred to me to take the beans to them so I loaded up a crate and presented myself.

Snap! I broke a bean in front of the boss. And another one, snap!

'See', I told him. 'Young, tender and fresh.'He was definitely interested. We wrangled politely over the price and agreed.

'How many kilos have you there? he asked.Very promptly, quite sure of myself, I quoted, as everyone knew what the crates held,

'Twenty one.'He looked doubtfully at the brimming crate.

'Well, let us weigh them. Haven't you got some scales?'

No, not big enough apparently, so without a fuss he counted out the money and I went home very pleased that we had earned something for a change.

The new young workers who had picked the beans gathered around. They were impressed with the wad of notes I brandished at them, only to see I had charged for twenty one kilos when they had weighed them at fourteen. I was aghast.

Back to town I hurried where I explained my error, and handed over the money while the poor man stood dumb-struck. Never, ever, in nearly forty years in business had he had such an experience. Whereas before I had been a customer, now I was a friend. Every time we went there afterwards, we were warmly welcomed and given red carpet treatment. I imagine he enjoyed telling it to all his cronies, that unique experience, as an after-dinner joke. Peculiar people, these foreigners.

Generally vegetables in Greece are big, too big. Money again. The more weight, the higher the price. Very few growers take a pride in the taste of their produce. It is the looks, and the weight. Many do use manure, generally because they have animals. Their vegetables are excellent, and they know it.

The lazy ones find it easier, possibly cheaper if they have no stock, to use artificial fertilisers. Year after year they lam it on, till the fields are dead and their produce is as synthetic as the fertiliser.

Occasionally you will come across a real tomato. Huge, deep red, it is juicy and the taste? Not a vegetable at all, a fruit. Sweet, tangy, it can be mind-blowing it is so good. Most of the time though, the tomatoes, mass-grown are pale, watery and tasteless, needing an imaginative and clever cook to give them any zest at all.

They do know about the advantages of natural fertilisers. The Greek peasant is a clever person who works so hard, he has no time to fill his head with rubbish. He has learned from his forefathers and from experience. He will grow a patch for himself and his family, while he sells the synthetic stuff on the market.

In our early days, Stamos heard that he could make his fortune by growing potatoes. He had level and good land and water. We went to Naxos, that windswept bug-free island where seed potatoes come from. We learned all we could. Yet, at the back of my mind lurked some fear that we were doing something wrong. Search though I did in my memories, it evaded me. Stamos and indeed his family, were on such a high of optimism, he would not have listened anyway. Only when we utterly failed did I remember.

We stored the sacks in the cave, ideal being cool and shady. The seed potatoes were not like any I had seen before. They were dreadful, almost unfit for pigs. Many of them were mushy, rotten and stinking, a foul job to deal with. Our group of young people toiled away valiantly, except for one.

A Greek friend had asked me to take her daughter for some time, 'to practise her English'. It did not take me long to understand that the harassed mother just wanted some peace and we seemed an easy touch. At first, the girl made a pretence of being helpful, then found some English magazines. Sitting on top of the sacks, she totally ignored suggestions that she get back to work and carried on reading. Each one of us was thoroughly disliking our task, and it irked to witness that lazy girl opting out while we toiled.

At lunch time, I surprised my helpers by telling them that I would be serving the meal. Normally, it was self-service. In Greek houses the mother always dishes up. Knowing pretty well the appetites of my youngsters, I doled out accordingly. When I came to Athena's plate, I gave her just one potato. She looked at it, then at me.

'Only this?' she enquired.

'Yes,' I replied coldly, 'and you have not even earned that.'

All along the table the young people carefully buried their faces in their plates and tucked in. A rough justice, but justice was done. To general relief, she went home.

A wily old potato grower came to advise us. He was pleased to instruct Stamos, an agricultural engineer, on how much chemical to use and so forth.

'It says two spoons for five gallons,' he explained dishing out the spoons. 'But,' a crafty wink, 'why don't we put four?' Two more went in.

We sat and cut the seed potatoes, a disgusting smelly business and filled huge two-handed buckets which were full of small holes. Then they were dipped in the vats of the solution and set to drain before going to the planter.

I looked at the bottle of chemical after the old boy had left and was appalled to see that the 'spoons' required were Tea Spoons, not Desert Spoons as he had used.

It was more than likely poor fellow could not see very well. Either he did not realise he was short-sighted, or, for whatever reason, couldn't contemplate wearing spectacles. Certainly he could afford them, but maybe just did not want to spend the money on them. Either way, I am pretty certain he would have put in extra chemical as a matter of course. Hence so many vegetables are blown up magnificently by hormones or whatever, the farmer gets his weight and his money, and who cares about the health of the nation?

If I filled a whole page with –

Life is very hard in Greece.
Life is very hard in Greece.
Life is very hard in Greece.

Anyone, who has NOT lived and worked in Greece couldn't begin to understand.

Of course I am not referring to the rich city slickers. I am writing about ordinary people, the majority, country people and the life I knew, loved and struggled with.

Stamos cleared the old orchards planted by Uncle Frederikos, a crying shame, for there were many rare and wonderful trees. Years later, I was blamed, of course.

Mordor. 'Tzoungla', as many Greek friends described it, (jungle). Whatever it was called, it was an overgrown tangle of totally neglected and unproductive trees. Having spent months labouring on the younger orange trees in front of the house myself, I was relieved, for I'd had enough. At day's end, I ached all over from my efforts, not forgetting my poor hands.

Pruning all those hard citrus trees would have taken many months of skill and effort. Which was only the beginning; next came the tedious job of clearing the branches. We had no help whatsoever at that time, so it somehow had fallen onto me. That then would have just been the beginning. Irrigating. Feeding. It would have been at least three years before the trees could have recovered and borne fruit. So out they came, leaving land clear for new ventures.

The thing about potatoes I had forgotten, is that one must never plant root crops in land recently cleared. Not only was the land full of twitch grass, it was also full of every bug and nasty worm in the book and we certainly learned the hard way. The few we did harvest were full of holes, and totally unsaleable.

We were however, saved from complete disgrace by a deep frost which wiped them out well before they were ready. Very useful, to be able to blame someone, something, for our own mistakes. But it was galling, and a terrible waste of money and effort, none of which we could afford.

Stamos and his family were shattered, their dreams and calculations were put away. They had not heard the wise old saying

'One year a-seeding, seven years a-weeding.' And goodness knows how many years of seeding had gone by unnoticed.

The other saying, which in this instance was a clout below the belt,

'Don't count your chickens before they've hatched.'It was a very sad experience, a bitter lesson indeed. We really could have done without it.

Greeks love sweet things; the shop windows are piled high with a huge variety of delicious and irresistible cakes. The root of this passion must come from the not so distant past when honey, that scarce luxury, was the only real sweetener to be had. While shops provide luxurious cakes, the women, who rarely have manageable ovens, make their jars of preserved fruit. Guests are always honoured with something sweet, the sweeter the better. Every good wife will rush to the cupboard and bring forth tiny plates and spoons, and serve up some syrupy confection of her own making with a glass of cold water. It could be orange or pergamot peel, grapes or quince. Each woman has her own family recipe and each year she makes sure to tuck away some speciality to serve her visitors. Basically they are candied fruit, for they simmer in sugar syrup for days. The variety is astounding, and shows the imagination of the woman. If there are no 'glykos', sweets, (yet another Greek word used in our lives, glucose), there generally is a box of 'loukoumi' (Turkish Delight) to offer.

There are many factories who prepare these preserves and we used to provide them with what we could. Every spring the calls would come.

Neranzakia, tiny round green bullets which would otherwise grow into marmalade oranges, fetched a good price when tiny, almost nothing when ripe. Sikakia, small wild figs. Pergamot, that strange, orange-coloured, lemon-shaped fruit with a powerful aromatic smell all of its own. We had all of these and in spring, when nothing else was in production, we used to sell them if we could.

My first time we were asked to take some examples of the neranzakia, I picked what I considered was an honest selection. Shocked at my stupidity, Stamos scrabbled through my bucket and hurled the larger of them away.

'Only take the tiny ones,' he instructed me sternly, 'never anything bigger than this.' Another offending baby orange was deftly flung far. 'And, when you fill the crates, put the bigger ones underneath.'

We had a problem, or should I say, I had a problem. For it did not suit me to be dishonest and not show the buyer our spectrum. I never learned. I did however learn how to make the neranzakia, and they really were quite interesting. First they had to be well pricked all over with a needle, each and every one. Then they were soaked in water, changed several times, till I suppose some of the bitterness poured away. Lastly they were simmered for ever in a sugar syrup. They looked almost black by the time they were done, and being home-made the syrup was very dark too, unlike the pretty green syrup of the sweet factories. The praise I got gave me pleasure, although I felt the work involved was dull and not particularly complicated.

A call came for baby wild figs. We had two or three trees but Stamos assured me it would not be worth it, for they paid so little, and it was difficult picking. Then Maria phoned asking for money. I decided to pick little figs.

I had been well warned about the acid milk which exudes when the figs are picked. In the hope of not being burned, I put a good layer of cream on my arms, neck and face before I started. Later, glowing like the rising sun, on fire indeed, I realised it hadn't helped at all. By the time I had filled my crates, that evening and the early next morning, I was bright red and itching all over. Pleased however with my efforts, I drove to the factory in Loutraki in order to give Maria the money, when she arrived for lunch. It was a smart, town-centre factory of some repute. Not a scruffy little village affair as some we knew. The owner, a dapper, mean-mouthed little gent, spotted me, threaded his way across the factory floor and immediately set about deriding my fruit. The crowded factory was open-plan and busy as a hive. Everyone working there seemed afraid of him, yet, looking at me, their eyes were kind. Being country people, no doubt they had noticed and understood my burnt skin.

The price quoted on the phone had been twenty two drax a kilo. He went through the crates like a demon, experienced fingers plucking the slightly bigger figs out and throwing them down with abuse. My stomach churned, I hated him, the rude, miserable money grubbing, mean little old devil. I stood, looking into the middle distance while he made mince meat of me. It crossed my mind to walk out and toss all the figs outside his grand front entrance in protest. Then I remembered Maria. He ended his tirade by offering me seven drax a kilo and marched off.

I stood there shocked. I was so hurt. I just was not used to be treated like that, or being shouted at so roughly. What could I do or say? I was a poor farmer, he a rich towny. I, as every other peasant who supplied him, had worked and picked to make him rich. A wave of distress swept up inside me at the injustice. I breathed in deeply for fear I would weep in rage, and that would never do. Then the manager, who had been hovering, came up to me, looked at my face, arms and figs and said very quietly,

'I can only pay you twelve drachma a kilo,' then turned and called a porter. 'Get working on these quickly, because they are nice and fresh.'

Well at least Maria got some money, if not as much as I had hoped for.

Another time, again burning and red, I took an order of wild figs to another factory. As the boss was not there, I was told to leave the crates and the money would be sent. When we rang a week later, we were told that the figs had been so old and stale, they had been thrown away, there would be no money. Did they get used? Or were they put to one side and forgotten? This is how we were treated. This is how hard it was. This kind of story would repeat itself many times over the years. Really I do not know how the Greek peasant can tolerate it. Yet, perhaps I can. They learn to give as good as they get, shamelessly. They cheat at every turn, they make and break promises vigorously and lie theatrically. Bravo them!

It is the most vicious of vicious circles. No one trusts anyone, so everyone cheats, and subsequently gets treated badly.

Generally the bosses know their workers will cheat them, so they pay them as low wages as possible, accordingly. The workers know the boss will pay them too little, so they cheat him. This is from the very top of the scale to the bottom. If anyone starts off, (as I did) being honest, they will lose out. It is join them or die.

Historically it is so well established, I doubt it can ever be changed. After a few years of being treated badly, I confess I more or less joined the masses and retaliated in kind.

One lady we knew opened a very select boutique which did well for the first few years. Being an honest person, she filled in her tax forms, and paid up. Most of her sales came from tourism, which due to the political situation, then hit an all time low and her business was in the Doldrums. When she filled in her tax forms accordingly, she was simply not believed.

'Pay up, or go to jail.' Not wanting to go to jail, she paid up.

Another family, Anglo-Greeks and very good friends, had a similar experience through the death of a sister. A widow, she had lived in a simple, small flat, but in quite a good area of Athens. Her brother, a truly honourable man, elderly and not in good health, diligently attended to her estate. Not wanting to leave his wife and daughters with the irksome responsibility, he promptly paid her death duties. Twelve (12) years later, a really huge demand arrived for duty on the furnishings of her flat.

My friends were struck dumb. Furnishings, what furnishings? Everything in the flat had been old and shabby, certainly not antique. Of course they had taken small family mementoes for themselves and their children. The few pieces worth giving, went to the sister's friends, her neighbours and the concierge. The rest, useless junk, went into the bin. The sum demanded was so large, if it weren't scandalous, it would be funny.

That a man in his eighties should be harassed for taxes on the estate of his deceased sister after twelve years is bad enough. For worthless sticks of furniture it shows that there is something very wrong.

This sort of situation reigns supreme. The honest soul is so much in the minority, bribery and corruption so rife, that if he fails to play the game, he will lose it.

During that first visit to Greece in 1969, when I sought to

understand the Greek psyche, I was lucky that not only Emilios tried to explain it to me.

Another friend, a well travelled, cosmopolitan man, son of a high politician told me the following.

When a Greek tells you something, he is really thinking something else. And, when he gets to do it, he will do something quite different.

Stamos and I had endless tussles over these matters.

'Say what you mean and stick to it.' I might announce, fed up with the prevarication of whatever situation we were arguing about. It was hard for him.

On the one hand he liked the British, finding their manners 'gentle', thus making life easier and generally more pleasant. At other times he would rage, hating what he described as 'softness'.

'Courtesy, or just a smile are passports to the world.' I capped my argument. Which might cause him to glower and march off, or laugh, and hug me. It all depended on the mood of the day.

As with every normal mother, I often ranted at my children.

'Lazy, useless boy.' Or something to the same effect.

'You must not say that,' cut in an anxious Stamos. 'He is young, he will grow up, do not say such things.' Insinuating that my sons were lilies, not healthy young fellows well used to their tough mum.

'If I don't say them, who will?' In the early days, surprised, I might counter. 'How will he grow up into a decent man if I do not guide him? Who but the parents should rear their children, to teach them discipline so that they can cope in the big wide world?'

'But he is a good boy.'Of course he was, I knew that. He was also lazy! 'What?' I raged on, 'is wrong in telling the truth?'

'Truth?' roared Stamos, the philosopher. 'What is truth? Who cares about the truth?'

It was no good, our cultures were too different. Gradually, I was beginning to understand, the truth must be avoided at all costs. Shut your ears, eyes and mind to it. Turn your back on it. Walk around it, under and over it, but avoid the truth at any price. Directly opposite to how I was brought up. (Help!)

'If you tell one lie,' I hammered on fruitlessly, 'you have to tell three more to cover it up.'

A total waste of breath. This was a habit in the blood, born of centuries of persecution. I was just an idiot foreigner who knew nothing.

A Greek woman friend told me an old Greek saying which goes:

Truth is bitter (in the mouth).

Too right.

Chapter 15

The Mountains

My love affair with the mountains began very early in my years in Greece and may have stemmed from my having been born in the foothills of the Himalayas. Of course, the Greek mountains are nowhere as high as the Himalayas, but they seem so and are very beautiful, wild, fresh and if distant from humanity, clean.

Kostas, the kindly shepherd who had engaged us as taxi service for his sister-in-law's wedding, offered us the use of his house. Unbelievably primitive, we were nonetheless glad of the chance to stay there. Indeed we did, several times in summer and we even spent a New Year there, and very cold it was too. Like any empty and unused house, it was not inviting. One just had to imagine how it had been with parents, perhaps grandparents too, and lots of children living there. Spread out on the broad, scrubbed floor planks would be fine and colourful rugs, spun and woven by the women. Not only on the floor either, for all the blankets were hand made, warm and heavy. Bags of stores and herbs hanging on the beams and distaffs with wool set in a corner, ever ready to be used. Gleaming pots and pans, upside down on high shelves together with the wooden and ceramic water jars. Sadly, there were many ruined houses where such everyday things fell and lay rotting, because they were not considered of any value. Without shame we collected the abandoned treasures which we found. Scrubbed and polished into new life to be admired and wondered about, I still have a few of those long abandoned treasures.

Kostas' house was totally bare, one room with a wooden floor and four rough walls. There were poor-fitting shutters on the windows, and the ceiling was not lined in any way, just the huge ceramic tiles laid on simple bough roof timbers. There was no water or electricity. No furniture except wooden plank beds, a couple of very low, round nomad tables and a few little stools. Ever a poor sleeper, I thought the night away for it was so cold. It was incredible lying on the hard bed, gazing up at the ceiling, seeing the brilliant stars through gaps in the roof tiles.

A typical Sarakatzani house, it was built of roughly cut stone and mud, with a heavy red tiled roof somehow sustained by slender timbers. It is a subduing thought that all the tiles were brought by mule, from the nearest clay pits which, as far as I know, were not very close. Most of the houses were built to the same design, just larger or smaller. Kostas' was medium. There he and his siblings had been brought up during the summer months, going down with the flocks when the weather grew too cold, to winter in the plains. There was a school in those days, set between a tiny, very ancient church and the magnificent just old church. The old school room now rarely gets used, perhaps for occasions. It must have been an idyllic childhood, even if they did begin to work with their parents at a tender age. Kostas always spoke of it with nostalgia, but he was a rare one. Most of the others I talked to only remembered the hardships, of which I am sure there were plenty.

Every house was built to the same design. The front and only door faced West and the windows had no glass in, just simple wooden shutters, which were usually kept closed. There were two, at the most three, rooms apart from the area underneath, which was for the animals. Just one room, the main living-cum-sleeping room, had a wooden floor built over the stable. There is always a small trap-door in this floor which goes down into the space below, a simple rustic wooden ladder as the stair. Presumably during harsh weather this saved going outside. Also perhaps some warmth from the animals filtered up into the living room above.

Fixed wooden beds lined the walls, above which were set good pegs supporting all clothing, which to keep off the dust, are always neatly draped with sheeting. The remaining room had an earth floor, practical as this was generally the cheese and store room and the mud floor just soaked up spills. Apart from the wonderful smell of wood smoke, there was the curious, slightly sour, smell of milk that has gone off. Perhaps it came from spilt whey or from the barrels of fetta.

Every house was built on a slope, the down-side creating the stable where the sheep were kept, not just at night but also in the heat of the day. This to escape the dreadful biting flies, and in the dark was surprisingly, wonderfully cool. The only other time I saw something like that was one summer, when driving in Finnish Lapland. Extraordinary long branches and leaf covered barrow-like structures, similar to the benders of the Sarakatzani, gave refuge from the myriad insects to huge herds of reindeer.

There was always a hearth on the north wall, the over-mantel often strangely elegant as in a French country house. Simple wick lamps were the norm, paraffin lamps with their fragile funnels were used for special occasions. Later I was intrigued to learn an interesting way to help them not to crack from cold draughts. A long old fashioned U shaped hair pin was hung on the rim, so the heat equalised. It worked too. Electricity did not reach that village for many years so it was, as with most real country folk, up with the sun down with the sun. During poor weather, the cooking took place on the hearth, a simple fire with a trivet or grills with a very low stool set beside for the cook. Using the simplest equipment, meals always tasted wonderful. A crude pair of tongs, usually made from iron or split bamboo, would turn the chops or whatever. In fact, meat was not very often on the menu. Life was very simple there, and to our way of thinking, food was very limited.

Without refrigeration, they used dried food and what they grew or produced themselves, with the exception, that is, of flour. For every woman had her sour dough pot well wrapped in damp cloth, in order to provide that most basic and delicious of foods. Amongst the piles of goods loaded on the mules and donkeys were sacks of flour. Now and again a miller would drive about the far villages, enjoying leisure and hospitality while word flew by bush telegraph that he was there, parked at the kaféneon. For bread was and still is the staple. No Greek meal is without bread.

The first time Stamos ever took me out, we went to a Japanese restaurant set in a lovely old garden in the Plaka in Athens. He was pleased to be there, for when he had been a boy it was where he had taken English lessons. Happily he described the teacher, a very short little lady, whose hair was piled up on top of her head to try to make her look taller.

Sadly the pleasant mood did not last long, for all too soon I had what must have been one of my first experiences of just how impossible he could be. For of course no bread was served. And he wanted bread.

'I don't care if this is a Japanese restaurant or not,' he raged at the waiter. (Do I or don't I remember his banging the table?)

'We are in Greece, and I am Greek, and – I WANT BREAD.'

Very embarrassing. A poor waiter was no doubt sent hot foot to a neighbouring restaurant, for he returned very shortly with some awful pappy white bread. So peace was restored.

It was an education to see how those mountain folk had created a life in that wilderness, simply using what was round and about them. No electricity, no gas, no piped water. Yet they built ovens and cookers and cooked and baked and made wondrous dishes and cheese in and on them.

There was a 'fou-fou', built outside, well away from the house for safety against fire, sometimes cleverly incorporated with an oven. A large structure, it was in fact the usual mud beehive oven carefully built over with stone for protection from the elements. Much depended on the energy, initiative or finances of the family. Some ovens were most excellent and roofed, with even two fou-fou, as a two plated cooker, a luxury, in front. Waist high, the fou-fou was simply built with rocks and mud on the apron of the fournos and the good wife could be cooking two things at the same time, with even the oven in use, if it were for a feast. Because the cheese pans were so huge and when full so heavy, that fire was always on the ground. Surrounded with big stones, perhaps to keep the fire contained as well as to support the pan, two people had to lift the pan on and off. It was amazing watching the old shepherds and their wives working.

Some of the real nomads, who had no house but lived in benders, returned each year to their regular summer quarters. It was touching how they cared for their flimsy little homes. Well fenced with wood from the forest, they grew flowers and herbs in the tiny yard, keeping it swept and spotless.

They cooked on the same circle of stones every year. Set in the ground, they might have to repair it in spring for they even make their bread on it as, of course, there was no baker for many miles. As a good fire died down, the food would be set on trivets over the ashes, a large metal dome covering it all. More ashes were heaped up around the edges to keep the heat in and first, marvellous loaves, then a succulent meal would emerge as usual.

Water was collected from the springs which were dotted about the village. This was generally the women's job and there are still, occasionally to be seen, fine ceramic, two handled pitchers called 'stamna'. Often plain, many had delightful coloured designs on them.

181

There were also small wooden water barrels which were transported by mule or donkey. Most work was done outside so wash-day was generally a companionable affair near the well. Each woman had a wooden trough set on a low wall or trestles in which she washed. This trough usually doubled for bread raising. It was an unspoken rule never to pollute the wells.

Sanitation, was non-existent. Presumably there were designated, unsanitary corners near each house. In the past the village was very well populated, so it must have been quite a public affair. Now there is piped water, even if with a simple garden hose, and many of the houses have some sort of sanitation, but, which I fear would not pass any laws.

One spring, we decided to drive to the mountains just for the day to get away from our chores. We had several young people with us and the day promised fair. As we trundled higher the magnificent fir trees grew taller and more dense. We were happy to find ourselves climbing in snow, except that we kept passing abandoned cars at every other bend. At one point there had been a minor landslide leaving barely enough room for us to pass. Holding our breath, we crept forward and across, glad it was early and the mud was still frozen.

To our horror, on arriving at the village, we found it almost crowded, with the fine day others having had the same idea. Some were locals just up to check on their houses and maybe to do a little pruning. Others, incongruous in city suits and silly shoes, were towns-people up, we were shocked to learn, to make plans for building summer houses.

'But how can you even think of building a new house up here when there are so many splendid old houses crying out to be restored?'

They, shocked in turn, looked at me in disgust. Restore an old house? Ugh. Oh no, no, no, they were going to make an Alpine house, with steep roof, ducky shutters and a little veranda like in Switzerland. Our hearts fell for we were already dreaming of how wonderful it would be to do what we suggested, restore an old house.

We had a lovely day, exploring high and low under an intensely blue sky and the fierce, pure sun. There were a few tiny birds about and one hungry cat, no doubt deliberately left to eat the mice. Occasionally we were alerted by the ugly call of a grey-headed crow flying over. As evening fell so too did the temperature, rapidly. Gathering our brood, we set off to go down and home. As we reached the outskirts of the village there stood a delegation, a motley collection of would-be hitch-hikers.

'And what are you waiting for?' asked Stamos in a steely voice.

As one they pleaded for a lift.

'Are you quite mad? (One of his favourite sayings.) Do you think I will risk my family and my Landrover to take you lot down? Certainly not,' slipping into gear again he eased forward. 'You walked up, you walk down.'

Poor things, how their faces fell as they began to trudge through the slush and mud after us.

Cautiously we set off down the hill, the road now quite terrible, a morass from the day of sunshine. At the landslide, we crept fearfully along with bated breath, and safely through. Then, quite suddenly having made up my mind, I asked my beloved to stop, and ordered everyone out. Unusually for me, I gave Stamos his orders. Very firmly I told him to go back to the village and collect them. He was either startled at being so bossed about or acknowledged that apart from being my vehicle, it might be rather wise, so without a word, he manoeuvred the landslide again and disappeared.

We waited shivering on the side of the track in the sudden evening chill and it seemed ages before the Landrover returned. Quite a different gang of faces peered beaming gratefully at us. Nonetheless, the descent was hairy and it was a relief to drop them off along the way at their respective cars. The plan was for us all to stop at the one open café, half way down the mountain to buy us a drink.

There are two cafés side by side, pretty well in the middle of nowhere but at a small cross road. The owner of the upper one,

Yorgos, lived nearby so took his chance and in winter opened on weekends, in the hope that some hunters would stop and give him their custom.

Happy to see us, he encouraged the fire and saw to our orders. Cold, we were glad of the warmth, and it became quite a merry party. The city slickers, their feet wet and frozen in their silly shoes, were all smiles and gratitude. Using their few words of English, they told us how grateful they were for the ride.

'It was worth risking death,' chortled the happy Stamos, just to see their faces when I reappeared.'

'Gentleman, gentleman,' announced one spiv, beaming at me and indicating Stamos, the hero of the day. (Gentleman my foot, I thought sourly.)

Mine host Yorgos had once washed dishes in America, where he had picked up some ideas on decor. Proudly he showed me his collection of artifacts, weavings, glitsas and so on; certainly he had made an effort to make his café attractive.

Over the years, when I was restoring one of the despised village houses, I often passed him walking down from his orchards. As Greece had not yet joined the EEC, and money was very scarce, the cafés had hardly got off the ground, I always gave him a lift, for he had no car then. Sadly, greed caused our friendship to come to an end when he made the great mistake of grossly over-charging me in order to impress the other customers in the café.

Two of our lads, Brian and Philip and I came down from measuring and stopped to warm up at Yorgos. We shared two bottles of light beer which were served with bread and just a little cheese. The bill was so high, knowing the prices, I was really shocked. Realising that Yorgos was intent on impressing the several old bucks also in the café, I decided not to make a fuss, so paid up and determined never to go there again. And I never have.

Later, when the weather was warmer, the café next door opened so we went there. Having not only had exactly the same fare, but indeed more, we were charged less. So indignant was I, that I assured Nikos and his wife that we would always stop at their café and inform all our friends to do so when on their way up to the house. After explaining the reason, Nikos was very quiet before he spoke.

'I do not know why he does it, Kyria. We make such a good profit here, it is not necessary.' I later found out that Yorgos was his brother.

There is a sequel to this story, which happened years later when I was going up to the old house we were so happy to have bought. A young fellow rushed into the middle of the road and flagged me down. Was I going past the cafés? (Where else? There was no other way up.) Would I be so kind and take him and a lamb?

A sneaking feeling told me that this was one of Yorgos brood but I said nothing and agreed to take him and the lamb. I waited some moments till a handsome carcass, all ready for the spit and well covered in paper, was hoisted into the back of the pick-up. Beside me in the front, the lad chatted away and invited me to have a coffee when we got to our destination. When I asked which café, and he told me it was Yorgos, I thanked him and quietly explained why I never went there.

'Even if I am a foreigner, my husband is a Greek farmer. We have all the same problems that you people have. I was always kind to give Yorgos lifts before he was rich enough to buy a car. He never offered me even a coffee, instead he robbed me. It was wrong of him to over-charge me. Just once, which was once too often. I was very hurt, having always given him a lift.'

The poor lad was incredulous and upset, even trying to assure me I that I must be wrong.

'Ask him then,' I persevered. 'Watch his eyes. He will of course deny that he over-charged me to impress his other customers, but his eyes will give him away '

Thereafter I just drove past and Yorgos would look away. Silly man.

So many times this happened in one way or the other. A little finger resting on the scales. Miscounting. A bad piece underneath. Masses and layers of wrapping. Every little subterfuge to gain just a few grams here and there.

Happily all this foolishness was balanced by others who were honest and warmly generous. Glad to know me and to my have my custom, wanting, needing indeed, to keep it, they erred on the side of generosity. So life was a balance, and I learned who not to go to the second time.

During one of my trips home, I bought Stamos two pieces of fine wool cloth in Scotland. A little local tailor made them up and did a wonderful job, particularly on the country suit which was a quiet tweed, the second was just dark. Stamos felt and looked marvellous and was immensely pleased with himself.

At last he was to go to Britain for the first time. Despite his many years being educated in France, he had never crossed the Channel. Really country bumkins, far from the city and news, we did not even know that it was to be the Queen's Silver Jubilee. Therefore as we landed and went our different ways, I told him that if he had any trouble with immigration, he should wait for me to come around.

Well! He was out before I was, no doubt being mistaken for a very well-heeled gentleman tourist in that fine suit. We did laugh.

And were we impressed? For London welcomed us with flags aloft everywhere. The days were miraculously mostly fine. We checked up in the newspapers and joined the crowds and even saw the Queen. Then he was utterly charmed with a party in the square in front of the house where we were staying. More flags and bunting. Rows of sheet-draped tables, and makeshift benches. So much goodwill, it was deeply touching. Hordes of children raced about underfoot while their multi-national parents cheerfully set about providing goodies for the feast. It was truly an occasion to remember and I recall Stamos dancing with TWO little girls at the same time, to their mutual delight.

We collected another Landrover, still second-hand but not quite as elderly as the first. Realising that with his blind eye he really was not so safe, I only allowed him to drive on motorways where there was plenty of leeway.

He loved it all. The roads, oh but they were marvellous, hanging out of the car window he pointed like a kid.

'See, see! Look, look!' at this or that.

Then the cats, my goodness, the cats. It was a hoot.

'Stop!' he'd yell, and hang out of the window again to gaze in admiration at some gross moggy sunning itself on a wall. Until that time with Stamos, I had not realised there were so many fat cats in Britain. Compared with even our well-fed farm cats, they were giants.

We stayed with friends up hill and down dale getting the warmest welcome from everyone. At last we went to a tiny, very old family house in Northumbria, which had remained almost as primitive as on the day it was built. Having heard glowing reports from all of us who so loved it, he gazed in shock and disbelief at the lack of every mod con and his enthusiasm waned dramatically. Quite apart from the lack of twentieth century amenities, during my absence it had been used and abused by a lot of so-called friends, and was in a filthy and sadly neglected condition.

Upset that this special little house should be so disappointing for him, I speedily set to with vigour and took two and a half days to clean it. During which time, not surprisingly, Stamos threw a mighty sulk and took himself off to walk on the fells. Eventually, probably realising the work might get done more quickly, he joined me.

Spotless, gleaming, warm and homely, we sat exhausted in front of the fire with our evening glass of wine.

'And!' his voice raised in contempt, 'after all that filthy work I can't even have a bath.'

So I left him to his wine and went off with intent. As quietly as I could, I filled the coppers, stoked up the range, un-hooked the tub from the dairy wall and got everything ready. While doing this, I sourly remembered all the primitive places he had taken me to, where there wasn't even a chemical loo, let alone a tin bath tub. Ha!

At last the water was boiling, so I poured first cold, then hot into the tub. Next, I set a little stool beside the tub with soap dish and nail brush, and lastly put the maiden (the Northern word for clothes horse) around, well draped with towels for warmth and privacy. Lastly, I opened the glowing fire box door and called him.

'Your bath is ready, Sir.'

There followed a long silence except for watery, soapy sounds.

I sat and gazed out of the tiny stone mullioned window at the magnificent, ever changing view and thought for the thousandth time, how very blessed we were to have such a house. A cough alerted me from behind the maiden.

'Judakimou.' (My little Judy.) 'Thank you for my lovely bath. NOW, I understand how you feel about this house.'

A clean and contented man emerged and peace was restored; I too was grateful.

We went the few miles into Scotland, visited friends and drove on to Edinburgh which Stamos loved. One evening we decided to sleep in the Landrover near Queensferry, so booked into a rather desolate camp site. It was by then early autumn, and rather cold and bleak, so we found a hotel and went in to warm up. Alas I now made a silly mistake, because I enthusiastically introduced him to the joys of Newcastle Brown. Forgetting that Stamos could not hold his drink, I soon regretted it. Instead of getting sleepy or romantic, he took the third course, and became thoroughly belligerent,

'You have to get on with my children,' he raged at me.

'You failed to teach them to respect their elders.'

'You must get on with them.' he repeated.

'No,' I replied firmly, 'we have to meet half way.'

'You have to get on with them,' he persisted. Or was it the good beer talking? 'You should have taught them manners.'

'They are Greeks,' he roared. 'not polite British.'

'And more's the pity,' I muttered miserably.

So here was ugly drink loosening his tongue. Obviously he had been harbouring these dark thoughts for a long time, just as in the Mani, the first time I had seen him over the limit when I had been so shocked at his rudeness to the young Germans at the taverna. Now I just watched him sadly, irritated that yet again, the demon should ruin our holiday.

Distressed, I walked over to the bar and ordered coffee for him; a good move as it turned out for I met the young manager who was, yes, surprise, surprise, a Greek.

Suddenly the sun shone. Two refugees in a strange land fell as brothers on each other's necks. Well, not quite, but they really were so happy to meet. Of course, with traditional Greek hospitality, we did not spend the night in the cold Landrover on a camp site. We luxuriated instead in a lovely room, en suite, with TV (which himself loved) a machine to make tea and a bowl of fruit.

Our drive back to Greece was in some ways quite sad, for having not been in France for twenty five years or so, Stamos found that many things had changed, many not to his liking. He had been educated there during his early twenties, a most impressionable time. Having got through the horrors of the war and civil war in Greece, it had seemed as paradise. It is sadly, so often like that. Perhaps memories are better left intact.

In Italy, weary of driving, I longed to get off the motorway, down to an elusive river which meandered far below us. Eventually we found a little-slip road and left the hurtling traffic. Even then, the river seemed unattainable till an old boy on a scooter stopped to help us. Struggling to remember how to say 'river' in Italian, somehow we made it there, with him leading. The next half hour in the gentle evening light was a delight. Sitting on the rocky, river bank, I don't know how we managed, yet we did actually 'talk' together. It was a warm, sun-lit evening, conducive to friendliness. When our guide heard that Stamos was Greek, he embraced him, telling him with passion how Greeks and Italians are brothers. Two index fingers were rubbed together in demonstration. We talked, arms flying, I desperately sifting for words which might help the charade. It was lovely, one of the really good memories.

Next day, we pulled into a market to buy fruit for the few remaining days of our journey. There I bought a fine wooden basket, which they told me was for the sower to carry his seed for broadcasting. A shabby old man sidled up to us stealthily and I wondered, what now? He then produced from the folds of his vast black coat, a curious piece of stainless steel, well punctured with treacherous nail holes. He then demonstrated in mime, with an imaginary lump of cheese, that it was a grater. So, despite not needing or indeed wanting it, we bought it out of sympathy for him. Obviously in need, he must have worked hard in its making. No doubt he would drink the proceeds, but he had not begged. He had created something with his hands, probably from the drum of an old spin dryer or some discarded machine. Being a handywoman, I was impressed with his effort. I still have both wooden basket and grater, although neither has been properly used. The basket is blue and holds the candles in our little church. The grater, unused, is just a dusty memory, which somehow I cannot bring myself to throw away.

Chapter 16

Escape to Iceland

Back at the farm, once more, we cleared up the inevitable mess and once again started work. I recall that there was not one clean sheet in the cupboard, the dirty linen basket overflowing. Obviously there had been much entertaining in our absence.

Soon, and thank goodness, a fresh batch of young foreigners began to arrive. Unbidden, via the bush telegraph, they trailed up the drive and valiantly threw themselves into whatever tasks were on.

Sadly, Stamos' the family did not appreciate these young workers. I never could understand why. For they were fun. Hard-working. Undemanding. Almost all of them. It might have been some unconscious jealousy. A resentment against these enterprising usurpers; which is what they were considered. Could it have been that it was pretty clear how clever and hard working they were? An example? For most of the young foreigners had worked really hard, perhaps for years, in order to take off, to travel and see the world, to go walkabout. Certainly, with their help, the farm throve and grew tidy and became a farm of which Stamos was very proud.

Our relationship continued deeply loving. I never expected or asked for marriage. We were mature, independent people with such a strong bond, a legal document did not seem necessary. Besides, it was common knowledge that we were both married to others.

Why then, at that time, was Stamos always urging me to get a divorce? He was so persistent, almost childishly so. A mystery I could not understand. I would eventually, when the tangle of lies were unravelled. Curiously, while he continuously pressed me, he never mentioned getting one himself, so I assumed this was another Greek quirk. (He, of course, being independent in the affair, or 'the goose and the gander'?) Eventually, succumbing to his demands as usual, I did obtain a quiet divorce, and inevitably wondered, 'what now?'

My being free might well have been the cause for another bout of unpleasantness. I became ill from a constant barrage of nastiness. I was barely acceptable as a mistress, while it was quite another matter being the unpaid housewife, cook, farm worker and banker. Innocent, not understanding the hatred directed at me, I learnt in time, that at all costs Stamos would be prevented from making me his wife. However, as there was no divorce on his side, a marriage between us was never mentioned. I truly was not bothered. There were some real advantages in being independent, and we were happy as we were.

Sadly, the constant drops of poison had begun to work. Whenever Stamos went to Athens he returned thoughtful and miserable. Whenever his brood visited us, the atmosphere was thick with antagonism.

'Friends', constantly advised me that I was doing it all wrong, and told me what to do. It seemed my attitude was poor. I must work harder at being a door mat. A whipping post. To give, give, give, everything without question. To turn the other cheek. Exasperated, I remember retorting to one of these 'friends', a single and childless business woman, that I would never dream of advising her. I was merely a mother, farmer and housewife, and having no knowledge of running an office, would never have the impertinence in advising her on how to run hers.

Sadly, as it transpired later, this remark caused me to make a bitter enemy. Although she always appeared friendly, her true feelings became evident as I gradually heard the tales she put about in order to harm me.

Lonely and hurt, I slowly came to the end of my tether. Weary of the struggle, not really understanding, it eventually drove me to leave Stamos. Poor man. He was as desperate as I. We could not understand what had happened to us. Why were we to part? Why must I go away? But in order to preserve my sanity, I decided I must go, at least for some months to give us space. I remember saying to him,

'When you have sorted out your family, then I will come back.'

It was a black time for both of us, hoping against hope for the impossible, that the problems would be miraculously solved. Some hope! The youngsters had too little to occupy themselves. They seemed to have no hobbies, no direction, only dreams and abandoned studies. All they did was to gossip, make mischief and torment me.

Years previously, I had read a little book whose name I forget, by a dotty English woman, whose name I also do not remember. It was charming. An adventure in the Thirties or thereabouts, a diary of how she went by ship from the north of Scotland to Iceland, and journeyed across it on a pony. Of trekking across great waste lands and lava beds. Being welcomed by total strangers at distant little farms, far and wide. Being passed on, on to the next habitation, ever to be taken in and welcomed. Of always being wet. She wrote with enthusiasm about the magnificent and ever changing skies and wondrous rainbows. Of her courageous pony. Sleeping on hard, horsehair-stuffed sofas. And always, the unstinting help and hospitality of the generous people.

It so intrigued me, that I dreamed of going there to see for myself. In my youth, when visiting my father in India, I had met some Icelandic friends of his. The husband worked for Fisheries, and had his charming family with him. Being the first Icelanders I had met, I remember them well. Especially the younger son who impressed me by announcing firmly, apropos of nothing, 'And – we – do – not – live – in – igloos!'

It was so quaint, so unexpected. Funny how little things stick in the mind. Apart from them, Iceland and her people were all a great fog and ice-shrouded mystery to me, and one I yearned to explore. So why not?

Directly due to all the miserable past months, now I would receive joy. I phoned the Icelandic Consul in Athens and made my plea. I had no idea whatsoever, where or how to start. Help!

So astonished by my stumbling request was this kindly Greek, he just handed me over to his Icelandic wife. So began a life-long friendship and not only with her, but with her country.

Remarkably, I did still have some money. Sadly, leaving a miserable Stamos, I went first to England, then Scotland. Unfortunately, my dream of going the same route as the writer, was not to be. For there being no boats for intrepid travellers, I went the only way, by plane, Glasgow to Reykjavik. My new friend the consul's wife had arranged that I should stay with friends of hers, the husband a writer, the wife working for Icelandair. They lived in the country outside Reykjavik, in a most charming and practical house with two of their five sons. The arrangement was that I should cook in exchange for my B & B. For Svanhilda hated cooking, and tired after the days' work, daily gave her sons fish, which they hated. It wasn't hard to please the boys with long experience of my own sons and of cooking at the farm. My economic bent also pleased my hosts, for with one extra mouth to feed, (mine) the housekeeping bills were less than usual. It did however often prove quite hard for me, because ever used to vast quantities of vegetables, I suffered mentally and physically from lack of them.

'Vegetables please.'

A daily cry, when presenting my list. So a jubilant Sigurder would present me with half a cabbage. Oh dear. Impressed by their magnificent greenhouses, all heated by hot springs, I was aghast that they only grew flowers. Yet they all seemed so healthy despite lack of vegetables; a question of what you are accustomed to I must suppose.

The growing season being very short in that northern island, not very much does grow outside. I was lucky to be shown and was fearfully impressed by the root cellar which the neighbours had, and where they stored their small, incredibly tasty home grown potatoes.

Missing Stamos acutely, I nonetheless dug in, determined to learn all I could of this strange new country, feeling very privileged to be there, taken in as one of the family and in no time, the community.

My friends got me a job at the local woollen mill where I learned about the special Icelandic sheep and their magnificent fleeces. It was hard at first. I was lonely, and it was quite a problem getting used to the noise, the machines, everything. However, everyone was so kind, I soon became accustomed to it.

Having arrived early in the New Year, I was enthralled by the snow everywhere, with perhaps a mere three hours of daylight to admire it. When I began work, a ten minute walk down the hill, I called for Margaret, a neighbour and arms linked, we struggled along supporting each other against the wind and to keep upright on the icy road. Together with another mill friend, Esther, I was drawn into local events, heard the men's choir and went to church. Sometimes I was taken for drives in the country at the weekend and one day I watched the antics of a group of youngsters in three jalopies which amused me greatly. Obviously they all had the same station on their car radio, as had we. On a small frozen lake, they played 'follow my leader' and danced. It was a hoot, so graceful, swinging this way and that, timing their skids in harmony. I had never seen it done before, and certainly never since.

Lucky to be introduced to diverse people, I was saddened once, so far from Greece, to come across a story, very similar to mine. A charming, clever and handsome woman, had suffered from the children of her man to such an extent, their relationship ended. We tried to comfort each other, but how, when the pain is so severe? She and her little daughter had to live alone, away from lover and father. Such a wickedness surely would in time, reap its own reward. What, I wonder happened to those insensitive kids? And did the sad couple ever manage to find happiness together eventually, with their little daughter?

Stamos wrote to me every day. Amazing. I doubt he had written as many letters in his whole life. He also phoned me once a week, so we kept closely in touch. There were some older ladies at the Post Office at Mossfellsveit who were very kind, even to phoning me at work to make sure I had received today's letter.

Occasionally I went by bus to Reykjavik which is when I gawped at the magnificent scenery, never getting enough of it. That an ice-bound land could host so many exquisite colours on its snowy mountains was incredible. The sheer expanse of it, range after range of varied and exquisite muted colours. It was hauntingly beautiful.

Through my host, I found myself invited to a film festival which I much enjoyed. This in turn gave me the exciting opportunity to accompany some of the film people on a day trip to the Westman Islands. Having quite recently been spellbound by the tense news of the volcanic eruption and subsequent first time ever dominance of man over the huge forces of nature, it was a thrill to look down from the little plane and see it all laid out below us.

To the west lay, jutting from the sea, an all black cone, the new island of Surtsey, the world in the making. Having avidly read what I could about it during its birth, it was a special chance to see it. In time, I would name a dreadful, mad and infertile black goat after it. But that is another story. It was a bonus as a farmer during my Iceland stay to see on Haemai, the tiny seedling trees planted by the school children, growing in the warm, fertile new earth of the volcanos's slopes.

In the field below the house where I stayed, was a barn which housed some sheep and horses. If I was at home mid-day, I delighted to see the farmer let them out, a special moment, for with a mad rush, they leaped and bounded to be free outside. They then all tore about for some moments, round and around, kicking up their heels with joy. I was intrigued however by the young horses who came out with caution and delicately picked their way over the ice, obviously very afraid of falling over. I was told that the horses are broken very late, although much handled and very tame, for the first thing they have to learn, is to keep upright. Many of the sheep stay out all winter eating mosses which they scrape from the rocks beneath the snow. Sadly many are lost of course. Yet many do survive, no doubt thanks to their wonderful double layered fleece.

Once I went into a huge barn which appeared three quarters filled to the sky with hay. The smell, oh the wonderful smell of sweet hay. There is nothing which comes out of a bottle which can compare with nature's fragrance. Despite the harsh climate and short summers, they make sufficient hay for the whole, long winter. The milk and butter were the best I had ever tasted. A sharp contrast to the awful margarine and evaporated milk I had reluctantly become used to in Greece.

Since the earliest days, the Icelanders have depended heavily on their horses, strong, loyal creatures that they are. Until quite recently, the only beast of burden, they even now go where no vehicle can, across the rugged rocky landscape. Brought by Vikings originally, they must have been the best and the strongest to have survived the rigours of the sea voyage and the subsequent harsh elements. Sigurder told me he thinks that they are descended from the original European horse, for they are identical to the chariot horses on ancient Greek carvings, on painted vases and murals. Short in the leg and extremely strong, they carry big men with ease.

Another kindness came when a friend arranged for me to ride on one of these superb Icelandic ponies. I felt like a giant on his back and foolishly feared that my feet would touch the ground. But he was so strong and so firm footed, it was a wonderful experience. We rode out to a huge river delta, which being from hot springs was not frozen and the flats were exposed silt.

It was then that I remembered I had received an unexpected and curious letter from a dear friend of Stamos in Corinth. Not that I think Nikos wrote it, for he spoke no English. A simple working man, he originated from the Mani, so was special. 'Nikos Tyres' we called him, to differentiate from all the other Nikos, for of course that was his business, he sold tyres. His one roomed shop was on the main street, chock-a-block full of tyres of every shape, size and condition and most of the work took place outside on the pavement. His little desk was squashed against the murky window, and when you needed help, he would somehow scrabble his way out from the chaos, his round face alight with greeting. He actually resembled a Michelin man, rotund and cheery. He was ever hospitable, a true Maniot, insisting on sending for a tiny cup of coffee, or a soft drink.

But Nikos was a very special man with hidden talents, for he played the Spanish guitar as a master. Many was the time I happened upon him during a quiet moment, to hear his stubby fingers coaxing glorious music from his well worn guitar. Apart from his music he had another hobby, not least, he collected sea shells. Sadly I never saw them, but Stamos who had, told me his huge collection was from all over the world, exquisite and impressive. He and Stamos were real buddies. An odd pair, the squire and the tyre dealer, they had in common great hearts and fine minds. It was a true friendship. Right at the beginning of my time at the farm apparently Stamos had told him that this was his new wife. And Nikos, one of the rare gems of my early acquaintance had said,

'That is the best news I have heard for a long time.'

So of course and back to the letter.

'Dear Mrs Judith, please send me shells,' came to mind when I found myself riding on a bare river bed. Due to the warm river, for the first time in my stay, I could see the earth and not just ice and snow. Greatly daring I got down and did collect several huge shells, possibly rather common bi-valves, and what a job I had hanging on to my horse! Then what a struggle it was getting up on his back again, trying not to drop the muddy shells as he frantically tried to join his mates who had disappeared over the horizon. Which was indeed an added bonus as it turned out. For to my astonishment, we RAN, the movement unique to Icelandic horses. It took me seconds to realise what was happening. He just took off, smooth, fast, and for me a first, it was splendid, marvellous. So dear Nikos got his shells and I my ride. Out of sorrow comes joy. I am ever grateful to all those generous Icelanders for those four unusual and hospitable months.

I began to make plans to leave, for my time was up. The Easter holidays approached and I wanted to be with my boys. But the best laid plans, particularly with Stamos for a mate, never happened. He phoned me and announced that he was coming. To Iceland. I did not ask him from where he had found (one of his favourite expressions with money) the fares. Apart from missing me, he was apparently so intrigued with my enthusiastic descriptions of my host country. He wanted to see it for himself.

Having regained my equilibrium, I felt a curious nervousness when he arrived. Nothing had changed, except that being far away from the source of our aggravations, we could just be happy. Naturally after mere hours, it was as if we had never been apart. On a previous trip to England I had bought him a good sheepskin jacket which he was glad of. On hearing of his intended arrival, I had made him a balaclava, of which he was most scathing. Until that is, it blew 20 below, and he gladly wore it.

With a 'nothing ventured nothing gained' decision, we tracked down the Co-operative Store's vegetable buyer. I understood that every town had a Co-op, it was the best known shop in Iceland. Things had been so bad in Greece with sales of fruit, we thought it worth a try to try to find a new market for our wonderful oranges. We spoke at length to a nice young man, but to no avail, for he wanted ripe sweet oranges before Christmas. Ours were barely ripe then, and would be at their best months later. We learned that Spain supplied them earlier, so our efforts were to no avail.

'Let us get married.' Stamos announced to my surprise one day.

'Oh,' said I, 'have you got your divorce then?'

No reply.

It was then, and still is now, a mystery to me, why facts, large and small, were distorted, often beyond recognition. The inability to tell the the simple truth. For some reason, it had been avoided. So what was the truth? Will I ever know? In this case, is it indeed necessary to know?

'Why do you want us to get married?' I asked. 'Are we not just fine as we are?

'No! Because I want my children to understand that I want you for my wife.'

'How can you marry me when you are still married to Eleni?'

'Because I am not married to Eleni and never was. We were never legally married,' he announced flatly yet firmly. 'For she was already married to another.'

Gradually it came out in dribs and drabs. There was the chaos of war. Greece was over-run with foreign armies. There was much hunger and hardship and people survived how they could, even to consorting with the enemy. This was followed by even worse, the tragic civil war. During the destruction, so much, including papers, were lost. Only witnesses could say if indeed and when a marriage had taken place. It was a harsh time of sorrow and desperation. Who knows what lonely, loving people had married and taken comfort in each other, despite their differences. Then perhaps inevitably, through world events out of their control, they were forced to part? Who knows. Love has no barriers.

Stamos told me that Eleni had married a German officer, a great sin at that time in Greece. He was, so Stamos said, the only man she had truly loved. When war drew to a close, he had left with his retreating army. Was he killed, did he already have a wife, or did he decide just not to return? We shall never know now. Poor Eleni.

Eleni and Stamos had met in France after the war while he was a student there. She was some years older than him, a cultured woman from Alexandria in Egypt who spoke French and English perfectly. Did she go to Northern Europe to try to find her husband? 1957 was not a good time at all. So she met and set her cap at Stamos. Eleni said that they were married in Paris. Stamos said they were married in Athens. Which one was telling the truth?

His family, deeply disapproving, had refused to attend. It had not been a happy or successful marriage, so I realised that basically, all the pretence was to protect their children, loving them, as they always did. No one really cares about legitimacy nowadays, but still, Stamos seemed to mind enough to fabricate and live a lengthy lie on their behalf.

Our friends arranged everything. I prepared a wedding feast, Greek of course. We went into Reykjavik on a lovely day for a civil marriage, and Sigurder was our best man. A handsome judge dressed in a fine mid-blue robe performed the ceremony. We were both asked if we were free to marry each other. With a clear heart I replied that I was. When Stamos was asked, he answered 'Yes,' in a strong voice.

To this day I sorrow that he had to suffer so many years of soul destroying pretence. Yet, it probably protected him from making another mistake, for he was an attractive and delightful man. Certainly, if his poor long-term mistress, who had been such a pest to me in our early days had known, his life would have been made unbearable.

So later, although I found it very difficult, I held my tongue when he was accused of bigamy, perjury, the lot. That was how he wanted it. What mattered was, that we knew that we were legally married. What it came to, he wanted his cake and . . . He wanted to be married to me. He wanted to protect his children. Over the years it was hard not to give the game away, ignoring the flack, the snide remarks. I played my part as he directed.

We were married in March 1978 according to the law of Iceland. It was a beautiful ceremony. I remember some of the lovely and wise words.

'Be kind to each other for as long as you live together.'

Simple and lovely. Quite a hard one too.

Afterwards, my hosts opened their house to our guests. It was a happy gathering. We provided a Greek meal, with ouzo and retsina.

Friends arranged for us to stay in a cabin for ten days. On arrival we had to shovel the snow from the door to get in. It was perfect. Once we called on a small farm, friends of friends, and were given warm hospitality of traditional pancakes and syrup. Intrigued with their farming methods, we saw their cows all inside, standing on sloping, opened up rubber tyres. We visited a geyser and rejoiced at the spectacular show it gave us.

Married we might be in every country in the world, but at that time, there was no civil marriage in Greece. Civil marriages were just not recognised. Marriage and divorce were controlled only by the church. You could marry three times and divorce twice. So the church reaped substantial funds, all around. Wealthy people found it easy and left the country and married outside. Poor people suffered or lived in sin, which of course in that society was not easy. But, as was our case, civil marriage was simply not considered legal. The ex-wife was still the legal partner in all matters including inheritance. It would change, but it took years to do so.

There would be another charade with Stamos' divorce. Truly, he was an excellent actor, for he soldiered on, in order to keep up the pretence so that we could marry again. Another charade, we held it in our little church. Unnecessary, but, that was how he wanted it and he usually got his way.

Related people too, were in the iron hand of the church. I knew an excellent young couple who were distant cousins and who, despite being devout, left the Orthodox church, to get around it. They then joined another church, who permitted cousin marriage, and as far as I know, lived happily ever after.

Despite our marriage not, at that time, being legal or acceptable in Greece, it made us happy. We left Iceland with gratitude and regret, for at that time we were not to know that friendships made then would last, despite the passing years, and the hand God dealt us.

So it was, after a brief time in Britain, happy and full of optimism, we once again drove back to Greece to start our married life together.

Chapter 17

Gold

No sooner had we arrived home on the farm, we did a quick dash around to see if all was well. To our shock and horror, we saw that not only had someone destroyed the marble tomb of Stamos' grandparents, but that the altar of the church had also been vandalised. We were bewildered. A marble column base which had been set under the huge flat altar stone, was thrown down, revealing an empty cavity. What if anything had been in there? Treasure or a relic? Despite the church being roofless, having cleared away the debris, I had always kept it neat and clean. Who on earth would do such a thing in such a deeply religious country?

Stamos, ever ready to fear the worst, immediately became morose. He said it must have been done by pious people who were angry with him for his neglect. Now this I could not believe. What sort of statement was this desecration? Huge effort, substantial tools and considerable strength must have been used. I did not agree with him despite having no other suggestions. It was a mystery. Until the day by chance I mentioned it to a neighbour.

'Oh,' he said, 'so they came to you as well!'

He then explained to me that there had been some foreigners around in a big van. Young people, Germans. They were around and about for days, as if they were looking for something. Then they were observed camped in his olive grove above us, near the tiny Byzantine church of Saint Theodoros. There is no way to drive to the church which is in the middle of little fields and orchards. All very well fenced, with only a really narrow high fenced path, it can only be reached by foot.

One day he saw them drive off at speed, and went to investigate what they had been doing. It is a poor little church, very little used and with nothing of value in it worth taking. The fine domed painted ceiling had been severely damaged for a long time. Christ's eyes had been stabbed out, and time had taken its toll. The story goes, that during Turkish times, one night some Greeks took refuge in there. Surrounded by Turks, they somehow managed to escape in the dark, and in fury, the Turks desecrated the church in revenge. Nothing in the church had been touched or taken, but on going around it he found at the back, a newly excavated, neat square hole. Of a size which could have accommodated two ammunition boxes.

Every village in Greece has its story of GOLD. Either from the ancients, the Turks, or latterly the retreating forces of either Germans or British. Many was the time a Greek peasant asked me to bring a metal detector back from England, for he was sure he knew approximately where the gold had been hidden in his village. Needless to say, I refused, being well aware of the consequences should I be found out. Things have a way of getting out, nothing is kept secret for long.

It may well have been the Germans who hid their gold when they left our farm. It was a super hiding place so near, yet quiet, tucked behind the tiny church, and an old soldier must have told his young people the details of where to find it. A small road, an old church So they came up our drive searching, to our deserted farm and wickedly vandalised our church and the tomb. I imagine they were quite desperate with their early lack of success and must have been on the phone quite regularly for clearer instructions. And finally, finding the cache, they fled home with their loot, this time victorious.

Quite apart from gold, Greece is full of and very strict about ancient artefacts being taken out. Woe to the unwary who swims, snorkelling, in protected waters. On one of my frequent visits to young French in our local prison, I met two older Dutchmen, ordinary, respectable chaps who had in all ignorance done just that, so spent two months inside. What a way to end a holiday! What a shocking experience, poor things.

Many was the time we heard of farmers who ploughed up artifacts, and being poor, the temptation to sell them was great. A near neighbour was putting in some drainage when he came across a strange circular stone. Investigating further, he found it was the top of a beehive tomb. Very ancient, and oh dear, very special. But he didn't know that. All he knew, was that his was huge luck in finding GOLD. For inside were some amazing things in remarkably good condition, and they were on his land. Therefore it was his, or so he thought, a solution to all his problems. Poor foolish farmer that he was, he began to try to sell it. Trouble. Inevitably people talked, word spread and in no time at all the antiquities were confiscated, no reward was given, and the poor fool was banged into jail. An example indeed.

Having worked for archaeologists, whatever shard of pottery, fragments of glass or stone I found in my work on the farm, I asked my ex-colleagues, now friends, what it was. Then, into a box they went, mere fragments, only of interest to me, but knowledge and never, ever, leaving the land where they were found.

Sadly, no farmer reports anything interesting on his land nowadays. It is simply just not worth his while. If he does, it probably would be fenced off and he might get a peppercorn rent for it. Or not. It will lie idle for years and years, while either the authorities try to interest a foreign school of archaeology or it will be forgotten. The trouble being there is so much which is ancient waiting to be investigated. Any dream that he might be compensated is just that, a dream. Say nothing, ignore it, go on trying to make a living out of the starved earth and at all costs avoid the authorities. Greece not only has more ancient sites than it can cope with, it is also a poor country.

The rugged mountains of Greece are pitted with caves. Many are still used by shepherds but I imagine many more are deserted and lost. Talking with some mountain friends one day, I learned about the war and the civil war and how many fugitives had hidden in them. Some caves have water in them, a blessing from heaven, and many ancient churches perched on inaccessible mountain sides must be built on very ancient holy sites. One man told me that he found some pieces of pottery in one such place. Excited, I asked to be shown them. But he shook his head and told me that in fear he had smashed them, not wanting to be found out. OH! Oh! One wonders just how many wonderful things have, over the years been destroyed by fearful people, and so lost forever.

Knowing of the terrible history of our area, it was no surprise when we found human bones after ploughing. One can only suppose they were unnatural deaths, otherwise they would have been buried near the church instead of various odd places. For such a small farm, it apparently has had a long and varied history, most of it harsh. It became our quiet habit to place all the bones in a box in the church, and later, when it was restored and used again, we re-buried them there.

My first memories of farm life come from the age of nine. Newly arrived in Britain, the war just ended, I had suffered a hideous first winter. Growing like a weed, there seemed never to be enough food. The boarding school where I was incarcerated was in the Fens. It was bitterly cold, the heating being almost non-existent and my chilblains blossomed. I remember our dormitories and the shelf with our wash things, where our face flannels hung frozen, stiff as dried fish. As far as the eye could see, lay flat brown fields interspersed with dykes over which blew the icy winds, from Russia. (So we were told.) Many of my schoolmates were the daughters of farmers and it may well have been by their thrift and generosity, that we survived. No one believes this, but I assure you it is true. A pig farmer father supplied the school with BLUE potatoes. Unfit for human consumption, originally designated for his pigs (presumably coated with gentian violet? Whatever.) We were glad of them, and the blue mash dished up tasted all right to hungry children!

The first summer in England however, was in sharp contrast, a time of joy. I can only remember those endless golden days of harvest. A skinny, freckled-faced child, sitting on the fender of the binder, poised, stick in hand. For it was my grisly job to sock the poor, maimed rabbits sharply behind the head and put them out of their misery. I feel such sorrow for the present-day children, where just about everything is forbidden, out of bounds. Glued to screens of various types, they can never know the pure delight in nature, which we did. Never has bread, butter and strawberry jam tasted so good. Never has water, straight from the stream, been so cold and pure. Those precious days in Sussex made me a country woman. Hardly born and bred, but the seeds were sown. As it turned out, better later than never. Years passed and I lived on the clay of East Anglia, where again farm life went on round and about, ever filling eyes, ears and mouth.

Fate, sending me to live on a Greek farm with Stamos, then gave me years of delight and endless toil. In the beginning the main difficulty was supplying Stamos with the courage to start again. He had got out of the habit of work and delighted in abandoning the farm at the lightest suggestion. The state of the farm was daunting. It needed everything from cash to energy, but most of all, courage. Weeds abounded, waist high, indeed the thistles were amazing, over two metres high. On our return from Iceland, there it was, a thistle farm, for no work had been done in our absence. The thistles were about to seed, a terrible sin to permit not only for our land, but for the entire neighbourhood. I became very vocal and hurray, successfully persuasive.

First we ploughed a double furrow around the perimeter. Then we filled every container we could find with water, and armed who ever was at the farm at the time with a broom or what ever and stood them at equal distance all around. Next we phoned the fire brigade to ignore all calls from neighbours. Only to come, if we called. This agreement became a regular habit thereafter, to our mutual satisfaction. Then I took over, having seen it done in the past, the right way. One end of a long hawser was firmly tied around a straw bale, the other end was attached to the back of the little tractor. A trickle of petrol was poured in the centre of the bale and it was set alight. Off Stamos drove, much enjoying himself doing something positive and having learned something new. Right around the perimeter he went, while the tall, dry thistles quickly ignited and set up a fearful roar.

Inevitably the neighbours arrived hot-foot and hysterical, adding to the row. Those of us on the big field boundary stood on duty, ignoring them, eyes narrowed against the smoke and made sure no flames escaped. It worked. A flattened, blackened field lay smoking before us in no time, and a jubilant Stamos then set about pacifying the astonished and indignant neighbours. Now we could begin to farm again.

There was a small empty field near the road, and I determined to plant it up with vegetables. Donning a pretty blouse, skirt and head scarf, I began ploughing, making very sure that my furrows were absolutely straight, for it was a matter of pride, being a mere woman, I got it right. Passers-by crawled along gawping and incredulous. Too busy really to notice them, I like to think that some even crossed themselves. The horror of it! The shame! Whatever was the world coming to; a woman ploughing!

Then there was the local bus. An extremely beat up, little light blue job, unfit for main road travel, it had been banished to the villages.

As it trundled by, it seemed to lurch and veer, as every passenger leapt to my side, every face pressed to the murky windows to SEE. I loved it, well who wouldn't, except when at night I blew up, reacting to the pollen of the luxuriant weeds with an appalling dose of hay fever.

It was the same with the pruning. Women were just not clever enough to do that either, although, and bless him, Nikos thought otherwise in teaching me. This was generally considered man's work. As was driving, ploughing, you name it. I dreaded the arrival of a male visitor to the orchard, for his horror was tangible. He usually tried to grab my secateurs or pruning saw and launched at my little trees to show me the right way, his way, to do it. When in the passing years, one thousand apricot trees stood magnificent, neat and orderly, pruned and productive, their tune changed. One or two were even reluctantly generous in their praise, turning over my hands to see the calluses with kind amusement. But, it still was not quite right, and their women would never be permitted in this man's world. I was a foreigner and therefore different, hence I was excused the temerity of competing with them.

In later years when Lily the pig regularly gave birth to up to sixteen piglets instead of the Greek average of seven, I was often wooed with gifts in exchange for them. Indeed that is how we came to own peacocks, guinea fowl and an assortment of other lively exchanges.

One day I overheard good friend farmer Mixalis, chatting away to Stamos as they admired our latest litter.

'Funny thing about these foreigners isn't it?' hanging over the pig sty, smiling at the antics of the rotund little dears. 'Perhaps all the love she gives her animals does have an effect, for look at them, so many and so well' Followed by copious spitting in their direction, just in case the devil was lurking about.

As time went on, I employed all sorts of gadgets to make life easier and to improve the stock. At first they brought their lambs, kids and calves to me to be castrated. There was nothing gory about it either.

Just a gadget and strong rubber ring slipped over the offending articles and that was it. A few weeks later, their bloodless and shrivelled up masculine appendages just dropped off. Later I gave some of my shepherd friends their own gadgets, with instructions to keep the rubber rings in the fridge so they wouldn't perish in the heat. I was a mere step ahead of them if they had but known, avidly reading my monthly English farming magazine, and either on my trips home buying the goods, or persuading incredulous and long suffering friends to bring them out when visiting.

Later still, when we had cows, I snipped off extra teats from baby heifers, and all too soon, neighbours arrived with their calves for me to do also. I found it a most scary operation in the beginning. First a shot of pain killer, then very sharp scissors, and, according to the book, a great snip to get out all the mammary gland. This left a terrifying and huge hole, which at first frightened me horribly, though luckily I did not panic although I was thoroughly alarmed. Yet after a few days with regular treatment of antiseptic spray, the hole closed up and healed surprisingly quickly and neatly, so with relief, I too had learned something new.

De-horning was simple in comparison for I used an American chemical, and not hot iron which I found far too frightening. First I carefully clipped off all the hair on and around the horn bud, then spread on the powerful caustic cream. It usually worked well. Horned animals can cause such mischief by getting caught in and ripping up thorn fencing and the Greek shepherd is a busy soul.

Our first attempt at keeping a goat was a disaster. A huge black creature with long horns and uncertain temperament, she was sold to us as being in kid. As mentioned before, I named her Surtsey, after the new volcanic island off Iceland. Hopefully, the island will in time prove more fertile than she was. Her fine belly waxed on the plentiful food she had, but the months went past and no movement was seen so we guessed that alas she was just plump and not kidding. Meanwhile I had begun to milk the two sheep, a novelty to me, anything rather than the awful evaporated milk we used. Surtsey was sent packing, and we began looking for another nanny goat. It was a relief when she went, for we were all scared of her as she did not hesitate to use her horns as they should be.

Our 'kibbutz style life attracted not only backpackers, some of Stamos' Greek friends began to send their young to us as well as mine. These young Greeks thoroughly enjoyed the life on the farm, but they never stayed long.

We rose early and breakfasted on tea or coffee, home made muesli, bread and jam, marmalade and later, when we had cows and plenty of milk, great dishes of yoghourt. Sheep's milk is wonderfully rich and high in fat, so makes a super yoghourt. The cows, when they arrived, being Guernseys were just a little lower in fat than sheep, so I used to add a tin of evap. to 'thicken' it. Just a big tablespoon of yoghourt starter from the previous batch was kept back each day and gently creamed with a little warm milk. Then a large ceramic pot was filled with warm milk and the starter, stirred, then well covered with a rug and left to set in a warm place. When it was ready I used to gently stir it again to redistribute the cream which had risen to the top, and put it in a cold fridge over night. It was delicious. If we were flush we had honey and nuts on it, the Greek way. Sometimes I would add a tin of condensed milk, so it was rather sweeter. However it was, it always went down speedily.

They ate well, our young people, and my goodness were they appreciative! Most of them having been on the road away from home grub and comforts, they really tucked in, enjoying everything. Naturally their appreciation was a great encouragement to me to keep trying. As we had walnut trees and just a few stray almonds, it was a quiet, happy job sitting in the fine shade under the walnut trees in front of the house cracking away. Ever attended by the now appreciable flock of fowl and of course, the dogs, there was always a fearful scrum when we threw a maggoty nut down. Every creature vied for them, risking being beaten up in the process.

212

There was a nice brown hen who showed up one day with a fine brood of chicks to our surprise and pleasure. She was a very good mother and gave us much amusement. Locating a fallen walnut, smart bird, she would stand in front of it, chirruping away, as if ordering it to open. Anyone going by would then stamp on it, and Mrs Hen would then call her chicks in her special 'food children' voice and they arrived hot foot and joyfully made very short work of it. No other creature would dare to intervene, being well aware of her sharp and ready peck. One day we were having lunch outside as usual, and there was a treat, home made baklava. Maria had taught me how to make them and although getting enough nuts cracked was a long and tedious chore, they were so well received, it was well worth the trouble occasionally.

'Oh Judy,' said Tineke, one of our good Dutch girls, holding her piece up in the air, 'your baklava are wonderful.'

Whereupon a hen leapt up and took it, to our shock and amusement. As it was the last piece, the poor girl was not happy.

Our fowl were an odd lot, many having been bought from the tzingania, and certainly were without pedigree. The Rom would rattle up the drive, loudspeaker blaring, their trucks, smelly and overloaded with fowl of all sorts.

'Kott-es. Papp-yes. Heen-ess. Gallopoula!' (Hens, ducks, geese, turkeys.) 'Ta kallitera, eftina.' (The best, cheap.)

Even if I didn't buy anything from them, we always gave them hospitality, at the same time as bullying them to fill up the water troughs in the truck. I was after all, the local rep. for the Animal Welfare. One chap who I liked and trusted, had the fattest wife I have ever seen. She was huge, breathless and obviously unhealthy, for perched on the edge of a creaking chair, she moaned non-stop of her many aches and pains. She was however, his pride and joy, and a great advert as to his ability to keep her well. As usual dressed in the full, colourful tzingania outfit, a light cloth (mantiya) was draped over her head. Sparkling like a Christmas tree she wore elaborate gold earings, chains and numerous rings buried in the fat of her fingers, all their fortune.

Although, obviously, turkeys were regular fare in Greece, for why otherwise would they be for sale, I never ate it in a Greek home or taverna. I do not think they have developed any tradition as have we at Christmas, or the Americans have at Thanksgiving. So I assume that turkeys are a rather recent event in the Greek diet, like potatoes, and indeed very many other things which took time to reach what was historically a deprived and poor country.

I usually bought some turkeys if they were available, or, if times were hard, did a deal, a 'bazzari' with grain against the fowl. They were usually black and white, and I have no idea of what, if any, breed they were or where they originated from.

One, who escaped the pot, I can't think how, came to be called Mrs Turkey, and was the only one of her breed I ever became fond of. A plain, great gawky thing, she pottered around freely with the rest of the fowl, the hens, ducks, guinea fowl and peacocks. Having had little experience with turkeys, I was delighted when she began laying lovely big speckled eggs and unfortunately in my ignorance took them all. They were marvellous in all baking and made superb omelettes. Of course without a turkey cock, the eggs might well have been infertile, unless she had previously mated with one of the long gone deceased males. So alas, by the time she went broody, she had no eggs to sit on. With a mind of her own, she determinedly sat herself on the low wall of the old cistern by the front of the house, where so many other mothers brooded, and where I suspected water lay deep below. With barely a wisp of dry honeysuckle to shade her, she sat through the blazing heat of July and August. Now and again she got up and went to find a drink, looking pathetic, thin and tatty. On one of her little excursions I ran to have a quick peep in her nest. Horrors, oh dear! Two walnuts and a stone! Poor thing, oh poor thing.

August passed and I feared she must die for she did not eat and looked utterly wretched. At last I decided I must hatch a plot of my own. Making a comfy nest in the corner of the kotetsi (hen house) I put in six duck eggs. That night, with as little fuss as possible I carefully lifted her, took her to the kotetsi, and sat her on the new nest. With fear and trembling I looked at her in the early morning and saw with relief that she was sitting tight. On with the rest of the plot.

Not far away from us there was large and well run hatchery run by a nice man which produced only white fowl. Armed with several large pots of jam and marmalade which I knew he liked (all home-grown, home-made naturally), I went and asked for any rejects. Bless the man, he sorted out those with any black on them and somewhat amazed, I gladly accepted forty chicks. Back at the farm I waited till evening and all was more or less quiet in the kotetsi. On my knees in the clean straw beside Mrs Turkey, I first slid my hand under her and removed a few duck eggs. Then, with a handful of chicks, I carefully slid it back under her again until all forty were more or less covered. Sitting on my heels I held my breath and waited. Silence, then came a very strange, soft sound, 'CCCcccrrrrrrrrrrrrrr.'

It was of course, turkey mother love, amazing. Head under one wing, she looked at her new born, a miracle indeed. Two chicks ventured out. She stretched her neck and picked one up. Aghast, I watched fearfully, sure that now I would have to quickly remove them all, for was this the beginning of a massacre? Of course it wasn't! Carefully she tucked the wayward chick under her wing and fluffed up her straggly feathers to cover them.

Wonderful, marvellous, who could believe that this pathetic, ugly bird would become immediately, on order, the perfect mother. Her hot and hideous waiting was over and she was rewarded with a huge and lively family who she completely accepted and adored. They wandered up and all over her, they pecked at her eyes and beak while she turned not a feather. When I deemed that they were large enough to let out of their little area of the kotetsi, she took them out for route marches, ever protective and ferocious if any other beast came too close. It was a hoot to watch her striding out on the land, her kids struggling along on tiny legs behind her like a wake. There was a suggestion of Saint Trinians and yes, she did in many ways resemble the delightful, 'jolly hockey sticks' Joyce Grenfell.

We had some excellent home-grown chicken on the table for some time thanks to Mrs Turkey who was allowed to go into happy retirement. That old girl made me change my mind over turkeys which I had always considered stupid, vicious birds, only fit for the table. A childhood memory in India of being chased, terrified, around the tennis court by a huge cock turkey, might well have helped. Bribes, in the form of gold or silver gifts had to be returned after two days, often accompanied by pitious mourning from my mother. But eatables were kept, and now and again handsome cock turkeys arrived with great baskets of vegetables. As a seven or eight year old, that particular one seemed extremely large and I remember my father comforting me with.

'Don't worry, we shall soon eat him!'

Now, entirely due to her, the valiant Mrs Turkey, I think that on or off the table, they are grand.

Chapter 18

Wishes Granted

Considering that I am a lucky woman with a gift in my hands, I always took a keen interest and delight in Greek hand-work. It was so interesting to see the similarities in so many crafts from other countries. In the mountains, wood was put to every use, uncannily alike, for example, those in Scandinavia. Not that they were considered 'arts and crafts' as do we nowadays. Necessity had ruled, usually producing sturdy, handsome and thoroughly practical everyday utensils. But the human eye had to also be satisfied and even the decoration was similar. Like everything, times change and there is little hand work done now. Just the occasional old shepherd carves away at a glitsa head (crook head) as of old.

A hill village not so far from us was mainly inhabited by Arveniti. They are ethnic Christian Albanians who were thrown out of their land by the then pasha, who insisted that they convert to Islam, or go. They went, to Greece, in the sixteenth century and have retained their language and many of their customs.

Traditionally the Greeks mistrust them. Even now they are considered incomers and past sins have never been forgotten.

Nothing changes really, for the recent invasion of the worst type of Albanian into Greece must well be a repetition of what happened those hundreds of years ago. Thieves and murderers they were then, and thieves and murderers they are now. Really!

Nonetheless, we had some most excellent neighbours who were Arvaniti, even now speaking their own language, at least in the house. Stamos told me his family were also originally Arvaniti, and when he was vile and or cheated me, his wife, I wryly thought that the old tales must certainly have sound foundation.

That hill village had a most gifted saddler. His samaria were not only very well made, they were unique as he studded them all over with brass pins in decoration. They were magnificent. Might this custom have come with a forefather from Albania so many hundreds of years before? Why not? I never saw others as fine elsewhere, so like to think that due to the isolation of his village, the art remained. So impressed with his work was I, that I began to fret that it would be lost and perhaps by now it has been.

I dreamed of getting videos taken of every traditional Greek craft for posterity, just in case the young may one day wish to do them again. Of course and sadly, as with far too many of my dreams, it never happened.

Most of the saddles one sees in use seemed too cumbersome and heavy, and often the donkeys were left out all day with theirs firmly strapped on. Dwarfed by them, the little things pottered around their field while the master worked. Eventually I learnt that it was not done just from laziness or neglect. The back area and kidneys were well protected from sun and rain by the saddles, which were really not so heavy being made of wooden slats, straw and cloth. The lining underneath was called samariskuti, a marvellous extremely thick wool felt often made in glowing colours. I took to creating things out of this stuff for presents, hats and so forth, for it was cheap and lovely to work on.

Then a good friend of mine who was an artist in Athens offered me her loom. For very little, I joyfully purchased it and brought it home 'in a hundred pieces' and with the very able help of Antony, got it all up together again. A splendid loom, it was a marvel of invention. I could imagine a clever woman saying, 'Kosta, if you can do that, (or this), it will mean I can work faster and more smoothly.' And Kostas must have been a superb carpenter, for he did it.

It looked like a great four poster bed with a seat in front. It had a flying shuttle, such a luxury. It had four pedals and its own bobbin winder. I was thrilled with it, for it was another cherished dream satisfied and I was ever grateful to Eleni for it.

Where to put it though? We decided that the huge landing upstairs was the only and indeed ideal place for it. In those days it was common to see looms set up in all kinds of odd places. Balconies, under houses in the cellars, even in courtyards well covered up. Already by the mid seventies when I was first living there, Greece was entering Modern Times with a vengeance and looms were definitely going out of fashion and being banished. I suppose the older peasant women were just so used to working, ALL the time, they had to find something to do when things were quiet. I fear in this I really was a true Greek peasant, for I hated lying on the beach, or sitting outside doing nothing when we had guests. Fortunately there was always some small chore handy to occupy me. If it wasn't cracking nuts it was stringing beans or whatever. If no domestic chore needed doing, then out came the spinning wheel. At least being a bundle of nerves is productive!

With the arrival and erection of the loom, here was a new and joyful task. First to learn about it, for I always thirst for knowledge of this kind. Having got the hang of it with enthusiastic and rowdy help from Mrs Petropolous, now I began to teach the girls who were interested. It was very pleasant sitting up there with the French doors opened to the magnificent view of Akro Corinth to the West, with often a welcome breeze too. Some of the boys also wished to learn how to weave, excited with the new art. Unfortunately none of them understood that their little lengths of self expression could not be instantly cut off and given to them to take away when they left us. For all their work went onto the roller until all the warp was finished. So each one wrote their name and address on cloth or paper and carefully stitched it onto their piece so that when at last, maybe a year later, the length was all done, I could unwind the roll, cut it up and proudly send off their little works of art all over the world.

A cry for help came from Mrs Petropolous, literally. After shearing, they had to wash their fleeces in order to sell them and they had no water.

'I'll have to take them to wash them in the sea,' she cried. 'We have no water, what can I do?

Stamos to the rescue, for he really was deeply fond of her. An old galvanised tank was brought near the house and a hose filled it with icy water in no time. Then Mrs P. arrived with Margaritta, her eldest daughter, laden down with wool. Shoes off, skirts hoiked up, into the tank they climbed and began treading the fleece, while the the water was being continually topped up and filthy now, slopped over.

When it came to slaughtering Mrs Turkey's brood, both Petropolous arrived. We did it in stages for there were so many of them and it was done outside as was the usual custom in Greece, using a walnut tree to hang them on. It was such an excellent arrangement helping each other, and is really as it should always be. I was so happy to have home grown chicken, but our freezer was not so large, so I de-boned them, packed them neatly to freeze, and used the bones to make soup. One thing which made me shudder however, was what they took away, all the while smacking their lips. The cockerel's combs she assured me were very tasty, likewise the feet. I obviously have never been really hungry because neither appealed to me.

It was another Mixalis, a shepherd who lived nearby, who found us our next and most successful nanny goat. A first kidder, he brought her to us shortly after the birth as he wanted to sell the kids. Soon enough we discovered that was not the only reason for his kindness, for she put up a tremendous fight and would rather stand on her head than be milked. One of the boys knocked up a splendid milking stand, where her head would be fastened through two planks as a guillotine, but just over a feed bucket. It was a nightmare, a battle royal. She was a big, tall girl, strawberry roan, aristocratic looking with a disdainful air but at least she had no horns. It needed five people to milk her at first, so I well understood why we had her. Each leg had to be held while I tried to milk with frequent accidents to the milk pail. I took to giving her a thump on the neck if she misbehaved, yet very soon just needed to raise my fist, so she winced in anticipation and ceased her nonsense. At that time the eldest of my five goddaughters arrived from England. A lovely, tall girl with strawberry blonde hair, I named the new goat after her, Serena. Anything but serene, it was hardly applicable at the beginning, but as time went on she became not only an excellent milker, she once even gave birth to wonderful quads. Serena goat soon calmed down, became part of the family and was a really good friend.

I began to feel rather unwell. Not ill exactly, but fragile. Having thrown caution to the winds in the vain hope we might at our great age produce another child, I had been aware that all was not right with my body, my age I supposed. A combination of age, for by now I was forty, and hard work obviously prevented me from holding on to those minuscule forms of life, so small, I barely knew they existed as they slipped away. Until a stubborn tiny soul hung on, and I began to wonder if perhaps we had managed it after all.

Fragile! It was as if every shred of energy in my body was concentrated on the preservation of this new life. Where I had always been to the fore in whatever task was to hand, now I dragged myself about uselessly. Stamos began to scold, watching me in disbelief as I drooped about barely even doing my own domestic chores. So impatient was he, I became quietly indignant, so kept my suspicions to myself.

At last I told the girls and bless them, thrilled, they took to protecting me, doing my jobs and generally helping me to rest, which was obviously what was needed. The worst times for me were when driving with Stamos. The landrover was hardly the most comfortable vehicle, and neither were the roads brilliant. After any trip I was trembling with weakness and twittering with nerves, exhausted and near to tears. All the while he raged at me to shut up telling him to go slower. Men!

After six long weeks of this charade I realised I must tell him. Somehow it seemed so difficult after his unpleasantness and what seemed a long silence. I waited till siesta.'Well,' I began tremulously, 'I suppose I must tell you.'

He glared at me.

'What have you broken now?' he asked roughly. (I am not a breaker, and never have been.) I began to cry.

'Horrible man,' I uttered, 'Savage!' feeling that this was all wrong, not as it should be. 'I have to tell you,' I blurted out, 'that I think that we are making a child.'

He stared at me astonished, then slowly he reached for me and first kissed my mouth, then my belly. He was thrilled! All tenderness suddenly, there was a total turn around in his attitude towards me. My lassitude was gently understood and I was urged to rest instead of toiling. We girls had some good laughs.

Now he drove so slowly, the landrover was always in fear of stalling which made me almost as nervous as his usual break neck speed.

Both of our families were small, there were few children, so he was really happy at the prospect of a new child. No doubt anticipating a joyful reception as I was, he told me to inform the elders of his family. Delighted to do so, I rang up, and gave my news. Silence. Then. 'Oh dear, but what will we do about the inheritance?'

Shocked silence from me too. I felt my heart hammering with distress, this was not what I had expected, anything but this. No joyful words came, no congratulations and no love. I was so hurt. My heart became hard then and as if from afar, I heard my voice retort. 'My child will need nothing from you. My family will look after it, you can keep your inheritance.'

I did not tell Stamos of the response I had to our news, for he would have been furious and very hurt too. Yet they were not alone in their disapproval of my pregnancy. Indeed my in-laws reaction paled in comparison to that of my father. For when I finally told my parents, I had it all over again, even to my father saying he hoped that I had come home to have an abortion. It was most distressing.

Just once more we had a crisis when I feared I was losing the child. I put myself to bed and the anxious young workers, placed breeze blocks under the foot end. They were sweet in their concern, and the house was strangely quiet.

Stamos came in looking anxious and old. 'So that's that,' he said dully.

Surprised by his very real concern I replied, 'No! That is not that.

After a few days he took me to a local clinic to be examined. Having worked in a maternity hospital in Athens, I should have been prepared, but I wasn't. It was frightful. I was helped up onto a black Rexine couch, no cloth, no paper, just my bare seat on the shiny surface where no doubt dozens of other rumps had lain.

'Baby,' he announced. Well I could have told him that.

With rest and care, still in one piece, I began to feel myself again. Now that I did not work 'like a dog', I realised with joy that I could instead spend many hours at the loom. At last my home-spun wool could be used to make something worthwhile, perhaps a little blanket for the baby. So there I sat clacking and clicking away happily until the day when I heard a call from below. It was Mrs Petropolous come to visit.

'Come up and join me,' I called down, 'I am at the loom.'

She appeared at the top of the stairs, her face red and furious. As a virago she fell upon me, tugging at me to get up. 'Siko, siko!' (Up, up!) she yelled, 'Don't you know that you must not use the loom when you are pregnant? You will surely lose the child if you go on.'

Bewildered with this strange information I did get up, and went downstairs with her. On careful self examination of this information, I thought that perhaps there was some truth in what she said for certainly I had had some worrying twinges recently. Was it just folklore or was there sound sense in what she said?

Then I remembered something which had happened very many years before when I was a teenager and was visiting my parents in India where my father worked. I was sewing with my mother in the upstairs sitting room when the bearer came up with a card. A salesman was below selling foreign, electric sewing machines. He came up, a very pleasant young man who spoke good English. He carried a small metal case which opened up to a neat little sewing machine. They were ridiculously cheap and my mother bought two. One for her and one for me. I was very chuffed.

Intrigued, my mother then asked him why they were so cheap.

Smiling wryly, the young man explained. Apparently treadle sewing machines were suspected of causing miscarriages and infertility, which is why men came to be the main machinists. (Perhaps the rocking of the pelvis with the treadle might cause trouble?) Now either it was the stingy husbands not wanting to fork out for an expensive item such as a sewing machine, or, there was a real fear that sewing machines did indeed cause infertility.

It came to pass therefore, that ALL sewing machines were suspect! Only women past child-bearing, or men, would use them, hand, electric or treadle. So here was this intelligent young men selling off his excellent Swiss machines, for a song. I had mine for years until I gave it to Maria.

I found it most interesting comparing these stories which came from such different cultures of lands so far apart, and deduced that with sure peasant wisdom, there must be some foundation to them. Sadly, I stopped weaving.

Two cheery Australian nurses came to stay. I enjoyed their lively company and one day, when Stamos had gone to Athens, suggested that together we demolish the ugly, utterly dull and useless fireplace and build another more elegant and serviceable one. Ever optimistic, we got as far as just the demolition by the time Stamos returned. To my surprise, he was enthusiastic and we succeeded in erecting a rather handsome French country-style over mantle which worked far better than the old. I still know and occasionally see Ann and Jude and now delight in their children.

Our joyful anticipation was apparently not shared by the family for once again I came under fire with all sorts of silly unpleasantness. Feeling very vulnerable and not my usual tough self, I wept easily, and could not cope.

The day came when I felt I could no longer tolerate the continual barrage of venom, so packed up a small bag and weeping, told Stamos I could not take any more, and that I was going away for a while. Where to go to was another matter. For knowing that Ruth was in England I could not stay with her. I just knew I must leave the farm for self preservation.

'Are you quite mad?' he shouted at me as I left.

'I will be soon if I stay any longer in this house', said I and walked down the drive towards the road.

By chance a taxi passed so I took it to town. There at a bus station stood a long distance bus with KALAMATA written on it. I caught it. In those days it was a very long and tortuous drive. The twists and turns of the mountain roads were exhausting and by the time we arrived hours later at Kalamata, I was trembling with fatigue. There were several hours to wait for the next bus south to the Mani, so I rested and had a light meal. Then! Suddenly I remembered that Debbie, a lovely young cousin of my ex-husband was due to arrive the next day, and that it was her birthday. Now I love birthdays and always make a fuss of them so I rushed to a nearby shop and bought her two local mantiya (scarves) and using printed paper from the shop turned inside out, wrapped them up and posted them there and then. Having abandoned her I felt that this small recognition of her birthday, might be a tiny compensation.

Still waiting for the bus I sat reflecting sorrowfully on the new events in my life. At all costs I must preserve this child, however old I was. However unwelcome it apparently was with Stamos' family, we wanted it.

Then an unpleasant incident took place. A man in his thirties or so, came and sat beside me and began uttering filthy invitations. I was shocked and cross and tried not to indicate that I could understand him. So I was paying the price for those many naughty girls who gave all foreign women a bad name. Not unlike the sewing machines!

At last in early evening I arrived totally shattered at the village. On my way up to Ruth's house along the stony paths, I rested now and again, sitting on convenient boulders. A couple of women friends passed by, and I told them my news and why I was there. They were so reassuring in their comfort and told me that the rest here would do me good. At the house I settled in with relief and had a good night's sleep.

The next days were pure joy. From early morning they came bearing gifts. One after the other, having spread the news, the women came with small plates in their work-worn hands. Some I knew well, others barely, just by sight. Their gifts, covered with a cloth, might be: half a loaf of sour dough bread or two eggs or a dish of horta or a lump of cheese or some fruit. Then they stayed awhile and sat with me on the terrace overlooking the sea, reasuring me that all would be well, but that what I must do, was rest. Even now tears come to my eyes when I recall those wonderful, generous women. So close to reality and to the harsh earth, it was they who supported me and rejoiced in my coming child. I can never forget their kindness. Now, when they laugh incredulous at the huge young man of our making, I tell them that he is surely part Maniot, having been nurtured before birth by their warm generosity.

It was the wrapping of Debbie's parcel which gave the game away. To my great surprise Stamos and Debbie arrived two days later, happy and grinning with their unexpected little holiday. All, once more and for the time being anyway, was fine and dandy. Love and joy flowed, and we had a late feast for Debbie's birthday.

Not having very much faith in Greek medicine at that time, I decided to go home to have various tests done, and to book myself into a hospital for the delivery, the same one where I had given birth to my first son twenty two years previously. Apart from all this, I had to visit my parents, an annual affair, particularly as my father was not in good health.

We booked me a one-month return ticket with the plan I should go back to London at seven months for my confinement. All sound planning, none of which in fact happened.

So I said my goodbyes to the wonderful neighbours and our dear animals and at the airport cheerfully told Stamos I would see him there in a month's time.

'Take great care of yourself,' he told me earnestly, holding me close most tenderly. I smiled at that beloved and cranky man who so recently had been roughly goading me to pull myself together and get to work.

I would most certainly take the greatest care of myself, for I was sure, being a son maker, that this would be another boy. Now, I could do the perfect thing and name him for that excellent man, Uncle Frederikos. He who had no child, he whose shadow I had met for some strange reason, on my very first day at the farm. 'Over the hill' I might be, but I would do all I could to sustain the tiny life growing within me. So off I went for one month, which in fact became one year.

Not knowing what life had in store for us, we confidently parted with great love, he to return to his life on the farm, and I to medical tests and my parents in my own country.

BOOK II

Chapter 1

Back to Reality

At last we came home. We drove across Europe in late April, 1979 with our precious cargo, Frederikos, a minute and peaceful little boy. It had been eighteen years since the birth of my last son who had weighed in at nine pounds. Despite being indignant and utterly fed up by being told how 'old' I was, how 'high risk', on and on, I did eventually accept that they were probably right. Certainly it had been a hideous pregnancy, horribly uncomfortable and very different from my three others when I was in my lithe and healthy twenties.

Having left Greece the previous September, for a one month sojourn in Britain to check up that all was well, it was a blow to find it was not. I was firmly told that if anything went wrong, ('due to your age!') they would not be responsible. So what could I do? As we so wanted this baby, I simply stayed. Within days, Stamos had shut up the farm and left it in the kindly hands of our neighbours.

We were pretty heavy on our friends that year, that was for sure. Yet how greatly blessed we were in having them. For not only did the noble Petropoulos watch over the farm and care for the few animals that we had at that time, we both stayed with an old and

231

treasured friend of mine in London. The original one month's hospitality stretched for seven, and my fairy Godmother, Elsie Magarshack, let us stay with her in her warm and cosy home in the tiniest, snug bedroom. Little had I known as a mere nineteen year old, when I first met her and we did pottery together, that our friendship would last warm and strong, for so many years. We had such fun together despite the many years between us and eventually and cheerfully concluded that despite our respective ages, we were both, in our souls, still sixteen. For ever!

The arrangement was that I did the housework and cooking and we paid a nominal fee for our **B & B**. Another long-time friend, who had actually been my jeweller in the past and owned Knowles Brown, the most fascinating shop in Hampstead High Street, was instrumental in our survival. For he employed Stamos, in the building of a splendid workshop at the back of his premises. It had been Peter who had encouraged my study of gems, and Peter who offered me a little afternoon job in the office above the showroom.

It was a vile and snowy winter and I was ever fearful of walking on the icy pavements with my growing tummy. Elsie and I used to hang on to each other and she became quite chirpy as time went on as not only could she keep up with me, but she could walk faster.

Then the day came when I was standing at a filing cabinet when 'the heavens opened.' It was Thursday afternoon, and I was due to stop work the very next day so that I would have six weeks to organise myself before the expected arrival. Horrors! I gazed helplessly at the growing pool forming around my feet, darkening Peter's lovely apple-green carpet. Having not experienced such before with my previous three birthings, I began to weep, knowing it was far too early, and that they had been right; I obviously was too old for this sort of thing.

Panic stations ensued, all quite funny in retrospect. Having realised what was happening, Peter hustled me downstairs, through the shop of astonished customers, and out into the street. Mark had been sent hotfoot for his car, his NEW car I must add, his pride and joy.

'No!' I said firmly, gazing at the pale-blue velvet-lined seat I was being urged to sit on. 'I will not ruin Mark's new car.'

We glared at each other. But Peter would have none of it, and swept off my cloak, draped it on the seat and shoved me in. Quite how I don't know, perhaps it was incidental, but a howling police car arrived. Waving aside the gathering crowd and having ascertained that no murder or robbery was being committed, the police escort then swept along in front of us, down the hill to the Royal Free, still howling. All very embarrassing.

I honestly do not think that Frederikos would have survived had he been born anywhere else. Finally, on Saturday evening he arrived, foot first (trust him!) tiny, but alive and well due, I am certain, to the great skill in obstetrics of a young South African doctor, who was obviously a master of his craft.

'It is all right,' Stamos reassured me later, when I was wakeful and fretting in the early hours. Having been to have a good look into the incubator in the premature unit, he was immensely pleased with his new son. 'It isn't all white any more,' said he jubilantly, 'it's all rose.' (RoZe of course.) For Richard had allowed Stamos to stay in the theatre, quite against the rules, and I had noticed how he had winced, as a very white, apparently dead baby, was held up by the leg.

'Why did you make that awful face?' I asked later.

'Because I thought that they were cutting it up,' was his reply.

At 2,250 kilos, (five pounds), he was a dopey, floppy and very ugly mite. While being fed with tubes in his nose, he lazed about until the date when he should have been born, before coming to life. A charming Greek lady intern doctor loved him dearly, telling me that 'if this one had been born in the mountains, oh yes, he would survive.'

So, we had made it, and after two months, we decided we could risk driving him across Europe, home to Greece.

We were quite a sight. For my old friend Annie had found me a pram, or should I say rather, a perambulator. A great white swan of a thing, a reject, far too large for modern homes, it perched on top of the Landrover roof rack, to the fascination of all who beheld us.

When at last we pulled up in front of the big house, I again noted how sad it looked, uncared-for and bleak. The first soul to greet us was Morag, dear loyal hound friend, she gave us a wildly vocal welcome, even weeing all over the place in her huge excitement at having us home.

When at last she had calmed down, I brought out the cocoon in which slept the baby. Choosing my spot on the bare earth, I sat down cross-legged, the baby cradled in my lap and invited Morag to meet 'my puppy'. Sniffing all about him, tail wagging furiously, he was accepted.

Despite the original lack of enthusiasm from the Greek family, now he had arrived, their attitude was very different. He was welcomed with open arms. Which was indeed comforting for me whose own parents had shown bare interest in their new grandson.

Indeed I was shocked to be asked, 'What colour is he?' (Were my widely travelled and cosmopolitan parents so very ignorant?) He was in fact a Greek baby with deep green/brown eyes, from Stamos' mother and he had the lightest of olive skins.

Now I learned of a new and most charming Greek custom. 'To Golden the Baby.' Every new baby is welcomed with a gift of money and the inevitable spitting, 'Ftu, ftu', to ward off the devil. In fact, I had just once before and only recently come across it. During our weeks after leaving the hospital we had rented a tiny house in Temple Fortune and the owner of the Cypriot fish and chip shop around the corner had slipped a fifty pence piece into Fredo's pram. 'How on earth did this get here?' I asked Stamos. Very pleased with the gesture from a stranger, Stamos explained the lovely tradition to me.

So it was that everyone who saw our new son presented him with a note, or coin, depending upon their standing.

Every morning the little boy would be wrapped up and left out in his huge pram carefully draped with a cat/mosquito net. Inevitably, Mrs Petropolous was deeply shocked. Shrieking in indignation she would scoop him up and stomp into the house, railing at me for having left him outside.

'It is so healthy for him. This is what we do in England,' I tried to explain.

'Well this is a Greek baby.' She always had an answer.

Fortunately she did not come over so very often, so as every old fashioned English baby, he was parked under the walnut trees and left to sleep whatever the weather. Every day we sprayed the bare earth in front of the house to lay the dust and one day I remember apparently being distracted for a moment for I sprayed the pram which brought forth furious howls of indignation. It was difficult not to laugh while comforting the shocked infant, for the water, coming up from a very deep well, was icy cold.

That was a golden summer of great contentment for both of us. Stamos was in top form, happy, proud, well and full of plans for our future. It certainly helped when I received a somewhat unexpected and very handsome windfall.

He came home from town one day, his one eye glazed with longing, for he had seen a TRACTOR. The very first John Deere in the district. His tiny, little old blue one still worked, and we all loved it dearly. Fine for rotovating, it was hardly a real working tractor. Now not only was Stamos the hereditary squire of the district and French Consul, he was also a French-trained Agricultural Engineer.

To sell the very first John Deere tractor to such an august person, was plain and simple free advertising. A very, very, reasonable sum of money was asked.

In thanks for entertaining his visiting guests, my ex-boss, the archeologist Paul Clement, often presented us with a case of Kair champagne. It was the local brew and, although not of the finest vintage, it was very pleasant. On the day the new tractor arrived, for of course I had to let him have it, we gathered around with a bottle in welcome. Sitting on the tractor, the glowing Stamos held the baby Fredo on his lap, and even he had some. We stood around with our champagne in plastic cups toasting it, and liberally sprinkled the bonnet of the gleaming new machine, for luck.

By now, young people had begun to arrive and help out with whatever was going on at the time and life was full, busy, and lots of fun. My sons came to stay and made friends with their new half brother and I have charming photos of them carrying him around on their hips in a sling. Years later, when at the same age that they had lugged him about, the chunky, six foot five inches Fredo could have floored them. But then, in 1979, he was the dearest little fellow, quite the doll of our extended family.

Our young workers were a mixed bag. At times we had mostly Brits, or Dutch, with a smattering of other nationalities coming and going. They were as our own children. We felt responsible for them, and they were valiant in their efforts towards us. We had so many good kids, and that summer the Dutch seemed to abound, such a good natured gang they were too, and ever appreciative of my cooking.

They willingly practised being parents, bathing Fredo, doing the nappy changing and feeding him. It was the quaintest sight seeing him, fast asleep, draped over the substantial belly of Willem, in the orange orchard. He was our most loyal worker and friend, the maddest and best Dutchman of them all.

A tradition began, by chance as they do. We started having The Tripian Games every year. A water sports event in the cistern, which included straight racing, plus other daft competitive games. A lot of time was spent working out tricky manoeuvres involving flour and chocolate, tumblers of orange juice, anything for a laugh. The kids threw themselves into it, organising teams with their usual gusto. These batty occasions will never be forgotten and anyway we have a splendid record of them on film.

As I have said before, it was a huge cistern, created by the clever Stamos from an ancient wine cellar. Used for storing pumped up, icy water, in order to irrigate the land, the first days it was anaesthetising, it was so cold. By the time it thawed, it became murky with algae and although warmish, was nowhere as pleasant.

Every afternoon at five, siesta over, we congregated at the cistern. As I walked across from the kitchen, my baby began kicking his legs in anticipation. He loved it. But I had to introduce him to it gradually, inches at a time so he grew accustomed to the cold. Otherwise he would roar. Surprisingly, my mother sent two tiny plastic rings which just about fitted him so, once used to the cold water, in he went to pootle about with his many foster siblings in close attendance.

Five metres deep, a few even learnt to swim in it, no doubt from self preservation. For there was frequent horseplay and the unfortunate non-swimmer had to watch it. Once they threw in one of my bottle-fed lambs, then I was told to jump in to see if it would follow me, even in the water. It did. I firmly drew the line however when they suggested pushing my old mare in. Idiots.

Then that moron Willem decided to check just how deep the cistern was. We could have told him, but no, he decided to find out for himself. Damn fool boy. Taking up a long, iron builder's bar, he pushed it into the water.

We had plenty of experiences on the farm, but never a death. If he hadn't been wearing rubber wellies, no doubt at all, Willem would have been electrocuted. For the top of the bar touched an electric cable which fed the irrigation pump. Bang! All the electricity in the surrounding area was blown. Oh my goodness, what a scare. But nonetheless, we laugh over it still. Dear Willem. (The clot.)

One day when things were quiet and Stamos had gone to Athens, I was alerted by the furious barking of our pack of dogs. The second son of Xrysoula, our best Rom fruit picker, stood outside. A gentle boy, he was quite the opposite to his thug elder and only brother, who was an all-time thief. Now, he seemed to be in deep distress and it took me some time to work out what was his trouble. What with the hysterical dogs, his Rom Greek and my lousy Greek, it was hard. His urgency and terror were distressing. Piece by piece I came to understand what he wanted.

Xrysoula was being held at the police station. He had been sent to fetch us for help. She would be transferred to the women's prison in Athens, that evening. By repute, this was a terrible place, quite different from the cosy little local men's prison, down the road. So it was up to me to intervene. With Stamos away, despite really not knowing what it was all about, I was their only hope.

So I drove into town with him, the baby on his lap, flummoxed but willing. As I entered the building, the boy held back and crept away, too afraid to come in with me. I was on my own. It really was a heart-rending sight seeing her, head bowed, sitting in a corner, a figure of total dejection. Determined to fly her flag, I kissed her properly on both cheeks. Hesitating, for it would never do if he was seen to reject her, she held her arms out for Frederikos and, bless him, he happily went to her, an old friend. Our relationship now established, I had to understand why she was there. And more, why she was to be taken to the women's prison in Athens.

Apparently they had never paid for the permit to build her 'house'. Eyes wide, I asked the man behind the desk to repeat himself.

A permit? For that shack? A tiny, four-walled box, topped by a leaky tin roof required a permit? It never should have been allowed to be built in the first place. It was a stable, a poor one at that, not an abode for human beings. But, if it was not settled today, she must go to prison. I looked at him helplessly, for even for us, it seemed like quite a hefty fee. At that moment I just did not have it.

'Surely,' I pleaded, 'this is her husband's responsibility?' For well I knew that the useless Yannis spent lots of time in prison anyway, so who cared if he did another stint? But no, the 'house' was not in his name, but hers.

I had less than half the amount of money required on me and the banks were closed for the day.

Pushing what money I had across the desk to him, I eased off the two gold bangles given me by my sister which I always wore, and shoved them over too.

'Let her come home with me,' I implored. 'Take this money and my bangles for security, and when the banks open in the morning, I will bring the remainder.'

He was a kindly bobby, perhaps a little surprised by my involvement and concern with a mere tszingani. He took the cash, pushed the bangles back at me and told me to take her and he would see me in the morning.

As we left the building, the younger son swiftly joined us from the shadows and we drove home to the farm. I dug into the fridge and set a small meal before them. Oh but we were so relieved.

I drove them home, up to the rocky plateau to a strangely quiet Rom village. 'Tripina', someone called. Then as one by one they saw the car, me, Xrysoula and her son, like wild-fire the whole village came to life. People erupted from every shack and tent and rushed across to greet her. It was like the arrival of the Queen of Sheba, a tumultuous welcome, and for me, deeply touching. For the Rom women are the very heart of the family and home. While the men spend plenty of time in prison, it is very, very rare for a Rom woman to do so. They rarely commit true crimes, restricting themselves to petty pilfering, and that usually, just to feed their children. So there she was home again, Xrysoula the poorest of the poor, even in Rom society, she was given a true hero's welcome.

If, when this journal gets published, IF, ever it is made into a film, I would like to choose the music for that blessed afternoon, The Arrival of the Queen of Sheba.

The following day I went to town at dawn to avoid the heat, took out the required money from the bank, and settled up at the police station.

A couple of days later Xrysoula came up the drive, skirts swinging, full of purpose. She explained that now she wanted to do something for us. She could never repay us, but a deed? Could we think of anything? We thought. For of course this was serious business, there was honour involved. Finally we decided that we would like a bell tent, such as the Rom use in summer. It was happily agreed on. We bought yards and yards of the correct canvas and handed it over. Apparently many of her family and friends helped her stitch it, all by hand, a fearfully hard job. It was a beauty. Everyone was pleased. Honour was restored, Xrysoula now had a legal home, and I yet another weird and beautiful experience.

Just in case I should forget to mention it later on, I am happy to tell that years later, I actually gave her the pair of golden bangles. It seemed the right thing to do. As I pushed them over her thin, work-worn hands, I made her promise that she would never, ever sell them, (or give them away). Nodding hard, smiling broadly with delight, she said that she would always keep them for good luck, and for memory's sake. To this day she swears that she still has them, but I haven't seen them since.

Not long after the police station incident, Xrysoula appeared again. They were going fruit picking in the North. One of her seven daughters was to be married. Would we act as her family? What a lovely project thought I. Then we learned that the groom was in prison, and that the ceremony would be held there. Well!

A lovely seventeen year old Rom girl presented herself one morning. She was fourth daughter of Yannis and Xrysoula, their seventh child. Delving into my great treasure trunk, I unearthed a frothy delight of an evening dress, white lace and turquoise silk. I had used it but once at a fancy dress ball. It would do very nicely as Panaiota was about seven month's pregnant. She was delighted. We then set about making the net bonboniers in order to do things properly. Happily taking up the offer of a bath and hair wash, we dressed her and took her, a truly radiant bride, the mere mile to the local prison.

The gates clanged behind us.

I was pleased to see fruits of handicraft labours, occupational therapy no less, laid out on a table, to tempt the visitors. They were ghastly. Coarse, synthetic wool in vibrant colours had been made into all manner of gee-gaws, place mats, oven gloves etcetera. I suggested to Panaiota that she might like one. All eyes watched earnestly through the barred door, for this was cigarette money. After some indecision, she chose the least lurid, which we paid for, thus making one prisoner happy.

The groom, Leonidas, was a good looking lad, and his horrible mother had managed to dress him up very smartly. Apparently she was most displeased with the union, basically because Panaiota came from a 'poor' family. Yet never mind that her foolish son had not only stolen a police car, in his drunken state he had left it parked outside their house.

It was a charming ceremony. The prison had been burnished and properly prepared. A white cloth gracing the dining table, which with a handsome cross and two fine candle-sticks on top, served as the altar. Two amused town priests officiated. We flung rice as was the custom, although it was perfectly evident this bride was fruitful. The inmates held the candles, made the right responses, and were happy to receive the screws of sugared almonds. Afterwards I handed a small bag containing a meal to the bridal couple, who were allowed fifteen minutes together, although the wine was not permitted. Happily they talked, only to be roughly told, 'Speak Greek.' For of course they were speaking in Rom.

It had been a real family affair. The groom's father, two brothers, an uncle, and various lesser relatives of the bride and groom shook our hands beaming. This small interruption in the boredom of prison life, made everyone happy. Apparently the event also caused the groom to get out of prison a fraction earlier, so he was in time to escort his wife to hospital for her delivery.

The very next day, they called by at the farm; Leonidas patently disappointed at not having the expected son, gladly joined us in

241

drinking to the health of his daughter. When I asked Panaiota why she had come out so soon, she said she did not like the hospital, so left immediately. She showed me her adorable, one day old baby. A chubby, soft brown little girl, I was asked if I would be her Godmother. I accepted, feeling greatly privileged. Ten months younger than my baby, it was ideal for us all, for she had all his hand-me-downs, although she was tiny and he, a long fellow. She was his only little friend for a long time, and they loved each other.

By then, we were making progress with restoring our little church, but Panaiota was desperate to have her baby baptised. It seemed that she had the devil in her, and only by being baptised, could he be driven out.

I approached the priest in Examilia. He was never in apparently and never returned my calls. At last I tracked him down and asked if he would baptise the Rom baby. He must have heard what I wanted via the bush telegraph and was quite obviously most unenthusiastic. At last he coldly agreed to do so at his church, at such a time on such a day. All my instincts rebelled. A man of God, he was there to serve the people. His manner was hardly holy, and foolish me, I wondered why.

'Please excuse me asking you if we may hold it at the little church of Saint Theodoros above our farm?' (also in his area) I asked politely. 'It will be a small group, needing little space.'

'No,' he replied, eyes glittering unkindly. 'There is no electricity there.'

So, and the story of my life, I laughed gaily, totally unaware that I was not dealing with a truly good man.

'Oh do not worry about that. I will buy lots of candles and bring a little gas burner for the water heating.' Then, blindly blundering on, 'after all, you have only had electricity in the village for a few years, and Saint John had none at all.' (Oh dear, will I never learn?)

'Go elsewhere,' said he, and turned his back.

Suffer the little children to come unto me –

I was shocked. Why? What to expect from such a humbug of a man? Call himself a man of God? More like a man of the devil. So we went elsewhere, to another hideous church nearby where the priest was a splendid, jolly, Greek Australian.

'Call me Father Nick!' he said cheerfully. Thankfully, we did.

We went through the trunk again and Panaiota chose the baptismal gown which I had worn. We all trooped to the next village to attend the ceremony. The little star looked adorable in my pale cream, frilly, lawn dress and bonnet and yelled blue murder, as is correct, to chase off the devil. I made some promises which to this day I do try to keep on her behalf but it isn't easy, for she remains a very wilful little madam. Father Nick did the whole ceremony beautifully and thoughtfully translated much of the service into English for the benefit of the group of our young people who happily attended. Stark naked, she was well dunked in the font, her hair was snipped and a lot of olive oil was poured all over her. Father Nick blew in her face, 'the breath of God?' and some salt came into it too but I can't remember where, or at which stage. Anyway, by the end of the ceremony we now had a little Christian, albeit a highly indignant little Christian, called Anastasia Judith.

Which is how I became Koumbara to all her tribe, related by God probably to most of the Rom in Greece. And I have to say, I am very proud to be so.

Chapter 2

Re-Building

Periodically, Stamos 'went mad' with the whitewash bucket. It would be a quiet time, and as a professional, he went through the house, room by room, till it was dazzling white. Not long after our many months away, he was again hit by the decorating fever and the saddest thing happened, which caused a cloud to cross his soul, seemingly never to completely lift. The clearing up of his children's rooms caused him to throw away a lot of rubbish, including some letters.

One always hears the sound advice to never, ever, read other people's letters, for you are bound to see something unpleasant there. The whitewashing activity stopped suddenly, and he came downstairs white faced and still and silent sat by the fireplace. He looked so old, sad and utterly miserable. I could not imagine what had caused his sudden and complete change of mood. He did not speak or smile, just sat as if critically wounded. At last he told me the cause of his distress. Foolish but oh so human, he had read a letter. A letter, from one son to the other. The words are embedded in my mind.

'He came like an American daddy, with money pouring out of his pockets, trying to buy our love.'

During our months in London, in order not to be too heavy on the wonderful Elsie, every weekend we had taken off somewhere. Many other friends gave us hospitality, so that Elsie could have her home to herself at weekends. Then one day Stamos asked me if I minded if he visited a student son and his wife.

'Judaki mou' (my little Judy), 'would you mind if I took some of our savings? Perhaps to help them, with their little house?'

Of course I did not mind, and anyway, he was earning more than I. He went, and returned wonderfully happy. He recounted how they had bought wood, together built shelves, gone to the pub, met lots of young people and had a lovely time.

Right then there was no comforting him. Yet I determined, at the very next opportunity, to question my step-daughter-in-law, an honest girl, about that fateful weekend. She was genuinely aghast, for apparently, it had simply not been like that.

'It was a lovely weekend,' she told me. 'We were all so busy and happy together. It was wrong of him to write such a thing, for it just wasn't true.'

Poor Stamos, he was really broken, for he so loved his children. I cannot imagine my own pain, if any of my sons were to feel the same about me.

So he threw himself into the farm, with cash in the bank from the recent windfall, his dreams were at last a possibility. Plans were drawn for a barn, the permit clearly painted on a notice, correctly stuck in front of the foundations for all to see. Like everything Stamos did, it had to be the biggest and best. His was to be an enormous barn. My objections were waved aside. Mixalis had a huge barn, he must have one also. When I ventured to say that all of Mixalis' family, were 'workers of the world,' (and ours were not), I again got short shrift. A true Sagittarian, Stamos always reached for the stars.

245

We were however incredibly blessed that year with a few young men who were not only enthusiastic, they were gifted and knowledgeable builders. Brian lead us all. Only in his early twenties, he was a natural. At last, and again, the church progressed. Stamos announced that as all Greek churches had a veranda to sit in, we must also have one. It was during digging out the foundations that the kids uncovered, just under the surface, the remains of a baby, shreds of the shawl it had been wrapped in still evident. We wondered about it. Obviously buried a long time before, had it been a still-born child? Or had it died in infancy and the mother been too poor to bury it properly? It cannot have been a murder, for obviously whoever buried it there, behind the church out of sight of the house, must have been a deeply religious person. I gathered up the fragile fragments and put them together in a box with the other human remains which we had found during our work on the land.

Stamos, (in his element) and I drove to Patras to buy timber right off the docks. Roof beams and lining for the church and beams for the kitchen extension

Two teams laboured independently on the two projects, church and lean-to. But this began to cause mild friction, for the church builders, (the devils) considered themselves superior to the lean-to builders. I, having grizzled about the lack of shelter directly outside the kitchen for years, was delighted that at last we were to have one. A splendid, full length, open room, there to store wellies, sacks of this and that, fridges, you name it. A proper, farm necessity.

'So how is the lean-to going?' drawled the holy ones on arriving back from the church for lunch.

Or, 'What progress with the shed?' The gang working on the kitchen extension became annoyed. For even if their lesser and despised task was not to the glory of God, it would please Judy.

I racked my brains for a satisfactory solution to this minor but irritating problem. Feelings had to be soothed, for really they were doing a most important job. Whoever heard of a farm kitchen just going OUT, into the elements, without any form of store or shelter immediately outside? Then I hit on a fine solution, a proud name. As it had taken Cheops years to achieve his pyramid, so it had for the house to have this highly necessary extension.

We called it 'The Cheopery'. It was a good sound, everyone agreed. A notice was painted and stuck up in the entrance. Pride was restored and there were no more derogatory remarks on 'shed' or 'lean-to' bandied about.

Even the bathroom got a face lift. A large and damp room, the walls yearly turned black with mould and had to be whitewashed regularly. Stamos lined the end wall with rather clinical, plain white tiles, interspersed with some colourful, hand-painted majolica tiles which my godmother had given me. Rather superior souvenirs from Spain, Don Quixote and Sancho Panchez, they relieved the whiteness, and the little Frederikos and subsequent grandchildren delighted in looking at them.

The pressures on just one, albeit large, bathroom and loo were enormous, especially with a baby to change, for I kept all his gear there. Once more, our excellent team of lads to the breach. Behind the bathroom, a bush loo and shower were erected to everyone's satisfaction. No loo ever had such a view, for due West over the apricot orchards, rose the impressive and beautiful hump of Akro Corinth.

Over the years, other bush loos arose here and there on the farm, extraordinary but sensible little structures of bamboo and make-do.

Almost all the young people treated the farm as their home, and us as surrogate parents. The little Fredo also got his share of attention. I well remember watching a young Australian trying to teach him to crawl. Magued, originally a Copt from Egypt, strung a cord under his tummy, hoisted him up and tried to show him where to place his feet and hands. Lazy baby just objected noisily, inevitably doing a belly flop. For why should he bother to walk when on offering a smile, he had so many willing hands to lift him up? He did eventually crawl for a short time. Then, as a drunken sailor, he walked when he was ready, at the grand old age of sixteen months. Stamos and I smiled warmly at each other while watching his unsteady progress and were very proud, as if he were our first. Which, of course he was.

Nineteen eighty is well remembered on the farm for the coronation of Queen Beatrix of the Netherlands. It was also the day when we gained yet another dog. A very small one this time, naturally called Trixie. I had gone to the Rom camp for something, and the usual gaggle of kids hung about the pick-up while I spoke to Xhrysoula. I half noted a boy holding a substantial rope from which was attached a very small, cowed, black and white terrier. I saw too that her leg had been broken.

'What is it with the little dog?' I asked.

They all replied together, loud and un-clear so I did not understand.

'Take it,' said an older woman on the fringe of the crowd. I looked at the little dog with pity but knew I must not take another creature home; we had enough.

Business done, I made to leave when once again the little dog and I looked at each other. A small, deep moment of contact passed between us. I got out of the car, scooped her up and left.

Els, Willem's girl, cared for her in the Well House for the first days, for with her leg and her fear, she needed peace, quiet and security. I have no idea how old she was but somehow she survived with us, even with her gammy leg, for ten more years. A wonderful, loyal and loving little dog, bright and clever, for after all, Trixie was named after a queen.

On the big day, the whole farm was taken over by the House of Orange. Every human, animal and machinery was bedecked with orange ribbons. I rushed to town to buy cloth and made a couple of Dutch flags. The mid-day meal was entirely orange, and I remember pouring egg yolks into the mashed potatoes to get it right. A party was held. A telegram was sent, and eventually we even had a thanks for it.

For I love occasions. All no doubt resulting from a deprived childhood when left in England at school, my parents disappeared seemingly 'for ever'. To this day I love spoiling people for occasions, especially their birthdays, all because of the ones, (oh pathetic), I missed out on.

The First of May, is another big day in Greece. In the past when money was very short, children used to make steffania, (flower wreathes) mostly from the glorious, bright yellow corn daisies which abound at that moment. Standing beside the road flagging down motorists was a great joy when, for a few drax, they sold some.

Nowadays every house has its steffani hung on the front, there to stay till next year. I used the same wire ring every year, growing ever plumper with the build up of flowers. We used the first of May as an excuse for a break from our labours and took off into the poor little vineyards above the farm around the old church of Saint Theodoros where the wild flowers were magnificent. Spring is something so special in Greece. The flowers are somehow far more vivid and colourful than anywhere else. The poppies seem almost to be an electric red, they are so bright. Stamos was always the judge on these occasions. He prowled around the exhibits with deep concentration, and then presented the winner, generally with a huge bar of chocolate.

This was the best horta picking time and every Greek housewife, bored with the winter, would collect a few of her friends and sally forth. Revelling in getting out of doors, she returned home, her bags bulging, to feed her family. Each weed has its own virtue, and one, which amused me, was supposed to be good for male virility. Hence, clever ladies, they got the time off from their dull chores, and happy from their day outside, were probably softer, and more inviting to their men, so no doubt the weed was given the benefit. I taught many an incredulous girl how and what to cut and cook and smiled at their appreciation when the mess of greens was served up at table. Xorta, or horta, is the root of horticulture – the growing of green things. Stamos told me that Greece would not have survived without it during the terrible days of war. When I had heard, many years earlier, that they did the same in Italy, I had felt so sorry for them. To be so very hungry, to eat weeds. But then when I lived in Greece and better, learned to cut and cook my own, I found that horta is delicious, and much nicer than spinach cooked the same way. Boiled in salted water, drained well, sprinkled with oil and lemon juice, it is a very healthy feast. Much horta is cultivated now, long and somewhat tough and nowhere as good as the springtime weeds for free.

Oh and the hortopitta! (weed pies.) The country women all have their secret ways and in spring make huge round pies with homemade, rather thick filo pastry. Mixed with the finely chopped raw weeds are oil, salt, pepper, some chopped spring onions, a tablespoon or two of rice and a little fetta. It is quite a long and laborious job trimming and washing the weeds, and I remember that Willem was a most excellent chopper upper of them. But then, how he relished the pies.

Four English ex-public school boys turned up, one the nephew of an old friend of mine. They were a zany bunch, delightful, willing in every way, the more mad the task the happier they were. We were alerted when a shot rang out at the end of the land. High summer, it was very much the close season. The boys hot-tailed it, to find out if one of our dogs was the victim. They returned, Edward carrying a dead fox. Now, I knew we had foxes, for occasionally I saw them and I often heard them. Even if we kept the kotetsi shut at night, they came in the day and helped themselves to wandering fowl if the dogs were sleeping.

'Will you?' asked the eccentric young Englishman, 'cook this for me?'

Struck dumb for the moment, I then agreed, if he would skin it. A poor old vixen, thoroughly mangy and flea-ridden; I used all my culinary skills to cook her. Bay leaves galore, onions, garlic, it was no use. It was dreadful. I laid it out neatly boned on a big platter and passed it round. The brave took some, I tasted a shred. Yuk. When I visited his parents at their castle in England some time later, his father was incensed, indeed irate.

'You can't eat a member of the dog family,' he fumed. Unwisely perhaps, I contradicted him, telling him that dog, (not fox) was a delicacy in some parts of the world. He would not hear of it. But never mind, it was done and we had the memory of another mad experience. That night I listened to the sorrowful crying of her cubs and cursed the horrid watchman from the factory beyond the farm. For I knew it was he who had shot her and who casually shot so many of our dear dogs.

Birthdays and Christmas were big occasions on the farm, but I had a firm rule which caused great thought and resulted in splendid invention. NO money, was to be spent. The kids had little enough of it, so this was the law. At least they might use a very little money, for materials only. All gifts had to be made by hand. It was such fun. Furtive activities and strange requests all blossomed into extraordinary works of art. Once we had a spoon-making contest, (as we were short of spoons). Whittling took place in every corner. They were amazing. Either huge and rough, and fit only for giants, or small and fine and exquisite. I have some still. Another gift they gave us and each other were songs. After practising away quietly usually with guitars, on the day itself and if possible several times, they raised their voices and held forth, their offering, their gift. It was charming.

Whenever we went inland to visit Mixalis and Diamando, we passed a small house which had a beautiful big cart parked in a shed beside it. Every time I remembered, I had a little nag to Mixalis, for it would be such fun to have a cart for our dear old mare. Here and there throughout the small country roads one saw similar carts abandoned in various stages of neglect. Originally painted brightly with flowers, faces and patterns on a blue ground, they were now faded by the sun, yet still wonderful. Ever admiring things worked with the hands, I grieved sorely for these forgotten works of art and would have liked to rescue them all.

One day Mixalis phoned. The owner of the cart said to come and get it. The shed was falling down, it was ours. An optimistic group, we happily set off after we had rung Makis, our favourite truck driver, and arranged to meet him there. Sure enough, the roof was half down, so with a great deal of shouting and effort it was lifted and the cart pulled out. It was then, somehow and with plenty more shouting, hoisted onto the truck. As usual, Makis was very amused with our nonsense.

After I had grubbed about in what remained of the shed and salvaged what kit I could find, sadly in poor condition, I paid the farmer and off we went. Unfortunately the cart had been stowed shafts down, so the ends were rotten. No immediate and jolly trip by horse and cart could happen until they were replaced.

Having always loved Argos market, it was easy to find an excuse to go there. It was necessary to leave the farm early in the morning in order to get there when it was at its most lively, not forgetting to be there before it got too hot. We had often passed a carpenter's shop in the narrow back streets, and thought it might be worth a try to see if he could replace our shafts.

The dusty little street was lined with open-fronted shops of every sort, their eaves trimmed in the old way, with wonderful ceramica. Heavy end-roof tiles in the shape of icanthus leaves, or heads of Zeus or Hermes gazed down at us. All manner of little shops did their business half out into the street, including a small café where on my very first visit, we had rejoiced, together it seemed with half the market, over the purchase of our first lamb. The Landrover parked some distance away, we walked to find the old carpenter, two boys carrying the shafts.

Rows of tool handles were lined up on the pavement outside his shop. Mattocks, shovels and spades, already fitted with new handles, stood in rows waiting to be collected. For it seemed that this was all he did now. A handsome old man with the kindest face, he left his bench and came to see what Stamos wanted. Taking a shaft, he went back into the gloom inside, reached up to a rack above his bench and lifted down a plane. Fitting it into a groove on the shaft, he looked up smiling.

'I made this.'

We crowded into the coolness inside his workshop. The smell of wood was lovely. He and Stamos talked excitedly together about our new cart, and he happily agreed to make new shafts for it. All the while, my eyes getting accustomed to the gloom, I noticed above us, set on the roof beams, three more carts, or rather the body of carts.

Brand new, there they lay, thickly covered in dust. The old man spoke quietly, mourning to us that no one wanted them any more. Everyone had a rotovator, or a pick-up. The days of the horse drawn cart were over. Now all he did was to repair simple farm tools, replacing their wooden handles.

I stood, still gazing up, my brain churning. For while Stamos loved all machinery, I loved all wooden things made by hand.

'Surely we can use one?' I muttered, still gazing upwards. 'Maybe we can make a great bed for Fredo out of it?'

Catching my dream, Stamos organised the lifting down of the cart. Amidst much flying dust of ages and the inevitable shouting, down it came, to be taken out into the street for all to see. A crowd gathered, something unusual was going on.

Then Stamos held forth, loud and clear, arms waving, pointing to the cart and the tools. He was in his element.

'Are you aware, you people of Argos, that you have a master craftsman here?' The old carpenter bowed his head. 'Do you see what he is doing now, instead of creating these magnificent works of art?' The cart was waved at, then the tools. 'All he spends his time and his gift on now is mending mattock handles!'

I noticed the carpenter whispering into the ear of a young boy who ran off, shortly to return with an elderly and very comely matron, obviously the carpenter's wife.

'Look!' roared the orator, 'just look at the workmanship.' They all looked, felt the finely turned bobbins and nodded their heads in agreement. The carpenter and his wife stood in the middle of the throng and basked in the warmth of the unexpected attention and praise.

A boy who had gone to fetch the Landrover arrived, easing his way through the crowd till in front of the carpenter's shop. More shouting, more dust as the cart was once more dusted off. With every available hand helping, for it was heavy, it was hoisted onto the roof of the Landrover and tied down. A sensible but small sum was handed over despite much refusal. Everyone shook hands with everyone. The carpenter's wife was roundly kissed. The hold-up, having attracted the attention of the agricultural policeman, was sympathetically cleared. Waving our good byes, jubilant, off we went home, with another weird load on the roof rack.

As we trundled along, I was so happy and thrilled with our extraordinary buy. Happy too with my man, who with his sympathy for the underdog or has-been, had lifted the spirits of two fine old people. They I am sure will never forget him or that day, and neither have I.

Eventually the bed was made and used. A friend of Geoff's came to stay; Nick, one of those blessed people who can put their hands to almost anything, made two sturdy low trestles on which to stand the wheel-less cart. Other small alterations were made to the body and a new mattress was bought to fit it. There we were, the proud owners of a most extraordinary and handsome bed. Lucky boy!

Chapter 3

Children

The first birthday party we held for Frederikos was the beginning of a great tradition for all his friends in the area. For what we know of children's parties just did not exist in Greece. Because in the past most people were semi if not wholly illiterate, birthdays were rarely remembered or celebrated. The big 'fussaria' (lovely word which actually means – trouble) is on saint days. In the past, names were very strictly passed down in families and the old names usually were from the saints.

For by church law everyone is supposed to be baptised after a saint. For the centuries while Greece were under Turkish domination, it was understandably essential to stick with tradition. No doubt that after independence in 1830 the educated switched from Christian names, to those of the far and distant past. It is mainly amongst the educated even now, that ancient names are used.

In 1981, Stamos became a grandfather for the first time to a dear little snub-nosed girl who was named Kassandra, an ancient name. Undoubtedly it was acceptable with the jubilation of independence, to dig into the past and glorious history of Greece. Therefore, this like many other laws has thankfully been relaxed, for who, for example, ever heard of a Saint Fred? Nonetheless, with foreign or new fangled names, a saint day is also usually designated to everyone. I, whose middle name is Virginia, celebrate one of the great religious holidays for the Virgin in August.

They come around very regularly and everyone is well-wished or invited for the name day. The phone never stops. Sticky cakes abound. All the relatives, particularly including of course those sharing the same saint's name, sit about gossiping over tiny glasses of liqueur while the children run wild underfoot.

Everyone goes to church, especially if it is an important saint. Saints George, John, Michael and Andrew are top favourites. The bells ring, loud and long, indeed sometimes, several times a day, to summon the faithful. Everyone wears their smartest clothes. There is usually a panayeri, a festival centred around the church. In the small villages it is a feast with eating and dancing, with everyone contributing. In larger villages, there might also be some stalls selling all manner of junk and there often are some incredible antique swings and round-abouts which are turned by hand. The towns, as with everything else, are very commercial with glitzy stalls galore and have very superior, flashy and terrifying fairground rides run by generators. While the commercial side of these days is important, at least some stalls remember the Christian origins and sell garish religious paraphernalia.

The first thing which hits you is the music which is at TOP decibel, shattering. Nonetheless, panayeries are fun, make a break in busy, mundane lives, and even bring in a bit of cash for the smarter opportunist. A farmer might roast some whole lambs, kids or pigs, then sell them, chopped up, by weight, doled out in paper. They are then, like fish and chips, eaten by hand while the visitors wander about looking at the stalls. Splendidly messy. Others might bring plants, vegetables and flowers to sell. Having restored our own little church, we would soon be doing our bit to keep up tradition. We

256

however, would be offering old fashioned hospitality, definitely without the commercialism. It was fast becoming evident that not only were we both hopeless with money, neither of us had a shrewd bone in our body.

Fredo's parties continued with being a huge success as he got older, with musical chairs, blind man's buff, statues and so on, none of which the local children had ever played before. The birthday cake being another new phenomenon, caused great excitement. The candles were a big hit, particularly the automatically re-lighting variety, having to be blown out several times amidst squeals of joy. TV has played a huge part in showing the masses what people do in other countries, so birthday parties were known about, if not normally held.

Many years later, I was to discover with delight, just how great was the influence of television. Attending the wedding of goddaughter Emilie, I volunteered to do the flowers. Without a car, it was arduous trailing to the market and back lugging masses of flowers and greenery. Having done the baskets for the church, vases for reception and the bride's bouquet, I was left with an inevitable pile of broken flower heads and odds and ends. Thoroughly weary by then, I had removed myself to the peace of the garden. Being a frugal soul, I decided to salvage what I could to make sprays and buttonholes. I was a useful guest, for speaking Greek, albeit kitchen Greek, I was interpreter between the Greek in-laws and the other English guests who were valiantly toiling away to make it all possible.

Roula, Emilie's mother-in-law came out to see me. I showed her the boxes of sprays and buttonholes and explained them to her.

'The sprays are for the important ladies.' I held out a fine one. 'The best are for you, your mother, Ruth.' Then picking up a smaller one I carried on. 'These are for your sisters and cousins.' Then on to the buttonholes which were much of a muchness 'And these are for the important men.

'Eyes glowing, hands held out caressing a spray she breathed.

257

'Oh Julia, just like in Dynasty.'(I loved it, oh how I loved it! It really made my week.)

When Fredo went to school, a new gang of town kids were invited, going mad in delight with all the space we had to offer. At first, I was appalled when the parents or grandparents arrived too, sat themselves down in our saloon and expected to be waited upon. They must have thought me incredibly rude when I told them that as I would be busy with the kids, could they return to collect them at six. Whether offended or not, the elders soon understood that foreign parties were different, so in time did not expect to be entertained by me. Meanwhile the children had a glorious time and vied to get invited every year.

Christmas was really a non-starter then, while now alas it is a 110% commercial affair with lurid junk imported from the East strewn about in the market places. Over the years, so as not to feel homesick, I always decorated our big living room with loads of greenery. It was so simple to cut a wayward branch from a cypress, stick it in the corner, and pretend it was a proper Christmas tree. Fredo's first Christmas is memorable and all that greenery reminds me of a ghastly experience.

Those lucky people, as myself, who have always lived in peace, cannot easily understand the suffering of the other half of the world. To read, watch on television or hear about conflict, only part of the mind takes it in. For we weren't there, and it is well nigh impossible to fully understand the terror or tyranny of the time.

Greece has had a varied and often brutal history, some very much in living memory too. They really must be a very forgiving people as now they seem to get on with their lives, looking the other way when they are reminded. A civil war, brother against brother! Unimaginable sorrow. The colonels. Utter wickedness. Tyranny is always slow to fade and somehow the little Hitlers seem to survive in the shadows waiting their chance. The bully-beef apparently also manage to hang together, ready to support each other to exercise their brutality. The victims too, with fear embedded in their bones, are always waiting, available.

The far and distant root cause which brought about this experience was directly due to a great earthquake. Our area is often shaken with them, for two earth plates meet under the sea, deep in the Corinthian Gulf. The quakes are usually small, but just occasionally as then, very dramatic. So it was in the second century, when what is now called Ancient Corinth was destroyed by a huge tidal wave. Debris dumped by the retreating water caused new land to form. It was alluvial, entirely sandy soil in fact, on which now stands our town of New Corinth.

As long ago as Saint Paul, the people of Corinth were considered awkward. Things don't change. In retrospect I laugh, but then, oh dear, it was all deadly serious, as matters in small-town affairs tend to be. Feelings ran so high, the only crime not committed so Stamos told me, was murder.

Inevitably what was a small town, became a big town. The drains in that sandy soil were totally inadequate. The place stank. It was a regular occurrence to be held up, when shopping in town, or to have to make a detour because a sludge-gulper was blocking the road, emptying cesspits. It was grim, incompetent, unhygienic and smelly and the problem grew and grew. All the while the town council talked, and talked, and nothing got done. The top dog, a wealthy man (of course) waved aside demands for a new sewage works and decreed that it was far more important for the town to have a sport's centre. The land had already been bought and fine plans had been made. One wondered what favours had been promised, what bribes might have been given. War raged spasmodically, and slowly but surely the sports centre grew. So too did the problem of the sewage.

Now everyone knows that farmers moan, indeed they are famous for it. Although the townspeople thought that we farmers were rich and enjoyed a wonderful life, one of our brethren who was drowning in debt, as no doubt were so many others, unable to cope any more, abandoned ship. Perhaps he had to find a dowry for a daughter? Or his roof was falling in? Or perhaps like us, he was struggling to pay his bills, still waiting after two years, for the money for his apricot crop? So to solve his problems, he LET a small piece of land to the council, a mere kilometre out of town, for the dumping of the town's sewage.

In a country where everyone knows everything that is going on, they watched and waited. When the bulldozers had dug their pits, the great day arrived. Together with all the neighbouring farmers, my husband set off on our prized new tractor to block off the road. A great assortment of machinery and life gathered before dawn. Big and small tractors. Rotovators, with or without their chariots tacked on behind. Fitting in here and there were trusty pick-ups, vans, motor bikes, donkeys and carts. There was much good natured shouting and arm waving. They settled in place, waiting. The sludge-gulpers came and finding there was no access, they went and they dumped their loads elsewhere.

Intense meetings began taking place. There was much support far and wide, for the dump was patently far too close to the town. What was more, it was too close to the huge army camp where the youth of Greece were incarcerated. It would not do, for how could our boys defend hearth and home with such a health risk? That proposal was withdrawn which brought about a lull, while the sewage problem grew and grew.

Then came whispers about another struggling farmer who had secretly signed a contract with the council. His land was even nearer to us, the extent of pollution was greater. More little farms would have their wells affected.

Our farm then became the centre of operations with Stamos at the controls. They came and they talked, and talked and talked, sitting under the walnut trees while I dished out beastly little cups of coffee ad infinitum.

For 150 years, Stamos' family had led the district through thick and thin. Now Stamos, certainly the most literate of the lot, was the leader of the opposition with a vengeance. The new site was going to be much more difficult to defend, for it had five roads leading to it. Every man and vehicle had to be drawn into battle. The council, no doubt hearing about it from its spies, called in THE LAW.

Squads of police cars arrived from nearby towns. Top brass, shimmering with gold epaulettes and braid strutted about. The army too were there in force, suitably draped with their arms at the ready. Last but not least, the dreaded armoured cars arrived from Athens. With them too, came memories of the recent past, bad old days.

This amazing show of brute force was directed against a group of unarmed and generally harmless country folk who were, after all, just trying to protect their water supply. It was shocking. Shameful. We withdrew. A very sober cavalcade moved out. Then the whole shebang, armoured cars, police and army, escorted the sludge-gulpers to deposit their loads of stinking and untreated sewage.

Understandably, all this had brought back many old fears. For it had not been so long before, during the era of the colonels, when friends had disappeared in the night, never to be seen again. Or had they re-appeared, wrecked from their tortures. No one dared to object openly, but the freedom so heavily won, seemed very thin.

Meanwhile the council got on with their sports centre and again, plans for a proper sewage system were put on the back shelf. In time, they must have heard that the new dump was causing anguish to the neighbourhood as despite it being winter, the smell and flies grew.

Then, the unfortunate man was well and truly set upon by his neighbours. Obviously as he and his family lived nearby, they too must have suffered. Cowed, ashamed of his actions, the man went to the council to withdraw his permission. Whereupon the council threatened him, with imprisonment for breach of contract.

That night, someone (who no one knew but everyone knew) took the law into his own hands and set fire to the wretched man's barn and car, completely destroying them both. There was, the next day, a great deal of quiet, yet sympathetic smirking amongst the farmers who sat under the walnut trees. If the law can't support the righteous, the law will be taken into the hands by the right.

Now began a new chapter in the tale of The Havouza. This is the Turkish word for cesspit, and is still used. The council, bravely supporting their poor fool, now took thirteen farmers to court. All those hours of talking, they had brought it upon themselves and Stamos was on the top of the list. In order to gain public support, they had produced a poster explaining all the ghastly details. Not only were these widely handed out, they were stuck up everywhere. Alongside black-bordered death notices, on lamp posts in town, all along the roads, wherever possible. Needless to say, it had Stamos' splendid humour written all over it. Alas, having not wanted to actually name the head of the council, they labelled him, 'The Shit Shoveller.' Not only did this cause much merriment, it naturally caused grievous offence. This was the sort of label which sticks forever. War was declared.

The council accused the thirteen farmers of 'causing trouble in the town.' The intelligent judge soon realised that all thirteen were just good men, doing what they deemed was right for their own. It was an expensive business, but we won the case.

Unbelievably, in double quick time, another charge was laid against them. This time it was for 'inciting violence'.

Remembering my very first visit to Greece in 1969, when Iliara was born, I insisted that Stamos listen to me. I had been much impressed by her Cretan uncle, the gentle George, while I stayed in Iraklion. In the crisis with Simos, who had suffered a severe accident, George had held his audience by not shouting, which is the norm, but whispering. Now I tackled Stamos.

'Do not shout!' I told him, actually having to shout to make him listen. 'Speak slowly and clearly and softly. Then, they will all be quiet, and want to hear you.'

Wonders, he listened, he did and it worked. The lady judge must have been charmed by his lovely voice for she said, 'Now that is a man!' (I purr at the memory.)

We won again, yet, even then, it was not the end of the story. The Shit Shoveller was determined to have his revenge which is how I learned of tyranny first hand.

We were all unwell with severe colds, yet even so Stamos had gone to Athens. I was concerned about the baby and rang him to come home quickly in order to drive us to the doctors. He arrived home just as the light was fading around four so I asked him to put the two sheep in while I got the baby ready.

Then I saw a wisp of light flash past the window. I thought it was a police car, and as we occasionally had them round for French nationals in trouble, I did not think twice about it. But when Stamos did not return to the house, I looked out and saw that the sheep were still in the field so went to put them in for the night. The Petropoulos passed by with their flock on their way home and I asked them if they had seen him. They had not. A mystery.

'I think that the police have taken him,' I told them, puzzled. Their faces a picture of alarm, they went on their way.

If Stamos had been taken to sort out some French, why hadn't he, or the police informed me? Surely he would ring, or return shortly? I waited, cradling my sick baby, growing increasingly indignant for I dare not take him out in the cold Landrover without Stamos' help. As time passed, I grew anxious.

It began to occur to me that this was nothing to do with the French, but something to do with the havouza. I was incredulous that a man should disappear from his home in a police car, without his wife being informed. I simply did not know what to do. I knew no one. I had no local friends who could help me, so in desperation, I phoned Stamos' sister in Athens. A woman of the world, she would know what to do. After some time she called me back to tell me that Stamos was indeed being held by the police.

Now it was Friday evening, the weekend stretched before us and nothing could be done. I was distraught, shattered at this appalling injustice and mal-practice. My sister-in-law thankfully had however, organised for a paediatrician to come out to the farm to attend to the baby.

There in the big room, close by the bright fire, our only heating, I waited and wept. In the corner stood a huge, home made Christmas tree. All about me, the natural green decorations hung cheerfully, reminding me of other happier times in another place. The sound of a car arriving alerted me so I opened the front door to the doctor. I did not know him, for up till now, ours had been a very healthy baby. I learned later that he had been trained in Germany, so he took in the festive scene without comment. He appeared grumpy, possibly because he had been called out on that cold night. Again later, I found him to be a very cheerful man. It well might have been the sight of my swollen eyes and red nose. Alas I was never one of those fortunate women who cry with delicacy.

'What,' he asked gruffly, 'is the matter with you?'

Getting a grip on myself, really glad to have someone to talk to, it poured out.

'My baby is sick. My husband is in prison, and, I want to go home.' More tears. He did not seem a very sympathetic man, which was just as well or I might never have stopped.

'OK about the baby,' he said, 'I will see to that. Sorry I can't help you to go home. But, why is your husband in prison?'

More tears, then, out it came, 'The havouza, the beastly havouza. I think.'

He nodded, examined the baby and wrote out a prescription. I paid him his fee, and asked the taxi to go to the chemist and return with the medicine which he did. Alone, I settled down for the evening, utterly miserable and still unbelieving at what had happened. There was no war on, no dictator, no colonels, yet this was what they did. I hated this country. I hated being there. I just wanted to go home. I wept anew.

There was a knock on the door. Our precious neighbours stood there, all dressed up in their Sunday best. Having completed their milking, they had come to accompany me to find Stamos. Dear, brave, loyal and wonderful people.

Oh what a country of contrasts! So much hatred and evil, and so much loving kindness. Gathering my wits I thanked them profusely but told them 'no'. They must on no condition get involved. I sent them home, relief all over their kindly faces.

'Lock all the doors!' they called as they went.

'I never lock doors,' said I.

'Lock all the doors tonight Kyria Julia, please, so we can sleep.'

So for them and for once, I did. Shutting down the fire, I trailed up to bed, my little boy in my arms. At least I thought, he was all right and hopefully on the way to recovery with his medicine.

A long time later, sleepless and as if in a dream, I heard the familiar and beloved whistle. Stamos stood outside whistling away and I ran down to let him in.

Of course it had been a put-up job by the poor, offended Shit Shoveller. Being Friday evening, with all the courts closed, the judges off, he had sent his heavies to bring Stamos in. The reason given was that we did not have a permit to build the barn. Monsters! Of course we had, and there it was, stuck in the earth clear for all to see. Stamos told me that they had literally jumped him and hauled him into the car. He knew that if he put up a fight, he would get the worst of it and a one eyed man is far more vulnerable than others.

Ah but for sweet chance; a sick baby and that excellent doctor. Having in his youth been quite a rebel himself, (we heard about it later) he like Stamos was a great one for the under-dog. On leaving me he went straight home to phone a judge acquaintance of his, explained the situation and demanded, 'Get Tripos out!'

The judge rang the local police station and said, 'Let Tripos out!'

And, oh ho, they did!

Occasionally when I meet the Shit Shoveller in the street, I greet him cordially. The sports centre flourishes, and at last, the town got its new sewage system, so, for the moment, all is quiet.

Greek law totally mystifies me. When I first met Stamos, he told me that he was fifty five, but on his papers, he was fifty three. (Now have I got that right? It is all so confusing.)

I gawped, trying to take it in.

'How do you manage that?' I asked.

He carefully explained. When he was a youth, already a one-eyed youth, having had an operation to remove an eye, his parents were understandably afraid for him, should he be called up by the army. So they went to court and swore on oath that there had been a mistake in his birth date.

'But surely,' said I, 'no self respecting army would even think of taking on a one-eyed boy?'

I got no reply.

We were to come up with this same matter when a son wished to leave school a year early. After long and noisy discussions, Stamos, who would do anything for his children, agreed that he would go to court. History repeated itself. Again, and I suppose on oath, Stamos told them that he had made a mistake over the birth date of his child, and that he was in fact, one year older than stated on his papers.

'But, surely you can't do that?' said I incredulous, still ignorant of how things are done in Greece. He could, and he did.

'Is this wise?' asked the sympathetic judge very seriously.

Stamos assured him it was. Hence, by a stroke of a pen, the lad suddenly became one year older so that he could, and did, leave school. So now there were two members of the family who had two different ages, one according to fact, and the other, to fiction. Amazing.

Chapter 4

Dreams of a Mountain House

Aware that my handsome windfall was dwindling alarmingly, for Stamos' attitude, 'What's yours is mine', caused me deep concern, I did two things. The first, for my 'old age' I organised £10,000 to be put safely into bonds in England. The second, was seriously to begin the search for a house in the mountains. Despite liking the sea and loving to swim, I am a mountain person. It might have been something to do with being born in the Himalayas, or, perhaps having been Tibetan in a previous life, for altitude suits me.

We drove to explore the nearest range, Zyria, due west from us. Of course we already knew it, having been lent a house there by Kostas, the shepherd whose sister-in-law's wedding we had attended in my early days. These were unusually luxurious times for us, for together with some of Stamos' family, we stayed a couple of days in the mountains in a charming, government hotel. I remember putting the baby outside, stark naked, on a yellow sheepskin rug which Alison, one of our girls from New Zealand, had sent him. We listened from behind the shutters in our room, as he crowed with delight. We then heard the shrill arrival of an indignant Greek lady. He must have been pleased to see her, charming her with smiles, for she soon stopped her scolding as she sat beside and talked happily with the little fellow. It surely must have been an unusual sight, a lone baby sunning himself. The word 'therapia' was clearly trotted out, for not many Greek mothers would expose their naked babies to the mountain air.

It was so very beautiful and unspoiled and we determined to find something which would be easily accessible in the hot summer, if not in the snowy winter.

A call came from Kostas.

'Ella, ella!' (come, come or hello, hello) he shouted in the correct country way. Speaking from the one phone, situated publicly in the kaféneon, he tried to lower his voice so that the whole village wouldn't know his business. He had found us a house below the village, set in one stremma. It was just four walls, but it had good floors and shutters. He agreed to make arrangements for us to meet the relative who was selling it. Liking Kostas and trusting his judgment, we felt that we were on our way.

When we saw the house, we realised it was exactly as he had described it. Stone-built with heavy ceramic tiles, it was an oblong box with an upstairs and half a downstairs. On a slope, as all mountain houses are, we had the greatest difficulty in reaching and climbing up to get in at the front door. Sure enough there was one big room, part of which did have an excellent, newish wooden floor. Set on magnificent great beams, the roof timbers were in contrast, rather spindly. The wooden shutters, as usual with no glass, were well made and fitted with good iron fastenings. One wall, on the south end, was crumbling and needed urgent attention. For, as with all the old houses, it was simply built with rough-cut stone, cemented with mud. The one-third north end of the room, which had originally been the dairy, was no longer divided by the regular wood partition from the living quarters. This area had one window and as usual for a dairy, an earthen floor. Underneath, half dug into the hillside and reached by a trapdoor and wobbly home-made ladder, was the cellar. This is where they had kept the sheep. As it was merely the stable, it too had an earthen floor and one tiny window. But oh heaven, it was wonderfully cool.

The house belonged to the mother-in-law of Kostas' cousin, another Kostas. He was prevailed upon by Stamos to sell us the rest of the land around, which was his, bringing the plot to two stremmattas. This was a rough piece of land, just under an acre, bounded by scrub hedge and which sloped down to a stream. There was just one tall, very old walnut tree which gave some shade, and very soon sported a fine swing. It was not a very productive tree, lacking care and water, but it had a remarkable feature which I have never seen before or since. The walnuts it produced had THREE-part shells, not two halves, as is normal. There was no electricity at all in the village at that time, but there was a well, way above us, so we understood that we could manage to bring down water with little trouble.

Having handed over my tiny house in Northumbria, a not dissimilar bothy, on a hill with no water or electricity, to No 1 son, Antony, this house was to go into No 2 son's name. So it was named 'Spiti Sebastian'. As Sebastian was studying law, we thought he should go along to sign the papers, an experience for him and to assist Stamos with the legalities.

They set off early one morning to the meeting of the vendors. It was to be held at a lawyers' office along the coast, at the foot of the mountains. Stamos had the cash rolled up in his back pocket. I mean real cash, no cheques or anything modern, for this was how all Greek men carried their money.

They arrived home that evening extremely grumpy. Inevitably, the vendors couldn't agree on anything. Arguments raged loud and long. As there were TWENTY of them, it was not surprising. The further three owners had disappeared into the maw of the United States and could not be found. An appointment for the same time, same place, next week had been arranged.

'Can you give me the money for the house Judaki?' said Stamos.
'But I have already given you the money,' I replied surprised.
'Well I have spent it,' said the love of my life.

I could not believe my ears. He had spent it! The money for the house, gone! Furious but speechless, I went to the bank again and drew out the same sum, amazed that I was to have to pay twice. Obviously I still didn't know him.

They went and they returned, once more having suffered the same uproar, with yet again, no one agreeing on anything, let alone signing the sale. Stamos told them that if this happened the next time, the deal was off. Sebastian vowed never ever to practise law in Greece.

I swiftly and firmly removed the cash from Stamos' paw. Twice was enough I thought. I refused to pay for one, ramshackle old mountain house THREE times.

Sebastian had to go home, the Easter holidays over, but we did eventually get the house, signed, sealed and paid for (twice! I still can't believe it). I was however really happy, for not only was there something tangible to show for my windfall, it would be a godsend in the fearsome heat of summer. It was a mere hour and fifteen minutes drive from the farm, a great bonus.

If it had not been called 'Sebastian's House' it surely could have been named 'The House of Contentment', for this is what it came to be to the many who stayed there over the years. The legal documents are a hoot. For together with very poorly written signatures there are thumb prints and crosses. The sums handed to the distant relatives were so paltry, it was embarrassing. But it was done at last, and now we would have to begin work, plenty of it.By now our already small families were reduced further by the loss of Stamos' parents, and then not much later, by the death of my father.

I can never forget one day when we were visiting Stamos' parents who were spending the summer across the bay in Loutraki, we had such a very moving experience. Although his father had met me several times, being very old, his memory was poor.

'Who,' he asked Stamos, indicating me, 'is that?'

'This is my new wife Baba.' replied Stamos.

We then watched transfixed as the old eyes crinkled and tears fell.

'You didn't invite me to your wedding.'

Oh dear oh dear, I almost wept too.

We went for a short package-deal holiday to England, actually the last time I saw my father. Just before leaving, two young people arrived from Australia. Nuffy, (Nauphsika, daughter of Greek Cypriots immigrants) and Peter, on his way to England to see his folks. As Nuffy spoke some Greek this would be a great help to the young workers we were leaving on the farm. I was however, absolutely appalled by how loud and rough the girl was. (But more of Nuffy later.)

To our alarm, on our return our luggage had gone missing, including Stamos' smart new black suit. It arrived on the morning of his father's funeral, thank goodness, so he was able to attend it properly dressed.

It was a lovely day, and the old First Cemetery in Athens was quite beautiful. Filled with magnificent mausoleums and beautiful marble statuary, it is a place of serenity and history. I had attended just one funeral there previously, that of Aunty Pouffie, Emilios' aunt. Her funeral service was so gently conducted by the Anglican priest that Stamos, who had never been to a Protestant funeral before, was fearfully impressed. So much so, he told me, that it was the kind of funeral he would like when his day came.

Stamos' mother, old and frail at the end, at least had the pleasure of getting to know the little Frederikos. A very blonde and charming little boy, they really seemed to like each other, which naturally made us very happy.

We postponed his baptism because of her death. The little restored church was magnificent, snowy-white with deep-blue wooden trim. Fredo was a walking, if not talking, baby of nineteen months when at last we held it.

Having met the shade of Uncle Frederikos on my very first day at the farm, I more than willingly agreed that my last child should have his name. Not that I like the anglicised version, but Frederikos sounds much nicer. It is the custom in Greece to give family names to the children, so at least I was doing something right. If he had been in a peasant family, he would have been called 'beba' by one and all until his baptism. Only during the baptism when the priest calls out his Christian name, is the child properly named, and thereafter called by it.

To my surprise, we had some real unpleasantness when I announced I wished my precious postscript little son to have one English name, James, amongst the three Greek. James with a Latin 'J', as with my name, a letter which does not exist in the Greek alphabet. Frederikos James Stamos. Having chosen the godmothers without consulting me, Stamos now wanted to be entirely in charge of the naming. I stuck to my guns. Which brought about the wrath of God on my head. Whenever crossed, Stamos could really be quite nasty.

'So you are naming MY son after an old lover of yours,' he shouted at me. Not clever, I hate shouting. I did not even bother to assure him that I had never (alas) had a lover called James. Indeed I had in the past never even known one. The only James I knew I had met recently and in Greece. He was a young fellow, son of the then British Ambassador and friend of the children. I won that battle surprisingly, and Frederikos James Stamos walks tall, with all his names, to this day.

Stamos had befriended a very fine old priest called Father Pirunakis. Roughly translated, it means 'little fork,' the AKIS, showing he was a Cretan. He was, so we were told, a rebel, a man after Stamos' heart. A truly good man, one who did what he considered right, he did not hold with being told to do otherwise. We were, Stamos assured me, greatly honoured that he agreed to officiate at the baptism.

Work hotted up with preparations. A great deal of tidying up took place, rotovating the weeds, rolling the land about the church, whitewashing all the trees. Most foreigners are amazed by this, which is the habit in other Mediterranean countries too. The trunks of many fruit trees are whitewashed in order to cut down the bugs, and to protect the bark from the hot sun.

Daring to go into the village church where the priest had said – 'go elsewhere', we measured up their 'pews', Greek churches don't have pews as we know them. They have long rows of strange, tall seats along the sides of the church. You are not supposed to sit during a service, although they can be very many hours long. But you can just lean your seat on the narrow plank of these pews, and they are generally reserved for the elders. We made a row with six seats, one for each of the four brothers of the previous generation and two of the present, Stamos and his sister. I carved all the initials into the rather difficult wood, and was very pleased that he insisted that my initials were to be beside his. The plan was that we would eventually make four more pews, for his four children, to place on the other side, but alas, it never happened.

We went to Athens in search of a font, to a most amazing Aladdin's cave, full, it seemed to the eaves, with church paraphernalia. Apparently when rich patrons bestow gifts on churches, the salesmen take away the old, unwanted items, obviously paying the priest on the side. Much is said about the foreigners who steal from Greek churches, and it might well be true occasionally. Foreigners get blamed for a lot of things. Every forest fire is their fault; yet if the truth were known, it is usually due to a cigarette stub thrown from a car window, or glass in the endless rubbish discarded in ditches along the way. I once actually saw a neighbour of ours leaving his plot and driving along our track, throwing a fag out of his pick-up window. We lost about an eighth of that field of wheat due to his thoughtlessness

Looking around in the Aladdin's cave, it was obvious that the vast majority of treasures in that place were indicative of what really happens. Each corner was piled high with marvellous old things, higgledy-piggledy. Candlesticks of every shape and size from tiny to magnificent. Holy pictures, incense burners, lights, candelabra, you name it, there it lay in an abundant confusion. Any spare space on the floor was littered too, a horrible muddle. We gazed around in awe, for all we wanted was a font, a koulumbythra. The owner and I picked our way through the morass to a heap in a corner where there was a good selection to choose from. I quickly decided on the smallest, a copper one, the oldest and most simple. We did not take it away with us then, for they kept it in order to restore it, which they did beautifully. It looked lovely. Glowing red, with all the dents bashed out of it, our name was printed on and it had gleaming brass carrying handles. When it was delivered to us, the man donated a small, hanging candelabra, indeed he even came to the ceremony, which was nice.

Although restored and pristine, the little church did look rather bare compared with the usual Greek church which is generally overloaded with gewgaws. It was a little difficult being tactful with the several well meaning folk who arrived with hideous offerings. I carefully explained that as it was such an old and simple church, we did not want anything new. I pointed to the newly arrived old koulumbythra proudly. I fear they were not impressed but on the whole, they got the message.

I phoned Father Nick, and asked him to come over to advise me. Standing in the open doorway, obviously appalled by the empty space before him he bellowed, 'You carn't 'av a service 'ere!'

Stamos and the two Petropolous were standing with me, very shocked. For after all our huge works, our efforts were patently not appreciated. Stamos, red with indignation, puffed himself up and roared.

'When you enter my gate, you sweep your feet!' (Which roughly translated means, 'when you visit my farm, you watch your step!')

The Petropolous were really upset now, and crept away. For

despite knowing Stamos very well, they also knew that it just is not done to argue with or shout at a man of God. Not prepared for any more nonsense, I elbowed my tactless husband away.

'Why?' I spoke very clearly, 'why do you suppose I have called you Father Nick? I need advice from you. I need you to tell me what to do, what we need, what I must find. For you know that I am a foreigner and do not know the ways of a Greek Orthodox church.'

Thankfully by then Stamos had disappeared and with Father Nick's feathers smoothed down once more, we went around the empty and diminutive church together and I promised to do what I could.

In the house stood a tall brown clerk's desk. It was useless, served no purpose whatsoever and Stamos agreed that it would do nicely to hold The Books. Apparently it had originated from the days of the distillery. Using the turquoise-blue paint left over from the door and window frames, I painted it; then using some gold paint, added just a hint of gold trim. Then I remembered the handsome wooden basket which we had bought while driving home via southern Italy. A basket meant for carrying the grain when sowing by hand, almost symbolic, it would do perfectly. So that got painted blue as well, and is still used to hold the soft brown candles for the faithful to use. When I had first cleared the ruined church, I had found two broken old iron tripod candle-holders. Tall, spindly and rusty, I had them repaired, cleaned them up, fixed two large round empty fish cans on top and painted them black. Filled with sand, they would do nicely to press the candles safely in.

It was such a busy time, for not only was I having to get the church all dolled up, guests were arriving from far and wide and apart from being a busy wife and mother, I was also the hostess and cook-general.

And then there was the problem of Uncle Frederikos. I had not known about him, having been told by Stamos that the farm had belonged to his grandfather. So there I had been, that very first morning, very tired from a cold and sleepless night, sweeping. And there he had stood, his back to the fireplace, a tall, well-built man, all in black wearing some sort of white cravat. Except of course he was not there, for he had died in Leeds in England in the nineteen thirties. For some reason, I had provoked an echo, shade, ghost, call it what you will, who in English, and with great courtesy, had asked me who I was and what I was doing. I had learned later, when I had asked Stamos if his grandfather had been a tall, well-built man, and he had replied that no, he had been rather short. But his Uncle Frederikos had been a big man, and he had told me that he lived at the farm for years. It was then I first heard the name, Frederikos.

I never saw or spoke with him again, although I thought I did sometimes feel his presence while I worked on the land. Yet the idea came into my head, from where? 'Bring me home.'

On our way back from Iceland we had visited Leeds, found the cemetery and eventually his grave. The merest germ of an idea, a seed, was planted and grew. After a lot of fussification with signing of papers, paying bills and so forth, it was arranged. Not alas returning his bones to his homeland, as would have been correct, because apparently British law does not allow it. So we went through the palava of having him exhumed at dawn before the cemetery opened, cremated and finally, sent to Greece. It was rather an unusual undertaking and needless to say, would never have came about without that wonderful windfall.

Word got around as to what was happening and in a quiet way, without my realising it at the time, my kudos went up further. First it had, by restoring the church, now by bringing home the remains of the greatly respected Frederikos. Stamos was very pleased. He felt it just the right moment too, the return of the elder, and the baptism of the younger. We designed and had made at a marble factory nearby, two simple, very robust, head-stones. One to replace his grandparents' tombstone, which had been vandalised by the gold seekers, and the other for Uncle Frederikos.

A few days before the baptism, a note arrived from the Post Office that there was a parcel to collect. Leaving the girls in charge of child and kitchen I went to town to collect it. What should have been a three minute job turned into hours of hot and frustrating to-ing and fro-ing.

'What is this?' asked the young man at the Post Office looking puzzled.

After examining the parcel I told him that it must be the ashes of my husband's late uncle.

'Take it to the Customs,' he ordered me, handing me a sheaf of papers.

I drove down to the port, parked nearby and went into the Customs House. It was something like a scene from purgatory. Well, as I imagine purgatory is. For it was full of people milling about as I was, all clutching papers. Every little room was full, and through the cigarette smoke you could just see a weary soul at a desk, trying to sort it all out. I noticed with wry amusement that there were notices all around the place saying 'No Smoking'. One office was for cars. Another for imports of trade goods. Another for ships arriving at the harbour and so on. It took me some considerable time to discover which room I was to go to where I gratefully found a chair to sit on and await my turn. At least overlooking the gulf it was cool, for sea breezes filter in and there is always something going on out there to watch.

At last it was my turn. Offering the small parcel, I explained what it was and that the Post Office had directed me there to clear it. The woman examined it and the papers, then gave them back to me. This was out of her field. First I must take it to the Government Health Office to have it cleared before she could.

I drove back into town and located the Government Health Office. After climbing three flights of stairs, because the lift was broken, I finally sat down in an open-plan office full of people. Hot and sticky, I put the parcel on a desk by me and waited. The man before me done at last, I repeated my needs, offering the papers and indicating the parcel.

'But what exactly is in it?' the new official asked, perplexed. For there is no cremation in Greece and when the day of judgment comes, you are supposed to go UP, all in one piece. I began again, airing my few new words, for of course neither had I known much about cremation, ashes and so forth before.

'They are the ashes, the physical remains of my husband's late uncle which we have brought from England, where he died, to re-bury here, in his own home.'

The man frowned, apparently not familiar with any procedure which might enable him to clear this. A small distraction was taking place behind me. The man's troubled gaze strayed from the parcel to the woman sitting behind the desk. I turned and looked at her too. Now I did have some small experience of epilepsy, and thought that the poor woman was having a seizure. Leaning right back in her chair, uttering pitiful cries, her head jerking, her eyes rolling, she was flapping her hands wildly. Poor thing. Anxious, I looked back at the man to see if he was going to do anything about her.

'Oh do take that thing off her desk!' he said in disgust, returning to the papers in his hand.

Looking back at the woman I then realised that indeed she was having a fit, but an emotional one. All because Uncle Frederikos' urn of harmless ashes were sitting on her desk. Incredulous and trying not to laugh, I removed the offending parcel and the squawking stopped. (Grief!)

'This is nothing to do with me or this office,' now pronounced the man. 'Don't you have a doctor friend who will sign the papers for you?'

Bureaucracy! All because, so I had been told by an educated Greek friend, of the hundreds of years of Turkish rule, when no one would ever make a decision for fear of getting it wrong. To avoid trouble, they just passed it on to someone else to take the responsibility. This is what I was dealing with in the late twentieth century. Next, I drove to our doctor, a very good man, this one trained in England and thoroughly practical. Ever busy, he quickly signed it, definitely the most speedy transaction of the day.

Back to the customs at the port, another signature, (with, or did I imagine it, mute congratulations.) And finally, back at last to the Post Office for the final paper, and, bliss, but hours after I had left it, back to the farm.

Quietly, strangely moved by the experience, we set the little urn on the altar, hoping that Uncle Frederikos was at last happy to be home.

That evening without fuss or ceremony, Stamos gathered the human bones which we had found about the farm and stored in the church and buried them together, with his uncle's remains, in front of the little church.

It was a good feeling. Something which by modern standards was a complete and utter, sentimental waste of time and money, it had been done. We were then, and I am still, rightly proud of our actions. As he had never married or had a family, we were doing the duty of his children, now even to the naming of a son after him. He had been a fine man, greatly respected, and he deserved it.

Chapter 5

The First Service at our Church

Frederikos' baptism was the first of many feasts we held in and centred around the little church. This was a practice run as it were and I for one had lots to learn. For a start, we never knew how many people would come; it really was Open House. (The highways and the hedges.) All Stamos' relations and friends came from Athens. All the smart cars rolled up full of cousins, second and third cousins. Childhood friends came with their spouses, children and friends. For it came to be a regular grand day out in the country and was a way at last, for Stamos to repay hospitality. So too did the neighbourhood come to our celebrations, in beat-up assorted agricultural vans and pick-ups, making a regular mixed bag of high and low folk, including my Rom koumbaras.

I was advised that the problem of catering equipment was easily solved by hiring everything from town. A singularly unattractive woman rented out all one might need quite reasonably. I discovered later to my cost, how she made her extra bit. The list of 'missing' items she presented to me afterwards was ridiculous. Sour faced, she stood her ground, (silly woman) until I paid up vowing never to return to her and I never have. Instead, over the years I collected a mass of utility crockery and cutlery, only resorting to disposable plastic mugs instead of glasses.

Despite that sourpuss, many good things happened which warmed my heart. Maria's boyfriend's parents generously volunteered to make the Christening cake. Starting with shelling the home-grown almonds, it was not only a valiant effort, the cake was delicious. As the lady cook who made it was English, she knew exactly what to do and it was a wonderfully rich fruit cake, not known in Greece.

We had, on our way home from Iceland, bought a small marquee in which to sleep our extra workers at harvest times. Having enquired for such a tent here and there without success at last a jolly man approached us. He told us, having been a clown in the past, he had a small marquee which he no longer needed.

So we followed him to a row of garages where first, still smiling, he had to unpick the chewing gum which kids had shoved into the lock. Fortunately it all went on the roof of the Landrover. Poles, ropes, canvas, the lot and was thereafter of great use. For the baptism, it looked very grand set it up just in front of the house.

Anne, an old girlfriend of mine came out from England, one of the two who Stamos had invited to be godmother. It had been she who had been such a help when I had been rushed early into hospital. Stamos had gone home for business, promising that he would be back in time for the birth. It was she who organised the loudspeaker summons to the taxi sent to meet him at Luton. As royalty, it brought him straight to the Royal Free. Mind you, for the amount of help he was during the days I was in labour, he might as well have stayed in Greece.

Having had my first son twenty two years previously, also in the Royal Free, I had learned that rowdy mums are never popular, so ever after I kept my mouth firmly shut. Years later, while in the delivery wing and fearfully worried that I might lose this precious child, the noise had been so dreadful, as a scene from hell, I was really

281

distressed. One woman was screaming, another was sobbing, and a pretty young woman was swearing like a trooper at the top of her voice. I became aware of what a protected life I had led, as half of her tirade was of such an incredibly rich vocabulary, it was completely new to me.

Then, and can I ever forget it, in came a young doctor.

'What the devil's going on Dolores?'

What a splendid phrase. Miserable though I was, it actually made me laugh.

So Stamos arrived, fully expecting everything to be over, and here he was, the poor soul, having to sit about and wait beside a sorry and intact wife.

'Hold on as long as you can,' said the excellent Dolores, the tiny black, head midwife, 'every hour counts, he is better in there than out here.'

Stamos grew ever more despondent.

'I have never been so bored in my life,' said he, to my disbelief.

'And you think that I am enjoying myself?' I asked incensed, remembering my previous three births and my sympathetic and diligent back-rubbing ex-husband.

'Go, oh go away,' said I. 'Go to the father's room and watch the TV.'

Which he very happily did, later to give me a glowing account of how comfortable and civilised it all was. There were reclining chairs where the feet went up, there was an excellent TV, colour no less, and, a machine where he could get hot drinks. So as not to allow them completely off the hook, there was also a phone, so when births were imminent, the fathers could be summoned from their creature comforts.

In time, he would be entirely forgiven his insensitivity during my travail as his caring attentions to his new son became evident.

'You see to the top half,' he would say, 'while I deal with the bottom.' Which he did with his usual diligence. During these unsavoury operations he was often heard to call the little angel,

'Skatoulaki.' Which means 'Little Shit.' As with many innocent beginnings, it stuck, for the Little Shit, now being a hefty lout and a Big Shit, is still called, Skatoulaki.

Anne took Fredo to the beach every day so that we could get on with the work involved for such a big party. The day before the baptism he fell over, getting a good cut between the eyes. Nonetheless with his blonde hair fetchingly fluffed out, he looked angelic. He did not wear my old baptismal robe which was far too small, but just a delicious, frothy white day robe of my father's. And boy, didn't he know he was the star? He smiled so graciously all the time at everyone, loving the attention.

By now he had learned to cope with the noisy enthusiasm which his smiles brought forth from admiring peasant friends. It had been embarrassing when he was tiny, when all too often, shocked by the racket, his smiles had turned to tears.

'He smiles, he smiles!' they would yell into his face, frequently loudly clapping their hands with delight. I learned that Greek babies are careful with their smiles for, apparently, just that reason. Smiles bring forth such pleasure that poor little terrified scraps shake, stop smiling, take breath and then roar in fright. So smiles are reserved for familiars, it is better not to smile at strangers. Poor dear Mitsos Petropolous who so loved little things, was mortified when his noisy appreciation of the smiling Fredo ended in tears.

The day of the baptism was however, quite different. A glorious day, our many guests were delighted with everything, including the sunny baby who smiled at all of them. That is until he was put through the indignity of being stripped, dunked, oiled, the lot. Then, in his smart new grown-up clothes, he rested in his godmother's arms sucking his thumb and whinged.

Our church being so very small, Father Pirunakis happily ordered the koulumbythra to be brought outside. The area directly west of the church is like a miniature theatre, with the land as a half moon rising to the spitaki behind the tombs. As there were very many people at the ceremony, some of them stood on the higher level to get a good view. I remember Father Pirunakis pausing in his prayers, to demand furiously that a group of young men standing on top put out their cigarettes.

'This is a church!' he shouted at them. 'And this is a holy service before God.' They quickly put out their cigarettes and I was very impressed.

We then had a buffet feast which was laid out in the big tent. A totally un-Greek meal that first time; a cold collation which in fact being very different from the norm, caused much interest with the locals. This was followed by champagne and the excellent Christening cake accompanied by toasts to the boy.

That was one occasion, so different from far too many others, when I only remember happiness and total family harmony and cooperation. No harsh words were spoken, no black moods were directed at me. It was a truly happy day.

Apart from the inevitable stack of boxes of sticky cakes presented to us, Fredo was given some nice presents. Just one I remember well, because it showed such imagination and understanding for the needs of a little boy. It was a huge, red, wind-up tin car, brought by the children of a local hardware store where we always shopped. It was really so clever of them for he loved it, the top favourite.

One major mistake I made that day was to hand out blankets to everyone who asked for them. It is a firm habit in Greece to have a siesta after lunch every day and being in the country was to be no exception. Our guests happily lugged their blankets off into the orchards to lie down to sleep under the trees. As it was early autumn, every weed was topped by its seed head and now, rotovated in for the occasion, the earth was full of them. There are several weeds which when young, have their uses, if not for the animals, then for horta. But the seeds, oh dear. Beastly little hard balls covered in hooks of various shapes and sizes, they seem to survive for ages. It took me for ever and ever to de-weed all those blankets.

Now our church was restored and quite beautiful, our neighbours began asking if they too could hold services there. This pleased me enormously, and the evening before I'd drop everything, rush over and give it a good sweep and bang the lovely Romanian rugs. Which was just as well, for some of our visitors took their religion very seriously, half the time lying prostrate on the floor.

Amongst our guests at the baptism were many of our young foreign workers including Kiwi Dave, one of the fournos builders. He was the self-appointed official photographer, hence we have a splendid record of a great day. They were an excellent gang, who as family, helped us with the festivities.

After the celebrations were over, we three went for a week's holiday to Crete. During the glorious days of spending my windfall, Stamos had bought two mini vans. A white one for us, and a yellow one for a son. One memory I have of that holiday was driving down a mountain in the pouring rain. Having become used to the robust Landrover, the little van must have suffered. We finally reached the edge of a village and were hailed by a cheery crowd sheltering in an open shed. Smoke and steam were belching forth. People were arriving every few minutes with great dripping baskets of grape pressings. For it was the vine harvest, and everyone was busy with it. Mud, cow dung and water were being mixed by hand into a dough. A great copper vessel had its lid taken off, the pot underneath was filled with the sludge and the top was cemented back into place using the dough. Amazing. The fire underneath was stoked up, more smoke and steam billowed about, and I, oh joy, had learned something new. Another first for me, it was a great and traditional STILL, for they were making raki. Stamos answered all their inevitable and many questions before we were waved off with, of course, a bottle. My thanks to them were photos, several batches of copics, which I oont later.

Back home again, another girlfriend came from abroad to stay with me. Stamos was absolutely charmed by her but then she was charming. Miri had been my best friend at school in England, something which irritated my parents, for she was a foreigner, from the Middle East.

'We make such sacrifices to send you to a good school and instead of having a nice English friend, you pal up with that foreigner.' (I am ashamed to remember it.)

Children do not normally note races or creeds and I certainly did not. She was my friend and I loved her and was loyal to her till her tragic and early death. Stamos drove her to Delphi, then I took her to Olympia. We wanted her to have a really happy time. For Miri was dying and when we talked, as good friends do, she told me that she thought that her illness stemmed from misery. She told me of how, when her children were young, her diplomat husband had taken an older and sophisticated mistress with whom she just could not compete. I grieved with very mixed emotions. We went to an island, taking the little Fredo with us and delighted in going across to Turkey by caique. I remember our laughter while getting wet from the spray, sitting cross legged, side by side, backs to the mast, the baby asleep sheltered under my dress in my lap.

It was a happy little holiday, despite my anger at her. For Miri listened to no one and, refusing surgery, spent all her time and money going to quacks the world over. We talked endlessly and discussed relationships between parents and children. I had briefly known her father, a splendid man, but I never met her mother who I gather was not a warm-hearted woman. It was distressing to hear Miri talk about how, now she was dying, it was wonderful to get so much love and attention at last.

When she wanted to have her hair washed and set, knowing a girl in the village who was a hairdresser, we went there. I was amazed, having supposed that she was a professional in a small way, at least according to village life. Astonished at how primitive it all was, I watched Miri, highly amused too, leaning over the balcony, having her hair washed with a jug.

Our holiday ended too soon, but at least I had the pleasure of having one of her young sons to stay with us a couple of times. Handsome and charming, he was so like his mother in every way, it was a small compensation.

The farm was working well, we might even be solvent in a few years. Land, which had been so desperately neglected for so long, needed huge works done on it to make it prosper once more. With the injection of cash, it ran smoothly with decent machinery and proudly-growing little apricot trees. Great quantities of new irrigation equipment were bought and had to be learned about. Clearing up corner by scruffy corner we progressed, our young workers valiantly, slowly but surely undoing the neglect of ages. Although I did not really understand why, Stamos did not wish to employ Greeks and no Greeks seemed to want to work for him. Perhaps they were too expensive to employ? Or having to pay their agricultural insurance was too high? Other farms, merely had family working. He suspected a Greek looking for work. When we had no help, he inevitably sent me out to find some. Whatever the case, Stamos really liked the young foreigners. We either had none, or too many. Later, if this was the case, I would pack them off to the mountain house which kept everyone happy. They were always free to come or go. Only very occasionally did we ask any to leave, and that was because they were no good, unpleasant, dishonest, and so forth.

Having learnt how to prune the very hard citrus, I now taught some of the Dutch girls how to prune the grossly overgrown mandarin trees at the side of the house. Once pruned to half their original size, they were whitewashed and looked wonderfully neat. We now hoped for big mandarins for, although full of pips, they were really tasty and Greeks love mandarins. Having been so neglected, the fruit had been very small and unsaleable but even their time would come again quite soon.

With winter, came calls from an Athenian travel agent asking if we could receive some groups of French farmers. With the advent of the Common Market, this became quite a regular occurrence. They began as friendly affairs and were fun, a break in our day. Stamos tremendously enjoyed speaking with our guests and playing the country gentleman. While he discussed world farming matters, I served up coffee and home-made biscuits or wine and snacks.

With his being the honorary French Consul, we found ourselves providing free hospitality to hundreds of strangers. With my being the honorary representative of the Animal Welfare, I in turn found my chemist and food bills were getting out of hand. We began finding the honorary part of our lives, quite heavy.

When the call came to expect a bus load of BELGIAN farmers, I objected.

'Why?' I demanded, 'do we now have to entertain Belgians too?'

I recall the surprised Stamos quickly getting the message and phoning the travel agent. Poor thing on the other end. I nonetheless was delighted on hearing my normally head-in-the-clouds-husband, wholly supporting me. A very modest sum of money was suggested and happily accepted. From then onwards we were never out of pocket and I have to say that the Belgian group was absolutely delightful.

Occasionally the French cooperatives arrived with wives and children, which was nice for me. Then we might put on a meal and they stayed for a couple of hours and we even made some money on it. It showed, in this case anyway, that as you sow so do you reap. A good thing came out of all that entertaining.

One day there was a call from a stranger. It is important to note that it was mid-day on a Thursday. Shopping hours in Greece are to us, Northern Europeans, unusual. Due to the heat, some shops are open in the afternoons after six, some not. Now and again all the laws concerning opening and closing hours are changed, inevitably just when I had at last, grown accustomed to them. Eventually I made it a habit to do all my shopping, first thing in the morning. Then everything is open, it is cool, and it may even be possible to get a parking place without a struggle.

'My name is Per,' said the strange young voice, then named a Scandinavian agency for whom he worked. 'When I was at a meeting of tourist guides in Athens just now, I heard that you sometimes take foreign groups for lunch.' Cautiously I assented. 'Can you,' he went on (and hark to this), 'have fifty Danish farmers for lunch tomorrow?'

Gob-smacked, as we say in the North of England, I looked at my watch. Noon! The shops closed in one hour. Not possible, really it was not. I told him so.

'Please, oh please,' the anguished cry came over the line, 'what will I do with them. Please say that you will have them?'

Now I am a capable woman and I am a good cook and, yes, I enjoy a challenge. But this, it really was impossible. I ran through the difficulties with him. Chairs and tables, crockery and cutlery, wine, quite before even starting on the food. Silence.

Suddenly and extremely unusually for me, for I am totally unworldly, I asked him, 'What will you pay me?' Silly question, for they always ask, how much do you want. He did. I thought rapidly. Generally we were underpaid. Well someone had to make a profit along the way so we were usually cut pretty fine. Steeling myself, and with great courage I came out with, 'One thousand dracs a head.'

I swear that I heard the sound of hands being thrown up in the air. 'So much!' he gasped.

I thought rapidly. They were Danes, and damn it, much richer than we poor Greeks. One thousand dracs was peanuts to Danes. I worked myself up in indignation. One thousand dracs, for a three course meal in a beautiful place with wine included, as much as they wanted? Suddenly hard and careless I heard myself boldly saying,

'Take it or leave it.'

'I'll take it, I'll take it,' squeaked the relieved Per. It was arranged. In twenty four hours we would receive a bus load of Danish farmers and families. It was the beginning, had I known it, of a long and excellent partnership with lovely people.

It was also a frantic scramble, and I actually had to borrow the money from our young people for my purchases. I rushed to town, shopped furiously and a little extravagantly in my haste and began preparations in the hideous heat of the afternoon, instead of taking my siesta.

As always, the young people ran to it, erecting tables from all sorts of old doors and electric cable drums with white sheets acting as table cloths. The seats would be straw bales duly covered with rugs. We'd manage. First thing next morning, some of the young drove to buy the wine from Nemea, (where Hercules slew the lion.)

It was a most successful lunch. A beautiful day, and everyone was all smiles. Next morning there was a call from Per.

'I want to thank you for giving our guests such a lovely time and excellent meal,' he said, his voice warm and trouble-free. 'I will never, ever argue with you about money again, for it is the very first time we have not had one single complaint. Will you please, (here it comes) have a group for lunch once a week?'

Marvellous! A steady, regular if small income for five months in the year. Wow! They would never know just how much their presence helped us to survive in the coming years. I made it my habit to really strive to give them exciting, Greek food and they loved it all, not forgetting the excellent wine.

We always bought the red, known as 'brusco', in sixty-litre barrels, a most excellent full-bodied wine. If ever Dr Clement heard we were going to Nemea, he always asked us to get him a couple of cases of the same wine but in ¾ litre bottles. Those twelve, pretty green bottles with their fancy labels, cost him more than we paid for our sixty litre barrel of the same stuff. Draught wine, straight out of the barrel is called Xyma (or Heema.) It had a little tap on, so was easy to decant into jugs and was a great compensation in our hard-working lives. We had wine with lunch and supper, and it was surprising how most of our young people learnt to drink for enjoyment, rarely drinking to excess.

We often made the visit to the wine growing area of Nemea, as an outing. For ours was a family farm, not a factory farm. It was about an hour's run, so we often took a picnic and made an excursion out of it. Occasionally, if we were few, we ate at the one taverna in the middle of Nemea. Here an excellent old girl, Kyria Athena I think she was called, cooked memorable and inexpensive meals. Nothing fancy, always varied, they were just for the locals, for tourists were very thin on the ground in that backwater. Mine host, a shadowy figure who drifted about doing little, was a canary fancier. I once brought him a canary all the way from England in the back of the Landrover. He was very pleased.

Generally however, we went up to the tiny monastery perched on the cliffs high above the town. A collection of fine old buildings, there had been an old hospital there during the Turkish rebellion. The tiny church is another holy and ancient place, simply for its pool of water which filters down from the rock plateau above. We would find some shade and have our picnic admiring the wondrous views, then rest or explore, glad of a change of scenery.Once we had a most unpleasant experience there. A woman far below, presumably picking horta, so it must have been spring, began shouting at us. We could not hear or understand what she was saying so eventually ignored her. Then a police car swept up, telling us that they had received a call that there were foreigners stealing from the church. Fortunately Stamos was with us that time, so the matter was quickly resolved even if painful. As the caller had refused to give her name, the two bobbies consoled us that she must be soft in the head. Nonetheless, it cast a shadow on our day.

When we went to collect the wine in the early days, the factory was a very primitive place, it was a wonder that their wine was so very excellent. A few women toiled in a huge open barn, keeping warm in winter by burning old pallets in a barrel. They came to know us well and we always got a kindly welcome. At whatever harvest time we went, we made sure to take them boxes of oranges or apricots. The arrival of our baby boy caused great excitement. With cries of delight he was handed from one to the other. They like so many others, just laugh when they see what the little mite turned into. In the summer, never wearing shoes, they discovered his web toes. We were amused to see them when he was born, and horrified when a family elder had said they must be cut. Never! Such dear little feet. If it had been his fingers, it would have been quite another matter.

Inevitably with such a small and friendly place, the ever-smiling man at the gate heard about THE TOES. The very next time we went to collect wine, he drew us to one side to examine the baby's feet. Grinning broadly, sitting on the stone pavement, off came his ancient work shoes and grubby socks, and there, lo, another set of web feet were happily displayed. A brother!

Although the spanking new wine factory at Nemea is nothing like the draughty great barn of old, thank goodness the wine is, as always, excellent.

Chapter 6

New Experiences

Early in 1982, at about 11 p.m., we had gone to bed but were not yet sleeping. In the summer the scratching of a mosquito bite might lightly joggle the bed. But there were no mosquitoes in winter. The joggling grew, and grew, and with a start I realised that the bed was shaking, indeed the whole house was shaking too, and hard. One of Stamos' sons thrust open our door shouting, 'Out, out!'

'Go', he said, 'I'll get the baby.'

I saw Stamos lean over the cot, which was on his side, so I ran out, across the big landing which, always a bit like a trampoline, now bucked and bounced. Dragging the back the heavy woollen curtain at the top of the stairs I too began calling, 'Out, out.' Young people emerged from the bedrooms in various states of undress, staggered across the unsteady landing, and down the stairs. There was no sign of Stamos so I called him urgently. He appeared in what felt like hours, stark naked, for that is how he slept, the baby well wrapped in a blanket, almost making him decent and we struggled down the stairs together

When I asked him later what had caused him to take so long he replied,

'I wanted to wake the baby gently.' (Marvellous! Dear man.)

It was mere seconds, that frightening earthquake, yet it seemed to stretch for ever. We congregated in the kitchen where the light still swung, for Stamos, having built it himself, knew it was the safest place in the house. Eyes wide we gazed at each other in shock. Then we giggled nervously. The sounds of the world filtered in, a cacophony of alarm. Every living creature was crying out in terror.

I truly thought that the roof had caved in and the Loutraki mountain had slipped into the sea, the noise had been so horrendous. Later, when I saw that not only was the roof intact, the mountain was still there, I was really surprised. Over the next weeks with the continuing quakes, I eventually realised what was happening. Every single stone, tile or branch was rubbing together. Millions upon trillions of surfaces scratching each other brought forth a sound, a roar, as the end of the world.

We realised that it had been a big one, but as we had no radio, didn't know how to find out? With great daring we went back into the old part of the house and turned on the TV. For a while it was blank, then a courageous newscaster appeared. Sure enough there had been a major earthquake in our area.

Little New Zealander, Sue, known as Munchkin, arrived from the Well House. Despite being half underground, she too had felt it. All day she had been patiently helping me prune the apricot trees and I had been in the deepest pit of depression, unable almost to speak.

'Please believe me, Sue,' I remembered saying to her, 'I am not in a bad mood. Neither am I cross with you in any way. It's just that I feel so very depressed, a great weight on my soul.' (Maybe ha ha there is going to be an earthquake.)

The lights went off and on and off, and thankfully on again. The phone, miraculously still working, began to ring. Many friends from Athens, on hearing the news, were checking if we were all right. Local friends began to arrive, terrified in their jerry-built apartment blocks, feeling safer in the country. We knew there would be more. Sleep for the night was over.

Exhausted with nerves and lack of sleep, we took stock the following day. Amazingly we had come off unscathed. The old house, the upstairs lath and plaster, the downstairs stone, had just shivered and settled again. The cistern, thankfully full, was fine. All our neighbours were safe; we had all merely had a fearful shock. I utterly failed when trying to phone my mother to say we were safe as all the lines were jammed. So later that the morning I went to town and sent a cable to my sister in London saying that all was well.

Calls came from all over the world. 'Are you all right?' Europe, Australia, America. Friends, relations and countless old kids warmed our hearts by their concern.

Reports came of fearful injuries suffered by terrified people leaping over balconies, mainly broken legs and pelvises. The army camp down the road, which I would consider a well-built complex, had its quota. People were panicked stuck in lifts, caused by the electricity going off and on and off again.

So few were killed, being in early spring, it truly was a miracle. We drove across the bay to check on my sister-in-law's house. We were shocked on our way to pass what had been a big hotel which was now totally destroyed and looked like a club sandwich. All the floors had collapsed, one on top of the other. Between the layers of crumbly concrete were pressed and hanging out beds, mattresses and carpets as sliced meat and lettuce. It was shocking. Had that earthquake happened a month or two later, when the hotel was filled with tourists, there would have been appalling loss of life. A great scandal. Despite strict building regulations, there was more sand than anything else in that construction. Even the iron used was flimsy. No doubt it had been built on the cheap and more than likely palms had been greased in order to waive the necessary inspections. As there hadn't been a big earthquake for some time, complacency was the norm. Well, we were lucky that time, it doesn't bear thinking of what might have happened just a little later.

Stamos' sister's summer house appeared fine. Another well-built old house, it was presumably the same age as ours as the staircase is identical. Some of the thick panes in the newer porch were cracked, and so in case any possible thief might consider going in, we bought glue and stuck strips of paper over them, just to show that the house was not deserted. Being a busy and tidy soul, those empty little tubes of glue went into my bag, where they hung about for ages. Eventually I thought that if I had an accident and anyone looked in it, they would think that I was a glue sniffer. So it got cleared out.

The quakes went on, just one other big one, which brought down more poorly built and already shaken buildings and many small tremors. Anyone living in an apartment block simply vacated it. Even in Athens, miles from the epicentre, the squares, parks and even the roundabouts in the middle of the city soon blossomed with tents. Anybody who had folk in the country, descended on them. There was great camaraderie; as in war time everybody helped each other where they could.

The TV stations sent out teams to speak with the refugees in their tents. Obviously one old lady so amused them that they popped in her delightful interview between other programmes several times each day.

'Where do you come from grandmother?' the interviewer asked. She mentioned her home village.

'Have you ever experienced such an earthquake before?' (Now for the jewel.)

'Oh no!' she replied, highly indignant, 'we don't have this sort of thing in our village.' It didn't matter how often they showed it, we laughed every time.

A village high on the other side of the bay had been badly damaged. We took them sacks of oranges, from pure neighbourliness, well before the government was offering to pay for such supplies. To our horror, they complained, saying that the oranges were rubbish. Well I know that there are miserable hearted people the world over. Nonetheless, we were surprised and hurt by their lack of appreciation of our spontaneous gesture.

An empty area between us and the town soon blossomed with tents sent, I believe, by the Red Cross. A stand-pipe was erected and a row of loos built. Soon every tent flourished a puffing stove-pipe and it became a really friendly little village. When Easter came, not long afterwards, we watched them celebrate in true village style and probably better than when they lived in the town.

Teams of government architects toured the whole affected area. When they reached us, they viewed Stamos' various scaffold supports with amusement. Armed with paint and brushes, each building received their official verdict prominently painted on the front in big letters.

A = Perfect.

AE = Needing attention.

EE = To be demolished.

Ours, being an old house, received EE! In fact it was probably more stable than most. It still stands and with many new supports, will probably do so for years to come.

Eventually grants were made for re-building. I know we did get one, but do not know what Stamos did with it.

Stamos and I slept in the church with the baby for a couple of months. We lived in the house by day, but as evening fell I remember walking across carrying Frederikos and answering to the little Athenian owls.

'Toot,' they said, and 'toot,' I answered. Fredo thought it was a good game.

I was speaking to my mother on the phone one day when I felt a tremor coming. I just managed, 'I'll ring you back,' and fled before it hit. After it had passed, when I called her back, my mother told me how when they lived in Pakistan, they always used to have one of those pretty, bead decorated nets covering their bedside glass of water.

'The beads tinkling on the glass warned us,' she told me. Very clever.

Every tiny farm sprouted a Rom-type shack in order to house the townspeople who were too afraid to move back into their flats. All summer it seemed as if the countryside around us was busy and happy with refugees. Later, as repairs were done to their homes and the tremors ceased, they filtered back to town and all became quiet again.

Unfortunately, all the water pipes were suspect, so instead of sludge gulpers blocking the roads, a fresh water tanker took their place as it did its rounds. Every home left its cans on the doorstep to be filled with drinking and cooking water.

We could actually see the snow capped peaks of the mountains to the west, and wondered how that area had fared. With thick snow lying on the heavy ceramic roofs, there was a strong chance that many of the old houses had collapsed. As spring advanced and cars could get up there, we heard from Kostas that his old family house had fallen down. Ours, thank heaven, had not.

Brian had been home for the winter, and returned with a ready-made family. A wife, son and daughter. It was lovely for Fredo to have two resident children for company for although older than he, they were very kind.

To my great surprise, Stamos announced one day that we were to be married in our church by a Greek Orthodox priest. He did not ask me; I was told. As we had already had a civil marriage in Iceland, there seemed no need and certainly, I felt content and secure. But he insisted, saying, which was true, that civil marriage was not at that time, legal in Greece.

There had been between him and his children, much discussion about a divorce from Eleni their mother, all centred on money of course. I kept firmly out of it knowing it to be all nonsense and having given him my promise of silence. For as perhaps only he and

I knew, theirs had not been a legal union, Stamos had told me that Eleni had previously been married to and divorced from a Greek. Then, in the war, she married again, and obviously very quietly, for it was understandably deeply frowned upon. Her second husband, a German officer, he told me, had been the great love of her life. It could be, while travelling with the retreating forces that he had been killed on his way home to Germany. Or perhaps he had returned to a previous and legal wife there. Who knows?

For us to go through another marriage, appeared more fuss than sense to me, yet he seemed irrationally determined that we should do so. In a way, I am grateful to him for that, for although it has been of absolutely no use what-so-ever to me as it turned out, it was good knowing how much he cared and wished for it.

A small ceremony was arranged. The congregation were few so it could be held inside the little church. I asked if we might borrow the wedding rings of Stamos' deceased parents, just for the ceremony. We needed all the luck we could find. Unfortunately, it being term time, my boys could not be there. There were the young people on the farm and the Petropoulos, some French visitors and only two members of Stamos' family.

Halfway through the service, with a great deal of noise, the younger family member dramatically stomped out in a monstrous show of displeasure. Shocked, it took some moments before we all collected ourselves together so that the service could continue. If I was offended, then what of poor Stamos? Once again, he was devastated and later in the privacy of our room, holding his head in his hands he mourned the dreadful behaviour of his child.

It is all too easy to think that it was really his own fault and that he should have been tougher with all his children and taught them how to behave. The truth was that he was afraid of them. That was his greatest tragedy. Hating rows with them, he eventually gave in every time, but naturally he tried to avoid disagreements with them in the first place.

It had been that same child, then in mid twenties, who when we were in the little rented house in Temple Fortune had bunked on us. Free board and lodging. I also did a packed lunch every day, as my sister had organised a job. We were miserable with the black moods and rudeness. There was no sign of gratitude. Not even a little toy for the baby, a bottle of wine for Stamos, or flowers for me or chocolates for my sister. It should have been the happiest time for us, safe with our new child and we had worked so hard to save up for it. Sadly it was anything but, while our uninvited and unwanted guest stayed and made us miserable. As I was breast feeding, it could have been my distress which resulted in a very colicky baby. He shrieked interminably, pushing out his tummy button, the first of my babies to have an umbilical hernia.

'All that baby needs is love,' I was told by that stupid boy.

Shocked by this gross impertinence, I was amazed to hear this from one who only seemed to know how to hate. If I had been the bitch I was alleged to be, I would have opened the door and said 'Go!' But I was not. That was not my job, it was Stamos's. I felt we did our very best by providing food and warm accommodation, for it was bitterly cold that winter. Why were we being subjected to this dreadful tyranny? Stamos should have said something, if only to protect me. It was he who should have opened the door, but he could not. His life seemed so filled with guilt over past mistakes, he had no moral strength to cope with it.

It had been distressing then and was again at our Greek marriage. It would be, had I known it and tragically for all of us, a situation which stretched for evermore. Parents can fail their children in so many different ways. Poor Stamos, if only he knew the extent of that failure.

However we were now twice married. Whether or not it was for my money, as the chief trouble-maker informed me, it at least made Stamos happy.

Plans now got under way to restore the old house in the mountains. After several sorties to measure up, the boys made their drawings and their lists and we set about organising it. It was too cold for them to live up there yet, but we tried to collect the materials together. The roof had to come off, for although it was roughly lined with old boards, we could not only see daylight, but rain and snow would certainly come in. We needed roofing felt, and this brought me to another interesting experience.

One of the best things about Greece was the relaxed way business was done. Instead of going to a builder's yard and ordering whatever you wanted, then having to wait for ever and pay a beefed up price, you went straight to the producer. So I drove to a factory by the sea not far out of Athens, which made roofing felt. I asked for our order and I left with it, just 'off the press', still HOT.

I remember that Sebastian was there and that he found that his poor old van simply could not take that load up the mountain. It was too heavy. So out came half of the black, smelly load, to be left on the roadside. Up that particularly steep bit he went then back again. Until he got it all safely there.

A new tradition was forming, this time for me as I have a birthday in April. My birthday was to be a day off. No cooking, no work, they would do it all.

Son Antony was always begging me to get a pig. Pigs, he said, were very interesting. So we had one in my early days on the farm, by name of Papaligura. He was indeed an interesting if confused soul. For he really believed that he was a dog. He ran with the pack all day, and when evening came, squealed with huge indignation not to be allowed indoors, their special treat. He watched his mates through the glass, blissfully loafing in front of the fire but he, who was not house trained, was not permitted entry. How he fussed outside the French doors until, fed up, I'd let him in. When, inevitably once or twice he had an accident, I landed him a good one on the rump and hustled him outside again. It reminded me of Maggie, a past beloved Bull Terrier; when I thumped her, I got the worst of it. For she, like a pig, was very solid. Slowly, Papaligura learned to behave. After dropping a plop on the stone floor, he would squeal and run to the doors, knowing he had done wrong.

Alas, Papaligura didn't last for long for he was stolen, probably again by Xrysoula's eldest son. So with my birthday looming I distinctly remember saying that I would be happy with anything, so long as it was not on legs.

The day before, magical spring with sunshine and flowers, I became aware of the most terrible screaming from the field behind the house. Only on one occasion during my many years on the farm, dealing with so many and varied young people, was there even a hint of a fight. (Which I had soon put an end to.) Alarmed, I raced down the track to rescue whoever was being killed. It looked like a huge rugby scrum, heaps of young people in a stack. The noise was terrible. When at last seeing me they sorted themselves out, all laughing cheerfully, there was still a great noise at the bottom of the pile. A small pig was unearthed, screaming blue murder.

I was very annoyed. I had particularly said, 'No more animals!' There wasn't space in my life or money in my pocket to feed one more mouth. How could they? But Antony had been right, pigs are very special. I named her Lily. She was such a wonderful soul, a friend, indeed one of our extended family. Like many of our animals, she wasn't quite sure what she was, dog or human. She loved us and fitted in with our lives, giving us endless joy, and piglets, until her tragic end years later.

She had apparently been donated by the huge pig farm at the end of our land. The gentle, top man in charge of the animals spoke some English, so no doubt was badgered for her by the kids. She was what you would call an English Saddleback, pink hide with black face and black girdle. We knew next to nothing about pigs, except that they were remarkably intelligent and that they eat anything. When he advised us that she was old enough to go to the boar, off we went with her somewhat bewildered, in the trailer. That first time I do remember a flower wreath was made for her, the bride, but she ate it. Her visits to the pig farm to be mated were great fun and she came to know where she was going. She usually stayed for a couple of weeks, but her relief at coming home was very obvious. Once, ever busy, I must have left her too long, for when she came home we found her feet were in a terrible mess. She could barely walk and was in much in pain. No doubt the pen she shared with numerous other pig ladies was water/muck-logged. Anyway, we were grateful for the pig farm's generosity in taking her, as it turned out, with amazing success.

With the birth of her first litter, Lily caused an occasion to become a Super Occasion. A call came from Athens. Would we give lunch to a group of British? Most unusual and hurray. They were the European Members of Parliament from Brussels visiting Greece with their families. Having never had a British group before, I was delighted.

Early that morning I had been to see Lily who, being a close friend, I was very familiar with. Having absolutely no knowledge of birthing piglets, I nonetheless noted she was not at all comfortable. We were delighted with our guests, and were as usual, very busy hosts. Half way through lunch I asked one of our youngsters to go up to see if she was all right. She was indeed, birthing naturally as an old hand. The meal became ever more rowdy, as runners came with wings on their heels bringing the latest news. Glasses raised, full of the excellent brusko, everyone sang out,

'Seven – eight – nine!' and so on till we reached thirteen. Possibly a record in Greece, and if not, they must certainly have been the most drunk-to piglets in Greece.

When the meal was barely finished, as one, we picked up our mugs and the decanters and departed to the pig sty. Well fed, and well drunk, we all cheerfully hung over the wall admiring the clever girl and her adorable pink piglets.

I understood later that Sebastian, who by then was a fully fledged lawyer and working for the European Union in Brussels, ate and drank out magnificently on the story. Happy day.

303

Chapter 7

The Mountains

Where to begin with describing the glorious Greek mountains? I suppose they are not so very different from mountains the world over, yet I think they are very special.

Each village in our range had its own character. Some must have been mainly Arveniti, descendants of the original immigrants who came from Albania in the 16th century. These were Christians who would not convert, so they were driven out by the Muslim pasha and travelled to Greece where apparently things were more relaxed. Some villages were mainly Sarakatzani, a nomadic tribe which still exists from Rumania to Crete. 'Our' village, where we had Spiti Sebastian, was one of these. I find it is easy to recognise that race, for their complexion is generally fairer than that of normal Greeks. They often have fair or brown hair, light brown or blue eyes and a high colour. I once met such a man in our town. He had rosy cheeks and dark brown hair and I thought that I recognised him as being Sarakatzani.

'Are you Sarakatzani?' I asked.

'No,' he replied, 'but my parents were.'

On the whole, these people mixed well, but no doubt with age-old feuds lying just under the surface.

Villages had names taken from their churches or from the natural surroundings. Kastanna (said Kastanya), the place of the chestnuts; kastana = chestnuts. Karya, the place of the walnuts; karythia = walnuts. Some of the lower villages are inhabited all year, but the higher ones are still nomadic. It is far too cold with those simple houses and snow-blocked roads for any to stay. Mind you, the house two up from ours owned by the retired agricultural policeman of the village was an exception. A somewhat cranky man, he had, in his working days, sat out wind and snow storms all winter. One wonders quite why, for there were no animals up there and little enough of value for anyone to risk the journey to steal. Unlike most, he had no gift in his hands to pass the days with woodwork or carving. Instead he read his Bible and counted the letters, or was it words, on each page!

They were, until very recently, very simple villages entirely centred around the church. And what churches they are! Some are four hundred years old, tiny, more than somewhat battered; services are still held in them occasionally. Our village has just such a precious church, but then, in front of it is another. Huge, indeed magnificent and merely two hundred odd years old. The woodwork and the wall paintings are all very fine, they are not so cluttered with synthetic gold horrors as are too many of the new ones. It took me some time to work it out why the mountain churches are so wonderful compared with those by the sea. It is simple. The lower ones are done up by wealthy patrons for all to observe, while, and thank goodness, the higher ones remain as they were, now just for pious visitors and shepherds to use.

There is another church just outside our village which from above frankly looks like a large cow house, for it is roofed with corrugated iron. Yet inside! The paintings and woodwork are wonderful. The outlying arm of the village which it served has fallen down, now mere heaps of fallen rocks where houses stood, so it stands alone, yet is diligently cared for.

Yet another superb church stands above a village we pass through on our way up to Spiti Sebastian. Architecturally it is unusual, indeed it is splendid. The story goes that the village, only having a very small and simple church, asked the local pasha if they could build a larger one. He agreed, but on one condition. They were to build it within six weeks, in the style of a mosque. If they did not complete it within that time, it would be a mosque. Of course it was completed in time because, so Stamos told me, they had been working for ages on the quiet, preparing the wood beams and cut stone for it.

The magic day for the spring migration is 15th of May, and in autumn, after the feast of Saint Dimitrious, the 26th of October. Most mountain villages, as ours, usually have a second village lower down, with sometimes almost the same name. The people in the lower, larger village, are the same families with the same names as those in the higher. Very few now migrate, just a handful of shepherds go up for the summer, and down, for the winter. The exception being for saint days, which are religiously attended. With the recent prosperity, many have made their simple houses into smart summer houses, and go there for the really hot months.

Over the top of the mountain and down the other side, is another set of villages which are lower and inhabited all year. They too have lovely churches, and even hotels, some of them quite grand. It is a joy to go there, an excursion, or as we say a 'volta'. Braving the hideous road, more rock boulder than anything else, we go to shop, for our village only has a kaféneon with few provisions. Wine, ouzo and beer of course. No bread, but a few tins of corned beef, sardines, tomato paste, rice and pasta. The owner is a grumpy old man, definitely out to give short change to the rich foreigners where he can, so we just get our basics from him. At weekends he kills a lamb and gets out his soufla (bar-be-cue) for visitors from down and attempts to be jolly.

Over the mountain, the other villages have deep gutters on the sides of the roads full of fast-running water. Indeed there seems to be water everywhere. Apart from a couple of shops which sell everything, there is a Post Office and a small cheese factory. Theirs is of course feta and myzithera and very excellent it is. It is always a pleasure to pass laden donkeys or mules on their way to deliver milk and give the traditional greeting: 'Xeratai' (Heeratay). Xera is the ancient word JOY. So it could be 'Be joyful; Go joyfully; Come joyfully'. Such a truly joyful way to exchange greetings, and usually with a stranger. On our way back, the views are so glorious, inevitably we start belting out the tune from the film, The Big Country.

The first time I did that trip was in midwinter with Stamos. The sun shone brightly on the pristine white snow. The sky was an incredible blue. Apart from the occasional grey-headed crow, we were alone. There were no tyre marks on the snow, yet he was determined to do it, and it was terrifying. At one point he took a corner too short, got stuck and ordered me out 'to push'! If the Landrover had stalled and rolled back, that would have been my lot. But we made it. The snow weighed so heavily on the branches of the fir trees, that they lay flattened, half across the road. It was a hairy drive, but Stamos, as a kid in a Dodgem car, loved every moment of it, while I, terrified, covered my eyes with my hands. When we got to the village on the other side, he was even more pleased to see a row of pappoothes (grandfathers) sunning themselves outside a bar. We joined them for a drink, and Stamos happily told them of our ride. They were much impressed. Thankfully, we did not go up and back, but down the other way from where we were.

At four thousand feet, I found the air delicious, but found walking quite arduous. Some people seem to like to just walk, from A to B. My mother was like that. My father, who I suppose I take after, just crawled along, quite the opposite. He, as I, didn't miss a thing. The herbage is so wonderful, the wildlife, the rocks. Everything is wonderful, so why run? There is so much to see. I found my knowledge grew with every trip I made up there; on getting home, out came the books. Useless knowledge I do believe, is a very fine thing. Away from the muck of 'down', the slopes were rich in so many plants in which I rejoiced. I had much to learn.

On the farm on the 9th of May, or the weekend nearest to it, we had our first panayerie. Well now we had a lovely little church, we must do everything properly. I hasten to add that although most people know that the feast of Saint Nicholas is held on the 6th of December, ours is different. Traditionally it is known that Saint Nicholas stopped and rested at our place on his way to Bari. Hence he is known as Saint Nicholas of Bari. It would be nice to think it was actually our farm, but tradition is vague on that. His next stop, (he must have had a brilliant and very fast ship), was to the Ionian island of Zakinthos or Zante, which is its old name. They hold their feast for him, on the 11th of May.

Years later, after real research, I discovered the true story and include it here.

All our neighbours rallied around and we held a feast with the traditional lambs on the spit. I do not remember how many lambs we had that first time, or who the Papas was who held the service, but it went well. We were getting the hang of it. Many of Stamos' family and friends came from Athens and hospitality flowed as it should do. No doubt some blankets got well weed-headed again, despite being spring and my previous intentions.

Brian's wife had been at my elbow for some time now and learned not only to how to cook with great economy, but also how to please everyone.

My problem throughout was that I had no one to learn from. It seemed that no one in our area dried anything. So my efforts were hit and miss, and I might get there or I might not. With our trees in production, I had taken to drying apricots. I did not know how. I looked at the pale, sulphur-dried shop apricots and wondered HOW were they done? So, my own recipe was first to blanch them in boiling water, using huge wire baskets, then dump them in the cold bath. After draining them well, we laid them in the sun on the roof for about five days. It seemed to work, albeit they looked nothing like the bought ones. They tasted wonderful, much better, but I have to admit they were ugly. They were dark brown and flat. More like miniature cow pats, yet they lasted well in the great Ali Baba ceramic pots I stored them in. First I lined the bottom of the clean pots with bay leaves, believing this might help against bugs. When they were full of apricots, I covered them with more bay leaves then tied a strong cloth firmly over the top. They kept well, all year. A few signs of life were quickly removed by boiling water. As the old saying goes, 'What the eye don't see, the heart can't grieve over'.

These home-dried apricots were a great addition to our diet, adding variety and pleasure. Occasionally, at the end of preparing bread I chopped some up and hurled them into the last of the dough with an egg or two, some sugar and cinnamon. Fruit bread made a pleasant change. Apple Crumble of British recipe books got changed to Apricot Crumble House Speciality, and very good it was indeed, but not too often. It was mainly dished up for special occasions.

There was the famous day when the dried apricots came out to be made into the much-enjoyed Crumble.

'Now,' said I, 'for the custard.'

And Carol was heard to say, 'Where's the Bird's.'

Poor girl, the noisy wrath of many young people fell on her head.

'We don't have Bird's here!' they yelled in unison.

So she had a lesson on how to make simple, pouring, home made-custard.

Boil two pints of Milk in which there are dissolving four tablespoons of Sugar, a drop of Vanilla essence and a pinch of Salt.
Beat hard three or four eggs in a small bowl

and when the milk is almost boiling
add two tablespoons of creamed in water Cornflour to the eggs and mix,
then pour into the milk mixture AS IT RISES, switch off and stir well till thick.

All this reminds me of a young Australian we had. (I understand that they love custard in Australia.) He was always sent to the end of the self-service queue when it was apricot crumble and custard. Rex would then, as usual, overload his bowl and carefully stagger back to his seat, trying, amidst jeers, not to spill any.

Carol had to be taught almost everything, and learn she did. For there was only a tiny gas stove at the mountain house, two rings and an oven up there, apart from the wood burning fou-fou. All bread would have to be pan baked, and I would go up every weekend to replace stores. They were a valiant crew, Brian from England, Philip from Eire, and Ian, known always as Beanie, from the US. Carol was cook-general while her two children just did odd jobs.

A shimmer of excitement existed amongst us as we made our preparations for our migration to renovate the mountain house. It was a mammoth task. Our big Landrover looked very small compared with the vast trucks everyone else went up in. Mind you, they not only had their flocks on board, they had all but the kitchen sink. But the excitement was the same. A feeling of anticipation which we shared with them. Like going on holiday.

'We are going UP!' Instead of a flock of sheep, our livestock consisted of a puppy, two ducks and just one lamb.

I would have also liked to send up a milking goat, but it was too complicated. Ziggy, one of Morag's puppies went up with them and we nearly lost her for spring is a dangerous time. I always told the kids to thump their feet as they went along little over-grown paths. Snakes, waking up from the winter were a very real danger, and light footed Ziggy was bitten. Fortunately a local was nearby and cut her to bleed. Nonetheless she was very ill, blew up to twice her size and they really thought that she would die. After that I kept homeopathic snake bite pills up there, but they were never needed.

It must have been extraordinarily uncomfortable the first week or two. A good pit was dug for a loo, which would, in true old style be dosed daily with ashes from the fire. It was just above a crabby little old apple tree, which in time, got the message and suddenly began producing magnificent, bright red apples. Water was brought down by ordinary hose pipe from a well above. We got a smith to make a small galvanised cistern which was gravity fed from the spring. When full, it simply over flowed back into the well so no one could grouse. It was a very practical method except there was one boy up in the village who delighted in tormenting us. An only child, his parents were very soft and horrified when, complaining, I threatened to thwack his legs with the stick I was carrying. When he got bored, alas a frequent occurrence, he used to bend up a twig and stick it into the exit pipe of our cistern. It was quite a climb to find out what was wrong, and it was usually he.

We were one of five houses well below the village but not the lowest. Our views were uninterrupted and spectacular. The house behind us was not occupied and was in poor condition. Now and again one of the owners came, but I understood that as it belonged to him jointly with all his siblings, he could not sell it. Behind that house was the grumpy ex-agricultural policeman who had spent his winters there. He also rarely visited, preferring the comforts of 'down'. Mind you, his dog made short work of our ducks when he was there!

And then there was Pappoo and Yaya. (Grandfather and grandmother.) They lived up there every summer for as long as the weather permitted them to, loving it as I did. Their house was singularly ramshackle, but they did not seem to mind. When we brought water down by hose, we fixed a simple stand pipe on the corner of their house for them. They refused to have it brought around to the front, indeed it seemed as if rather than being pleased, it rather perturbed them. For they had a dear Jenny donkey, who every day went with Pappoo up to the well to collect water to bring down in two wooden barrels strapped to her sides. Eventually they disposed of her, which saddened them, particularly as they felt she was no longer well cared for.

Every spring Pappoo and Dimitris, his youngest son, went up for the occasional fine day to prepare the vegetable garden. This was a small well fenced area near to their house. There they yearly planted many vegetables for when they would be stranded up there, providing almost everything that they would need. We tried to do the same, but our fence was not strong enough so the sheep had a good meal instead.

At first, every time I went up, Fredo whinged, because it was a new and a generally busy and messy place, as a builders yard. We would fill a plastic bath with warm water and he would play in it for hours. The fou-fou nearby always had a great black kettle going all the time, so we could top up the cold water and keep him warm and happy. An Aquarian, a water baby.

Then he discovered Pappoo and Yaya, just around the corner, albeit a corner full of nettles. Hands held out before him, he would edge around the narrow path to their front door and into child heaven. As parent birds they were forever stuffing goodies into his mouth. When he came home for meals he wouldn't eat. I raged, uselessly. The bonus was that at last he was learning to speak Greek. For despite my pleas, Stamos always spoke English to him until he went to proper school. I never knew any of my grandparents, so I envied the mutual love and happiness between Fredo and those two old people. They were his grandparents, and that was that. As he got older, he held his own at school. Not only did he have grandparents, he had his own village.

There is just one more, new one-roomed house near us which should never have been built and is not worth mentioning.

The house progressed with the skilled hands of those excellent young men. Carol fed them, ringing me up from the kaféneon with orders for the weekend. Ham and sausage from the pig farm behind us. Bakaloa (dried fish) from the grocer and mince-meat from our regular frozen meat shop. Vegetables, boxes of tomatoes, sacks of onions and tomatoes, kilos of beans, beetroots, celery you name it, just as a grocer I drove up. Not forgetting the demijohn, or was it two, of wine.

The roof came off and went back on again. The crumbling end wall became a low French door out onto the simple new veranda which skirted half the house. A very small bathroom was tacked on to the end of the veranda, with hand-basin, loo and shower. We learned that the best time to have a shower was during the day when the water might get warm, even hot, travelling down the hose pipe in the sun. Otherwise it was icy.

On the west of the house where were the cellar and front doors, we made a simple kitchen underneath the veranda. We found a fine stone sink and fitted a hose tap to it. The little cooker sat there, with its gas bottle. Plenty of nails went in, in correct peasant style and all my pots were hung up. Sifting through a fallen house, I found an ancient 'piatothiki'. Piato = plate. Thiki = store. (The word 'thiki' is used widely, for example, Bibliothiki = Bookshop.) I lovingly repaired it and happily put up some pretty Samosware plates.

Outside the kitchen we put a huge electric drum table with whatever rickety chairs we could find. Near by was the fou-fou, a most excellent albeit primitive stove. This was a home-made, two-ring, wood stove, wood being readily available and free, unlike gas. Stone, mud and plenty of ingenuity, it was a simple but adequate cooker known the world over. As usual, for fire prevention, we made it on the little terrace beside and not too close to the house. It even had a little chimney, so that the smoke drifted away and not onto those sitting at the table. It was really good for slow cooking. Beans and lentils of course, but I also used it for other things including bread-making. There were several little damson trees just behind it, which I fear did not appreciate the fire. Yet even so, they occasionally did produce fruit.

This was the sitting and eating area, but at first, without shade, it was often too hot there, so we erected a square frame overhead using plain water pipe and laid bamboo on top. I had discovered four, (so useful) little honeysuckle plants in the field below and I planted one at each corner of the frame to replace the bamboo eventually for shade. Everyone who stayed there had instructions to water them which they seemed to appreciate, for they grew.

The major problem was drains. The shower and basin waste water had their own sump, just behind the fou-fou, which benefited the damson trees. The kitchen sink had another sump which benefitted the old walnut tree. It was a very simple yet practical procedure and to add to it, I set some mint to grow on top. We dug a good hole and filled it with smallish stones and I hope the old trees benefited over the years. The loo waste was quite another matter. We walked due west down the slope to the little field and decided that this would be the best place. Pipes were laid first under the path, then our little havouza had to be made. The ground is wickedly hard during the summer when there is no rain, and the boys took it in turns to go at it with pick and mattock.

Now everyone knows that every other village in Greece has buried gold. If it wasn't left by the Turks, it was by one of the retreating forces during the last war. We had already had personal experience of young foreign vandals desecrating Stamos' grandparents' tomb, and our little church, in their search for gold. There is a strong tradition that there is indeed gold somewhere about our village, dropped by aircraft but never located.

As always, the papoothes spent their time outside the kaféneon gossiping endlessly. Their work-days pretty well done, they enjoyed the sunshine and company.

'Why, is this foreigner repairing an old shepherd's house? Why not on the coast? In the town? Why here, where there is nothing?'

Up spoke friend Spiros, the kindest of men; he had spent some time in Canada and delighted in chatting to the kids as they with him. It was he, with his wicked sense of humour who gave the old boys food for thought.

'Because she knows where the gold was dropped of course!'

So the grandfathers arrived at our place and daily stood themselves around the growing hole which the boys were digging. The boys meanwhile, somewhat amazed by their audience, dug on with new strength. Sadly no gold was found, so eventually the old men departed, disappointed and still perplexed.

Another thing which worried them, was why wasn't I, a rich foreigner, doing a fancy, modern job of renovating the house? Across the next valley there were recently done-up houses with all the trappings of German or Swiss mountain houses. Ducky rustic iron strap-work door and window furnishings abounded. Roofs became suddenly very steep, very alpine. Yet all this woman was doing was to repair the old house to make it habitable. Well yes, she was installing a WC in her bathroom and there was a shower instead of just a wooden bucket or a hose pipe.

While I was determined to keep the old house as much like the others as possible, they were disappointed with my efforts. We got our very simple but adequate septic tank built. Before the top was sealed I brought up a bucket of really stinking offal from the slaughterhouse and tipped it in to get things working. As long as it wasn't taken advantage of, it worked fine and did not overflow or smell.

Later on when staying there during a very hot weekend I heard the loo being flushed and crept to peep out from a crack in the door to see who had done it. Some locals who had relatives staying from Australia or the US were apparently giving them a guided tour. Visitors had to be entertained and here was evidence to prove that ours wasn't such a primitive village. There was no question that our house did not look nicer than most, because we took care of it. But the introduction to the first flush loo in the village amused me greatly.

Back at the farm midsummer, I answered the phone to a cheery voice.

'Hello there, it's Pete!'

Pete? Who on earth is Pete? My hesitation must have got through for next came, 'Nuffy and Peter, remember?' I did. Horrors, that loud girl!

'We're on our way back to Oz, waiting for money to come through and hating Athens. Can we come?'

'No,' is not one of my regular words. They came, and I quickly realised that something had happened to Nuffy while she had been in England.

'What ever has happened to you Nuffy?' said I, tact also not being a regular gift, 'You are SO nice now!'

Which she accepted with great good humour.

'Yes, even Peter says so!' she cheerfully replied.

They stayed for several months, valiant and positive helpers and we became and have since remained, close friends

There was much to-ing and fro-ing to the mountains from the farm. Any spare kid was shipped up there to help. After any great labour, with for example a crop, the young were rewarded by a quick trip, there to cool off and relax. During these lulls we began the long job of 'paving' the area around the house. The bare earth floors of the kitchen and terrace were a problem, for whenever it rained it became a quagmire. With imagination and quite some effort, it soon began to look and feel good with stone slabs. Called plakakia, they are to be found everywhere along the mountain roadsides and for free. Whenever we went for a volta (drive) eyes were alert for not too large, flattish stones. It is astonishing just how much one needs. We gathered them slowly, doing the terrace step by step, area by area, and it was much admired by all our neighbours. Indeed we were told, that this is how it had been done in the past.

But nowadays, the Greek houses round about were in far too much of a hurry to delay by such slow activity. Concrete is always slammed down, quick and practical. In a few years the frost gets in and it cracks, eventually to fall apart. Our floors if bumpy, were not too hard to sweep, lasted and even looked attractive.

One year, we had a fine crop of damsons. Apparently it does happen now and again, according to the spring weather. Our few trees were laden, and loving to preserve the earth's bounty, I eagerly watched what the village women were doing. First they laid newspaper out on any flat surface they had. Then they sprinkled the rather small 'damaskina' all over. Every few days they tossed and turned them, all the while watching the weather of course. For when it rains in the mountains, it rains. Then, when they are shrivelled and dry, they hang them up in little bags on nails on the roof beams. There they sway in any light breeze, together with the other fruits of the earth, frugally stashed away for winter.

Yaya told me that when, in cold weather, they are bored with the eternal fakkes, (lentils) they throw a small handful of damsons in right at the beginning of cooking and it gives the thick soup a wonderful flavour. I have done this a couple of times and she was right. The taste of onion, garlic and wood smoke combined with the tang of damsons is delicious if unusual. I don't know what else they did with them, for they were so small, seemingly more stone than fruit. I must find out.

Chapter 8

Loss

Not long after the grand migration, two of our young people, boy and girl, walked up to the mountains with my old mare Diamando. With a tent and their gear on her back, they travelled for several days, a great experience in their young lives. They told me of how, one night on spotting a fire burning on a hillside, they approached it. There they were warmly, if incredulously, welcomed to share hearth and hospitality. Apparently their whole journey was punctuated by everyone they passed with enquiries of, 'Who are you, where are you going? Why?' (very Greek!)

I thought this would be wonderful for Diamando, to be up there in the cool in green pastures. I also thought it would be fun for the young people up there to ride her and maybe to use her for carrying things. It was I regret to say, a total disaster. I inadvertently committed not one but two crimes. How ignorant can you get?

No sooner had the three gone off than Jenny, the little old donkey who had simply arrived years ago, started calling. Her friend! Her Diamando! She had gone and left her chum behind. We had actually thought about sending Jenny as well, but she was too old, she simply would not have made it. We never had any idea where the little party was, for it was a difficult route with deep gullies along the way. We comforted Jenny as best we could, but it was no use. After crying endlessly for a couple of days, she simply lay down to die.

Everyone on the farm was concerned and constantly visited her. We held up her head so she could drink, which she did. I was appalled when the blue-bottles began bothering her, trying to lay their eggs on her, even before she was dead. The very same hand-crochet bath mat which I had sat Emilie on in those first days when Jenny arrived, now came in useful. Wet, I laid it over her head where it kept her cool, and kept off the flies. She died, and I felt the most cruel and thoughtless wretch. It just hadn't occurred to me that she would mourn so, or that being such close friends, they must not be separated. We of course knew that it would be just for a few months. How can you explain that to a beast?

So that was another grim job for the lads. They buried her where she lay, at the end of the farm. It is a small comfort that a cast-out old donkey did, at the end of her life, have some contented years with us.

That was the daftest idea I ever had, as it seemed to go on and on, for it didn't end there. Diamando adopted the lamb as her chum, and seemed content enough. She was not a lot of use, also being old, except the children enjoyed her. She was a tall horse, Spanish to look at, black and white. The villagers were astonished to see the unaccompanied little children perched on her back, happily urging her along.

Then the day came when the lamb was slaughtered for some feast or the other, and Diamando lost another friend. Now we really were in trouble, for she took to escaping and wandering off. I constantly had calls, 'Kyria, Kyria, your mare is at –' and I'd have to leave everything, to Stamos' rage, and drive in the heat to find her, goodness knows where.

At the end of summer I made yet another mistake. In retrospect I wonder if another was possible. There were no jolly kids at the farm to volunteer to walk her home, so I engaged Spiros who, with his big truck, would drive her down. I put her saddle on, thinking it would help to make her feel more secure. I travelled in the back with her. It was a grim drive, particularly coming down the mountain roads. But we got her home safely where I fussed and spoiled her, yet as time went by, I felt something was wrong for she did not eat. I am just an animal person and work by instinct. I have never been really horsy, so frantic, I dug out my books, for I believed that she had lockjaw, and she had. Apparently older horses do sometimes get this after travelling by road. How could I know? I fled to the vet.

What an all round disaster and she, poor love, was never really the same again.

In between all this, a letter came from my very dear old school friend, Miri. It was difficult to understand, for her writing was scratchy, for she had only learnt English after she was thirteen. I poured over it weeping, for she asked me to send her something, but what? All I did understand was that it was bad news.

'Go,' said Stamos. 'Go and see her for a few days.'

I went to see a travel agent in Athens, the tears always just behind my sun glasses. I explained about my dear old friend who was dying, that I so wanted to see her, be with her for a little time, the last time. By chance I had found a kind soul, maybe one who had a similar experience in her life, for she toiled for me.

A miracle happened, for she must have been an angel. A group had gone to Miri's country two weeks earlier and one place had not been filled. She could arrange to fly me there for just two and a half days, but I must return with the group. It was very cheap. I went. A short hop. I was nonetheless quite nervous as I had never been to Miri's country before and I did not speak the language. There was no reply from her phone, maybe it was out of order? Was she in hospital? Worse, was she already dead? I took a taxi from the airport to her address. It was a risk, because she didn't know that I was coming.

Whether it is genetic I know not, but each time I have come up against a deeply distressing situation where I want to totally collapse and weep, an inner voice says 'Be strong.'

All I wanted to do was hug her and weep uncontrollably, yet I did not. Despite my diverse blood lines, that one-quarter, True-Brit stiff upper lip prevailed. Soon, we were, as of old, good friends, chattering about this and that. She was so very pleased and surprised that I had come. We discussed our children, our lives, our problems. I told her that I had lost my father and how cross Stamos had been because he had left me nothing. She showed me the jewels which her father had left her for her security. Two marvellous if old-fashioned Cartier watches encrusted with diamonds and a superb diamond ring. I told her how lucky she was to know from these gifts, that her father had loved her so much and cared for her future. I also scolded her for not wearing them, for she just wore junk, as a Christmas tree. With her usual humour she retorted,

'What, do you want me to grow into a fat old lady covered with diamonds?'

Looking at her, all skin and bones I knew she would never be fat, and she would never be an old lady; it was very clear. I could hardly look into her eyes.

Be strong, be strong.

It was a happy two days. I cooked for them, we went out. She introduced me to her friends, she was so joyful, 'Meet my English friend, from school days, look she has come to see me.'

I'm so glad I went, but when the letter came that she had died, then I collapsed with grief. I don't know why, but her death affected me deeply, probably because she was my childhood friend, and that she was too young. She needn't have died, she could have had surgery. Stubborn! A while later her husband phoned that she had left me one of her three good pieces of jewellery. I really intended to write to say, 'have them valued and send me the one of least worth'. But I was so busy with child, farm, kitchen, I did not, which as it transpired, was a great pity, for it indirectly lead to so much more trouble and sorrow in the coming years.

One of her sons came to stay, who was so like her, it was a joy to have him. Fearful of the responsibility given to him as delivery boy, he handed me a small box. In it was a single diamond pendant on a chain. I looked at it surprised and said, 'I don't remember this.'

'Neither do I,' he replied.

It was such a busy time that it was some days before I looked at it carefully. Only then did I understand why we didn't know it. It was one shoulder from one of the watches, on close examination the cut was evident.

So I realised what had been done; the bulk of the watch had no doubt been sold. He was, she had told me, despite his very good job in the diplomatic service, always short of cash. I was sent the fraction of it. Yet in retrospect it is a miracle I was sent anything; he could so easily just have forgotten her wishes and not told me. So much sorrow whirled through my head. Yet I wasn't surprised. He had cheated on her most of their married life; now she was dead, he was still cheating on her.

For me, I had the most precious gift of all, that she had left me something, a token of affection. I said nothing to the boy of course, and just put the little pendant away, feeling it soiled.

Summer over, we had few helpers, for it was evident that the farm was now in spanking order and just ticking over. The mountain house, almost completed, was shut down for winter. Small works would go on there for years to come, but the bulk had been done and all by those super kids. It was almost a proper house now.

Another tradition began, a Christmas Carol Service in our church. I rallied all the expats, and many neighbours came too. I laid down all the rugs and flokatia I could find on the stone floor and set up all the candlesticks available. It looked so beautiful. Maria and Antony made and photocopied carol sheets. They were very jolly with just the old favourite carols.

Sometimes we were honoured by the presence of the Anglican chaplain, Father Bert, which much impressed our Greek friends. Our guests were a mixed bag, indeed not just Brits and Greeks, but several other races. One charming old Greek lady I recall who, despite not having one word of English, made a habit to come every year. Sometimes we had musicians, sometimes not. I provided mulled wine and snacks, which after our carols were sung, we sat about eating. For those of us away from home, it was a joyful interlude.

There is just one Greek Christmas Carol. Kids, indeed even poor adults, usually Rom, arrive outside the door around Christmas time. If they are lucky they will carry one or more triangles which they hit diligently and rarely in time.

'Trigona Khristouyena,' is sung at top speed and this how it sounds phonetically. Here is a rough translation.

Triangle, Christmas carols in the neighbourhood,
Christmas has come and the New Year – Heh!
Triangle, Christmas carols in the neighbourhood,
Christmas has come, and the New Year. Heh!

That's it! Over and over again.

It really is not so musical. One hastily gives them money just to leave. Pity, as it is the same as with the marches we heard from the nearby army camp. I do feel that the composers and musicians of Greece have great and unfulfilled opportunities

Occasionally a few youngsters, including Stamos' children, took it into their heads to spend some days in the mountains during the winter. It did not matter how well we locked the house, somehow people got in. Well I suppose if you are cold and desperate, you can achieve anything. Antony had brought an ancient pair of green-painted wooden skis from the north of England. One spring, I was astonished to find them gone, a newish, bright-red shiny pair in their place. Good luck, I thought, and wondered who had been mad enough to swap his smart pair for those has-beens. It was as a small migration again when they went up there in winter, for they would need everything, and plenty of it. That must have been while we still had a Landrover, otherwise it would not have been possible.

Which brings me to the eternal problems all foreigners had with their vehicles. As they came in with foreign number plates, they were permitted to stay in Greece for only one year. One had to be out for three months before returning legally. It was a continual headache. Stamos had long ago sold his one asset, a white van. Then to all our sorrow, for fear they would be confiscated, he also sold my first Landrover, a dear old wreck, then later, the second, somewhat healthier. In both cases the cash quickly disappeared, needed I was told, for taxes, or whatever. We now depended entirely on the valiant little mini-van. Later still, when the crops needed a strong vehicle for delivering to the factories, or to the dump, Stamos inspected every vehicle on the market, then decided on one which had been made to his high standards. A deposit was paid, and alas, another sum was added to our monthly burden.

A friend came with a smile, congratulating Stamos on his new pick-up, a fair exchange he reckoned, for Frederikos. For it was well known that the Rom sold their babies in order to buy a vehicle. We liked it. That was a most valiant pick-up too, which lasted for years.

Around Christmas I usually tried to go home to see my mother. I needed to go too, for it was often very lonely on the farm, for at that time we rarely had workers. Winter was not the normal travelling time with the world's youth. Orange picking did not start till later when they were ripe and sweet. Stamos went to Athens for his social life while mine was frankly nil. It did not do for both of us to be away from the farm at the same time, for by now there was too much of value to risk it. We had no fences, and all the machinery was open to the world in the unfinished barn. As it was, I fear we did lose quite a few things without knowing it.

Three trips north to the wonderful American Farm School had given us three dear Guernsey heifers. September, April and December (those being the months in which they arrived). Dear, kind girls, they did well on the abundance of weeds which grew everywhere between the trees while liberally manuring the hungry earth. The thought to bring down a Guernsey bull was impractical. While we collected one of the calves, a half grown bull seemed to sense our need for he bellowed at us, unexpectedly and long. Even the head cowman laughed. But with a short wheel based pick-up, one calf at a time was enough for that long drive.

It was, without a doubt, a mistake. Not having cows, but having Guernseys. At least, I console myself, I didn't do what homesick British settlers did in Australia with rabbits. At least I am sure that the injection of fine pedigree cows into an area of pure 'scrub' cows (despite what else they may have been called) did nothing but good in raising the tone. The south is a lot hotter than the north, and there isn't the rainfall. So it isn't surprising that most of Greece's cattle are in the north. We managed well enough, as did most people, with evaporated milk. Mostly from northern Europe, it took some getting used to and completely changed the taste of tea. A tin of evap., with three or four parts of water in a big jug, almost watered away the artificial taste. With the useless Surtsey gone, Serena turned out to be a winner, so with goat and occasional milk sheep, we managed.

When Stamos ventured, always the first in the district, into growing alfalfa, my quiet naggings grew to a crescendo. Being prepared to do the work, it in fact didn't take me long to win him over and the exciting day came to drive north to find her. Of course I wasn't prepared to take on any of the pitiful creatures available locally. Besides, I had heard that the wonderful and exciting American Farm School in Salonica had Guernseys.

Everything I had ever heard of these placid animals seemed good. Also, they didn't appear to mind the heat either. When we used to tether them out in the orange groves, near enough to a tree for shade, they always chose to lie in the blazing sun.

Thankfully, September, the dearest, easiest cow imaginable, came first. Always being busy, we only managed one trip north a year to collect our babies.

Eventually, the naughty September learned to CHARGE. I can just see her now, dear thing, getting the others organised. Heads down, all together, ready, steady, GO. And off they went through the fence, udders swinging, milk spraying, back to the cow house. (Damn it)

Everyone who knew about Channel Island milk was thrilled to have it available. At first we sold it in sealed plastic bags and had a good outlet. We truly lived off the fat of the land. Yoghurt, butter and cheese, butter milk to drink! A lot of work, but worth it. I learned to make every sort of cheese, by trial and error. The feta was excellent but yellow. Long after the cows had gone I was grateful for it. The barrels of cheese I had been forced to store, from lack of sales, helped me through the dark days. In a country where sheep and goat milk is white, the yellow colour of our milk and cheese was not, alas, popular. I even learnt how to make the rennet to make the cheese.

Often, when visiting peasant houses, I had been perplexed by curious dried nameless 'things' hanging above the fireplace. Eventually I asked what they were, and was shown. The stomach of a young lamb, killed when still suckling, is hung to dry for rennet. When it is opened up, stinking strongly, it contains a solid whitish substance perhaps threaded with the occasional wisp of hay. This is well crumbled and mashed with a little water into a smooth paste. Then it is put into a small bottle and shaken up with more water. This then is the feta starter. Very little is used. It makes a fine cheese. One can buy tiny pots of powdered rennet in the stores. It might be easier, but it isn't nearly as good.

So now came the problem of mating. There was no decent bull in the area. The only bulls indeed were Barba Yorgi's (Uncle George) who were very fat, thoroughly interbred scrub Holstein.

Ah woe is me, now I cooked up yet another dream which although it didn't end in a nightmare, was a great waste of time for too many. Why is the price of optimism often so high? How about artificial insemination I thought? It was a familiar idea from England, why not try to get some Guernsey sperm from there?

The fine old word PALAVER is fitting for that whole operation.

'Of course, no problem, NO charge!' said a generous AI centre in the UK. Son Antony to the fore. On a motor bike, with the liquid nitrogen bomb on the carrier, the dear lad met us at the airport. The pilot, bless him too, agreed to take it.

As ever, I had somewhat overstretched my weight allowance. For apart from Fredo's and my cases, I had a toddler's pushchair plus a sack of disposable nappies for the trip. I had succumbed to a great temptation and bought Fredo a small tractor. I mean a small one, heavy-weight plastic on a frame. He adored it and although his legs were not long or strong enough to pedal it, he somehow managed to shove it along. Then I had two dozen Khaki Campbell duck eggs for hatching, papers and all. Then, dare I go on, I had six apple trees, for the mountain house. For don't we all know that the best eating apples are Cox's and the best cookers are Bramleys?

The first rumpus was when someone at the check-in tried to remove the tractor. Fredo hung on grimly. I remember to this day the poor man on his knees grasping the steering wheel pleading. It was a tug of war.

'No!' said Fredo, a little chap who understood two languages perfectly but barely spoke either. 'No!' hanging on to his pride and joy.

'Please,' said the man, still pulling, 'I promise that you shall get it back later old chap.' He gave in.

A worried young man escorted me to the side with my trees, eggs, and Guernsey sperm. I was getting just a little afraid that maybe this time I was pushing my luck. The trees were a fraction taller than I, and I am not a little woman.

'What are you?' the next young man asked, frowning, 'a farmer or something?'

'A farmer,' said I nodding.Another young man appeared, not in uniform this time, but in overalls. He cast his eyes at the trees; it seemed that they were the problem. As in every transaction in Greece I hastily thrust the papers at him. Unlike a Greek, he ignored them.

'I am not sure about the trees,' he said, pursing his mouth with worry.

We both looked at them.

'Now look here young man!' said I firmly, then watched as his expression changed and his shoulders rose to make war.

'I know that you will do your best, so, if they get a little damaged, never mind, I'll just have to cut them back.'

His shoulders dropped and he actually smiled.

I bet that there are not so many trees in the world which have travelled by air in a coffin. Greatly relieved I cast blessings all around and they got home safely and I did not need to cut them back.

It occurs to me now, that what I got away with in the early 1980s would not be possible now in this new millennium.

So much for all our efforts. The AI vet came from Athens at the right moment, and we had another daft, mother and father of a session out there, as usual in front of the house. Alas, she didn't take. I heard later that Guernseys really are happier with a bull, and this is what we resorted to, one of Barba Yorgi's. A tubby fellow, smaller than she, he certainly managed entirely successfully, better than did the AI, (and all effort and kindness from so many for all those arrangements).

It can be very cold indeed in the winter in Greece. Any wind, tearing over the far off lovely snow capped mountains all about, was icy by the time it reached us. An early bird, I would go down at about five when still dark and make preparations for lunch with perhaps a note to whoever we had helping. Then, well dressed, I mean very well dressed, I set off to the big apricot orchard. In the pocket band around my waist were my secateurs and a pruning saw. Trixie always came with me and we began work just as the sun was rising. It was very cold.

I loved the work, indeed I got lost in it, a therapy. Every tree had its own character, and I struggled to help them to grow beautifully so that when they were laden down with apricots, they wouldn't break. As the sun rose higher, piece by piece off came my clothing, till I was bare-armed and warm. It was a huge task, seven hours every day, which left me feeling not only tired, but so well and satisfied.

Of course sometimes the hunters came to spoil my peace and I exercised my lungs by screaming as loudly as I could to chase them off. I never was hurt by them, yet it was disconcerting to feel the spent shot patter all about me. They were often so rude, so indignant when I demanded that they leave our land. Why should they? After all (flapping the paper at me) they had their permits. It might also have been the sight of a mere woman pruning, and the fine rows of trees throughout the orchard. Man's work! Always aware that Trixie, more afraid than I and ever ready with a valiant nip would get shot, I steely eyed kept up my demand.

I was only once rough-housed by one who tore at my headscarf till Stamos, alerted by my screams came running. It was quite a distance from the house. That time it did end in quite a fistycuffs, as he tore in to my defence.

Every mid-morning, the little figure of Fredo appeared, calling for me. He carried a basket in which lay a closed jam jar with tea in it, and some of my home-made oat biscuits. He and Trixie sat down with the biscuits and I with the tea. It is a cosy, happy memory, for he felt so important doing HIS daily job, to take out Mummy's elevenses. I went in for lunch for about an hour and then out again till dusk. Occasionally, when it rained or she considered she had had enough, Trixie made as if to go home, returned and looked at me. This nagging, which it was, went on until either the tree was done, or it was too dark to see or the rain too hard. Whatever the problem, it finally got me going and joyfully she ran ahead.

Not only did the trees look bonny, standing neatly pruned in their rows, I with sun and wind burn looked blooming. So much so, I was twice asked where I had been skiing. What? When I had finished with falling about laughing at such an idea, I showed them my callused hands to prove my healthy occupation.

But the pain, oh the pain. My right shoulder hurt abominably so that nights were a misery. While longing to lie down and rest my weary limbs, the actual relaxing was so painful. Some kind Dutch boys, osteopath trainees, who we had helped to get a job, came often to treat me.The next task in the orchard was to collect the prunings which we cut up and made into bundles for lighting the fournos. This was done by any girls we had, or Rom children, glad of pocket money and a meal. A light job, it killed two birds with one stone.

Quite often, bee-keepers came to ask if they could put their hives on the high ridge on our southern border. This suited everyone when the apricots were in blossom, a sensible reciprocal arrangement which might, or might not, get us a pot of honey. Stamos was a good farmer. Of course we sprayed, but as he put it, it was a 'kind' spray. Whatever he used would not harm the bees. Like most people, I have a healthy respect for bees. While I was rotovating between the trees, east/west, it always seemed as if I was directly in their flight-path. We often 'collided' before they went on their way, so I used to speak to them, in my head, 'Now then you ladies, you do your job, and I'll do mine. I have no intention of hurting you, so please don't sting me.' They never did.

Why then was Stamos always being stung? I told him so many times to talk to them, but he thought that I was daft. Perhaps they had little in common. Fortunately, by then I was well into making natural oils from the herbs I found. The best for these occasions and always carried in the box under the seat of the tractor, was called

Magic Oil. As I didn't know the name of the herb I used, and the results were magic, that is how it got and indeed kept its name.

I noticed a lovely plant growing, with slightly furry soft blue-green leaves, and decided that as it looked so kind, I would make an oil with it. While this was going on I burnt my hand on another kitchen task and this oil being near by, I quickly used it. That night I was surprised not to have the usual thump, thump of pain on the burn. So I searched in my books to identify the plant but to no avail. Ever dismissive of laws in the pursuit of knowledge, I dug up a small plant. After washing its root well, I very carefully packed it up and sent it off to the Physic Garden in Chelsea for identification.

Back came such a lovely, erudite reply in a tiny hand.

'Well it could be this – or it could be that – or but, until it flowers, we will not know.'

Being in the warmer climate of Greece I watched my secret clumps flower, and so I identified it first. It was a member of the Borage family, with, according to Nicholas Culpepper, endless virtues. The one I like best is 'Good for sword thrusts.'

Whenever the cows stood on my feet, out would come the Magic Oil. Covered with paper tissue and soaked well, the bruise would turn blue, but it did not hurt. We use it to this day for every wound or sting and it always amazes me how it really does work like magic.

Some of the greatest compliments I received in Greece, were when the farmers or shepherds sidled up to me with a nudge in the ribs,

'Kyria, kyria if you please, give me a little bottle of your healing oil.'

If just a very minor part of my life's work, here at last was success.

Chapter 9

Good Happenings and Bad Happenings

With spring approaching and another panayieri to arrange, we were pleased when Makis (truck driver) asked if his fifth daughter could be baptised at the same time. What was more, I was invited to be godmother which I happily accepted. It would be quite a Do with both the feast for Saint Nicholas and a baptism.

And this was just the beginning. Maria announced that she and David would like to be married in our church on the same day!

Meetings and discussions went on interminably. Luckily Maria's mother-in-law was English too, so we could work things out very easily together. I understand the poor father-in-law was once again set to cracking almonds for the wedding cake.

There was a query about Maria's mother. Relations between her and the family had always been poor. Nonetheless I said firmly that she must be invited. She was, but unfortunately demurred.

Invitations were on a card with the two languages printed on either side. I sent a lot to past favourite young people, not really thinking that many would come, but just to inform them of what was happening. And what fun to have a wedding invitation, if you turned it around, in Greek on the mantle piece.

Replies came. One of particular interest came from a family who were Morris dancers. They would come and as their gift, would dance at the feast.

Stamos got in touch with Father Pirunakis and asked him to officiate for the day. My sister-in-law, who was to be the koumbara, (best woman), an important position, was in close touch with us over all the arrangements.

Everyone who organises a wedding will know that no matter how hard one works to get things done in time, the days fly past. We seemed to achieve so little although we felt we were managing much. There was no question of booking the caterers, this was going to be a home made job from start to finish.

Then it was Easter, and, as is always the way, unexpected hiccups came hard and fast to interrupt the smooth progress of our tasks.

With Stamos' involvement with the French Consulate, we were pretty familiar with prison and law courts on behalf of foolish young French. It might have been just a little cannabis plant to them, but it was a lot of trouble for us. Greece is very tough on the drug scene, particularly, we understood with foreigners. As Stamos disapproved of handing out bills to these unfortunate people, some more unfortunate than others, we were more often than not, out of pocket. He had no salary from head office, just the honour. It was after all, an honorary consulship. How, nonetheless, when some poor soul had everything stolen from his car or was near to death in hospital, were we to ask for payment?

I made friends with the local prison with visits and supplying books, clothes and sometimes food. Yet with all our young people and the scrapes they got into, so far none had ended up inside. But that was now to change! Not that he was really, one of ours, but he was temporarily.

Here is the tale about Thomas, an Irishman from Cork. He was befriended by one of the youngsters working on the farm, just before Greek Easter, and brought home. This is a time of such jollification, a time for hospitality, so it was quite in order. I liked him, a gentle lad with a sweet smile and soft Irish eyes. It was a joy to hear his accent. Having been in Greece for a mere two weeks, he was actually quite happy to be where he could understand what was going on.

The great night came. Candles in hand, we all piled into the pick-up, and off we went to the big church on the edge of town. There were the usual crowds expected at Easter, a merry throng, from the most ancient grandfather to the tiniest toddler. Everyone was dressed in their finest, a really social event. It never fails to move me. The intense, unquestioning faith. The ancient rituals, and the chaos.

The moment when Christ arises is midnight. There is no synchronism of watches. Every church has its own moment. Bells clang forth wildly. Ships in the harbour also celebrate. Sirens blare, bells ring, and ferocious firecrackers explode, often under the feet. It's a glorious five minutes of abandoned celebration.

'Christ is risen. He is risen indeed!'

Thomas was delighted with the service, the event. They were a happy bunch in the back of the pick-up going home, nursing their candles to keep them alight. At about 2 a.m. we made our way, satisfied and contented. First we lighted the lamps in our church. Then we went to the front door of the house to make our smoky crosses under the lintel. Christ was in our house. And so to bed.

That Easter, we were invited by several local families. We intended spending a little time with them all so as not to cause offence. Also, being quite a gang, not to be too great a burden on any one family.

We went first to Mixalis, who lived nearby. He was a big jolly shepherd who wore an impressive handlebar moustache, as of old. He had, at the tender age of sixteen, 'stolen' his bride, the slightly older and round-faced Katina. It had been a happy and fertile marriage. Most of their family were there, a lot of handsome children and grandchildren. They welcomed our crowd without batting an eyelid. The kids were delighted to be in on such a really Greek occasion.

334

The yard had been well swept and hosed down for dancing, so the soft smell of sheep was not unpleasant. A couple of spits were being turned and all the family were milling about trying to be helpful as well as being good hosts.

We ate and we drank. We danced and started all over again. Regretfully Stamos and I had to move on but the youngsters were so happy, they wanted to stay. Pleased and not a little flattered, Mixalis waved us off. Of course they were welcome.

A battered and sleepy party drifted in that evening to have some simple supper and to talk about the day's events. Most were suffering. Young and foolish, they had happily drunk everything offered to them. The aspirins were passed around. It took a little time to realise that Thomas was missing.

'Perhaps he went back to Athens,' I suggested. But no, a check on his back-pack showed he had not. Oh dear. I phoned Mixalis who told me that Thomas had left in a somewhat sorry state, at about 5 p.m. A whisper said that there was some disagreement over a girl. But where was he? Someone suggested that he was asleep in a ditch and would show up in the morning. But no, a quiver of anxiety filled me, I was worried. It is a habit. I have the earth-mother sense when something is wrong. It never fails me. Sure enough, late that night, a call came.

'Did we know an Irishman called Thomas?' My heart failed. Relief and trepidation.

The familiar procedure began, we were after all, old hands. As Stamos had gone to bed, I went to town to the police station to see him, A VERY sorry sight. With two black eyes, real bloomers, he was pathetically pleased to see me but also pretty sheepish.

'I don't remember a TING (that lovely Irish accent), not a ting!' It was quite a business getting the story out of him, reading between the lines, and eventually arriving near the truth.

It was obvious that Thomas had had a great day. He had drunk all and everything offered to him. Retsina, wine, beer, ouzo, twee little glasses of brightly-coloured poisonous-looking liqueurs. As he was no doubt a well brought up boy, how could he refuse? The mixing of drinks is a common mistake with foreigners. I too have suffered gravely, in fact just from mixing retsina and ouzo. Two and a half days of hell with a head split in half almost. I warn everyone about it. But of course, they must learn, as I did, first-hand.

Poor boy. But he had enough sense to start off home, that is in the right direction. Walking boozily along, he had passed a truck, a big one too. Climbing into it, finding the key in the ignition, off he drove. Still in the right direction. It was basically this fact alone which saved the day. But we weren't to know that then, or that he didn't even have a driving licence.

The owners of the truck, well known to us, were the local fishmongers. In a jiffy they had commandeered a friend's car and given chase.

Poor Thomas, he didn't have a chance. A row of fine cypress trees stopped him. Those poor trees sustained some ugly injuries, visible to this day. Apparently he leapt out and began to run, the fishmongers giving chase. When they got him, they sat on him and eventually dragged him off before the law. We never were quite sure where he got the black eyes from. It could have been on impact or being sat on and thumped.

All I could do, worn out from worry and lack of sleep after the long eventful day, was to reassure him. We would do our best, as if he were our own. One last job was to dash home for food and water and some medical supplies. Prisoners have to supply or pay for their own provisions. It is a poor country. Fed and watered, wounds attended to, I left him, calmer but still shattered and still muttering 'Bizarre!'

Early the following day we went to see him. I attended to his wounds, fed and again reassured him while Stamos talked with the police. One very real fact in Greece, more so then than now, is how precious vehicles are. Simply because they were so very expensive.

We understood that the whole fishmonger's family had been involved in the purchase. They were incensed and enraged. That the culprit was a foreigner didn't help. They would get their pound of flesh willy nilly. I shrank. Stamos as always, took on the role of supportive father and gave as good as we got. It was as usual, a very noisy confrontation.All the while the poor wretched Thomas kept repeating, 'It's bizarre, it's bizarre!'

The situation was not good. Our lawyer, Kostas, was away for Easter. The court case would be held on Tuesday morning. Without much optimism we were more or less obliged to employ Kostas' old father.

After a poor attempt at cleaning him up the next morning, we went in to the court house to support our wished-upon son Thomas. The chief judge was a large lady. The offence was a major one due to the high price of the truck. We hung about in the hallways awaiting our turn. The fishmongers were there in force. They began making demands to Stamos which were quite outrageous. It was quite obvious that they had worked themselves up into highest dudgeon. In their eyes, the accused was a foreigner and therefore rich. Finally Stamos lost his temper and yelled at them.

'Every time I see your faces you go up another ten thousand drax. I don't want to see you! I don't want to hear you! Let the judge decide the damages.'

Mixalis had come, very clean and handsome, his moustaches combed. A loyal friend, amused, he was there to help.

I was called to give evidence, which was to be the first of many times, had I known it, that I would be trying to get our young people out of scrapes. Not knowing Thomas at all really, posed problems. So I dwelt upon the Irish. I quietly explained that how, on my several visits to their very Christian country (I laid that on!), I had found them a delightful, pious people. It was however, well known that they were perhaps a little too prone to enjoy their liquid refreshment. My Greek not being too good, some useful mime came into it (hand holding glass). I struggled on.

Although the boy was little known to us, during the two days he had been our guest he had been easy and mild-mannered. Certainly not a raving alcoholic. His first visit to Greece, he appeared to be charmed with everything. Greece; the Orthodox Easter with its fun and fireworks. (Not knowing what firecracker is in Greek I merely said 'boom, boom' and got a dirty look from the judge!) He loved the people, the hospitality, the climate. But he was a kid, on holiday.

He can't have realised that he must not mix his drinks. This was a new experience; alas he wanted to try out everything offered at this happy time.

I confided with them that in northern Europe, we did have quite a problem with our young people. Having a comparatively easy life, compared with Greece at that time anyway, they often had more money than sense. A lot of them drank too much. This was sympathetically taken in. I wasn't just defending our lad, I was acknowledging that WE, had a problem.

Then Mixalis came on. He spoke very decently about the group of young foreigners who had spent many hours with him and his family on Easter day. He claimed that they had all enjoyed themselves hugely, and that no one had misbehaved in any way. However, he looked across at me, agreeing with my statement that Thomas had imbibed all and everything. It was quite obvious that the boy hadn't a clue what he was doing, mixing his drinks. That, had been his mistake.

The fishmongers came next to tell their story, richly embroidered. The lorry was a wreck. (It really was not.) There were decaying fish everywhere, waiting to be transported. Being Easter they would have to wait for the truck to be mended. What, could they do without a truck? They got some pretty scathing looks for all that nonsense. A likely tale. As if some alternative transport couldn't be arranged. They lost a point on that one.

Then our lawyer, old Mr Filipides came on. His son and partner being away, it was up to him to fly our flag with honour. Oh but how could I have doubted him? A fine old man, he quietly began with reason and logic. As an orator of old, like an ancient Greek, he held forth.

Couldn't we SEE (arms waving) that this boy wasn't a thief? A soft fellow, visiting our land, enjoying our Easter, unaware of the pitfalls of our terrible drinks! IF indeed he had been a thief, surely he would have driven the truck to Athens? Or Patras? But NO! He just made for home, his home in Greece, to the house where he was a guest.

Of course he had not STOLEN the truck. He had just BORROWED it! The genius. Oh excellent and wonderful Mr Filipides.

At last Thomas rose to his feet, supported by an interpreter, black eyes making him look quite pitiful. He earnestly told of how sorry he was and repeated his claim of really not remembering a 'ting'!

The accounting came next. Some pretty hefty demands for the truck. Our lawyer, despite being a friend, must be paid something. Court costs. It added up. He had his choice. He could pay the fines, the court costs and the damages or spend three months in jail.

While Thomas reeled with shock, we sighed with relief. It was far better than we had feared. We shook hands all round. Even with the fishmongers, who to this day cheerily greet me.

We then sat down with the manacled Thomas to try to work things out. Stamos simply couldn't understand him, despite his brogue being an easy one. I translated. Quite a reversal from the norm, a pleasant change.

Being an artist, on his first tour abroad, this 'bizarre' situation had happened. The very idea of prison appalled him. It was agreed that I should try to call Ireland for a loan of something over €1,000. (One thousand pounds.) Not his parents he insisted, who with seven children wouldn't be very pleased. But he thought that his Uncle Gorry might help?

He was led away to the cells, calling desperately over his shoulder. 'Try! Please Judith, TRY!'

For some unknown reason Eire didn't take reverse calls. We were, with the wedding coming up, pretty strapped for cash. I waited till Stamos was having his siesta, and crept downstairs to phone directly to Uncle Gerry in Eire.

Poor man, it must have been quite a shock. A long distance call, from Greece and from a strange Englishwoman. Asking for one thousand two hundred pounds to bail out his nephew Tom. Heaven knew who I was. (I could be a thief myself.) Properly hesitant, he took my phone number and said he'd call me back.

Within the hour the call came. But not from Uncle Gerry. Instead a cheery voice introduced himself as a Mr McCarthy, of the Garda and a friend of Uncle Gerry. He was checking me out. We got along like a house on fire.

'He isn't a BAD boy, Mr McCarthy,' I told him earnestly, 'just an idiot.' He agreed. 'In fact I'd say from short acquaintance, he's a real softie.' We agreed again. 'A week, or even two inside won't do him any harm. It's a nice little prison, near us. We can visit him often. But longer? No, I don't think so. It might bruise him and I don't think he needs or deserves that.'

Very definitely, we agreed again.

'You are a woman after me own heart', sang out Mr McCarthy (which warmed mine).

I was cordially invited to visit, if ever in County Cork. I still mean to do so.Poor Uncle Gerry. Dear good Uncle Gerry. He sent the money so promptly that Thomas had little more than a week to endure his incarceration. Quite an experience, not all bad. Something no doubt he can laugh over now and for the rest of his life.

Honestly, I do not deny that this was an unfortunate incident, but justice was done. It simply isn't ON to travel in other countries, steal, borrow or cause damage, for any reason. However funny or bizarre it was, basically Tom was at fault. It is not enough to blame the demon drink. He came back to the farm, like a beaten puppy, very soft and grateful.

Of all the amazing things I had been given by the young people, The Lectern for the church was one of the most interesting. Two pine trees had pressed together and naturally sealed. When they fell, the kids carefully sawed them up to make a curious piece of art, tripod for legs, with two branches aloft. On the top two branches, we fixed a shelf for the Bible, and on the other, an old scrap-iron four-piece candelabra. Properly painted up, it made a useful and interesting, if different lectern. Tom, an artist after all, got to work and did some charming decorating on it for the wedding.

Three weeks before the Big Day, we received a telegram.

'Much regret that I cannot officiate at your daughter's wedding. Christ is Risen. Papa Pirunakis.'

Oh my poor Stamos! Down he went, down as usual, into the lowest depths of despair; he was distraught. Father Pirunakis was not coming. Stamos was quite convinced that this was personal, and that something had occurred which had turned the good priest against him.

The phone rang incessantly. It seemed that everyone he knew was being called upon to solve the mystery. Why could he not come? Why now, should there be a personal vendetta against him?

'They want to hit me,' he mourned. 'It is a political move to hurt me through my daughter's wedding.' He would not be comforted. I was thoroughly at sea. I could not understand how all the family and friends were in such a state, there had to be a logical explanation.

Then at last word came through Mary, quite one of his nicest friends from his youth. A friend of a friend of hers had found out that poor Father Pirunakis was ill. His throat was so bad, he had been ordered by his doctor to cancel all engagements. Relief swept over everybody. Stamos almost recovered. So although there was nothing political about it, we were still left without a priest for our very special day.

Then, out of the blue the idea hit me. UP the Union Jack!

'I will go and ask the bishop if he will come,' said I. Such a brain-wave! This was not at first greeted by the wild enthusiasm I had expected. Perhaps, surprised, it was gradually however greeted with a glimmer of hope.

I rose early, did my chores, took quite a lot of trouble over my appearance and drove to the bishop's palace. It is a fine building near the sea, one I had often driven past but this was the first time I was to enter. I was met by a black-robed young priest who enquired my business. He disappeared and returned. Then he led me into an anteroom which was full of fellow supplicants. I sat down, now actually there, feeling rather fearful.

The other supplicants were mostly elderly Rom or gyftis. With nothing else to do I observed the subtle differences between them. Gyftis are gypsies, travellers, not blood Romany. Both peoples have a hard life and their mutual hatred of each other must in some way give them strength. I noticed that some held medicine bottles in their hands. Most were fat old women, as usual traditionally dressed in flounced skirts and tops of vivid if tatty material. I noticed too, that they were not as usual laden with jewellery. Indeed they seemed to wear none. So either they were genuinely poor, or had the wit to remove their gold while asking for alms. I used to be so indignant when on the underground in Athens, gyftis, their gold teeth gleaming, used to beg from me.

The young priest ushered each supplicant through a door at the far end, then, after awhile, out. It never seemed to be my turn. I remember I wore a soft blue cotton dress. It was strange for me to be just sitting. I never sat. Life was far too busy. While I sat I grew perturbed, for every time a supplicant moved up, went in, came out, the young priest moved me to the back of the queue. Why? Anyway, it gave me time to practise what I was going to say. Time passed.

At last the room was empty and I was ushered into a light and cool study. The bishop sat behind a large desk. A handsome, pale and austere looking man, he no doubt knew exactly who I was. That it was I who had restored our church, and brought the ashes of Uncle Frederikos home. Living near a small town where everybody knew everything, it is likely and he was most civil to me, which was a great relief. It helped that he spoke perfect English. I had heard that he had done some of his studies at LSE, where Sebastian had been. It made a bond. I came to the point.

'Your Eminence. Thank you for giving me your time. My husband and I have six sons between us, and just one daughter. She is to be married soon, at our little church of Saint Nicholas of Bari on our farm. It will be a great honour for us if you will agree to officiate.'

He told me a little of Saint Nicholas; it seemed he was happy to talk. I told him that one of my sons had been at LSE. Then he opened a huge appointment book, all white, and ran a finger down to the date, the 8th of May.

'What a good thing you want me for that day, for I am busy the next.'

I told him we would like the ceremony at five o'clock, if it suited him. It did. I was so pleased, smiling broadly in happiness, for this would restore Stamos' good humour, delight the in-laws and make a special day even more special.

I can't remember if I shook hands with him, I can't have, but I do know that I did not kiss his ring (ignorant woman). But he smiled me out very graciously and now, relieved and joyful, I with wings on my heels, flew home with the news.

'Hurray, hurray! The bishop is coming for Maria's wedding!'

The day was saved. Everybody was delighted.

Chapter 10

Maria's Wedding

Our lives were normally busy, but life before the wedding it was a frantic whirl. The phone never stopped, people were coming and going endlessly. There was still a farm to run, animals to milk and feed. I worked. And worked.

I had noted a large fridge outside a closed taverna on the fringe of town belonging to a young man we knew slightly. I suggested to Stamos that we ask if we might borrow it. HOW, after all, would I manage otherwise? It needed mending. It was mended. Now, and once again, the Cheopery came in very useful; that huge thing was parked in there. The days before the wedding I would be baking brown rolls, from our own wheat of course, to stash in there. Then I learned that the Morris men were all vegetarian, so plans were made for non-meat dishes. I prepared huge Greek dishes of mushy peas and beany messes, houmous and goodness knows what else. That fridge would serve its purpose.

The weekend before the big day it poured with rain, real monsoon stuff. We hoped and prayed that our weekend would be dry. Early May can be risky. Nonetheless, I approached the man in charge of the earthquake committee and begged the loan of some tents. He obliged, and they were collected and stored in the barn. Now if we were caught short, there would be substantial canvas for young visitors to sleep under.

Our excellent neighbours the Elliotts, who had a lovely villa at the end of our land, offered Maria's in-laws hospitality over the wedding. Marvellous.

Wine was bought, barrels of it. Crates of Kiar champagne too. Apart from our own production, offers of lambs, kids and a pig were totted up, for of course we had no idea how many guests would be coming. We expected this to be virtually an all-day affair. A traditional Greek lunch would be served mid-day after the morning services. After the wedding there was to be dancing and a buffet supper, in the barn. We rightly supposed that the locals would be around all day, and attend all the functions. We guessed that quite a lot of the Athenians would be arriving just for the wedding in the afternoon. Greece is not an RSVP country.

Father Nick was invited to do the service for the Saint Day, as well as officiate at the baptism. We were by now, and thank heaven, firm friends.

Suddenly, I was asked about a wedding dress for Maria. It had just not entered my mind that I was to provide this too, and I had done nothing. I thought about calling my sister to send one, but my sister-in-law thankfully took over. She found a lovely, very simple fine white lawn dress which had been her mother's and worked on that. It couldn't have been nicer. Stamos rotovated, then rolled all around the church to make a tidy surface.

Two local English friends, Jenny and her Aunt Barbara, offered to do the flowers in the church. The deluge of rain the previous weekend had given the herbage a huge boost; the farm was ablaze with colour. So we would be using wild flowers throughout. Perfect.

I was even organised with the funny mechanics of it. For beans of all sorts, lentils and rice all come in neat little plastic bags in Greece.

(Hence Xrysoula had often found it so easy to pop a couple from my store cupboard into her pantaloons.) I had horded these little bags neatly, just for the panayieri. They were ideal for keeping the wild-flower bunches fresh; tucked into the bags with a little kitchen paper dipped in water around the stalks and they looked good for several days.

My sister-in-law rang daily. We raced about, determined to get done what she wanted. Although it is merely eighty kilometres from Athens, our lives were worlds apart. We were going to have a country wedding, but it had to be good, for even if unofficial and outdated, Stamos was quite definitely, 'the squire'. And after all, he only had one daughter to marry.

Another call came from my sister-in-law in Athens.

'You must hire two hundred polythrones.' (Chaise-longues/long deck chairs.)

Now my sister always said that I was a Ninny and she should know, she's known me long enough. Well as far as the family was concerned, I supposed I was. No one else would have put up with the continual barrage of flak I got from them. As with many other orders I received over the years, my mouth metaphorically fell open. How the hell was I to hire two hundred polythrones? Ours was a one-horse town (and that horse was mine). Where, for heaven's sake could I begin to find two hundred polythrones? (It is pronounced – poly throne-ess, lovely word!)

I went to several shops in town to enquire. They like me were flummoxed. I had the promise of seven all told. I simply did not know what to do.

Then it dawned. Always resourceful, I felt the germ of an idea taking form. Now I knew that the huge hotel across the bay had polythrones, and I thought it might be worth a try to borrow some. Out with the charm. I rang up and asked a receptionist if the manager would receive the wife of the local French Consul. An appointment was made. On, once again, went the blue cotton dress.

It was probably my best day dress at the time. I drove across the bay and went to meet the manager who turned out to be a Greek from Alexandria. Now Stamos had always told me that they are the best of Greeks. He was most charming. So much so, I immediately confessed that I had used Stamos' official title just to get in and promptly put my request.

'Could I borrow two hundred polythrones for the wedding?'

However, always believing that nothing is free in life, I also told him that we had a band of Morris men staying, and they had agreed to dance for his guests in exchange. With a smile, he agreed to both proposals. Another summit reached.

The weather promised fair. Jenny and Barbara, our florists, toiled away in the church on the day before the wedding. Little bunches of flowers were tied, wrapped in wet kitchen paper, and put into the bean/lentil plastic bags. Anything which would hold them, was decorated. The whole lot was then finished by draping ivy on top to conceal the plastic bags. Corn daisies galore, mallow, cornflowers, a riot of all the field flowers, made our little church finer than any expensive affair. Everything looked different, natural and wonderful.

The young men dug a long pit for the souflãs, for roasting the meat. Our super neighbours, voices raised, were very much in charge. While the whole place was a hive of industry, I was seriously beginning to come to the end of my tether. (Understatement!) Requests were endless. Each person considered theirs the most important. The phone rang. Taxis arrived with people or gifts. I had to feed a swelling family as well as cope with the animals.

A fleet of young farmers cheerfully drove their pick-ups back and forth across the bay collecting the two hundred polythrones. Then, they dotted them all about the front of the farm amongst the orange trees.

Early on the morning of THE day, the neighbours, the Petropolous and Mixalis the shepherd, arrived to light the fires. It was at about four o'clock. We staggered up and made jugs of coffee to take around.

Just because I had been so charmed with the flowers in the church the night before, I escaped from the scrum for some moments to go in to admire it again. Oh but OH! It was full of bees!

Smelling the flowers I suppose, they must have entered by the two little side windows. It was amazing. I stood there listening to them, smelling the flowers too and wondering whether to laugh or cry. Instead I sat down on the altar step and decided to ask them to leave. Very politely, I silently explained the situation and asked, them, please, please leave, come back tomorrow.

Then went out, propping the door wide open. The next time I checked, a couple of hours later, they had gone!

Things were hotting up at the house. My sister-in-law arrived with a host of excellent women helpers. The kitchen was overflowing it seemed, the phone rang constantly, people arrived, questions, answers. There were just too many people!

I heard another taxi draw up in front of the house. Feeling I could not take one more person, I hid in the corner behind the door. It opened and a raucous voice called out,

'Anybody at home?'

I started crying, for it was Nuffy. After some good hugs and a lot of nose blowing, she left me and swept off into the melee. For Nuffy could speak Greek, albeit Australian Greek and Nuffy was a worker. Suddenly I did not feel alone, (silly expression with that crowd) for here was a true friend, an ally, and during all of that day, my right hand.

We gathered at the church for the Service for the Saint, it was all held outside as usual, so I need not have worried about the bees. But of course everyone went in to light their candle and to admire it. For the flower arrangements were truly charming and quite new to Greek people. Immediately there followed the baptism of my fifth god-daughter. With only sons, I had passed the word that goddaughters would be very welcome. I was proud to have Serena, Samantha, Emilie, Anastasia and now Marianna.

We went through the ceremony with the usual shrieks from the poor baby and laughter from us. A tubby little thing, she was too small to put up much of a fight, even so, she yelled! Dear little girl. As usual Father Nick conducted it beautifully.

The traditional feast was held on long white sheet-covered tables. Out of the pits came succulent roasted lamb, kid and pig, eight in all I think. The experienced shepherds, Dimitris and Mixalis were in control with their valiant wives behind them.

My Rom koumbara, Paniota arrived looking gorgeous, clean, bright and loaded down with jewellery. My little Rom goddaughter Anastasia hung on to my hand until she found Fredo, and then they were off. Then a group of Rom musicians arrived, I'm not even sure that they were invited but they played splendid Rom music on their ancient instruments while lunch was being served. I caught sight of some merry interaction between them and the Morris men. Some exchanges of instruments took place too. Poor Rom, three strings to a fiddle, battered and bent, they were delighted to meet these really friendly, strangely dressed foreigners who played so beautifully.

A smart woman who I did not know came up to Paniota and rudely asked her what she was doing there. But as I was near by I heard her.

'She is my koumbara, I replied, eyes narrowed, 'a special guest' (which quietened her). Even so, I told Anastasia and Paniota to stay close to me. Lunch dragged on, with runners to and from the house with plates galore. In all that hectic activity, the inevitable spoilt few Athenians came marching into the kitchen demanding coffee!

There was a lull after lunch, except in the house, still a madhouse, where the poor women were washing up like demons. It was quite clear that I did not have enough tea cloths. Outside in the spring sunshine, the polythrones came into their own. No orange tree did not have a replete guest asleep under it in the shade. Clever sister-in-law, it had been worth it!

Preparations in the bride's room got under way. As is the custom, countless lovely and laughing damsels were coming and going, giving support. The beautician mother of good friend Galatia was making Maria up. I had made her head dress, a simple wreath of orange leaves and blossom. As they were fresh, they wouldn't last for long, but they would get through the day. Her bouquet was the same except for the necessary blue; I had added some cornflowers. The soft pale blue did look pretty with the orange blossom. She wore my pearls. She looked absolutely lovely,

Stamos was now dressed in his dark suit, shirt and tie. It was quite unusual to see him looking so smart. When he came out of the house at about a quarter to five or so, I saw with horror that he was also wearing his fannella. A fannella is a thick wool vest, often long sleeved, worn by all the peasants, whatever the weather. And here he was, the squire, father of the bride, in his very best, and there for all to see ON TOP of his shirt, was his fannella.

'Get inside this minute,' snapped I, 'and take off that fannella!'

So shocked was he, for I rarely scolded him, that in he went like a lamb, whipped off the fannella and in record time reappeared without it.

The bishop and entourage arrived and I went with them to the church. The bishop then began to be robed at the altar end. I found the Reverend Jeremy Peake, Anglican priest in Athens and friend and I led him into the church to meet the bishop. Women (unclean) are not supposed to go into the altar area. (Who, I always asked, cleans it then?) So I got pretty short shrift until I drew Jeremy forward. Then we were all smiles and welcome.

When the ceremony was finished, suddenly, like a heavenly choir, a newly arrived group of strangers burst into song. Tony Elliott from the villa at the end of the land had organised them to come. Obviously a very professional group of ecclesiastical singers, they arrived in the nick of time. It was a total surprise and most beautiful. Greek plain-song I suppose, no instruments, just fine voices in perfect harmony. This surely was the gilt on the gingerbread, we were more than touched by that generous gesture. Everyone was impressed, not least I hope, the bishop himself, who then quietly left.

Looking at all the photographs of the day, I see myself in the morning during the baptism, then in the evening. I do not exist during the wedding ceremony. True, I was still busy, inevitably running to and fro trying to please everyone. But true also is the miserable fact that I was, even on that special day, being subjected to the old familiar unpleasantness. It had been brewing for days, even influencing the group of new young workers who I hadn't yet bonded with. Because of this, I did not really attend the wedding, just hung about on the fringe. When the ceremony was over, when the guests queued up to shake hands with the family, I quietly withdrew. For I did not want any accusation, that I had pushed myself forward. I was not Maria's mother, I was just a stand-in. I was not even family. I would not have it that anyone could criticise me for assuming any importance. So back to the house and back to work for the evening's feast.

Having sent out invitations far and wide, the Morris men did come and as their gift, danced for us. In the distance I did see the Morris men jumping up and down, clacking their sticks, the bride and groom joining them. I heard later that our Greek guests were somewhat amazed by the unexpected show. The few Brits who were also there must have been surprised too, but just enjoyed it as usual.

A friend of the family had offered to provide a disco in the evening so this was being set up. Every able-bodied soul was drawn into the transport of tables, chairs and benches. All these were hauled from the field near the church and put into the barn. I have had many very busy days in my life but perhaps that was the worst, for I have curious blanks about it. I do remember shoving tray upon tray of my brown rolls into the oven to crisp them up from the newly acquired fridge. I don't remember a lot. At one point I did change my dress for one more comfy, and with profound relief removed my smart shoes which were killing me. I truly do not remember what I served up for the evening meal. I do however remember dragging the British Ambassador to his feet and having a whirl with him.

There were three Ambassadors, British, French and South African, I think, and several Consuls. We were so honoured with their presence and our do must have been quite a change from what they were used to. It was also quite a sight to have their extremely smart cars parked out there in front of the house.

A sorry little incident occurred while the party went on in the barn. A gifty girl, presumably having seen the activity from the road, arrived and began going through the guests trying to sell plastic combs. No Rom would have done that. When Stamos saw her, his rage knew no bounds, he was furious and all set to get violent. I managed to get her to leave while he hollered away that he would call the police.

The three tiered cake was cut, toasts drunk and champagne flowed. Maria's mother-in-law, officially so now, happily told me that she thought it had been the wedding of the year.

'Symphony!' We were entirely in harmony in that.

No one wanted to leave the party and why should they? A fine evening, music, food and wine, why indeed. The elders crawled off, while the youth kept up their dancing for hours. We crept to bed exhausted, it had been a very, very long day. My feet hurt terribly, in fact I am ashamed to say that my toe nails went black and eventually came off. All this due to foolish vanity and toiling all day in those silly smart shoes. And they didn't grow back for six months.

Next day, the Morris dancers went up to the Rom camp to dance for them, which was greatly appreciated. That evening, the poly-thrones all safely returned, they danced, as agreed, for the guests of the hotel. Who, they told me sadly, seemed somewhat unenthusiastic.

We began the big clear up, it seemed endless. I toured the orchards with a crate and collected up glasses ad infinitum. Then back to the kitchen to wash them up, then out, for the next lot. How very untidy and careless people are. While I washed up, drained and dried, I felt the invisible daggers of pure hatred at my back, and just got on with my work feeling depressed. For that beautiful, successful, very hard day, had been spoilt for me just by this one malevolent person. Not only was I tired, I became sad, oh so sad. When Stamos came into the kitchen to see what I was doing, he saw my face and understood. Hadn't we after all suffered a similar situation together just after Fredo's birth? He kissed me and left. No words were spoken, they weren't necessary. For he surely understood that for me anyway, another special occasion in our lives had been ruined.

Half an hour later while still at the sink, and to my great surprise, my tormenter appeared and cheerfully asked how I thought the day had gone. Gob smacked, again. How to cope with this sudden switching of emotions? One moment all hate, the next bright and friendly as if it had never been otherwise. I said I thought it was a huge success.

Later I asked Stamos what he had done to provoke that total turnaround.

'I told him that you alone had, by your imagination and hard work, made the day possible. I told him that no one could have done more for his sister than you.'

I felt a great warmth and gratitude to Stamos who for once had so perfectly supported me. I basked in the love, peace and lightness of mood which pervaded our home. It was really nice while it lasted.

Stamos was wiped out and lounged about in the saloon happily taking congratulatory calls from all his friends

It was suggested that over the day, there had one thousand guests, but I, as the caterer knew it was more like seven hundred. (My feet knew it too.) Whatever, it had been, and using one of Stamos' favourite expressions, 'a triumph'.

Then the rot set in. We were utterly deflated. After so much organisation and toil, we were a burst balloon. The weekend after the wedding was exactly as had been the one before it, the monsoons came. We had been very lucky.

Nuffy, Fredo and I went to an island for a week. She did a drawing and took snaps of the dove-cots which abounded, and with a collection of my homespun, natural dyed wools, eventually made a most attractive, rustic tapestry. Later when back home, she even won a prize for it.

We returned with a deformed kitten who quickly joined the menagerie and made himself at home. Nuffy then went to the mountain house for a week before returning to Australia. The reason she had come was because Peter was at sea, trying to get his skipper's ticket and she had been feeling very lonely. A teacher, she had abandoned her school and gone to work on a shrimp boat as cook. In between feeding the crew, she also worked on deck. So albeit very lonely and missing Peter, she had earned a lot of money. I had written to her when I could, sensing that she really needed contact, and sent her an invitation to the wedding. Then, on the spur of the moment she booked her flight and came. I drove her up and left her for the week at Spiti Sebastian.

One neighbour I have not mentioned in the mountains lived below us with his wife. She was a sweet old woman, very deaf so shrieked all the time. I often used to hear her yelling at him, 'You are bad! You are a bad man.'

They had married late and had no children, which I fear was partly the root of their troubles. He was woman-mad! We heard that he used to go to Athens occasionally to the bazouki shows. Apparently he paid for favours with little barrels of cheese. Somehow, he got them out of their cheese room without her knowing, probably while she was out with the sheep. She immediately thought it stolen, and we, foreigners to boot as their nearest neighbours, were accused. Not surprisingly the old B happily supported her during all this tirade. I was sad when she hung a tatty old blanket over the entrance to the cheese room to forbid entry, for it was quite fascinating. Their fetta was excellent and how they did it I can't imagine. Everything was so ramshackle, her cheese cloths so old and stained. I'm afraid she didn't have a very happy life for he drank too much as well as everything else. Whenever he could, he used to come around so quietly we never heard him until he was there, right by us on the terrace. Leer? It was frightful. As foreign women had a bad name for being loose, (there is no smoke without fire!) he seemed convinced that we girls were available. So I am afraid all our young women at the mountain house had trouble with him. He would creep up to spy on them sunbathing. End of sunbathing. I did not actually like lone girls going there, for fear they might come to harm. He was a fool. When Fredo was young, I always had him close by me as defence when I went down to their house to buy cheese. Nothing daunted, he soon had his hand on my leg. Because we were all jolly, friendly girls, he thought in his crooked way, we were making advances to him. When Ann, she with the beautiful smile which she bent on everybody, asked me why he stood there with a five thousand drac note in his hand, I fell about laughing.

I can't remember when I started to call him 'Pattifingers' (from the old film *The Quiet Man*) but the mischievous Spiros heard me and soon it was all over the village. So I asked Pappoo and Yaya to keep and eye on Nuffy, who actually being a tough cookie really was fine. Unfortunately her quiet week did not materialise for she was bothered by all of them. Pattifingers came snooping around at least twice a day, and Pappoo and Yaya constantly went to check up if she was all right. Poor Nuffy, it turned out to be a most unrestful week.

When another crisis presented itself, the threat of prison again I believe, Nuffy unwisely lent Stamos money. Over the years, whenever she asked for repayment, her requests were ignored. I did, whenever I could, send her cash from England, but the bulk of that debt has never been re-paid, disgraceful.

355

Chapter 11

More of the Mountains

An all too frequent occurrence, mostly in the summer, was first hearing, then watching the fire planes going over. We might be working on the land when the familiar drone of the elderly prop jobs alerted us. They did a valiant job. There was no mistaking their noise, a deep, resonating growl. Fires are far too common in Greece. Precious forests which take so long to grow are wiped out in minutes. I would stand mourning and watch the planes going over and work out how big the fire was according to how many planes there were, and what size.

They are painted yellow, and the big two-men ones are Canadian. The small one-man planes are Polish and originally they were often used to crop spray. They had a nickname, 'The Flying Coffins' for and alas, a lot of them did come down.

Nowadays they also use helicopters.

I honestly suspect that most fires are started from careless smokers. There was the time when Carol and I were talking inside Spiti Sebastian when, unthinking, she threw her fag-end out of the window. A neighbour swooped down on us, scolding, and rightly.

Because a glowing cigarette end can cause a tiny fire which will creep along unseen for hours before it reaches something really dry. Then, and with a waft of breeze, it will ignite into a real fire and cause terrible damage. Otherwise, fire can be caused by glass left around amongst the rubbish. In the past, bottles were always returnable as Greece was so poor, everyone religiously collected together their bottles to return for a few drax. Now, much is non-returnable. Every church has a midden around at the back where horrid, tacky old bottles are thrown. Having carried olive oil as a gift from the faithful to light the lamps, they are too arduous to wash out, so are abandoned. Even a reflection from far off, can so easily cause a blaze. As I have mentioned before, foreigners are frequently blamed. Well, it seems that blame has to be put at someone's door. The really big, and simultaneous fires which do occur occasionally are frequently blamed on political activists. I just cannot believe it! How can an opposition do such a thing? It is their country too after all. Yet undoubtedly when fires do start approximately at the same time all over Greece, one does wonder. With several fires raging at the same time, the planes are very hard pressed to cope.

We were having lunch with the Elliotts one Sunday along the coast half way to Athens when we became aware that the breeze was HOT. Slowly, it became apparent that the sky due west was dark, then suddenly realisation dawned. Fire!

We drove quickly back to the farm, but no, it was further west, and my heart sank. For it was in the mountains. We called friends to find out and sure enough it was very serious, a front of many kilometres. The pitch pine trees were burning at a terrific rate and soon the sun was completely blotted out and sky above us was black as with a terrible storm. Later I learnt that the police had toured the threatened areas with loudspeakers and that our village had been evacuated. Except that is, for the shepherds. For they have their old ways to survive, and they had driven their flocks down into deep ravines, so that hopefully, the fire would sweep over them.

The planes were busy. It is an amazing sight to see them working. Just once I happened to see them from way above, which was very interesting. It was a small fire, on the outskirts of a village, not in the forests. Someone had obviously been tidying up an orchard and their bonfire had got out of hand. The little plane swept down to the sea, skimmed the surface of the water and rose. Then it did a circuit and flew to the fire and just at the right moment, it released its load. It was extraordinary watching from above, it was just as a toy.

We could not go to see if the mountain house was all right for about a week. Small fires re-ignited here and there so constant vigilance was needed. When at last we did go up, it was fearful shock. Miles upon miles of forests were blackened. Smoke rose, like a scene from hell. It was as I imagine it would be going through a war zone. What trees had not burnt to the ground were so charred, they would never revive.

The planes had stopped the fire two kilometres outside our village, a miracle everyone declared. Good piloting too.

Now began a huge labour and, as is always the way, out of tragedy some good comes. It took a couple of years to clean up. First, the mountains echoed with the sound of chainsaws. Men and machines worked on clearing the gentle slopes. Teams of mules struggled up the high slopes to bring down the wood. Great tall mules had logs strapped on their strong wooden saddles and would stagger down to meet the trucks on the road. There, at a pull of a rope, the logs would topple off, the poor mules dancing in the hope they would not get hurt. But poor things often did hurt their legs. I became friends with the muleteers and whenever we went up, I left fruit and vegetables in their hut for them. For it must have been quite a lonely task. They were, I think, all from the north, the mules too. I had never seen such mules before, great tall creatures they were. An unenviable task, for man and beast.

What had been a peaceful drive up, now was anything but. Logging cabins sprouted here and there, and great trucks loaded high would crawl down the dirt roads while we tried to keep out of their way. There were all manner of amazing machines, and of course, The Boy, was terribly thrilled. He strained to see around each corner what was coming up next. As most were totally new to us, we could not tell him the names so he cooked up his own. Every single machine was jubilantly called a, 'Dgu, dgu'.

One machine, which I can only describe as a giant pencil sharpener, was parked in a widening of the road. Here the charred, long lengths of tree were scraped semi clear of the burnt bark, to make a smoother surface. Everything was blackened, including the men. Ever curious, I eventually discovered what they were doing with the long logs.

All the cleaned straight poles were loaded on to trucks which then drove to the port of Volos. There they were loaded on to ships and transported to the Middle East where they would be used for telegraph poles. One man's loss is another man's gain. No doubt and hopefully, a good exchange was made.

When the slopes were cleared, the bulldozers arrived for the next stage. It was amazing to watch great steps being formed on the mountain side, a slow, precarious looking job. Puzzled, we watched each time we went up, till eventually we learned the reason. Magnificent re-planting then began. Not just the boring old fir trees again, but mixed forests, including broad-leaf trees of many kinds. We were much impressed and pleased. This really was a magnificent job of organisation by the Forestry Department. Once the little trees were in, next came the difficult task of watering them during the summer. Water tankers crawled along the roads while teams of women, pulling down long hoses, went from tree to tree. Of course not all survived, but very many have done. It will be a magnificent new forest before long. A gentle German boy called Andreas was with us on and off for a long time. He had a big old Alsatian bitch, a kind dog, but one who did not make travelling easy for him as many were afraid of her. He asked me if he could spend some time at the house, so I drove him up. As our neighbours were elderly, I had always told anyone who stayed there that they must not use up the wood round about but gather it from further away. The old ones needed it more than we did. So on our way up, we stopped here and there and loaded up the chippings and small logs left behind by the wood men, so that Andreas could be well supplied. We stopped off along the road and as we collected the wood, we tossed it into the back of the pick-up. Then as I was throwing a piece, a splinter dug deep into my thumb and hurt dreadfully. There and then I tried to get it out with a safety pin. Andreas tried. Two old shepherds passed by and they tried, all to no avail. A dirty old pin and lots of dirty old hands! By the time I got home my thumb was throbbing badly, yet the damned splinter was in so deep, we could not remove it.

Finally, and to my shame, two days later I crawled in to the hospital and explained my problem. Things looked pretty quiet there, thank goodness. A kindly lady doctor set to work on the now thoroughly swollen thumb. It was so painful I thought I would faint so ended up on a stretcher. Apparently it had done a 'dum-dum', going off in several directions. No wonder we couldn't remove it!

During July and August, I went up to the house as often as I could. Sebastian came out and together we put up a Heath Robinson division in the cellar. It was so cool down there, and with a tiny square window I thought it would make a fine bedroom. The beams were magnificent, huge and strong. I see them now.

The floor being earth was a problem, for by then I certainly did not have the money to floor it properly. Over time I laid very thick builder's plastic sheeting down, then every scrap of hand spun wool carpeting that I could find over the years. Topped with some lovely Roumanian rugs, it looked fine, even if it was a little uneven. The new wall looked horrid with our amateur hardboard tacked up, but luckily my old trunk produced another of my very special treasures, which came in useful. An old hand-embroidered cloth; you could see that it had been made on a narrow loom. Magnificent work, it covered the wall perfectly. I never knew what country it had originated from although I do believe it was an old Souzani. The flowers and colours were wonderful. I used to lie in bed and gaze at it in the gloom and wonder how many talented women had laboured over it. Then, just tucked in there, a clue to those, unlike me, who knew, was a tiny coffee pot. This made a separate bedroom which could, at a pinch, sleep four. It was magic to go up, to be able to breathe, to be cool and to sleep with a sheet or even a light blanket!

So we also had a proper storeroom, reached via the trap-door from upstairs by the wobbly old ladder and the cellar door. It was extremely useful for all the junk, gas bottles, herbs, skis and so forth. I proudly hung up my little bags of stores there, like a real village women.

Sometimes Stamos came up with us. He loved it too. But he always considered it his holiday, and did not do a thing. While as usual I worked away, he lay on the bed, all the shutters and doors open, and read. I used to call him Ali Pasha. It was indeed, a house of contentment.

Occasionally we had fantastic storms in the mountains. It felt as if the roof was coming in with thunder, lightening and deluges of rain. On one such occasion just the three of us were up there and Fredo called out, 'What is happening mummy?'

Quick thinking mum came out with, 'It's God, shifting about his furniture.' Which was well received.

In the bathroom at the farm there was a big old sideboard. Here we kept all manner of medicines, usually donated by kids on their way West, at the end of their travels. Whenever anyone was going further East, we would go through it and supply them with what they might need. Most however, were intelligent and already had their medicine bags properly equipped. There was the occasion when we were trying to find gyppy tummy pills, for two who were off in that direction.

'But,' said Kathy, a nice American girl who mucked in with the best, 'I've been there, and I wasn't ill.' We were interested. The

361

travellers got out their note books to write down the names of the hostels for future reference.

'Where did you stay?' they asked.

'The Hilton.' she replied.

After the laughing had died down, we asked ourselves WHY she was slumming it with us. I really do think that she was the one exception.

In the early spring, Flo, another kind German boy who had been away, reappeared with two very young Swedes in tow. He had found them in some distress, waiting for the arrival of their money. So he had taken them into his tent, shared his one sleeping bag with them, and as quickly as possible, had brought them to the farm. They were younger than most of our workers, sixteen or seventeen. Apparently they had saved up their earnings as paper boys, and were off to see the world.

During meals, we all talked of course, hence I overheard their plans. Next stop, South Africa. I was concerned, for at that time South Africa was a country in dire trouble. Two white kids on their own, knowing no one, with not so much money, were really asking for trouble. Now it was none of our business, but as it often happened, we tried to guide our young travellers on their way.

'It is a great big world, boys,' I told them. 'There are many calmer countries to visit, and closer. Why South Africa now, when there is so much trouble there, and you are so young. Why can't you wait to go there when you are older. Things might be quieter then too.'

I spoke to them as if they were my own sons. The miracle is, that they listened.

The softer of the two had a phone call from home. After he had spoken for some moments he called me. His father greeted me in admirable English (of course). After thanking me for advising the boys of wiser and safer travels, he asked if there was any gift he could send us. I thought rapidly. Then remembering the splendid plastic sledges of Scandinavia, which my boys had bought years before, I asked him if he would send our little boy a plastic sled. He said he would.

It arrived ages after, when I had quite forgotten all about it. A great big parcel, a marvellous bright red sledge; at the next opportunity, up it went to the mountain house to await the snow.

Unusually, I was up there alone with Frederikos. It was late summer and bliss to be away from the heat and toil of the farm. I sat on the front veranda with my spinning wheel, gazed at the magnificent views, and spun. I listened to the hundreds of sheep bells of unseen flocks in the distance, the occasional shout of a shepherd or bark of a dog. This was as near to heaven as one could get.

Fredo was pottering about downstairs. He had various vehicles which lived up there, so were old friends and well met. There was a yellow plastic beetle thing which he could sit on and scoot along using his legs. There was also a small trike, which he shoved along. The tractor was always left 'down'. He generally hauled the mountain vehicles up to the veranda, quite a feat, and scooted along, pausing at the front door, to be told, 'No traffic in the house!'

Then on to the French windows, where this order was repeated. It kept him busy for ages. For some reason it never failed to amuse him, or us. He never brought them in either.

On this day he seemed quietly cheerful pottering away in the store room, or on the terrace by the kitchen. The sounds were happy, so I grew complacent and went into a dream of serenity. With the rattle of my wheel on the wooden floor boards of the veranda, I didn't even note when his noises had stopped.

Then! A strange sound filled my ears, as an earthquake, or a truck unloading gravel. I stopped spinning and listened. The sound seemed to be going further away, down the hill, retreating until it all but disappeared.

Then! The most God Almighty row rose from the bottom of the hill. A flock of sheep, as one, opened their mouths and at the top of their voices, baa'd. Hanging over the bannister I tried to see what was going on. I couldn't. The sheep continued their cries of alarm, all one hundred or so of them. Gradually, interspersed with the baa'ing, I could hear my child laughing. And then, added to that, furious yelling from Pattifingers. My anxious cries of enquiry were joined to the racket.

It was a day to remember in our village. For sound carries in the mountains, and my, there were some sounds. Everyone up top knew something was going on. At the kaféneon they were alerted. Folk came hurtling down to see if we were all right.

Blessed child. Mad child. Stupid child! He had gone off down the mountain, in high summer, no snow, no greenery, just scree. He had taken off on the beautiful red sledge, and crashed into Pattifingers' flock of sheep. A soft landing for him, but, poor sheep, poor sledge! It had come all the way from Sweden, only to die before it had lived. For it was sorely damaged.

On the good side, Pattifingers was so happy to be quite the centre of attention that night. What was more, it was unusual to have something to talk about for once at the kaféneon. And no doubt for some time to come, to anyone who would listen. That mad Tripos child hurtling down the hill into his flock! Fortunately the sheep were unharmed, or I would have had a mammoth bill, for he was an old scoundrel. Miraculously, Fredo reappeared without even a scratch. Skatulaki, as Stamos always called him. (Little Shit). It was such a shame about the beautiful new red sledge.

Greece now a new member of the European Union, without a doubt everyone prospered. But oh dear, the waste, the criminal waste. Dumping was the new way to earn money. Not a lot, but enough not to bother to be decent farmers. I was incensed that tons and tons of our wonderful fruit would be simply tipped into a hole. In the winter, oranges, in the summer, apricots. Here we lived in a starving world, and we had fresh fruit which was so good, and no one wanted it. I wrote to Oxfam, the first big charity of the day, and asked them what if anything they could do about it. I reasoned that oranges would benefit the children of famine areas, while the peels would benefit any poor beast still able to eat. I did have a courteous reply, but not unexpectedly, pretty negative.

The European Union might give directives and organise payments, yet they were not very smart at following up what happened to the unwanted crops. It is no use just handing the job over; the harsh, bad old days still lingered in the minds of the men down the payment line. Why then should they pay to rent land on which to dump? Why should they pay to have holes bulldozed? Why should they pay to organise it all, and have the holes covered at the end of it? There was a much easier way, what is more, it was FREE. So no doubt, the cash would be pocketed.

A simple tour of the mountain dirt roads as a weekend outing, would produce likely spots, an easy solution. Wide areas where the trucks could dump, turn around and go home, were easily found. So our mountains were used, and two kilometres as the crow flies, there was a lemon dump. Day after day the loaded trucks arrived, backed up, tipped and pushed off. Easy.

In no time at all tiny, myriad fruit flies bred and multiplied. Our village, down wind I suppose, was over-run with them. It was terrible. The ceilings of the houses were black with them. Every surface was covered. Every shutter and door however tightly closed was to no avail. The milk and cheese suffered. It was indeed all but impossible to make the cheese. The people were desperate. Pleas to spray the hillside where lay the festering tons of lemons, were totally disregarded. It went on for weeks until I suppose, the situation died a natural death.

An old friend of Stamos and his lady came to visit from France. They were such a charming couple, with whom I am still in touch. Those two old boys from student days in Montpellier were so delighted to meet each other again. We gave them the key to the mountain house, knowing just how much they would love it. But they did not because of the plague of flies, and quickly had to remove themselves.

365

Something of this fiasco must have finally reached the proper authorities for it stopped and did not happen again.

With the end of summer, Maria came to stay, expecting her baby. I have one memory of that time which I deeply regret. It must have been a chilly evening, for we had lit the fire. Having never smoked in my life, I not only cannot cope with smokers, I actually physically suffer from cigarette smoke. Being just the step-mother didn't help, yet I did gently remonstrate with Maria for smoking over the years. No matter what I said, she did not stop, and now I saw that she was still smoking while she was pregnant. I was horrified. As her own mother was a chain smoker, and Stamos smoked little cigars, she had always ignored me, and did so now. Then I saw a whole, sealed pack of cigarettes on a small table near the fireplace. My hand came out, as an automaton, picked it up and dropped it in the flames. The whole lot burnt up in moments. I was ashamed of my action, but it was done. After some searching around the house, and when she had failed to find them, Maria asked me if I had seen them. My answer was,

'You know I do not smoke.' Which at least was true.

Once more the medical supplies in the sideboard in the bathroom came in useful. One of my great stand-bys was a urine dip test. Whenever anyone was under the weather, out it came, and there was at least a hint of what was their trouble. Doctors were expensive, and frankly, a lot of them were at that time not much use. For example when I had meningitis and was told I had flu.

Maria came down one morning,

'Judy, I don't feel at all well.'

Out with the dip test, a potty of pee. And oh dear, I could see that Maria was not as she said, at all well.

'Bed!' said I. To bed she went, until David came to collect her to take her back to Athens.

Her daughter was born, the tiniest little doll of a baby. They called her Daphne. Stamos was jubilant, two grand-daughters; he really now was a truly respectable papoo (grandfather). We agreed that as with everything else, we should share these little people of the next generation. The family was growing again. Three little ones, three middle sized ones and three elders. I would in a couple of years anounce that we had a grand-son, and then another. Sadly we did not see much of these childen as they were not living in Greece. But they did come out for holidays, almost siblings to Frederikos, for they were so close in years, just behind him.

When Fredo was at school and speaking Greek well, he assumed that all children spoke Greek. When we visited Kassandra his first niece, in England, he chattered away to her for some time in Greek. I listened as he slowed down, aware that he was not getting a response.

'Do you speak English?' he asked.

When she said 'yes', off he went again, in English. Now they were communicating.

One Easter, when the three of them stayed at the farm together, he was very much the uncle, the middle man and translator. For Kassandra spoke no Greek and Daphne spoke no English. It was actually quite charming to see how they managed very well to play together. Now, years later, the three of them, good friends, have both languages.

Chapter 12

Daily Life

My efforts to get Fredo into a playschool were a dismal failure. Friends recommended one near the sea. I was told to visit just as they were closing for the day. I arrived a little early just to see what the kids were up to. It was shocking, it was so cold. They were all bundled up in their overcoats, because as she told me, they were ready to go home. I edged my way around the room to feel the radiators, stone cold. There was one gas heater which was off. No, quite definitely not.

Then Stamos heard of a government school for children of working mothers. I was certainly that, so delighted I took him. There was a large playground with colourful swings and seesaws, sandpits and slides. The head was a really nice woman who I knew slightly. She agreed to take Fredo. I decided to leave him there for three half-days, or until he was settled. When I went to collect him, (it was not at all far from the farm), I began to notice that none of the swings, seesaws etcetera were functioning. Nothing worked. The frames were there but nowt else. When I went in, I found all the little children sitting in their chairs being read to. I asked to see their work, for there were no drawings or paintings stuck up on the walls as is usual. It slowly dawned on me that in fact there was little. No clay, sand, paint or pencils. Fredo began making a fuss going in the mornings. The women told me that he was happy only when playing in the yard. As he barely spoke Greek, the stories were lost on him. In the morning, he hung on to the mini, me, anything rather than go in. I was so keen that he should learn Greek, I really wanted him to. On the fourth day I just brought him home, defeated. He had learnt one Greek phrase,

'Then thelie' which means 'He doesn't want!'

So he happily ran wild at home, and very slowly did learn Greek somehow.

Our herd of cattle was growing and we were selling milk privately and to the yoghurt man, when he couldn't get enough sheep milk. My great mistake had been buying Channel Island cows, those lovely girls with their wonderful high butter-fat YELLOW milk. It just did not cross my mind that Greeks, being used to white milk from goats and sheep, wouldn't like it. We enjoyed wonderful home-made everything. Butter, cheese and yoghurt. I prevailed upon friends coming out to bring me small quantities of different English cheeses, then using them as starters, experimented. To my surprise it worked. We had some extraordinary and exciting cheeses.

Calves began arriving. We had so much joy and fun waiting for and attending their births. We sat up in turns at night, I as ignorant as the rest of them, freezing in anticipation. Our first bull calf, Vassilis (born on Saint Basil's day, first of the year) we left intact as a bull. The second, I castrated using the rubber band method. It was a pity because he was a better calf, longer in the leg, more Guernsey and less scrub Holstein. But as he came second, it was his destiny, for how was I to know there would be another bull calf?

We were so thrilled with our calves, we put them in the small field at the front for the world to see. People often said that they never,

ever saw cows in Greece, and of course they don't often, for it is too hot. But in the north, or in the mountains there are plenty. I brought electric fencing back from England. Every day we would take them out and switch on the little unit, making sure that the usual zig-zag signs were hung up as a warning to trespassers. Big galvanised tubs of water would be filled mornings and at mid day, and I was surprised when I began to find little coins in them. Stamos soon enlightened me, joyfully pleased with his fellow countrymen for their gestures of goodwill.

For yes, here it was again, a coin for a new baby and 'Ftu, ftu!' The spit in the eye for the devil, should he be about.

Word got about that there were calves to be seen, and the townsfolk brought their children and their grandmothers to ooh and aah. Not only were there no calves to be seen in the district, surely there were none as pretty as these?

Then the day came when we were alerted by terrible screaming, and an irate woman tore up to the house threatening to call the police. Holding the still screaming child by the hand, she claimed that we had electrocuted her. Oh dear! Down the drive I went, all the while trying to pacify her. Obviously they had not met an electric fence before. The husband was there, angry though not quite so vocal. I pointed to the warning signs, surely they had seen them? But no, she would have none of it. We had no right to have such dangerous fencing for the public to hurt themselves on. I led the father to the unit, switched off, and showed him the battery. He was amazed and impressed. I then drew the now quiet child close and showed her what we used to do as kids. Plucking a long grass I made a big thing of moving it slowly, slowly up to the wire until, BANG, I got a shock too. Then I switched off and took her in and introduced her to the cows and calves.

'Next time you come by, come and see me and we will switch off and you can stroke the cows again.'

They went off more or less pacified. Whew!

Much as I loved my life, I missed so much of Britain. I missed the jumble sales, the fetes, the church bazaars. I missed contributing, organising, donating, to all those things. I was lonely too, lonely for the good company of good people trying to do good where it was needed. Stamos didn't understand any of this, because Charity barely exists in Greece, but he went along with it to make me happy.

So we did have a couple of clothing sales and a wool exhibition on behalf of the Animal Welfare. Run by an English lady who was royally supported by some very civilised and kindly Greek ladies, it was a great success and lots of people came. Although they were bewildered at first, we went round with them explaining so they soon got the hang of it. The Do was held on the south side of the house amongst the mandarin trees which were used as clothes racks. My little exhibition consisted of all my natural dyed wool hanging on the trees too, my spinning wheels underneath. I served up 'English Teas', and I think they did well.Inevitably, our 'Old Maid' (well doesn't every family have one?), came to me with bitter complaints. Surprising, as this was one who genuinely did love animals too.

'Never, has such been done in the history of this family. Never, has our house sunk so low. What kind of disgrace is this, hanging up brassieres to sell in our mandarin orchard?' (Misery guts!) And there were NO brassieres.

This time, happy with the successful day and good company, I did not let the usual critisim bother me and go down into the usual depression. Instead I laughed at the poor thing. Neither 'old' or 'Maid', just one of those silly people always ready to make trouble. There was not ONE brassiere hanging up in the trees! They were good second-hand clothes which a lot of our neighbours were very happy to buy for a few drax. The money earned went to a good cause, to help the poor abandoned animals of Greece!' But it was no use. It didn't matter what I did, it would be criticised.

When Vassilis was about ten months old a phone call came from Examilia.

'Kyria, I hear that you have a bull?'

I hesitated, for to me, Vassilis was still a calf. I explained that he was ten months old.

'That is good Kyria, can I bring my cow?'

Well, this was a new one. I said he could and wondered if our lad was able to do his stuff. Not long after the call a noise alerted me, a fearful mooing was coming down the road, then down our drive. A poor man, exhausted, red in the face, sweating from exertion and hanging on to a very noisy REAL scrub cow, arrived in a whirl of dust. Vassilis started up a noisy duet.

She was a poor little thing, rather small and skinny with long, pointed horns. Of course he knew his stuff. Except she, poor thing, was more on her knees than up because he was such a lump. Word spread, it seemed we had something no one else had. Well didn't we know about it from our days of trying to get the girls bred.

We were eating under the walnut trees when I heard unfamiliar sounds from the cow house. I went to investigate. Himself was free and out and delighted to see me, he bustled up for a scratch. We had screen doors to the house in order to keep the livestock out. They were fairly light-weight things, with wire netting covered by fly screen. He firmly jammed his head on my chest awaiting the ear scratching and blissful, leaned against me. I felt the door going and going and uttered pitiful cries.

'Help, help!'

Wretched gannets, happily eating at the table, finally heard me, left their meal and came to the rescue to lead him back to the cow house. He was by then something under a ton, a softie, but even without horns, just a bit beefy to handle.

There is a nice photo of two boys actually sitting on him. Mick and his mate Philip were good boys who had stayed for some time on the farm. They cared for the animals and cheerfully did whatever else needed doing. Mick had the reputation of being a bit dozy. Harmless and kind, he nonetheless often appeared to be 'elsewhere'.

They returned from their weekend, a small squirming bulge in a pocket. Oh no! Not another creature to care for? We called her Micka, after her saviour. She was an enchanting and very tiny, fluffy black pup. We presumed that her mother had been a very young bitch and had not been able to protect all her litter from being stolen by a weasel or hawk which had later dropped her. The wounds on her body were superficial and healed quickly, but new-born, she needed every attention. My work with premature babies came in useful and as she was valiant and determined to live, she survived. At the same time Mixalis the shepherd had given me a very weak triplet kid to rear. I put it in a straw-lined basket by the stove and struggled with it, for it seemed that this one was determined to die. Then, for convenience I dumped Micka in with him. Peace! Success! These two little adopted siblings throve, always sleeping together except for at feed times. Mind you, it was essential that I got to the kitchen before anyone else, for there, every morning under the basket was a great lake to be mopped up. Occasionally I was late, and I would hear the bare footed Stamos roar with indignation as he waded through it.

'Why?' he demanded furiously, 'must we have animals in the kitchen?'

Not for one moment would I allow him to win this one, for they were doing so well.

'Because this is a farm, AND, it is WARM by the stove! And,' determined to finish the discussion for once and for all, 'this is MY kitchen. If I want to have an elephant in here, I shall have an elephant in here!'

The subject was dropped, to the amusement of the hovering youngsters, alarmed at the unusual raised voices. Sadly, all efforts to borrow an elephant from the odd circus which passed through, failed.

Of the very many young people who lived and worked with us over the years, ninety nine per cent were wonderful. Patient, conscientious, they gave of their best, even if for some, their best was not so brilliant. Some of them, scattered to the far corners of the earth, will always be as, 'our children'. Members of an extended family. Their loyalty and affection have sustained me through all the highs and lows. This I must admit because they felt like family, often during their own times of trouble. The best left, and always came back again, and perhaps, again.

Life as a farmer's wife anywhere is tough. In Greece it was exaggerated by the heat. It is horrible while working to feel the sweat pouring down the back of your legs, and down your front. My day began early, always before sun up. So many tasks were done more easily in the cool dawn. Butter was made using the batch of ice cubes made the day before. Being Guernsey, it was excellent butter. The cheese was made daily, all this of course when the yoghurt/cheese factories didn't want our milk as the sheep were in full production. All the while we lived like kings.

The day's menu worked out, being a diligent provider, I made basic preparations. Off I went to town, the parking easy just before the shops opened and it was still cool. Shopping holds no pleasure for me. I know exactly what I want and dash around as fast as I can. As the years passed I got to know the best shops, and I stuck to them. There never were enough hours in the day. One morning, hardly back home and laden down, my little son met me at the door, face full of importance.

'There was a phone call for you!' he announced proudly. 'It was Mick. He said it was VERY important. You've got to go to the police station.'

My heart fell. 'Why me?' I thought, mouth set, busily unpacking the bags and stashing everything away in the kitchen. Fed up at the prospect of inevitable and many wasted hours before me, I tried to ignore the insistent little voice following me about. After all, Mick was no longer with us.

'Please Mummy, Mick said PLEASE!' I felt my face grow sour. Mick had left some time ago. I knew he was still in Greece as he occasionally popped in. I was annoyed. I was busy. Why me?

At last, jobs done, an old hand at this game, I packed up some food. Plastic box well filled. Plastic eating irons. Water bottle and plastic mug.

I took my time for I was really irritated. Passing the Post Office where we have a box, I collected my mail, amongst which was a rolled up newspaper sent by my sister. Goodness knows how long the operation would take, it was just as well to have something to read. The kindly bobby on the gate met me like an old friend and led me through to the back and the cells. There appeared to be quite a crowd in there. I waited and listened.

Mick and another fellow were being spoken to by a very smart, English-speaking lawyer. Huge sums of money were being discussed. Spotting me through the throng, Mick cast a desperate look my way. Politely, I dismissed the lawyer, to his obvious relief. He explained that he had been summoned by the embassy. When he had gone, I looked at Mick. He looked very hang-dog. I realised things were BAD. I was annoyed.

With narrowed eyes, not prepared for any nonsense, I slightly raised my voice.

'Right. Now I want to hear exactly what you have done. I want the truth, the whole truth and nothing but the truth, or I will NOT – help – you.'

(You will understand at the end of this sorry tale why I have changed their names.)

Mick began, looking everywhere else but at me. They hadn't worked for a few days. They were broke and hungry. They were also rather drunk.

Interruption.

'How come you were drunk when you were broke?' No reply. A lull. A cough. Some shuffling.

They had decided to try to catch a chicken to eat. As they walked out of the village, they came to a small, well-fenced farm. Inside were a lot of livestock.

Timmy, the older fellow, decided to scale the fence. Once inside, his drunken efforts to catch a fowl were of course fruitless.

Alas, there was also a little billy kid there. Knowing that human beings mean food, the poor scrap ran forward to welcome Timmy.

There was a long silence. The two looked miserably at the floor.

'AND?' I demanded sharply.

'We killed it.'

'YOU WHAT?' I felt my heart hammering, my breath coming fast.

'HOW?' I snapped, now deadly quiet.

Although it had been Timmy who did the dirty deed, Mick now came out with the ugly truth.

'Bashed its head in with a stone.'

Even now, I struggle for composure. It is as if it were yesterday. I was furious. With the post in my hand, that rolled up newspaper (the *Psychic News* as I found out later) I totally lost my cool.

Screaming like a banshee, I set about the wretched Mick, beating him about the head and shoulders with the paper, yelling all the while. Truly, I do not usually lose my temper but this time all sense and dignity left me.

'How DARE you! (bang, bang) How DARE you! (bang, bang, bang!) You come to this country, you are a visitor, a guest, and you behave like a savage. You disgrace me, you disgrace your family, you disgrace your country. How D A R E you.'

More bangs!

Mick, arms up to protect himself, received the full wrath of a true animal lover. The blows rained down on his head. Pity it wasn't something heavier! In my fury, I was only half aware of a mad clatter and scuffle of feet descending the stairs from above, then a row of incredulous faces appeared at the door. They had heard my yelling from their offices upstairs and it seemed as if the entire police force had come to investigate.

At last, exhausted, I stopped.

Later I learned to my great amusement how that incident caused my esteem with the police to rise dramatically. They had even heard me on the fifth floor. In retrospect it is quite funny. At the time it was not! The audience filtered, smiling away.

Pushing the bag of food at them I told them they'd have to share it, for I hadn't known about Timmy. Thankfully they ate and we sat in silence after the storm. The two attending policemen wiped the grins off their faces and stood guard.

This time, there was no way I was going to fight for these two idiots. They had done wrong, something so utterly stupid and they must pay for it. Kostas the lawyer arrived. The lack of money was the main problem. Timmy, in his thirties, flatly refused to contact his family for help. Mick, at eighteen, was very scared and decided to try. The main difficulty was that his parents had just moved house, and he didn't know their new phone number. Another problem for me to try to solve. Feeling really grim, I went home, all set to prepare everyone for my absence in court the following day. And how on earth to locate his parents?

Blessed chance. Lucky Mick. One of our 'old girls', Tina, rang from England, just to say 'hello'. Having helped Tina through some bumps of her own in the past, now I appealed to her to find Mick's parents, and ask them to phone me very urgently. Willingly she agreed to be involved in the saga and was successful. Bless her. Thankfully, in double quick time the call came. A furious father and a tearful mother. It seemed that this wasn't the first time they had bailed out their wayward son. Father was against it, let him stew. Mother, as all mothers, was tremulous with worry. I was able to give an account of what had happened.

'That boy is always getting into scrapes.' mourned the mother. I made sympathetic noises.

'My husband says that this time, he has to go it alone.'

'Ignore him!' I stated flatly. 'Mick is a clot, but a nice one. Give him another chance. Don't let him go to prison, he's too young.'

Mother sobbed quietly.

So I told her the story about the *Psychic News* and the hideous exhibition I had made of myself by lambasting her wretched son. I actually even got some laughter out of her punctuated with 'good, good!' as she applauded my actions. Of course, as every good mum, she agreed to send some money.

Once again I stood up in court and gave evidence, not so easy in Greek. Mick had lived with us for three months. He had been a good boy, always caring for the animals well and with love. The other one was unknown to me. As discreetly as I could (Timmy, having been in Greece a goodish time, spoke some Greek), I suggested that he wasn't quite right in the head. At this, general and gentle murmers of agreement went all around the court room. No one had ever heard such a daft story before. Foreigners, particularly the British, really were most peculiar!

For, those two lads, in their befuddled state, had got their countries crossed. That crime, in Greece, could only be escaped from by a rapid exit. Their dastardly action having sobered them up, they 'should have' dumped their pathetic victim and fled as fast and as far as they could go. There was a big motorway nearby.

But NO! At heart true Brits, sobered and horrified by their deed, they had upped and off to the nearest police station. With the sad evidence in their bag, they had given themselves up. Brilliant! This honourable move now involved me, parents, and not least themselves, in a lot of trouble.

The furious owners came for their compensation. Together with showers of apology and sympathy, I handed them the price of the kid, plus a generous sum over that, as 'bus fare' Unfortunately I was to lose heavily on that deal one way and the other. They had heard about my magnificent Serena, the goat. They wanted her female kid, never mind that I wanted her too. Deeply reluctant but duty-bound, I parted with her at a silly price. They paid a part then, promising the rest later, which I never got. Oh ho.

Honour was sustained, they had their pound of flesh.

Finally our long-suffering lawyer young Mr Kostas Philipiddis. A well-travelled man, he understood the exploits of young foreigners. The money sent barely went around. Kindly he accepted half of what his fee should have been. But I don't believe in owing, especially with such decent people. When the next Easter came, half as a joke, half as payment, I gave Kostas one of our fine lambs for their feast. Well, nothing is free in life. He was very pleased with it. But, once again, I lost out.

We actually took Mick home with us. He had three great helpings at lunch, as if there was no tomorrow. The unfortunate Timmy, the elder, the true villain, was locked up. A tough lesson. For us, a silly waste of time.

So there was another batty chapter of my life. The moral is, when travelling abroad, 'keep your powder dry!'

Chapter 13

Mixed Bag

A beat-up old van trundled up the drive one day. Three young women asked for me, having apparently been directed to the farm because of my interest in herbs.

How to describe them? Odd? Different? Thoroughly peculiar? They appeared all of that, yet once we got to know them we found them most charming, although the peculiar remained. I eventually found out that one was English, one Scottish and the third Irish. The makings of a joke?

There were two little girls in the van too. One of about four, the other less than one. All three 'lasses' appeared to be breast-feeding both children. It was unusual. Quite apart from that, they looked incredible.

Having lived out of Britain for so long, I suppose I was semi-ignorant of the mad attire and haircuts of the youth back home. This trio had somewhat crazy hair-cuts. If I was amazed, what was poor Stamos? Up till now most of our youth were normal back-packers. Except perhaps for lovely Jonathan, who wore jewellery all over him which utterly fascinated Pappoo and Yaya in the mountains.

Could they be punks, I thought? Or Mohicans? Whatever they were, they were quite inoffensive and asked if they could camp at the end of the farm.

In a moment of madness, I had thought how pleasant it would be to make a summer-house at the end of the land, there to house guests, or even ourselves occasionally. An A-framed house went up on a solid concrete base. That was all. Sadly it never progressed and was a hideous waste of money, but occasionally youngsters did camp in there. The three girls erected their bender, inside downstairs, and had a very comfy home. It was fun getting to know them.

Now these girls were talented musicians who busked for their bread. Singing, playing the flute, whistling on tin pipes, banging tambourines, they made a lovely noise. They even learnt a Greek song, to the delight of the populace. When they were short of cash, off they would go for days, or weeks, and return to the A-house to rest awhile. They told us of a time in Athens when they were busking in a market-place and the police arrived. The elder little girl then set up an appalling row, weeping as if her heart would break. Whereupon the crowd (bless them) roundly turned on the police, so the girls escaped without any trouble.

They came and they went, never asking for anything and were no trouble. That is until a very hot day when Bridget rang telling me a terrible tale of woe. She had lost her flute. She thought she had left it on a bus. Help!

I was cross. It is so hard doing anything when it is really, very hot, but I said that I would try to help her find it. Unfortunately, because of the heat, my patience was low and I laid about poor Bridget dreadfully. I told her how I had a certain position in the town and how ashamed I was to be seen with her as she looked so peculiar. (I cringe at the memory.)

No flute had been handed in. I toiled on. Now to find the conductor of the bus she had travelled on. Having tracked both him and the suspect bus in the morning, I arranged to meet her at the bus station at four when he would be in again.

'And for pity's sake girl,' I raged, 'come dressed like a normal human being, will you?'

Four in the afternoon mid-summer is wickedly hot. Everyone should be sleeping. I trailed to town, just hoping it wouldn't be for nothing. Then I saw Bridget, and I had to laugh. She looked terrible. Far worse than in her usual batty outfit. She wore a ghastly old, old dress, faded and shapeless, and a similar dull scarf firmly anchoring down her wayward hair. Drab? No words could describe the total change. She really looked like Orphan Annie on a bad day.

After half an hour, the bus came in. I waited until the passengers were all out before accosting the conductor. He was as Bridget described, handsome, unusually fair and blue eyed.

'Have you got a flute on the bus which a girl left behind?'

He scowled at me, hesitating. Then his eyes strayed till they lit on the pathetic figure of Bridget hovering in the background. It was a miracle that he recognised her. The scowl turned into a broad beam. He turned back into the bus and opened his little private cupboard and drew out the flute.

'I was hoping to see her again.'

Bridget came forward and was emotionally reunited with her precious flute. We both thanked the happy conductor profusely; a little crowd had gathered.

'Well play something then, you idiot!' I told her.

So lifting the flute to her lips Bridget played a wonderful piece of Bach and as the joyful music flowed over us, all was well. All the occupants of the bus station had spewed out onto the pavement and we all stood listening, full of admiration.

One of the best, no quite the best party Fredo ever had, was because of those girls and their music. For they played for all the games, and handed out odd little instruments to those who were 'out' so they didn't mind so much. It was a total, never-to-be forgotten delight.

At the age of six, as with all children in Greece, Fredo went to school. A Greek friend of mine told me that as all Greek children get so shaken up and down on laps, their brains need another year to settle down. Hence they do not go at five as elsewhere. The important thing was that he soon made many friends. But, he had so much to learn, not only school work, for I had also failed him in all matters religious. However, he watched the other children and soon got the hang of everything. He loved it, all dressed up in smart clothes with a satchel on his back, off he went. The school is rather close to the farm, just over the level-crossing.

One really sad thing happened as a result of his mixing with the town children. Overnight, he hated the Rom, and from then onwards avoided all contact with them including my goddaughter, Anastasia, his good, old friend. I was really upset.

Every morning, or afternoon, they line up in front of the head teacher in the playground for a prayer. They then all properly cross themselves. Three times.

There is a shortage of schools in Greece. And, or, the population is increasing. There are just not enough school buildings, so two schools share. One week they go in the morning, the next in the afternoon. While the other school who uses the same building, does the reverse. It is very tedious, and in term life revolves around these changes.

During the heat of the summer, it must have been unbelievably hot in the class-rooms despite a veranda. There was a curtain which must have cut off some of the direct sunlight, but it also shut off any welcome breeze. The children and teachers wilted in the heat. I doubt that very much learning happened.

I discussed doing something about it with Stamos. If it had been in England, we would have had a parents' meeting, arranged some money-making efforts, and bought screens. Good strong bamboo screens on pulleys which could be put up or down according to the weather.Stamos looked at me as if I were stark staring mad.

'This,' he banged the table, 'is Greece, and they are Greeks. They have to get used to the sun and being too hot.' Then he ended scathingly, 'What on earth are you talking about?'

Crushed, I crept off and tried to forget the idea although I still thought it a good one.

Fredo enjoyed going to his school and was tremendously loyal to it although I thought that everything was appalling. There was no gym, so no gymnastics. No sports, no music, no art. The occasional young teacher tried to give them some push-ups against a wall, but it was all rather sad.

Homework, was a daily nightmare in every household. Any home you visited after school was a battleground. The poor mothers, anxious that their lambs did well, hammered them constantly. The children, worn out from school, drooped over their work totally without enthusiasm. I simply did not know where to start. It always seemed to be preparation for tomorrow's work so in the end I just gave up. He managed somehow until it became obvious that I had another dyslexic son.

Every child we knew had frequent extra lessons. The girls did Gymnastics, Ballet, French, German and English. The boys did Gym, Judo, Maths and English, whatever. All the parents we knew beggared themselves by paying for extra lessons each and every day.

Junior schools are co-ed while the high schools were segregated, in the country anyway. Private schools in the city might be a different matter. Basketball was a great favourite due to Greece having recently won it in the Olympics. Almost every other house has a basketball hoop on the side where the boys practice for hours. Apart from that, the average kid has little or no sport. With the sea on our doorstep, it surprised me that more was not made of it. The beach we usually went to has a long and very shallow shelf. It is a lovely place to swim, the sea is so warm, ideal for teaching young children too.

Occasionally even in winter I would take Fredo for a walk, just for 'a blow'. The flotsam is pretty extraordinary, very collectable. When Emilie or Daphne were with us, we used to collect cuttlefish to give to people who had canaries. Once, when there were none, Emilie collected twenty two odd shoes to give instead!

One winter Sunday after a fierce storm had subsided, off we went. It was wonderful to feel the fresh sea air as I strolled along and the boy raced ahead. Then, I noticed a bleached plank of wood on the high-water mark with a strand of seaweed lying on it. The weed appeared to be bleeding out a pink stain onto the plank. The rain must have caused it. I picked it up, then scoured the beach for more to take home. It was pretty elusive. Being a spinner and natural dyer, I was always on the lookout for dye materials.

I poured boiling water onto the mug of seaweed, and to my amazement, it turned the water into a deep claret red. Back to the beach to gather more. Then came a dyeing session of great excitement. The first batch produced a deep red. The next batch in the same dye bath, a fine pink. The third batch, a soft pink. The three skeins hung up glorious. What a find, but what was it?

All efforts with enquiries in Athens to the Maritime people and with other dyers produced nothing. It was too bad. How to find out, if there was no one who knew.

One of my dye books was written by the Keeper of Textiles at the Smithsonian Museum in Washington, Rita Adrosko. I carefully packed up a shred of the seaweed, samples of each of the three coloured skeins and, once again breaking the law, I sent them to Washington.

At last the reply came. Warmly enthusiastic, indeed grateful to be involved, I was told that the colour comes from an algae, which grows on the weed in warm, shallow seas. So, it was not from the weed itself. The next thing was their regret in informing me that I was not the first to discover this colour-giving seaweed. For Pliny the Elder had also known of and written about it. (Incredible.) What delight, such joy, that useless knowledge had given me and warmest thanks to whoever had taken the time and trouble to respond to my letter.

Thereafter I asked and asked, but with no luck. I could not believe that the intelligent Greek women did not know about it, somewhere.

At last success, but such strange information, coming out of the more recent past. We were in the North, and I thought to ask some women by the shore. They shook their heads. They did not know of it. Then a very old priest hobbled up leaning on a stick, his ancient and patched robe was faded to grey. A chair was brought out so he joined us. Having already discussed the matter at length, the women then asked him. He turned to me.

'When I was a boy,' he began, 'before Easter, we walked along the shore with our mother collecting such a seaweed. She used it for dyeing the red eggs.'

Wonderful! Even if unusual, I deemed it certain success.

It was the women in the mountains who knew and advised me on many colours, even if they no longer did any dyeing. I would hang my dyed skeins up on the damson trees so when they passed by they could see them. Inevitably they stopped and came to enquire how I came to get this or that colour. They were surprised at the lovely pink which elderberries gave, none of them having used it. In fact, latterly anyway, their main colour source apart from the garish chemicals, had always been walnut, which is easy, not needing a mordant.

Once, some of us were up there for the great summer feast for The Virgin. Unusually, there was bad weather, with horrific thunderstorms. I heard the bells ring at six and hid under my blankets. Then again at seven, when I dragged myself up. The day promised fair, although it was dripping wet. The rest of the family ignored my calls to get up to attend the panayieri, even for this special service. At eight, I ventured out with a strong glitsa and struggled up the slippery, winding paths. The early sun was causing the rain water to rise up in mists, it was very beautiful. At last I got to the village where I noted many pick-ups parked along the road. Leaving my muddy wellies and glitsa outside the door, I crept in. This was the large church, old but very fine. It was packed. A few people knew me and nodded. I crept closer to the altar to see better. A very old, white-bearded priest was holding the service attended by a young one. A few of the old men chanted or sang out now and again. The altar steps had been spread with a great white cloth on which were piled many loaves of bread brought by the faithful waiting to be blessed. The service waxed and waned. I understood not a thing but still found it very beautiful. Gazing up at the cracked dome, where incense gathered, I felt that truly God was there.

As I left, a small square of blessed bread was put into my hand and the young priest told me in a whisper, to 'wait'. What for, I wondered? Finally when they had all gone, he gave me three loaves, 'Because I know you have a big family.'

No doubt it was because he assumed me to be an ignorant foreigner who could not bake, but even so, I was grateful, for we had no fournos up there.

When we went down, back to the farm, Sebastian said he wanted to stay and go to the other panayieri. There is on every mountain-top in Greece a church to the Prophet Elijah, apparently taken over from Ilias, the sun god. Dimitris, Pappoo's son offered him a lift. So wearing his Ozzy bushwacker hat, Sebas began his toil up the mountain. Every vehicle who passed him up the rugged track offered him a lift, but, expecting Dimitris, he refrained. Finally when he reached the top, there was Dimitris who had somehow missed him. However! The gathered faithful and all those who had offered him a lift were much impressed assuming his walk had been an act of faith. Oh the accidental kudos Sebastian had from that walk.

I even sold some of Lily's piglets to a small farmer half way up the mountains to the village. He bought three, and I gave him the runt. Everyone was satisfied.

Dear Lily continued presenting us with huge and very attractive families. We made a little creep for them to get out of the pen and they went everywhere, only returning when they heard my cry 'Bay-bees.'

One lot took to going far and wide which became quite a worry. Once we thought we really had lost them and Stamos got very upset with me. Calls came from neighbours; they had just gone past, in this direction, or that. It was a worry. All thirteen of them streaked along, crossing the road like pink lightening, oblivious of the traffic. But being intelligent creatures, they always came home to mum.

One particularly large litter, sixteen, produced my one and only problem piglet. She was black, and her front feet were turned under so she couldn't walk. It seemed pretty obvious that she would be trampled on by the rest of them, and would never have enough milk. So I took her to the house and bottle-fed her. We called her Mavroula, Little Blackie. She was a very cranky piglet and while I was dealing with her feet, I had to put a rubber band on her snout to stop her from trying to take my hand off.

First I put plaster of Paris on her front legs to straighten them, but it was too heavy so off it came. Next, I cut up the curved flange of my precious pressure cooker, strapped pieces on to straighten her legs and it worked. In no time at all, her feet were straight and strong enough for her to run about.

I was shameless in my hunt for food for them. I carried her in a big taggari (shoulder bag) which rested on my hip. There she slept peacefully between feeds, warm and happy with the movement.

I would do my shopping, then ask if they had any left-over vegetables. Of course I opened the taggari to show them Mavroula, and charmed, they usually found something. I remember one nice vegetable shop owner clicking his tongue at me.

'Why Kyria, do you work so hard?'

I had to think for a moment.

'Because, it is my character.'

A cold store heard about my piglets and that I was generous in giving one in exchange for help with feed. It was a wonderful source of fruit and vegetables. Once he even brought me boxes of fish, the ice still packed around them. Well I don't approve of giving flesh to beasts so I quickly took them to the Rom camp where Xrysoula was thrilled and suddenly very popular by dolling them out.

Certainly we ate the good stuff, and if there was a lot, I took it to the Rom and the local prison where it was very well received. All our down-to-earth youngsters were impressed and joked with me that we were eating 'pig food'. I heard years later that just one was disapproving. Well no one was obliged to stay, or to eat our food. But it was probably because she was so disgruntled about everything that I actually asked her to go, and good riddance. It was something very rare for us to ask our young people to leave. I hate waste, and was grateful for the handouts due to the fact that they needed the space in the cold store.

Inevitably there were many windfalls in the mandarin grove, and I noticed that many peels were left about, and wondered 'who?' Then I saw the piglets, their dextrous elephant-like snouts manoeuvring off the peel and the fruit would go in a jiffy. Another thing perplexed me. They continually crunched on something, in their voracious search for food. I eventually realised that it was after rain, when the snails were out. So much for not giving them flesh to eat.

They loved it when we threw a clean bale of straw into their pen and romped joyfully with it. With the baler going well, Stamos passed the word he was available and we cleared many small fields in the area. Either we got it all, or it was fifty-fifty.

How I loved to show off carting it home on the pick-up. Ever more, ever higher, I crawled along, noting out of the corner of my eye all the incredulous old boys at the kaféneon watching me. Stamos always tried to make me take less, for he had once dropped a load of apricots by going around a corner too fast. But ever-busy, I wanted to cut down the runs, so made sure the load was well tied and managed it safely by dint of determination.

There was no piped water at the spitaki/pigsty, so I put an old bath in there which was regularly filled. We wondered why it was so often almost empty until one day, creeping up, we found Lily, in the bath. She was huge, the dearest pig imaginable, who loved company and best of all, being scratched till she fell over.

389

Why I did it, I don't know. From one good litter of piglets, I gave Yannis, Xrysoula's drunken husband, the biggest and the best. Handing over a small sack of powdered milk as well, as she was so chubby and robust, I felt that she might survive, even with him. It was moving to see how that tiresome man loved his pig. He stopped drinking, all his time taken in foraging or begging for food for her. He would take her for walks, as a shepherd, and she thrived. All the Rom in that camp, and another nearby, knew about her and also contributed what they could for her.

Any fruit picking they did, they always secreted something for Yannis' pig. She grew vast and was his pride and joy. What plans he had for her, I never enquired so never knew. Then word came. Yannis' pig had died. Xrysoula arrived at the farm, eyes brimming with tears which she wiped on her tatty dress. Yannis was inconsolable. The whole camp was in mourning with him. No one knew the cause. Had she, as so many of the dogs, eaten poison? More than likely.

One of his daughters came to ask me if I would give him another. Her father was inconsolable, he had so loved his pig. Now, he just sat outside their house crying all day. Sad though I was for him, I was cross at the waste. If I did give him another piglet, that too might die. But at that time, we had no more piglets to give anyway.

Chapter 14

Laughter and Tragedy

Our chicken house was pleasantly full. We let them out in the morning and they pottered happily all around the farm all day. They all put themselves to bed every night at dusk. The peacocks on the top perches, hens and guinea-fowl next, and the poor ducks got the worst of it on the straw-covered floor. They were a mixed bag, and generally quite peaceful together. Some I had brought in as eggs to hatch. Some had been given to me in exchange for a piglet, or other matters like help. When I had arrived at the farm years before, there had not been one creature there, just Stamos. Armies of ants used to march through the house, and there was an amazing assortment of bugs everywhere. Now with the fowl, we were almost bug-free. All the fowl's happiest times were when the earth was being ploughed. It was a hoot hearing Stamos remonstrating with the busy hens as he did his furrows.

'Move!' he would shout, standing up on the tractor waving his arms. 'Get out of my way!' But they didn't mind him because they were so busy finding delicious things in the newly turned earth. Twice he came in mortified, a poor dead hen in his arms. Twice more, two others, a guinea-fowl and a hen who were sitting on clutches of eggs were killed. We were so sorry, but accidents do happen, especially when they were had crept off on their own and were so well concealed in the long grass.

Living near to the big army camp, we were often invaded by families who had obviously driven a long way to see their sons, every six weeks. They would quietly drive in amongst the orange trees at the front, unpack, and lie about enjoying their picnic. Naturally our dogs would set up a racket, so we always knew they were there. A few well aimed stones kept them at bay, but of course the smell of food kept them nearby in the constant hope of hand-outs. I might pass the picnickers with a greeting and ask them to take their rubbish away with them. Huge indignation at that, although plenty of them did not, so I had to collect it up. I gained a very nice left-behind knife from one of those visitors.

Mother, happy to be visiting her lamb, would unload her super efforts of the past few days, and happily dole it out. Great round wheels of bread. Huge tupsia (baking tins) full of excellent pittas (pies). Great tasty red tomatoes, more fruit than vegetables. Olives, cheese, wine. A feast fit for the gods.

One day, having observed such a family party, I got on with my work but was disturbed to see someone hanging around the kotetsi (hen house). The dogs were making him so unwelcome I had to go over to make peace. He greeted me cordially.

They had come from the far side of Athens and were, as I had guessed, visiting a son at the camp. He seemed unusually busy observing the fowl. Very politely, he asked if he could buy a rooster. Now at that time we had but two, the rest having gone into the pot. Father rooster was truly magnificent. He had a fine ruff of deep peacock blue feathers. His tail was of many colours, shot with gold. He stood tall and wooed his wives with a great flourish, sweeping up the dust. Surely he was the ruler of the roost with a healthy crow and kept order magnificently. The other, a son, was a poor shadow.

Muted colours, he wimped about, terrified of his father, he always kept out of his way and was the last to bed.

I was delighted at the thought of an unexpected sale, for it meant a sack of chicken meal. Try as I did, I could not catch the wimp. Already a coward, my efforts caused him to flee in terror. Disappointed, the sack of meal evaporating before my eyes, I told the visitor that alas, no, I could not sell him a rooster.

'What about that one?' he asked, pointing to father.

Now I just could not sell a silly townee an old rooster. It would be dishonest.

'That one,' I pointed to father, 'is old. The other,' pointing into the middle distance where the wimp had disappeared, 'is young.'

'So?' enquired the townee.

I was just beginning to get a little impatient. Hot from rushing around fruitlessly trying to catch the wimp, and now this man was being awkward. I began again.

'That one,' again pointing to father, 'is old and tough.' Then with a wave of my hand, 'The other is young and tender. I cannot sell you such an old bird, he would be uneatable.'

He began to laugh. I simply did not know how to get the message across. Was my Greek really so bad?

'Kyria, kyria' (Mrs, Mrs), he was grinning all over his face. 'We don't want it to eat. We are building a new house, and we need it for the foundations.'

I stared at him. An inkling of his meaning filtered into my bemused brain.

'You mean,' said I, hands outstretched I began with mime. Holding an imaginary bird, I held up a phantom knife, drew it across the throat and held the bleeding rooster over the earth.

'Indeed, indeed,' he replied joyfully, relieved that this dumb foreigner had at last got the message.

I could not believe it! Here we were in the late twentieth century and they wanted a rooster to do a libation, a sacrifice, on the foundation of their new house. And Greece was such a Christian and religious country! In a daze I very easily tempted father rooster with a handful of grain, then caught him by the legs and tied them. Then I put a little feed in a bag and handed them over. A fair exchange, for a handsome note. We said goodbye and a very happy man returned to his family in the orange grove.

Still in a daze, I returned to the house to tell my incredible tale to Stamos. He listened, his eyes widening, then slapped his thigh and rolled about. With a great laugh he said, 'That is why I never finished the barn!'

Son rooster took over his father's duties after a fashion. Certainly he was never so handsome or successful.

One day, I glanced at Trixie in her bed by the kitchen door in the Cheopery. How she managed it and with which dog I did not know, but poor little Trixie had a new-born, dead pup beside her. Some time later I found that she had stolen a puppy from another bitch who was nesting under the fournos. Kneeling beside her I watched her cleaning it lovingly. But the little thing strove to find a productive nipple to no avail, so I had to take it back to its real mother. Poor little Trixie! Just because she was so small, she had no mate and no pups. Something had to be done. The call went out.

We found a very fine pedigree little dog, a miniature Pincer I think, and his owner was only too delighted to sign him up. When I called her, Dimitra came rushing from Athens and the marriage was consummated. To our great delight, Trixie had three lovely pups, a girl and two boys. The best pup, like his dad, went to Dimitra, while a neighbour wanted the other boy, I intended keeping the girl.

Willem's family were again staying at a hotel near by and came to visit. Henke had somehow gained himself the Greek name of Kyriakos (Sunday born?) so the boy pup was named after him while the girl was called Margaret after Willem's mother. I have stated before that I am not very good at saying 'No', and so it was again. Ruth arrived, and on seeing the enchanting little Margaret, badgered and begged me for her, as birthday present for Emilie. So Margaret became Tara, and was the happiest, brightest, greatly loved little dog, for years and Trixie was finally fulfilled, a real mum. Sadly, we were never able to repeat the breeding between her and her gentleman for, not long after, Dimitra and he were walking on the beach when he screamed and died. Probably because he was so light-footed, he had frightened and been stung by a scorpion and had had a heart attack. She was devastated.

Feeding the pack was a constant toil. I scrounged all and anything from anywhere, pressure-cooked it up then boiled it all in a huge pot with rice bits, powdered milk, bay leaves and garlic. The rice bits came in sacks from a very nice local grocer who was married to an Englishwoman. He told me that when he had been young, they had eaten the rice bits, for lack of anything else.

The fearful din from the pig farm at the end of the land always signalled slaughter day. Braving the racket and stink, I would take a bucket and wade through the gore, collecting what ever I could for the dog pot. I was appalled by the treatment of the in-coming pigs, but despite being the local rep of the Animal Welfare, being a woman (and foreigner) my words were totally disregarded.

A friend rang from Athens. Knowing of my interest in creatures she had heard of a meeting with a top EEC animal man. I must come. Eleni had been a friend right from the beginning of my involvement in Greece. Indeed I can say she was the only good Greek friend I had for years; it helped that she spoke perfect English. Not much older than me, she always behaved like an elder sister. She bullied me. Re-arranged my hair. Gave me super, cast-off clothes. (Some of which I still have.) Naturally, I answered her summons. We went to the meeting together.

Despite appearing a big, brash woman, I am in fact very nervous. Like a fool I got up to tell them about the pig farm on slaughter days. The guest only spoke English, so, trying to stop my trembling, I held forth with both languages, telling them all about it. How the trucks arrived, open-topped, full of pigs broiling in the sun. How they were then tipped, from quite a height, the whole load of pigs onto the concrete-floored yard. How many of them, especially the first, or those underneath, sustained injuries, mostly broken legs. How the men goaded them with sticks, poor things screaming, some barely able to walk, into the slaughter house. Anyone not observing that treatment wouldn't have thought it possible. And here we were, a member of the European Union. My stammered tale was apparently understood and was well received. Exhausted with emotion and effort, I sat down in my place where Eleni cheered me up enormously, by saying how proud she was of me!

Stamos had for some time been looking into the possibilities of having greenhouses. He tended to get a craze, then concentrate on it, disregarding all else. I as usual supported him in every way. I too wanted him to succeed in his bid to provide an occupation for his eldest son who had never settled long in anything. It would be good for him to become involved in a great new project, which hopefully, might cause him to abandon his regrettable flights of vitriolic fancy concerning me. I offered to send him to Cirencester for one year, all I could afford by then. My offer was, not surprisingly, turned down. It was a pity, for he was the only one of Stamos' children not to have the broadening of mind provided by some education abroad.

Just when life seems to be chugging along quietly, something happens.

We had a sudden family emergency. Maria was ill. Who would have little Daphne? There really was no one else able or suitable, so I did. With a six-year-old in the house, a two-year-old would fit in without too much trouble. Or so I thought. For this was a very nervous little person, who had a dummy in her mouth for twenty four hours a day. She understood everything in Greek, but could not be understood, if indeed she did speak, because of the dummy. As none of my four had ever had a dummy, comforter, call it what you will, this was quite beyond my experience. On the one hand she needed comfort, on the other she really should not have that thing in her mouth all the time.

Another problem I had to face was that Daphne was a sugar junky. I suppose that as Maria grew increasingly ill, she gave way to all demands, sweeties being the easiest. The first thing I had to do was to remove the sugar bowl from the kitchen table and put it high on the fridge, in order that she wouldn't reach it and spoon the stuff into her mouth. The other thing was that she had no conception what a potty was for. Enter Smarties! Well she loved sweets, so it was bribery and corruption from then onwards and it worked. The young people were all loving and caring and helped me with her in every way.

It was a source of much hilarity when Daphne would get up from her potty and exclaim jubilantly, 'Bravo, bravo!' in self praise. Unfortunately, at the beginning anyway, it was more often than not for nothing, but she did learn eventually.

In no time at all Daphne had abandoned the dummy, except at night and siesta. She began to eat and grew plump and bonny. The lovely old antique high-chair which all my children had used was brought out for her and she loved to hold court, sitting nice and high at table, thumping her spoon on it.

'Enriko!' (she couldn't manage Frederikos) she would call in a remarkably rich and plummy voice, 'Ela, mum, mums!' (Come, food.)

Then there were the constant difficulties with the telephone! Whether it rang or not, she swept upon it at every opportunity, crammed the hand piece to her ear and bellowed, 'Ella!' (come) in true peasant style. I had to buy her own toy phone, and eventually she got the message and left ours alone.

The first time we went to the beach she screamed hysterically for apparently she had recently had a bad experience.

'You stay in the car then,' I told her, 'We won't be long.' But watching us, the temptation was too great and before long she was reassured and happy.

Kassandra, Stamos' elder granddaughter came from England for Easter, so then, there were three. Somehow, even with the language problem, they did get along well, and with me for a granny, Daphne was learning English fast.

The National Day arrived, so with haste and ingenuity I got them all dressed up. Astrid, a talented needle-woman from Norway, laboured over Fredo's fustanella. (The full white skirt, of the men's national dress.) I remember it had sixteen panels, quite a task. Later, when Fredo marched with his class during the National and Oxi Days, we were so proud of him for he looked very fine. Unfortunately the sewing machine died as a result of all that hard labour (and was not repaired for eight years). Regrettably we did not inherit any traditional clothes from Stamos' family as it was too grand to have anything as rustic to hand down like the locals. But my sister-in-law had given me some very interesting old pieces of cloth. So it was a matter of sew and make do.

I bought some thin, very cheap red carpeting which I made into Fredo's jacket. After crochetting braid with gold fingering, I stitched it on, and dug out a red beret and festooned that with a long black tassle. Little Mary in Athens donated his fine red shoes with the big, black pom-poms. Honestly, he looked as good if not better than the rest of them. The little girls were much easier. Using left-over scraps of carpet, I also made them waistcoats with gold braid and Amalia caps. With frilly blouses and long skirts, they looked lovely, and certainly they thought so too.

We went to town to await the parade, our three dolls in high excitement. Daphne was extremely pleased with herself and ducked under the cordon and pirouetted in the middle of the road, admiring herself. I remember watching a burly policeman trying to remove her. Nothing doing. She came when she was good and ready. We have some lovely photographs.

With three little ones around, the young workers built up a simple platform in the old walnut tree directly outside the saloon and made a fine tree-house for them. The children loved it, even if I was always scared that they might fall.

Hot on the heels of the National Day came Easter that year. After we had been to Saint Anna, our regular church at Easter, the young people voted to go into town so I went home with the three little ones. We had set up all the candles in our church, so it was imperative that we get the holy flame home safely. Oh but that was a hairy drive! Three children in the front of the pick-up, clutching their lighted candles! The windows got steamed up very quickly and I was in a terror that someone would catch alight. But we got there safely and lit all the candles, to our great satisfaction.

If only, if only I had had a camera. So I just have to remember watching those three little people on the altar step, clutching their pretty Easter candles and chattering away. Our little church looked beautiful, ablaze with light and colour from candle-light on the huge pots of corn daisies we had gathered earlier. Everything was golden. It was a beautiful sight seeing the little children in it.

Every evening, we had a free show from Daphne on the scaffolding which Stamos had erected in the house after the earthquakes. With the enormous weight of the old ceramic roof tiles and old roof timbers, we now slept downstairs. We had brought down our bed and Fredo's cart bed was parked under the stairs. Daphne slept in a cot in the hall.

After her evening bath, sweet-smelling in pyjamas, it was her greatest joy and much to our amusement, she used to swing, like a little monkey on the scaffold bars.

'Kitta mama, kitta' (Look mama, look).

By the time Maria came for her, she was, with the aid of the carefully dealt out Smarties, potty trained. It had been fun having a little girl, but exhausting, for she was a pickle.

Things are always breaking on a farm. One day an underground pipe went, but where was it and how to find it? Stamos, having heard from me that I had the gift of dowsing, sent me to work.

The boys were digging in the obvious place, yet they didn't find anything. I took my rods and seeing the rusty thick iron pipe in my mind's eye, I walked, until, really in a most peculiar place, the rods dipped. I had found it.

'Here,' I told them, 'dig here.'

They looked at me frowning. It could not be there. It was too far out of the way.

'Right,' said I, turning to go back to the house, 'go on, go on digging where you are, till you reach Australia.'

They dug where I told them and they found it. They were a little annoyed and incredulous with me, so I told them of how I had discovered that I had the gift.

I must have been thirteen for I was visiting my parents in South India. They had me out in the winter holidays as they thought I could no longer cope with the summer heat, having grown accustomed to the cool of England. I had also grown unaccustomed to siesta. So it was we were 'up country' staying in a friend's bungalow and while they slept, I crept out to explore. It was scrub jungle, just small trees and creepers on a red earth. It does sound very unlikely, but I came across a holy man, with red marks on his brow, his head covered with ashes. He just wore a loin cloth and he was dowsing. I walked along quietly beside him. Of course as a little child I had spoken Hindi, then later a little Tamil. But this was Telagu country, quite unknown to me. It seemed as if he did not notice me, as he walked along slowly, concentrating on his task.

After a while the man turned to me and offered me his rods.

'You try now,' he said in perfect English. What a surprise! I learned later from my father's host that he had studied in Britain in his youth. I took the rods and he told me how to hold them, what to think for, deep in my head, deep in the earth. I was amazed when the rods dipped without my doing anything. He smiled at me.

'You have the gift too.'

Of course as way of pacifying the boys, we then had a dowsing session there and then. Using bent wire coat-hangers, off they went, up and down and sure enough to their delight, some of them also had the gift.

Another breakage brought about a funny incident worth recording. I never threw things away, I still don't. Squirrel Syndrome I think it is called. An old red rubber hot-water bottle had gone at the edges and although Stamos told me to throw it out, I first talcum-powdered it inside, then put it in a high cupboard.

One weekend when all the shops were shut, Stamos wanted to spray the fruit trees, then discovered that the flanges on the sprayer had gone. He thrashed about miserably trying to find an alternative until finally, he asked me if I could produce something. Out came the hottie, which made not one, but two perfect flanges and he had the grace to laugh. Being a squirrel did have its compensations.

My sister rang to say she had directed a friend of hers to visit us. We were very busy, but I offered to take her to see the mountain house, just for the day. It was late May and we were preparing for the apricot harvest. It was amazing how the trees seemed full of hard little green fruit one day, and the next, they were golden and ready to pick. This was a time for spraying and irrigating. The irrigating was a tedious job, shifting long lengths of white plastic piping, connecting them up, starting the engine by the cistern and waiting. Sometimes it would blow, with a loud bang. It could be anything. A little piece of dirt. A cracked rubber band. A poor connection. If it did blow, then it all had to be checked and set up again and tempers would fray. Doing it all once, was quite enough. But this was the moment for the apricots, it was imperative to give them enough water so that they could swell to their full weight.

Picking apricots was quite different from picking oranges; basically because apricots are a June crop, when it is very hot. They seem to ripen all at once, so it is frantic work getting them all off the trees and away. Oranges are a leisurely and cool spring-time crop when generally there is no hurry.

Making sure we had pickers was always a problem and on the rare occasion we advertised for them in the little English newspaper, the ad. always came out so late, that the harvest was well past before we got any response. Stamos often used to tell me to just 'go and find some pickers!' And some of our very best young friends were those collected from the highways and byways.

Another problem which beset us was crates. Those tough many-coloured plastic boxes you see everywhere, seem to move in their thousands from one part of Europe, not just Greece, to the other, many times. If you had no boxes, you could not pick your fruit. It was no use stock-piling them, for when you took them, quantities were recorded and they had to be returned. It was a continuous nightmare to make sure we were at the depot early, or they would be gone. One might have to wait a day or two before more came. And all the while the beautiful fruit would be dripping off the trees.

I got back from the mountains to be met by a group of very worried kids. Part of the irrigation had blown, just as Stamos was bending over it. I can't understand why he was doing that while the motor was running. It exploded, flew up and cut him in the eye. At least it was his glass eye. It would have been a major tragedy if it had been in his good eye and blinded him. They had taken him to the hospital, so quickly collecting up some homeopathic medicines, I raced there.

They were stitching him up by the time I arrived, I carefully put healing drops into his mouth. I learned later that they can't have been very experienced for they had not injected the painkiller in the right spot. I held his hands, for he was in terrible pain, and he twisted and wrung mine because of it. The next day my hands were black with bruising.

I learned some new Greek while all this was going on. The top doctor came to see how they were doing and asked about the eye.

'It is not his,' replied the young doctor, 'it is foreign.' (A foreign eye? Oh!)

I rang Athens, for a young relative was an eye doctor and it seemed a good idea to have him check over Stamos. So he went to see him and it turned out that apart from the unnecessary pain inflicted through ignorance as to where to put the pain-killer needle, they had done a good job.

Of course his medical papers went with him with the results of the blood tests. The grand Athens hospital, probably thinking that the little country hospital had made a mistake, took more blood and made more tests. And more.

So it was, because of an accident with the irrigation that it was incidentally discovered that Stamos had leukaemia. Goodness knows how long it would have taken to find this out if there hadn't been that accident. For outwardly, Stamos appeared the most healthy man in every way. Believing that cancer is caused by stress, I miserably wondered which of his many sorrows had caused his illness.

It was the Seventeenth of May, Nineteen Hundred and Eighty Three.

I write it out in full, for it was to be the blackest day in our lives. The beginning of the end for Stamos, and the beginning of the end of my life with him and in Greece.

Chapter 15

Good Neighbours

While Stamos was in Athens, I was barely informed of what was going on so I just got on with life on the farm as usual. Certainly I was anxious, not only worried for him but for the apricots which were 'staring me in the face' and getting riper by the day. Everyone knew of Stamos' accident and that, apart from the young foreign workers, I was on my own. Help and kindness came in from all sides. Neighbours flocked to my assistance. Including those who were successful, and had never been to Stamos, as had so many, asking for advice. Just because I had learned to prune, and our huge orchard of apricots was such a success, didn't mean I knew much more about them.

'Judy,' Yorgos, a neighbour from above the farm came to call. 'You must spray. I am going to town now to buy mine, shall I get some for you?'

I was so grateful, for of course I was hopelessly ignorant about such matters. That had always been Stamos' department; he was the agricultural engineer, he had always seen to it. The chemical was brought and paid for. I was given careful directions of how much to use and so forth.

404

With the help of an able youngster, we got the trees sprayed and in turn, irrigated by the good team we had at the time.

Another visit.

'Judy, you must be at the depot at three tomorrow morning. If you leave it later, you won't have any boxes.'

I went at three as directed, on the John Deere with the big trailer which Stamos had built. I was very kindly received and got all the boxes we needed. The word had spread, Mrs Judith needed help. Now we could pick our crop.

Worried though I was about everything, I felt very blessed with the care and kindness given to me by all the locals. So we managed with the apricots. Some went to the canning/jamming factories, but sadly, much was dumped. The EEC paid us a pittance to do so. Such a waste.

Contrary to the valiant neighbours without whose help we certainly would not have managed, I began feeling abandoned by the Greek relations.

It came to me slowly just how much I was disliked, indeed very probably despised by them. I felt that my situation was, as I imagined it would be in a harem, and I was very much a lower order concubine. For I was barely informed of Stamos' illness, or the future prognosis. There were vague snippets of information that the type of leukaemia he had was not serious, that he would live for a long time yet. I had the feeling I was to be denied any medical information, he was theirs, not mine. As time passed, that is exactly how it was. All I was told by the remaining elder, was that I must never, ever speak with him about dying. Like a fool, I listened.

Being an old fashioned biddy, with outdated ideas such as 'elders are betters', I did as I was told. All this however, took some time to digest. In my book, loving, caring couples always discussed everything. For heaven's sake, especially with something as serious as dying. My main problem was that I was always so busy, I did not even have the time or facilities to research his illness for myself.

When Stamos eventually came home it was as if nothing had changed except for some scars on his blind eye under the dressing. Nothing was different between us. I did not ask and I was not told. I assumed that I would be eventually, when he was over the shock of it all. But it never happened. I loved him, and looked after him in every way. The family came and went. I confess that I often felt really unappreciated, as an unpaid nurse, or a skivy, there to be given orders.

There was just one indication of how afraid he was for the future. All plans for the greenhouses were totally abandoned. Like the drop of a hat.

It was a quiet time on the farm, the apricot harvest being over. We went to the mountains, we went to the sea. We loved each other deeply. We were happy.

One day, returning from a swim, Stamos having insisted on driving, we had an ugly incident which left scars on the mini-van if not us. We were leaving the beach after a swim when suddenly, a huge motor-bike loomed and before we knew it, two burly men had pulled up in front of us, and confronted Stamos. Maybe he had gone too close to them? It all happened so suddenly, we were quite startled. They then began squaring up in front of Stamos, but, I suppose, on seeing the dressing on his eye, realised that it wasn't on to hit an injured man. So instead, they set upon the mini! Both were well adorned with gold jewellery, and as they hammered the poor little car, they dented it with rings and things. It gave us a fearful fright before they roared off. I wondered if they weren't on drugs. Thereafter the mini sported gold-inflicted dents for ever. Most peculiar, most distressing.

With autumn, we were on our own so most the work fell on me and I became desperate. I had recently made friends with more ladies in Athens through the Anglican Church, and one of them suggested that I approach the Refugee Committee for help. Neighbouring communist countries were opening their doors to let their people out, so we had many Hungarian, Polish, Yugoslav and Bulgarian holiday makers. Many of them, on seeing how agreeable life was 'outside', were 'jumping ship'. So Greece was becoming, at that time only in a small way, quite an oasis for the persecuted of those countries. As well as the Europeans, refugees were crossing seas, rivers and borders from the middle-eastern countries. A committee was set up to try to find them homes and occupations.

As time progressed, I was capable of doing much of Stamos' work, but not the really skilled jobs like hitching the tractor up with other machinery. But once hitched, I could manage to do most of it. Now I felt the urgent need for a good girl, one whom I could leave in the house with Fredo. A sound girl, who could put the potatoes on to boil. Lay the table. Hang up the washing and generally keep an eye on the kitchen to finish cooking the meals which I had prepared. I called Athens, to the Refugee Committee and spoke to a woman there, assuring her that the girl she sent would be treated as my daughter, while learning perfect English. Most of these refugees were wanting to move on to Canada or Australia eventually, so English would be a huge advantage

Having been brought up by an American mother, I had loved the story of Anne of Green Gables. Now while her foster parents had wanted a boy and got a girl, I wanted a girl and got a boy!

Andrew, a very decent young man arrived with his youngest brother Jacek. Apparently Andrew had come on holiday to Greece, liked it so much, so to escape the tyranny of the then Polish regime, he decided to bring out his three younger brothers. The family were devout Roman Catholics. Andrew had been in a seminary, while two sisters had been nuns. Apparently the family suffered gravely from its involvement with the church. So there they were in Greece, the three elder brothers working in the building trade in Athens, but, they were worried about the fourteen year old Jacek. He had some growing up to do yet. So here he was, a small lad, skinny-looking very nervous, with not a word of English. Well, what could I say? I could not send him back.

Jack, as he soon became, was to become my 'fifth son'. He was lovely in every way. Appreciative, kind, excellent with the animals and the naughty Fredo. Luckily for all of us, 'no' is not one of my favourite words. As for him, he arrived at the very best time for himself. Plenty of good food, sun and sea, caused him to grow, and he, far better than his brothers, was able to forge ahead in his new life eventually in Canada, for he did learn to speak perfect English.

When his birthday came, we gave Jack a great party. A huge cake with fifteen candles, presents galore. He was incredulous and very thrilled.

'Judy,' he said afterwards, clever boy having picked up English in record time, 'I never had a birthday party before. Thank you.'

Some time later he told me how he occasionally dreamt of his old home and his mother. Then frowning added, 'Although it was my mother, it was you too.'

Life went on, and inevitably money grew short. Vassilis, September's first calf, was sold at under a year, having impregnated the cows of the entire neighbourhood! I have a hilarious memory of struggling with a mating with just the little Fredo for help. Behind the house were some very old, gnarled mandarin trees which I had never got around to prune or indeed do anything to. One was beautifully forked, so in that convenient fork, I firmly tethered the cows. This was the only way I could manage the cow, and the bull on my own, more or less. While I hung on to the eager Vassilis, I remember yelling to the poor Fredo,

'Pull her tail to the side, pull her tail!' Thus are country children learned in the birds and the bees, very early.

A local butcher came and offered us a tempting price. Being honest, I explained that the fat might be yellow, as he was half Guernsey, but he was unperturbed. Just looking around at all the good feed with his experienced eye, he knew that our animals had been well fed. I didn't even have to try to convince him that the meat would be exceptional. It was, even though I had to pay full price for what I had back. That was the best beef I have ever tasted.

It was fun to assist in the developing cattle breeding in our area. We all helped each other, as well as fighting for better prices from the cheese factories. I became the local expert at de-horning and castrating. I even removed extra teats to the astonishment of us all, with no disasters! In everything to do with cattle, I was self-taught. I read, and I asked. I also simply used common sense!

The phone rang.

'Heretai!' (be joyful). The voice rattled on. Desperately concentrating, I at last asked him to stop and start again, slowly. It was Barba Yorgi (Uncle George) another cattle man, from whom we had first borrowed the bull.

'You want me to come over?'

'Yes.'

'You have a cow in trouble?'

'Yes.'

'She is giving birth?'

'Yes.'

'She is young, the first calf?'

'Yes.'

'Have you called the vet?'

A long pause. Then – 'No.'

I understood, even if it made me uncomfortable. The last time Barba Yorgi had calved a heifer, they had trouble. His cows are too fat. Anyone knows a fat mother may have trouble more than a slim one. This excellent old man and his wife love their cattle. Old and tired, they really should give up. I do understand. When it came for us to give up our girls, it was awful.

At last in desperation the vet. was called, who after his examination, decided it was a 'bottom first' presentation. Off he went back to town to collect his gear. She must have a caesarean. Four hours later he returned. The calf was in fact 'head turned back'. It was dead. The mother became infertile AND the vet had to be paid handsomely. A complete disaster all round. Which is why I was called. I gathered my things together. Antibiotics, soap, towels, gloves, disinfectant, etc. Donning an old pinafore dress with the shirt outside, it gave me a free right arm. Finally, grabbing my books without which I knew nothing, off I drove.

It was early January and despite our frequent wonderful weather, this was a cold day with a sharp north-east wind blowing. The poor beast was in the yard tied to a young walnut tree. The yard was a morass of mud, stones, tin cans, rusty wire, a virtual minefield. Taking one look at me she panicked and made it all but impossible to examine her rushing around the tree. At last, and thank goodness, she broke the frayed rope and made a dash for the familiar cow house. Happily we followed. With the other cattle inside it was marginally warmer.Well soaped up, I slid my hand into her. It was a long way down. She was such a fatty, it was quite a job. At last I found a little snout, two forefeet, one turned back but easily remedied. As I drew the foot forward, carefully so as not to break the water sack, the little hoof was smartly pulled back.

'It lives!' I sang out happily.

Then the waiting began. They had not slept for two nights, poor caring people. The fat young heifer was taking her time. But it was a live calf, and things were progressing, slowly.

'I'll get the ropes so you can rope it up', said Barba Yorgi.

'No!' I said. 'Be patient, wait, give her time.'

Every fifteen minutes or so, he nagged me again.

'Let's use the ropes!'

'NO!' I said.

'If we rope it up,' he persevered, 'I can call in a tractor and we can pull it out!'

Tractor! TRACTOR?

'NO!' I shrieked (tractor indeed!). I then firmly stood on guard at her backside.Three hours later we delivered a tired but healthy little bull calf. Bright-eyed and alert, he would do. Oh so happy, I rushed off, for my boy had to be collected from school.

It turned out to be a rather tiresome day. There was an electricity strike. Our water is pumped up by electricity, so I had to run around filling containers. Next, lighting lamps. We were privileged enough to have a quaint little milking machine on a cart. That evening milking was a nightmare, the girls did NOT like to be hand milked. At last, arms aching from the unaccustomed work, we finished.

'Shall we' I suggested, 'go and see Barba Yorgi and the new calf?' Delighted, four of us piled into the front of the pick-up. They met us warmly. Relaxed and relieved, they led us into the cow house to see the new baby.

'Oh Barba Yorgi!' I exclaimed in horror at the poor little shivering thing. 'Can you find him a blanket?' Without hesitation, the dear old man took off his own coat with which he covered the calf.

We then were invited into their 'house'. It is one room, about two metres by three. There is an area in front of the door which is 'the kitchen'. A stone sink and tap and a two ring gas cooker. Above the front door is a massive television which is literally STRAPPED up, with a few well-placed nails bashed in the wall about it as anchor. There is a double bed, covered with hand-woven blankets and a small table with a couple of chairs. Last but not least there was a good fire burning in the hearth.

Thea (aunt) Fotini is a lovely old lady. All smiles, she set at once to make a meal. It was pretty dramatic to see the pine needles being flung on to the fire, roaring up, so lighting up the little room. Next, with skill and speed she cut up potatoes into chips. It was a miracle the place didn't burn down.

'Patatoules' (chips) are greatly loved in Greece. There is an old story about one or other dictator, who wanted to introduce potatoes into the country, ages ago. The population were suspicious and refused to be charmed. So (the story goes) he planted a few acres of potatoes on his land and set an armed guard on it. Clever man, he knew his people. True or not, Greeks love them.

That happy evening, we drank Barba Yorgi's excellent wine and ate his olives and cheese, and fell upon the chips with gusto. They were happy to have a calf safe and well and I was immensely chuffed also. It HAD been a compliment to be called. It HAD been exciting, that moment when I felt the calf move so knew it to be alive. It was a good feeling to have been of use to these good friends and neighbours.

Several times that evening they announced that they would pay me. I steadfastly refused of course. Finally we gathered ourselves to go home. Sad to leave the warm room and gentle company, we donned our coats, for it was a cold night. Again they told me they would pay for my veterinary services. Again, I scolded. We were always broke but there was nonetheless some pride to cling to. Four of us squeezed into the front of the pickup and, about to take our leave with fond farewells, we were stopped by cries.

'Wait, wait.'

The two old people had their heads together whispering. At last, coming to an agreement, Thea ran in and emerged with something in her hands. Pushing it in through the car window, she cried out happily, There, there, you cannot go with empty hands!'

It will always make me smile, that 'payment', two packets of pasta! Marvellous.

Stamos was delighted as I and said we should 'frame' them. But this was typical of the true and wonderful Greek peasant. One rarely goes with 'empty hands' and never leaves either 'with empty hands' ! I like it.

Our number was similar to that of a local hotel (or as Stamos put it, a bordello). We did quite often have weird calls, always at some ungodly hour which brought swift and furious response. So when one night the phone rang, Stamos groped to it and yelled – 'What? Come, come! Go to the devil!' and slammed the phone down.

Some fifteen minutes later there was a knocking on the window. We slept downstairs at that time after the big earthquake, afraid that the upstairs was unsafe.

'Kyria Joulia, Kyria Joulia!' (A lot of peasants can't say my name, so Julia suffices.). I ran to the front door. It was Effi, a neighbour. Would I come, a goat was in trouble with birthing. Donning a 'Mother Hubbard' over my nightdress, I collected up my gear. Bucket, soap, cream, towels, antiseptic, antibiotics and gloves, etc. It was a beautiful moonlit night, and I walked easily across the fields, my wellies making flicking sounds against the high dewy grass. Making for a small light, I found the stable and went in. Vassilis and Effi, from the north of Greece, a charming laughing couple, were caring animal farmers. It was a low stable and a single light bulb hung from the corrugated iron roof.

A goat was lying on the none too clean concrete floor, so I went down to examine her. A head was jammed, with a pair of feet under its chin. I soon realised they were too small to be the head's own feet. With gloves on, I carefully pushed the feet back inside, and groped around for the feet which belonged to the head. Carefully flipping them out, the kid was born easily but, his tongue was swollen and he was very tired so we laid him down to rest covered up. The next one, 'Back Legs', came in a hurry, a busy little female, she was up and calling in no time. Two more, after that, all well. A good night's work. I was surprised and more than a little pleased to find a crisp banknote in my pocket on the way home. If that Nanny goat had been out on the mountain, there is a strong chance that she and her family all would have perished.

No sooner back in bed, when another caller came. It was a young Dane, part of a travelling Christian group who had quite a menagerie. A lamb on his arm, he explained that apparently it had been kicked by a pony, the eyeball was hanging out, the head badly bruised. Poor little thing. In pain, in shock, I harshly suggested he put it out of its misery and have it for Sunday lunch. You can't win them all.

413

Now and again, Stamos went to Athens for check-ups. At such a time, a circus came to town. Now I have to admit that they were pretty dreadful. I am sure it was the same circus which came every year, but it always had a different name. Lurid and dramatic posters were pasted up all over town announcing their imminent arrival. I thought it would be fun to take Fredo and Daphne, so with a scheme in my head, I loaded up the pick-up with bales of alfalfa and drove down to the sea. A large caravan was the ticket office, so I carefully parked just in front of it. They looked at me, then at the alfalfa, me again, then at the bales. They wanted some. I unloaded. A deal was struck. I ran around madly inviting every child I knew, including some of the Christian children. We went twice, thanks to the alfalfa, in all about thirty children. They had a happy time. The circus seemed totally unperturbed, perhaps it was a good thing to fill the place rather than have it half empty.

It was interesting to see how they all mucked in. The members of the high wire act sold colas and crisps in the intervals. The clowns set up and took down the lion's cage. Everyone seemed to have at least two jobs.

Then, to my horror, I found that Daphne had disappeared; I was frantic. I rushed out and scoured the beach, the whole circus area, the caravans, the lions' cages. Little devil! Well, when you lose a child, particularly someone else's child, your imagination does run riot. She was not to be found. So then I approached some of the staff. They mostly spoke Italian so I groped about in my memory and managed to make them understand.

The circus was halted in mid show. The master of ceremonies announced that there was a little girl missing. Her name was Daphne. 'Daphne? Where are you?'

She appeared. She had abandoned our common plank seats, slipped down and away and had been adopted by some wealthy Corinthians. And there she was, sitting in state with them in their box! Not only in the front seats, she was wonderfully happy, because they had been feeding her with endless chocolates. Definitely, Daphne was a chocoholic. She was most indignant on being returned to me and our seat in the gods. I was mortified and hung on to her tightly for the remainder of the show.

The following day some circus men came out to the farm and bought more bales of alfalfa. A clown came too, and begged to buy a duck for his act. I really wasn't sure about it but gave in and handed him a white duck who was in lay. No doubt he cooked up some jolly act with duck and eggs. But somehow we never went again in the following years, so I didn't know.

Chapter 16

Experiences

We were very lucky in frequently meeting interesting, indeed exceptional, people. It was always a pleasure receiving these unusual guests, for it not only broke up our working week, it lifted our hearts. A very special group of friends came, and brought with them two Tibetan Lamas plus their translator.

'Having been a Buddhist, in my previous life!' (What a statement.) Even so, I was more than delighted.

We were eighteen for lunch, I remember that amongst other things, I gave them baked fish. The Reverend Jeremy and Mrs Peake came, with their pack of little dogs. One of them, Eloise, was a Tibetan temple dog, and the Gagnchen Rimpoche swooped her up into his arms and joyfully cudded her.

It was a lovely autumn day, so we sat eating and talking outside. Through Tensing, the young translator, I told them about a vision I had about my previous life in Tibet.Then, we had prepared lots of food which we packed up and we rode on ponies to a great river valley, where the rushing water was white-blue. Many other people came, and everyone set up felt tents and entertained each other around tiny fires. The young people played games, and had mad horse-racing. Then at one moment, all the young men stripped off to their cotton long johns and dashed into the icy water.

While I was recounting this vision, the old Lama was nodding his head and smiling broadly. It was he told us, the spring festival. He also told me that my soul had wanted to be born again in Tibet, but that Darjeeling was as near as was conveniently possible in the circumstances!

When we had a quiet moment, I told the old Lama about Stamos' illness, and asked him to pray for him.

Another time when the Peakes called by, they came with Bishop John, the Bishop of the Mediterranean, no less. We sat around the table in the kitchen eating lunch and talking of this and that when I suddenly realised that I had, many years previously, met his sister in India. It was rather a funny little story which I told them.

We were going up to the hills the following day and I was in a chemists buying something when I overheard the woman in front of me. She was asking the chemist if he thought the things she had bought would reach her children in the hills by post the following day. There was some discussion. It was the weekend. The chemist looked doubtful, when I came to life.

'We are going up to the hills tomorrow,' I told her, 'Would you like us to deliver it to your children?' So it was arranged and we met the headmistress and her husband and persuaded them to allow us to take the children out. Everyone was happy, and so were we years later, amused at the coincidence, sitting around a kitchen table in a Greek farmhouse.

Then, more than twenty years later, in a new life, I met Bishop John again, he came to lunch, how wonderful are coincidences.

Life went on, every summer, from May till September, we continued to have foreign groups for lunch usually once a week.

The wonderful beehive oven which we had built, had come into its own. I could not have coped without it. What is more, our guests were highly amused with seeing their meal actually coming out of its cavernous interior. It has to be the most photographed fournos in Greece!

Sometimes, Frederikos would be persuaded to don his Greek national dress. He looked quite the charmer and was happy to pose for photographs, and occasionally to receive tips. Latterly, he was even a real help with serving, as a good Greek taverna boy should be.

One day late in the season when numbers were down, I was busy preparing for the group. The day before always involved the hard and fussy labour of preparing all the dips, pies and small eats. When the phone rang I asked Fredo to take it. I heard him in the hall, sounding bright and important.

'Yes I'll tell her', and to me, 'Forty people coming Mummy!' Panic, I had been expecting thirty. Half an hour later, the phone went again, once more Fredo went running. Again, this time getting quite squeaky with excitement,

'I'll tell her!' Sixty. Wow! Once again my shopping list had to be corrected. I generally phoned the orders and either collected late at night or, if pushed, the helpful shopkeepers delivered to the farm for me.

Once again the phone went. I could hear him in the hall. He was beside himself with excitement. Horrified, I heard him say 'EIGHTY!' I blanched. Oh no no no no no no! I couldn't do it! I went and took the phone and said so. There was a stunned silence.

'I simply don't have enough CHAIRS!' I explained. She laughed. Chairs? Who said anything about chairs? The last twenty were coming in WHEEL-chairs!

A couple of special vans arrived with tail lifts. Our guests were all seated around an assortment of sheet covered doors and electric drums. It was a merry party. As it was late summer, the peacocks had been moulting and hating to leave those beautiful tail feathers lying about, I had gathered them up. As our disabled guests left, I gave each of them a feather for luck. It was lovely seeing them off, happily waving their feathers in farewell. It reminded me of the film of little Dumbo the Elephant, with his magic feather.

The cows were in full production, and we sold the occasional calf, and hopefully all the milk. When we had no helpers, it was fearfully hard and I remember standing at the back of the pickup, with the churns on the ground. Some how I had to get them up and on board, alone. I sobbed and sighed and cried, just as had done Mrs Petropolous. 'I can't, I can't,' I wailed until inevitably that inner voice scolded. Oh just get on with it woman. So UP, they went, to be fastened on board. I was only half aware then, of what I was doing to my poor body, flogging it so unmercifully. My poor back. Time would tell.

When we couldn't sell the yellow milk, I always made cheese. It was stored in whey in huge churns, waiting for the rainy day (which be sure, came). Then I was given some of the dear little island cheese baskets, which inspired me to make something a little different. Courage and little cheeses in hand, I went to the big hotel on the north of the Corinthian Gulf (the one and the same where we had borrowed the polythrones). They looked nice, different, wrapped in vine leaves, pressed into the little cheese baskets. They tasted nice too. A head chef looked over them, cut one, tasted it and said 'Yes,' they'd have some. To my astonishment, a huge order was given. Nothing daunted I rushed home and set about the preparations. It really was a major task.

It was a hot, hot day, and with just the open-backed farm pickup for transport, I resorted to a tin bath-tub, bought and filled it with ice blocks, and loaded up the little cheeses. It was about fifteen kilometres away, so I raced against the heat.

Then came disaster. He asked me for my papers. I just did not know what he was talking about not being accustomed to doing business with such a huge concern. We had no permit to sell cheese. EEC regulations. I was dumbfounded, gazing at the ducky little cheeses laid out on their blocks of fast melting ice. What on earth could I do with it all? An impasse. The nice manager who I had met before and I stood silently staring at them in their neat rows on the submerged floes.

All that work. The excitement of the order. The joy the kids had sent me off with. And here I was, not having done my homework, stuck. My mind raced, there just had to be a solution.

'Can you give me a credit note?' I asked. 'So when an occasion comes, we can come over to eat in your restaurant and use it?'

Bless the man, no doubt having seen my terrible disappointment, and relieved at the solution, he wrote me out the note, and more cheerful, I trundled off home beaten but not down.

The occasion did present itself before very long. A sudden invasion of excellent old kids came to see us again. Willem and Els, Sebastian and Pippa. Young Jack, that special Polish foster-son. We must have been ten in all. Oh and for me, the sublime feeling of wealth! Of treating everyone to a proper night out, oh what bliss. I revelled in it. I also had the presence of mind to take along some little cheeses to the manager who greeted us warmly. The girls disappeared at one moment, and I understood that there had been some skinny-dipping far off in the shadows. What an evening that was, Greece at its very best.

We sat right by the sea, a warm night, perfect Mediterranean weather with a breeze to cool us. Ah gracious Poseidon. We ate and drank all the delicious things we never had at the farm. We danced, we swam. Jack disappeared and I traced him to the discoteque where I saw him gyrating like a dervish, totally lost with the mood and music. I suspect the waiters had instructions to make sure that ours was a never-empty well, for my occasional anxieties as when we must stop were always waved aside.

So much for cheese and the EEC. There is usually a way around things in Greece, thank heaven.

For me, an almost personal tragedy now befell us. Our apricot trees had a virus, it was called Sarka. It affected the fruit in a strange way. They looked all right, but they did not travel for they just collapsed from the inside, out. Everyone had Sarka, not just us. Apparently there was nothing to be done about it.

How to understand Stamos' character? He was such a lovely man, but there had to be a very powerful destructive force lingering in his soul. For his next step was to cut down all the apricot trees. No one else around us did, and they continued for years somehow getting and selling a crop probably by picking early.

Previously, Paul, the archaeologist, needed wood for his stove and asked me if he could buy some from us. Reluctantly I told him we had none due to our chain-saw being broken. Whereupon he insisted he give me a new one if I could organise his wood. Determined man that. So he did, we did, and everyone was very happy.

It was dreadful watching tree by tree going down. After years of pruning them, I knew them intimately. A couple of splendid New Zealanders and Jack did most of the work while Stamos directed operations. I think he also sold some wood to the local bakers. We had wood for fireplace and fournos for a good time. Even so, clearing that orchard was a long slow job.

During the cleaning up process, Ann from America came to see us again. As it was her birthday, we had a party in the field, with a huge bonfire of sticks. I suggested to Stamos that we ring the fire brigade to warn them not to come unless we called them, as usual. But he said as it was such a small bonfire, it wasn't worth the bother. Of course, within minutes of it reaching a great height, they arrived. Sirens blaring, lights flashing, they drove across the field in their trucks. I was mortified and ran over to them, plastic cups and wine jug aloft, and invited them to join the birthday party. They were very amused, congratulated Ann with the usual 'Xronia Polla' but demured, being on duty. This event added somewhat to the celebrations, and I am sure it is a birthday Ann won't forget for a long time.

Once again we grew wheat, a beautiful field. This was the splendid time when Stamos took Fredo up on the combine, a magic day. Then the trucks came and loaded up with the golden grain, then off they went to the mill near the sea.

'Alfa tria,' (A3) said the man in the tower by the weighbridge rather casually, trickling the golden grains through his fingers.

'What?' shouted the rather deaf Stamos.

'Alfa tria,' the man repeated.

'Ena,' yelled Stamos.

'Tria,' repeated the weighbridge.

Stamos furiously told the driver to move off and shouted to the truck behind. They would go to another mill.

'All right,' said the brute at the weighbridge, 'All right. Alfa ena, alfa ena.' (A1).It really was so tiresome. Nothing was achieved without a battle.

The crisis in our lives came hard and fast, like storm waves on the beach. Regularly. Sometimes big, sometimes small, but with regular monotony. Stamos used the word 'find' on these occasions. It was an odd word to be used in that context.

'I'll try to find some money,' or, 'Judaki, can you find some money?' It was also usually such an immediate crisis. If the electricity bill was not paid tomorrow, we would have no electricity, no water, I couldn't use the milking machine. It was endless. I used to imagine us walking along the streets searching, and the lovely Irish song often came to mind, 'And for all that I found there, I might as well be, –'

There seemed to be so many commitments quite apart from day to day living and farm expenses. There were the two old ladies, Eleni and our old pensioner Angiliki. Apparently when the andartes came for Uncle Frederikos, undoubtedly to kill him, a little servant girl saw them, ran to the house and hid him. For that act of loyalty she was properly rewarded with a piece of land near the army camp and a monthly pension. She was a dear old lady.

Disregarding memories of that wretched unpaid for fridge, many was the time when I bailed out Eleni. She would call, plead with me for just a little money, and whatever my situation, I always sent her some.

I seriously began to sell my treasures. How else to keep afloat? Pieces of English furniture, silver, jewellery. With every crisis, I would delve deeper. There was absolutely no question of asking or borrowing from anyone. That was against all my principles. There seemed to be too many ignored debts already. It was awful watching Stamos ill and worried; yet he never confided in me, so I never knew of his financial affairs. A critical mistake.

One weekend sticks in my mind like a sharp dagger. It must have been something very big, for he followed me around the house, ALL weekend, hammering. He must have the last of my money which was tied up in bonds in England. It was so serious, that apparently if he did not have it, he would go to prison.

'I must keep something for my old age!' I implored him. 'I have to keep something.'

But he was furious. Why did I need to keep anything? Hadn't he the biggest and best farm? Did I really think that Fredo and I wouldn't be well provided for in the future? Could I not trust him to make proper provision for us? On and on, powerful and determined. He was to have it. Wherever I was and whatever I was doing that whole weekend, he was behind me, demanding. It was terrible.

Exhausted, 'on my knees,' I gave in. He had had it all. I was now cleaned out. I had understood that he had virtually bankrupted his parents; now it was my turn. His sister later told me,

'I wanted to tell you not to give him everything, but I felt it wasn't my place.'

Too late! She had been more clever than I.

Years later, I regretted that foolish weakness more than I can say.

One Friday evening Eleni and Petros, neighbours with cows in Examilia, came to beg a bale of alfalfa. We sold most of it, keeping the tatty stuff for ourselves. Of course, inevitably we ended by parting with far too much to our disorganised neighbours. However, what are neighbours for?

'Did you know,' asked Eleni, 'that the EEC calf subsidy has arrived?' I didn't!

The cows and calves were mine, having paid for them. So also were the headaches involved. Times were hard as I was sorely pressed for feed. We were out of maize and the alfalfa was nearly finished. Delighted I planned ahead to fit in a visit on Monday morning to the Agricultural Bank in town. Lunch more or less organised, the cheese started, after dropping off the boy at school, I rushed to take my place in the queue. It is a nice old fashioned bank facing the sea. The interior is rather like an old British Corn Exchange. Big central hall, light and airy, there are few glass partitions and everything is very relaxed and informal. We chatted, shuffling along, for every one knows everyone.

I have a profound respect for the Greek farmer. They work desperately hard on their tiny plots, if indeed they have any. Shepherds such as the Petropolous have little, walking the verges every day, seeking out any neglected fields for their sheep. It must be quite a job keeping them fed, yet they do.

The gentle stink of beast hung heavily around us. It took me years to realise that the smell which rose from every countryman was not him, but from his animals. Greeks are amazingly clean despite their frequent and often serious lack of water. Anyway, it wasn't half as bad as say, the French armpit.

Eventually at the head of the queue, I got a warm welcome from friend Maria. Rustling though the papers she found mine and carefully peered at them. Then the smile faded.

'Oh, but I am so sorry Mrs Judith, but I cannot give you the money. These papers are in your husband's name.'

My heart fell. Why the hell weren't they in my name? Typical. I knew that much time wasting stretched before me while I did battle to sort this one out. I also feared that if Stamos collected the money, I wouldn't see it, and I urgently needed it for feed for my cows.

'But they are MY calves.' I uttered miserably.

The queue behind me, had shuffled closer to hear and were all sympathy. But after all, time was precious, they had their work to do. Clutching the papers I despondently left, knowing that if I didn't move fast it would be amen. Another thought crossed my mind. I gathered that Stamos owed the bank a lot of money, although I didn't know how much. If I didn't solve this problem quickly, if he had to sign for it, perhaps they would just confiscate it. Horrors, something must be done.

Nothing, but nothing moves fast in Greece. The boy had to be collected from school. The shopping had to be done. Lunch. The cheese. I knew I must somehow keep the mornings free otherwise I might as well just forget it.

Next morning early I took my problem to the government vet. It was he who had visited us to do TB tests, he who had seen that I really loved my animals, so he knew that they were mine. A nice young man, we tried to thrash over the problem and find a solution. A paper is necessary for just about everything you do in Greece, so he kindly wrote one out stating that in his opinion and experience, the cows and calves were mine.

The boy. The shopping. The lunch. The cheese.

Next day, I had to scout around to find the EEC office. A small affair in a small country town, I eventually found it in a block of flats. This was another nice young man, a stranger from the North. He took his time going through the papers. I explained the problem. They were MY cows, bought with MY money. Therefore they were MY calves. Apparently somewhat surprised by the large foreign lady before him, he went through the papers again sadly shaking his head.

'But don't you see' I pleaded on, 'if my husband collects the money, the bank might take it. It is really such a SMALL sum of money, but such a HUGE sum for me. I urgently need it to feed my animals.' I ploughed on to no avail. I recognised the blank look of hopelessness on his face as he just sat there.

Perhaps just to break the silence, he asked to see my Greek identity card. Having decided to have dual nationality, feeling that in some way it might be of help to me in the future, I handed over the little blue card. They are slightly larger but not unlike a credit or bank card. I remember how incensed I had been on having to give my fingerprints, like a common criminal. Having checked it, he handed it back. By then, the third day on this caper, my courage was failing. Yet one thing I had learned in Greece, if you really want something, you must be stronger than the other chap.

Miserably I sat fiddling with my card thinking of all the work which was waiting for me at home. It even has my parents name on it, my place of birth, all wrongly spelt. Then, my eye lit on something. The spark of an idea, a possible solution. It had been worth just sitting there. In Greece, every person has their father's name AFTER their own, for identification. Every WIFE, has her husband's name after hers. Now! If I put my name on the papers in front of Stamos name?

I leapt across to his desk, plonked the papers once more in front of him and made my suggestion. Beaming at me, (dear boy!) he said, 'Do it!'

Quickly, in my best Greek, several times over, I wrote my name, (which by the way has no resemblance to the Latin version.)

'Tzountith.' There, it was done.

Mutually joyful, we shook hands and I raced away. First I went to the bank where an amused yet admiring Maria quickly did the rest of the paperwork. I was solvent again. I really don't know where else in the world I could have managed it.

In another bid to contribute to our daily bread, I went into producing rabbits. In a fit of extravagance, I had some large portable cages made by another Yorgos, the blacksmith. I parked them under the mandarin trees by the kotetsi (hen house) and a miracle happened in no time at all. The mandarins had always been tiny pellets, more pip than fruit. Now with the rabbit manure, they swelled up magnificently, and we not only had rabbit to sell and eat, the mandarins were much in demand. We moved the cages each day, despite their being pretty heavy. I fed them proper pellets plus as much greenery as they wanted. It seemed to me that this was the correct way to farm.

One day Kostas, the one from the mountains, arrived and asked for a few crates of the best mandarins. For he was now involved in the market trading of fruit and vegetables. I was totally on my own, Stamos and Fredo being out somewhere. As Kostas would call that night, because he would leave for Athens in the early hours, I had to get a move on. One of Stamos' amazing and useful contraptions was a sort of tall trolley on wheels, with steps up to a platform. He was very clever with making things, and I hauled it out, for as usual, the best fruit are always the highest. Over my many years on the farm, my feet got into a dreadful mess from just wearing flip flops. I began work, the dogs as usual, hanging around being sociable. It was surprisingly slow, sorting out the largest, for I liked Kostas and wanted to do my best for him. Suddenly, while going up the little iron ladder, I slipped and fell over backwards. Both my shins got the worst of it. Skin right off, I swear to the bone, it was agony. Shocked, fed up, hurting, with no one about, I thought I'd have some self indulgence for a change. Lying on my back on the damp grass, my legs still stuck in the ladder, I bawled unashamedly.

Then I realised that I wasn't alone after all, for two of my best dogs had parked themselves close by me. I know if they could, they would have helped me. But instead they sat, staring at me, listening intently, turning their heads this way and that. Then finally they too started howling which made me laugh. I still have the scars.

Having doled out the magic oil and patched myself up, I began picking again. A strange car came up the drive. It was the young Scandanavian Christians. A miracle!

Seeing my wounds and hearing my tale of woe, those excellent young people were up the trees and on the platform in a flash, and the boxes were filled all ready for Kostas in no time.

Someone, somewhere loved me.

Chapter 17

Good Boys – Bad Boys

Amongst quite a few involvements with courts and prison, there is one wretched incident concerning two of our excellent boys from New Zealand to be told. Thinking of it still hurts. The shocking injustice of the whole affair is hardly credible. Even now I would like to correct the very real wrong done to them. I was and am deeply ashamed of Greece, my adopted country, for it. It was scandalous.

As usual, I blame myself. It was I who suggested that they take the day off and visit the town across the bay. Very much a tourist place, it might have attractions for them unavailable in our dozy little agricultural backwater.

Strapping cheerful lads, these two were old friends. One, half Maori, the other a Kiwi, they must have been the backbone of their rugby team. As with all our Down Under kids, they had worked hard for this world trip and now worked hard for us. They were also fast-drinking buddies.

Their sandals were literally falling apart. Firmly I insisted they buy some new cheap rubber ones, the Greek peasant footwear. No way was I going to allow our kids to set off bare-footed like hippies.

428

Happily they caught the bus for Loutraki while I dropped their old sandals off on friend Yorgos the shoemaker to be repaired.

Knowing it was to be 'curry night', they promised to be home on time. When they didn't arrive home that evening, the gentle Ann from America consoled me.

'Don't worry', she laughed, knowing them well, 'they'll show up when they've slept it off.'

I did worry. Dreadfully. Their anguish reached me from over the miles. I just knew something was wrong. By morning I was a wreck, while the rest of the family got on with the work unperturbed. Fearful of being out of earshot of the phone, I remained in the house and dragged myself through the chores. By lunch time, I was frantic. Allowing Stamos the shortest possible siesta, I hustled the little family into the car. Our normal program in summer was to go to the sea nearby, immediately after waking. So we set off for a change, to Loutraki.

Having dumped them at the beach, I rushed to the police station. Alas, I had feared right. The policeman at the desk was thoroughly unpleasant to me.

'THEM,' he shouted. 'Foreign savages! Barbarians!'

And where were they now? In the police cells of our own town. Damn it! Rushing back to the beach I again hustled my family out of the sea after the shortest swim and drove home. Gathering a meal together in plastic boxes, with plastic spoons and forks (the old hand at this game), I returned to the local police station. Unfortunately I knew my way around. I also knew the man at the gate, whose boy was in the same class as Fredo. Two kindly bobbies escorted me to the back where offenders were held prior to sentence. By now, tired from lack of sleep and anxiety, I called out roughly – 'BOYS!'

A frantic scuffle, for they were still handcuffed together and two pathetic faces appeared at a small barred window. Later they told me that my shout, 'boys', was music to their ears.

The first thing they asked for was water. The one thing I had failed to bring. Furious I turned on the two policemen. What kind of people were they not to at least give WATER to these young men?

The recent big earthquake had left the old water system of the town damaged and unhygienic. No one drank the heavily chlorinated stuff, everyone bought bottled water to drink. Lack of imagination and language had caused those poor boys to be locked up for almost twenty four hours without even a drink. It was criminal.

Furious, I rushed to the nearby bus station. Inevitably they had run out of bottled water so instead I bought cans of the fizzy drink called 'gazoza'. After struggling to push them through the cell bars, the policemen, perhaps feeling a little ashamed, unlocked the cell door and the boys were let out to sit with me.

Despite their hurting and swollen wrists, the cuffs being too tight, they gratefully ate and drank, their first sustenance for twenty four hours.

'WHY didn't you phone me?' I demanded, feeling indignant, tired and upset.

'We tried,' they assured me, 'And how.' Their requests to phone me or their embassy had been flatly refused. Entirely against all natural and international laws, those boys were just shut away and ignored. My feelings against my adopted country ran high. I demanded that they tell me clearly and truthfully the whole story.

They had enjoyed pottering around Loutraki. Once a rather elegant, old-fashioned watering place, it is now a busy, tourist resort. They had wandered around, bought a few souvenirs and a Greek shoulder bag. In the late afternoon, they went to the bus station, where they sat at a little bar and had some beers while they waited to come home.

Our Maori, the taller and gentler of the two, had a wisdom tooth bothering him. While they ate souvlakia and imbibed a lot of beer (it was hot), he took a pain killer from a sealed pack. Greeks don't like brown skin, associating it with the hated gypsies. Our Maori, whose mum was Kiwi, dad Maori, was the softest shade of café au lait.

The barman, observing all this, no doubt hating these tall, prosperous young travellers for their easy life, rang the story was that they were taking drugs.

the scene. A little pavement bar, tables and chairs out, a ers. Two relaxed foreigners waiting for a bus, drinking, ng, for their beers. Along came the law, three of them. foolish, they had obviously been trained by little Hitlers. ss, stupid way to behave. Tall and handsome young demi-gods in their society, what did they do? They our two innocents. They did not approach them civilly, the contents of their pockets. They attacked them, safety

urse, all hell was let loose. Our heroes, those tough rugby ling their own business, reacted quite normally. They put fight. The Kiwi told me much later, with a grin of satisfaction on his face, that they had floored them in no time, and reinforcements were called.

'The last thing I remember,' he said, 'was wrapping one around a tree.'

Highly understandable, but not very clever as it transpired.

I was mad! Before leaving the station I looked over the charges. They were dramatic. Not only had they injured policemen, they had caused a great deal of damage to the bar, as well as causing serious loss of trade.

Now I have to go off at a tangent. For as usual, we had 'friends' and thank heavens. Over the years, with the noble Lily providing us with excellent piglets and pork, I had heard about the New Zealand 'hangi'. A traditional and super way of cooking in a leaf-lined pit. Always interested to have a try at something new, I asked around. At last, using Stamos' consulship as an excuse, I rang the New Zealand embassy. Success. I was passed to a vice consul, an excellent lady, named Robin. Obviously a good cook and highly amused to teach me, she came to visit us.

The resulting hangi provided a superb feast for many and we had gained a new friend. Having slightly comforted the boys, and promising every help for their court case on the morrow, I went home and phoned Robin.

It is worth mentioning here that the New Zealand consulate had heard nothing. The next day, half an hour before the court case began, they received a call with the information. So in fact they were too far away to get there and DO anything to assist their boys! Scandalous.

It was wise little Ann who insisted that my day was not yet over. She was right. I had to go to Loutraki that evening to glean as much information as I could for the morning. Not having any idea which bar they had been at, I went to a couple, had a beer, got talking and finally found THE bar. I took the owner to task. Waving the papers, I asked to see the damage. Rather vaguely, he told me it had been cleared up.

The barman, a small, mean-faced little man who I thereafter called 'The Weasel', was watching from behind the bar. I soon understood that he was the cause of all the unnecessary trouble. Very quietly, very firmly, waving the paper, I insisted on seeing the damage. Busying himself around the bar, the owner repeated it was cleared up. Customers began to look interested, he and the barman were uneasy.

'You cleared up EVIDENCE?' I asked. 'Broken glasses, carafes, plates, cups, saucers.' Waving the paper about. 'You have thrown away the broken tables and chairs? Was it clever, when you are asking SO much in damages, to throw out the evidence?'

On and ON I pressed him, following him around the bar. At last, sheepishly, he offered to halve the sum demanded for the damages. (Damned nerve, but, the bargaining had begun.)

'NO!' I retorted, actually beginning to enjoy myself. (The snake.) Indicating the backdoor, and probable yard, I again demanded to see ALL the broken things.

VERY uncomfortably, for he wasn't a bad man, but just employed one, he told me with some apology that in fact, there wasn't anything broken, it had just LOOKED bad at the time. He would accept less than half what he had asked for. Casting a filthy look at the barman as I left, really angry by now, I spat out.

'I'll see you in court tomorrow.'

Robin arrived astonishingly early, and like the traditional mama, was loaded down with food. I remember laughing at her words.

'Well you can't go into battle on an empty stomach.' (Dear lady.)

We got early to court having done our best to freshen up the boys. The new rubber shoes I had browbeaten them into buying before going to Loutraki had been lost in the melee. They had been relieved of their new shoulder bag, newly acquired souveniers and ALL their money. Well, it was well known that the police are not very well paid. The lost property box came in useful but I put string in the shoes I had found for them because it was too early to shop for laces or get their mended sandals back. All things considered, they looked fairly tidy. It must have cheered them realising that their substitute family was there in force and ready for anything.

Once again, we found ourselves in the fine courthouse. The boys were led in. This was NOT what they had come to Greece for. The case proceeded with the use of an interpreter again. It was something of a farce, in fact it was ridiculous.

'How much damage was done?'

There was a preamble, but it came out at last,

'No damage.'

'Had they settled their bill?' They had.

The Weasel was closely questioned. The judges aren't in their position without knowledge of human nature. They pressed him. At last he admitted that it had been a 'mistake'! So he had made a mistake! (And our boys were paying for it.)

Now alas, the final card; the young policemen came on. Tall and fair, handsome, softies. They were well smeared with mercurochrome. It was embarrassing, laughable. The arms held up for all to see. Pathetic. A few scratches. A lot of 'red' (as we call mercurochrome!) Superficially dramatic. Poor lambs.

In my opinion those young coppers should have been reprimanded for 'jumping' the two innocent foreigners. The usual and correct procedure would have been surely to question them first. If they had, they would have seen the innocent pain killers and none of this nonsense would have happened. The whole police force should be instructed on how to arrest people in a civilised way. Not like Nazis or Colonels! And anyway, it was no way to encourage tourism.

Guests in another land, totally innocent, somehow they had broken the law. And having 'wounded' policemen, they were to be punished. I assume that the lack of water, food, or use of a telephone to contact us and their consul, was to punish them for the criminal offence of defending themselves.

They got three months, PLUS costs. We were speechless. I just could not believe it. Surely this wasn't the land where democracy was born?

Express letters to their homes. Telexes from their consul. Their hard-earned savings drawn out in New Zealand and sent to Greece by wire. They bought themselves out. Waiting for the cash to arrive, they did spend a couple of weeks in the local prison. The bush telegraph got a hold of their story so their fellow prisoners warmly welcomed them as brothers. In a country where for centuries the underdog admires anyone who fights back, those lads were heroes. Stamos, having been quite a rebel in his day, was proud of them. Even so, justice was not done.

Years hence, I hope that this story will amuse many little Kiwis and Maoris.

Fredo was going to school now, and although he thoroughly enjoyed it, he didn't seem to be learning much. I blamed myself, fearing that as a foreign mother I should have done more to help him. I had been firmly told not to teach him to read or write English, although he spoke it perfectly. Eventually, years later, it transpired that I had another dyslectic son, which apparently was not known in Greece, despite being a Greek word.

Every evening we lay side by side in our big bed while I read to him. At that time, I had very, very long hair. First I found that he had lice, then, oh horrors, so had I. At the chemist, I whispered, full of shame, that I needed anti-lice shampoo. To my embarrassment, he cheerfully yelled,

'Oh don't worry Kyria, everyone in town has lice!'

Aware that daily washing of very long hair was going to be tedious, I took up a pair of good sharp scissors and went into the bathroom. Sadly holding my long plait, I carefully cut it off short. Holding the severed hair in my hand, I went into the kitchen. Stamos looked at me in horror.

'When!' he shouted furiously, Ali Pasha, 'you want to cut off your hair, you must first ask my permission!'

I stared at him, mouth open, and then burst out laughing.

Was I hearing right? This was from my highly educated husband. Did he really expect me to kowtow like a peasant wife? Ask his permission? Certainly not. What ever was he thinking of? (Incredible.)

'Too late mate!' I retorted.

Another incident similar to that one came up when we were visiting Stamos during his occasional stays in hospital. The naughty Fredo had tried to kick a chum at school, missed him and hit the wall instead. His big toe was horribly infected, and I could not get it to heal. A young visitor who was a trainee chiropodist did his best, telling me that this was a well-known injury called 'Ostler's Toe'.

The hospital where Stamos was, seemed to be in a clutch of hospitals, and one day I noticed a Children's Hospital nearby. On impulse I swept in and explaining that we were country people, asked them to look at the toe. They agreed there and then to operate on him. Unfortunately they would not allow me in with him, and I cringed as I heard him screaming, and the accompanying yells of 'Idiot', from the doctors.

Shortly afterwards, seeing the poor bandaged big toe, Stamos was once again incensed. What did I mean by taking HIS son to hospital without him and without his knowledge? Again, I was struck dumb. Truly, I was flabbergasted.

During one of my visits to see Stamos in hospital, I saw for the first time, a most moving religious ceremony. Undoubtedly the same was held in our town, but living in the country, I had never seen it. Looking down into the street from the window, I was moved beyond words to see a slow candle-lit throng, carrying a tabernacle, pacing along accompanied by the slow beat of a drum. A canopied bier, as in an old fashioned funeral, it had just a simple Bible lying on it. The symbolic Christ. It was called the 'Epitafios'. It was beautiful and awesome.

As time went on, Stamos became subtly weaker, so much so that even climbing onto the tractor was difficult. I would give him a heave up and off he would go. How he loved that tractor. Then peculiarly, he began causing damage, ripping branches off trees, which infuriated him. So we came to an agreement. I'd do the slow, fussy, round-the-trees rotovating, while he did the straight runs.

Our system was that I'd do the early shift, come in to prepare the lunch and then he'd take over. After lunch, he'd have his usual siesta while I went out again and so on. It worked well, the farm was keeping tidy. He came in one day rather early and slumped on the kitchen table. Anxiously I told him,

'Go and get washed and leave a pee so that I can do a test. Lunch is ready so we can eat immediately.'

I gazed in horror at the dip-stick. Sugar! After feeding Stamos, which was exactly what he needed, I rang Athens and was told that it was not unexpected and that it was due to one of the drugs he was taking. Of course I had not been informed. Luckily I had some knowledge and some sense. Even so, I was offended by the lack of confidence. Ordinary domestic life began to get ever more difficult. No salt or sugar in his food. I was now having to cook separate meals for us, as well as increasingly doing more of Stamos' work. At the same time we still did not speak of his illness, or of death.

I felt very lonely.

Before Christmas, I had become involved with the Anglican Church Bazaar so we all went to Athens to attend it, a special treat. I had enjoyed making many things for it in the evenings all recycled of course, but fun and different. On one occasion I remember that we were invited to the ambassador's residence for a drink, and Stamos cheerfully arrived with a group of kids to collect me. Wearing his fanella as usual.

Our neighbours the Elliotts invited us over for lunch, I can't remember if it was Boxing Day, but around Christmas anyway. I thought hard what to take, one never goes with empty hands. Then I decided on making a big Christmas English mince-pie, something unknown, so different in Greece. By then we were out of wheat, so I used the very last of our own brown flour for the pastry. However, it was entirely home-made, my own mincemeat and flour, so it was an unusual gift. The Elliott's guests, intrigued by the unusual flavour, loved the mince-pie, and one nice man casually asked me what flour I used. Mournfully I told him it was the last of our own. I had not been clever enough to keep sufficient grain to keep us supplied.

A couple of weeks after, a huge truck arrived. I looked at the driver very doubtfully, for we were not expecting anything. He unloaded a large sack of brown flour. I frowned at him, telling him that he was surely making a mistake. But no. The flour had been sent by a mill owner who had met me at a Christmas meal when he had enjoyed my pie.

I was overwhelmed. Things like that at that time tended to make me weep. So little good was happening in our lives and here was evidence of such unexpected and thoughtful generosity. Not just

437

once either. Every two months until the next harvest, that truck came with a sack of flour. Blessings to that stranger for his kindness, for giving me happiness and putting real bread on our table at a black time.

In January, a group of boys arrived asking for work. Firstly, we did not need them, secondly, I did not like the look of them. After years of taking in back-packers, I was a pretty good judge of character. However, some friends had asked me to send on any workers, because they had a lot of lemons which needed picking up for the dump. I gave them my views, but they were not worried. They were caretaking a property for a nephew who was away and it was urgent. They collected the boys and took them to a nice little house nearby where they would live. The agreement was they would have one good meal a day delivered at about 2 p.m. They had to strip the trees and clear the grove for the going rate. The boxes would be collected and delivered daily.

Three days later I heard that it had been a total disaster. The trash, there is no better word for them, had sawn open a cupboard and helped themselves to clothes as well as drinking all the wine in the store. They had barely worked and had now disappeared. I was mortified. Furious, I was determined to track them down. Then I heard that they were drinking in Steffi's bar at our end of town. Any kind of injustice is like a red rag to me. How could they behave so badly to decent people who had offered them a good deal? It takes a lot to make me mad, but this time I really was.

They were sitting near the front window of the bar, somewhat sozzled.

'Right!' I roared in and banged the tin table, glasses jumping. 'Let me hear WHY you have behaved so badly? Why you broke into cupboards and stole? Why you didn't do the work you agreed to?' I went on I'm afraid, crescendo gathering in my rage. 'Why do you think you can come to this country and behave as monsters to these good people?I cursed them, their families, their country.

438

'Go home,' I roared, 'go home where they know what to do with rubbish like you. How DARE you come and let other foreigners down, how DARE you!'

Poor Steffi appeared and stood there, drying cloth in hand. The other customers sat hushed and spellbound. As if I cared! I carried on slating, them, pouring all the worst insults on them that I could conjure up. They had not only let me down, what would their parents think? They had also let down the rest of the back-packers of the world quite apart from their own country. SCUM!

Steffi's bar is for locals only, only very rarely do strangers go in there and more is the pity, for it is exceptional. Enormous barrels of wine are lined up on one side of the room. Tiny tin tables are covered with plastic cloths. A small section of the room is divided off to make a little general store. It is a calm little place.

Until I stomped in! My indignation at bad behaviour when young people abuse the kindness of the Greek peasant knows no bounds. Finally I banged the table and told them to get OUT of Steffi's bar, return the clothes, BUT, to pay first.

Placing an extravagant note on the table they left quickly. I never saw them again.

I sat down, exhausted. Mr Steffi came over, enquiry all over his face and put a little glass of brandy in front of me. Thanking him profusely, I earnestly begged his pardon, then began laughing, and told him and his customers, the whole ugly and infuriating story.

Vassilis Steffi was a lovely man, who I got to know quite well after that. I made to leave, again humbly apologising to him and the rest of the old boys, for my behaviour. They seemed very amused. He agreed that I might come again to speak with his mother and take some photos.

I had gained another friend.

Chapter 18

The Rim of the Vortex

Vassilis and Mrs Steffi lived at the back of the bar with his mother. The bar was a long low room, dim and cool, with one wall graced by huge barrels full of retsina. Mightily impressive. They were a really charming family. Some days after the rumpus, I called and met his mother, that bent little figure who pottered around in the background.

Born in eighteen eighty three, in the hill village of Saint John, Mrs Steffi senior was still going strong at one hundred and five. Having never met such an old person before, I admit I was very fascinated. Rheumy-eyed, not a tooth in her head; she had, however, fairly good hearing.

Stamos told me that St. John had a centuries-old reputation for breeding thieves and liars! Somehow I didn't feel it applied in this case. Certainly they were wonderfully hospitable to me. Perhaps, I had made my mark.

One day I went to take some photographs of her. She was having her lunch. All her life, she didn't take oil on Thursdays and Fridays. It being a Thursday, she was chomping away, surprisingly well with gums only, on bread, fetta and olives. Dressed totally in the inevitable very well-patched and faded black, black scarf on her head, she answered my greeting, 'Be joyful!' with a strident response.

'Heratai, heretai!' Be joyful, be joyful! Grasping my hand with hers, ancient, gnarled, and surprisingly strong. We adjourned outside into the early spring sunshine, the little courtyard spotless, sheltered and warm. Vassilis set a table and some chairs amongst the inevitable brightly-painted huge tins filled with plants. Sitting with us, for she was a little deaf, he acted as 'translator'. There was so much I wanted to know, this was such a privilege and experience. So we began at the beginning. Her early life and her family. He passed on my questions and she began.

'We were many,' she said, her hand doing the familiar circular movement which denotes it. 'Seven in all. I was the eldest. One, may the Virgin keep him, (she crossed herself automatically) died from burns when he was little. Another was killed in the civil war, so young, just a kid.'

More crossing. Her mind wandered, obviously thinking of those little lost brothers. Vassilis prompted her. 'The others,' she frowned, Vassilis put in a word or two, she nodded. 'The others, yes they have gone too, except?' Another prompting. 'The youngest, yes indeed, he is still alive. He is in the village, he still lives in our house. Indeed.' She looked at Vassilis who kindly told her, 'He is now ninety.' She brightened up and gave me a gappy smile. 'The youngest is still alive and he is ninety!' We smiled at each other, her face close to mine.

'Will you tell me more about your life, when you were young?' I asked.

She nodded again, pleased.

'Oh ho, my life!' hands up, waving. 'I worked, and I worked. Being the eldest child, I helped my parents. I milked the sheep and goats. I made the cheese. I tilled the land and planted vegetables. I tended our vineyard and trod the grapes to make the wine. I looked after the younger ones. Yes, I helped my parents always.'

It was a long and rambling account, always gently assisted by her son. As was the norm, she had spun and woven for her dowry. But somehow, being too essential to her parents, she married 'late'. This surprised me, as the wedding photograph, albeit faded and stiff, showed a very handsome woman. Her husband had been seven years her junior. As a mere boy he had gone to the States with his father to work on the railroad, 'somewhere around Oakland'.

They had married in 1917 when she was thirty four and he twenty seven. They lived on in the village where he was the blacksmith. He not only shod the donkeys and mules, he made the great wooden saddles called, 'sumaria'. Vassilis told of how he remembered helping. Over the next ten years she bore seven children, the first, Vassilis, followed by six girls.

'Have you eaten, have you eaten?' she suddenly yelled, grabbing my hand, remembering her manners.

'Yes, thank you, I have eaten.'

'Granted by God,' came the response. Which brought us to FOOD. Cheerfully, on she went.

'We took the froth off the top of the milk and soaked it with bread. Of course, it was home-made bread, simple, good, nothing taken out. We had our own cheese and olives, and sometimes we had 'bakalau' (salt fish). We had meat on four days of the year. Christmas, Easter, Saint John and Saint Dimitrios. If there was a wedding or baptism in the village, we might have meat then. We ate beans and we ate lentils. And of course, we had horta, oh yes, lots of horta!'

It was a rare treat to listen to that old lady. But she wanted to know about me. She was full of village curiosity and of course she could neither read nor write. Talking was most exciting, especially about something new. I had my little camera with me so we arranged her in a corner of the courtyard, alone, then with her son and daughter-in-law. Her wedding photograph was brought out, I really admired it; she was so pleased.

'Did you know,' she held my hand, 'Vassilis is bringing someone to take my photograph?' I nodded, we all smiled kindly at her.

In 1924 they had bought that little place. There were thirteen members of the family who all lived in the three rooms. Two sets of grandparents, she and her husband, and all the children.

In 1928, just before the feast of St George (23rd of April), it was raining very heavily one evening, when there was a big earthquake. Vassilis went on with the story. The four grandparents went with the children back to the village, somehow it seemed safer there. The parents stayed behind to make sure nothing was stolen. Having built the three rooms themselves, they knew they were strong and felt safe.

'Not,' said Vassilis with a smile, 'that according to today there was much to steal, but my sisters had all collected together their dowries, all hand-spun and woven, a great labour. So my parents watched over them.'

Which brought me to dowries.

'Yaya (Grandmother),' I asked, 'tell me about your dowry.'

She thought a moment, her ancient face creasing into a warm smile. Then frowning for a moment, she asked me for the third time,

'Are you from around here?' Vassilis gently reminded her. She nodded, 'ah yes, a foreigner, indeed, a foreigner!'

'My dowry, ah, my dowry! I made them all. So many fine blankets, sheets, carpets, rugs!' all the while the hand making the familiar circular movement.

'AND,' she looked at me intently, determined that I should hear this,

'Five – hundred – drachma!' (Truly a fortune in those days!) I showed my astonishment properly.

'Po, po, po! SO much.' I said. Satisfied that I was properly impressed, she reached for another olive and somehow, toothless, managed to eat it. The family drifted off to their chores in the little bar. The old lady and I remained sitting in the sunshine and she took my hand. It was a moving experience for me. That old, bent, work-worn hand, it was so cold. Carefully I chaffed it. How much work had it done? How much horta it had cut? How many babies, children, grandchildren, great grandchildren had it held? And how many dishes had it washed?

'Are you from around here?' she asked yet again. We talked a little more. She was contented. Vassilis had brought someone to take her photograph. I felt very contented too and very humble. It is the only time in my life that I have ever had the privilege of communion with such a very old person.

I have since heard that she lived to be one hundred and nine.

Our old pensioner Angliliki died. She was old and almost blind so was quietly mourned. We attended the funeral, of course, but her goddaughter arranged everything.

Now we understood that our excellent neighbour Mitsos Petropolos was gravely ill. He had suffered with stomach pains for three years, fiercely refusing to go to a doctor. Now it was too late and they removed most of his stomach.

We visited him in the local hospital and watched while his devoted wife poked morsels of food into his mouth like a mother bird. Home again, he disposed of all but his favourite sheep and spent his days snipping away at his orange trees while playing with his grandchildren.

His whole family was with him when he died late at night. We were informed immediately but told not to come that night to 'sit', as is the custom.

We called the next morning and Stamos gently rocked the devastated Angiliki while she sobbed. Then he went home leaving me there as family representative. He was very quiet, said little, but I could see that while he grieved, he was fearful too.

Mitsos was laid out in his coffin on the dining table in the middle of the room which served as bedroom, kitchen, dining and sitting room. Everyone, relatives and neighbours, mostly old ladies in deepest black, sat around him keening quietly. Angiliki wore brand new, all black-clothes. She was numb and exhausted and finally quiet. She had always been the tough, noisy one, who hounded her whole family, unmercifully, particularly her daughters-in-law.

How well I remember their elegant dancing at all the feast days we shared. A cloth held between them, hands raised, they circled the floor with such grace while occasionally Mitsos let out a wild whoop or whistle.

I remember their telling me of their marriage in the mountains, and how afterwards, they had walked to their new home. Carrying all their possessions, driving their few sheep, they walked for four days, sleeping rough on the way.

As just about their closest neighbour and good friend, I was, despite my ignorance, kindly included in the domestic arrangements being made for the funeral.

A great pot sat on the little gas stove where five kilos of freshly washed wheat was put to boil. I felt it a privilege that it was ours, for wheat, the staff of life, plays an important role in Greek Orthodox funerals. As the death had been expected, there was no need to postpone the funeral which was arranged for the following day.

Very many people came, all soberly dressed. They crept into the house crossing themselves, three times. Voices were hushed as everyone said to each other and to the family,

'Zoe sto sas, zoe sto sas.' (Life to you, life to you.)

Inside the little house two wall mirrors were swathed in black drapes. No one seemed to know why, when I asked. It was just the custom, maybe it was something to do with the devil. One said that a widow must not look into a mirror or the devil might take her too. Another said it was not right that she be vain at this moment. Yet another said that the devil himself might be hiding in there.

Mitsos' jaw was tightly bound shut, in case the devil might creep in and steal his soul. He might come in the guise of a fly, or a cat, and someone was always on guard with a fly swatter in hand. Should a cat appear, it is roughly shooed away. No risk is taken.

Two large candles were set up at his head and his feet. They were to burn until the he left the house to go for the burial. They would accompany the body to the church. After the funeral, they would be burnt at home for two hours for the next three nights or until totally used up. On no condition should they be thrown away, for they were to help the soul to depart.

Meanwhile, and for forty days, a small lamp would burn, the wick floating in oil on water. Three other candles burnt continuously, set in a bowl of wheat. I suppose in draughty houses there were many flames burning, just in case some should blow out. At all costs, the soul must be helped on its way.

Mitsos lay serene and very smart in his coffin. His widow told me later that they had bathed him entirely in about two litres of wine. Then, they had dressed him completely in new clothes, even to his shoes. I can't believe that Mitsos, who was so frugal and very practical, would have been impressed. The only thing she told me which were not new, were his komboloi, (worry beads) which lay twisted in his hands.

'I didn't see any as nice,' she told me. 'So I let him take his old ones.'

Before leaving for the cemetery, in order to break from his earthly home, three women did a curious passing of a candle around and over the coffin. Standing close, they did a strange weaving of hands, the candle being passed from one to the other. First to the left, swap the candle. Then to the right and back again. The circle was curiously broken several times, an interruption of movement. At last they stopped when they deemed that the ring of life was broken. It was strangely beautiful.

We congregated outside in the yard. The patched old concrete yard, where we had shared so many happy Easter and wedding feasts.

Suddenly a plate flew out of the front door and smashed dramatically on the ground. Turning to Soula, a Petropolous daughter-in-law and good friend of mine, I raised my eyebrows in surprise. Surely no one was having a tantrum at this moment? She replied with a half-smile. No tantrum, just another bid to frighten off the devil.

It was a long slow walk to the cemetery. Stamos not being very well, we drove behind. Everyone wore black, the women with black head scarves. Despite the short notice there was a good crowd, for Mitsos had been much loved. Traditionally the dead must be buried the day after death, unless there is any legal reason not to do so. This must be because of the heat and in the past, lack of refrigerated morgues.

The local cemetery is on the outskirts of town, our side. It is grossly over-crowded and overflows precariously down a slope. There are many magnificent old tombs and family vaults, many being extravagantly festooned with plastic flowers.

We shuffled into the small chapel of rest and filed past the coffin to make our last salutations, most kissing the icon laid on his breast; all crossing themselves. The coffin was laid before the altar with the two big candles burning at head and feet. The women had literally strewn Mitsos' body with flowers. Once more Stamos held Angiliki in his arms and oh, she did weep bitterly. It was a cold blustery day and many could not get into the chapel, so hung about outside where loudspeakers relayed the service.

Propped up there outside against the wall, were huge floral tributes from family and friends. Some were taller than a man, set on tripods and swathed with wide purple ribbons where the donor's name was written in gold. There was a big shallow basket where lesser tributes were laid, and I added my bunch of wild flowers, which I knew he would like.

The family lined up at the door as we filed out. The coffin closed, the priest led the way to his tiny plot. There he would lie for four years I was told, when the bones are removed and stored elsewhere.

The plain boiled wheat and baskets of semi-sweet biscuits were handed round. Everyone took a handful. What was left of the wheat was poured over the grave and covered with a mountain of flowers.

447

The mourners then straggled back to the house where miraculously, a wake was laid out. Tables and chairs were all packed into two rooms and everyone struggled for a seat. Baked cod fillets, potatoes, cabbage salad, bread and wine were served to about one hundred people.

At that time, only half understanding the pain the widow must be feeling, I went over for a short time every day. If I was going to town, I stopped by to collect her to drop her off at the cemetery. In her desolate state, all the village traditions and rituals were an essential. Whatever she did, even now, she did with her usual determination and energy.

She was touchingly pleased with my interest in all these matters, and instructed me with diligence. Perhaps it helped her to feel less lonely.

For nine evenings after the funeral, the family drove to the cemetery where they re-lit the candles and wept a little. On the third day, back at the chapel, another service was held, to release the soul. The other half of the plain boiled wheat was laid out on a cloth but not eaten. Without refrigeration it goes bad quite quickly and many are ill from eating it. Once again it was strewn on the grave where no doubt the birds and mice enjoyed it.

Next, Mrs Petropolous threw herself with a frenzy into cleaning her home. Everything, but everything had to be washed and scrubbed clean. Sheets, blankets, curtains and rugs. Ceilings, walls, floors and windows. It occurred to me that this was very clever occupational therapy for a grieving widow.

On the ninth day, another service was held. The same dull biscuits were served but the wheat this time was quite different. This time it was gorgeous. Full of titbits, it was delicious. Nuts and raisins, jewel-red pomegranate pieces, flaked green parsley, silver coated balls and lozenges, spices and icing sugar were all mixed together.

Next came the all important forty days' service and feast. Much as I appreciated how these rituals kept the bereaved occupied, I was appalled by the expense of it all. This time the pretty wheat was handed round in little paper bags printed with the deceased's name on. It was to remember him, 'with sweetness.'

The very first time I met this charming custom, I was accosted by a total stranger, an old lady in black bearing a plate piled high with pretty wheat, which she offered me. Bewildered, I asked her what it was all about. Delighted to explain it to a foreigner, she told me it was to remember her dead husband. Searching for the right words of sympathy, I was cheerfully 'put down'. He had died this day forty years previously.

At six months, there was another service with the handing out of sweet wheat. At one year, there was yet another service with the wheat and a feast for all comers. There is no cremation in Greece. The Greek Orthodox church believes that the body rises to heaven intact upon the day of judgment.

The final service would be at four years when the bones would be removed to their final resting place. Thereafter, the widow would celebrate the annual anniversary of her husband's death with making and handing around the sweet wheat. She would wear black for the rest of her life.

I was filled with awe by these humble women, who, not being able to read, kept up every custom by word of mouth. And every anniversary, however long past, was remembered and acknowledged, thus filling their hard-working lives.

Alas, our lives now spiralled downwards as in a vortex. Everything which could go wrong, went wrong. I was not managing at all. Not only could I barely earn the money we needed to survive, I was feeling ever more vulnerable in every way. There was no one to confide in. The family centred all their attention on Stamos, as they should of course. But I, in the background, the outsider, needed help too.

Still we did not speak of the future, yet I watched him as one who loves does. I knew exactly when he needed treatment, because his behaviour changed. It was almost a relief when he was in Athens because then I could weep and wail, be angry and forget about the eternal necessity to, 'Be Strong'.

Jack, a big lad now, had gone to work with his brothers to accumulate cash for his future life. I missed him in every way but we always kept in touch.

Caring for Stamos and feeding him properly was my main task. Fortunately, Fredo was a lively, normal child who kept busy at home and school without trouble. As the months passed, it became clear that without help, I just could not manage the farm alone.

Diamando, my dear old mare was getting old. We found her lying down, unable to rise several times. I feared her heart was failing. Try as we did to hoist her up with the tractor, it just did not work. So dear lovely girl, I had her put down. A bulldozer came, so she too is buried in a corner on the farm. I have such regret, why does one grow so fond of animals?

Then there was Lily the pig, another good friend. She had given us so many lovely piglets which we had sold, traded or eaten. I was having difficulty in feeding her. I refused to send her to the slaughterhouse, for she was as family.

Then the day came when a butcher in town wanted pork for souvlakia. He was a Sarakatzani, originally from our mountain village so I trusted him. When finally I gave in from pressure and total despair, I arranged that he should take her carcass. I didn't want to have anything to do with it and dear Lily went off thinking she was off on a jaunt.

You won't believe it. You will. He backed down on the deal. I was left with a huge quantity of pork which I did not want.

Worse, the men at the slaughterhouse told me that inside Lily there were thirteen un-born piglets.

Such guilt, such sorrow. That meat was the only meat we had home produced, that I did not eat. Dear Lilly.

Down I went, and down.

Then Stamos said we must sell the cows, because I could not cope alone and he could not help me. A tough guy came from just outside Athens where he had a big milking herd. He beat us down shamefully. When the truck came, my lovely girls panicked for they had never been on anything so huge or been so roughly treated. Impatient at their dithering, he got out a great bull whip and began lashing them. Blood spurted everywhere and furious, bursting into tears, I thrust the money back into his hands and told him to 'GO!'

But Stamos intervened and off they went while I wept in the house. Now he tried to take the cow money from me, my girls, who I had paid for, but I was adamant. How would we survive with absolutely nothing in the bank. The following day I drove to town and deposited in my bank, thus, I kept our family. I had always intended to go to see the cows en-route to Athens, but I never did.

At least that money kept us for the whole winter. Goodness knows how, during that year without the groups, we would have lived otherwise.

Chapter 19

Still Struggling

Slowly but very surely the farm was running down as time was running out for Stamos. After the cows had gone the excellent Scandinavians took our nanny goat Serena to add to their menagerie. Even while having the cows, she had remained as part of the family, for she was such a fine animal in every way. Prolific with milk and kids, she was also the calmest, kindest beast, and being thoroughly used to children, would be happy with them.

It was a slow and painful process, that 'giving up'. It was also very much a mixed blessing, for now we had no fruits of the earth to fall back on at bad times.

I was still being kept absolutely in the dark as to Stamos' illness and being so close to him every day, the deterioration was so very gradual, I barely saw it. When he went to Athens to see doctors, I remained at home carrying on. There was always plenty to do. In summer with the groups, and in winter, selling oranges and just ticking over.

It was perhaps due to the groups, as well as habit, that I kept on with sowing a little unused corner here and there on the land, with wheat for our bread. It was the minimum of work growing it. It cost so little to buy the seed and to harvest it. And after all with my mill and the fournos, it seemed the very best thing in every way to just continue baking our own bread as usual.

Each time I asked Stamos to help me to hitch the spreader on to the tractor, he found a reason not to do so. As the months went by, however gently I asked, he demurred, until it dawned on me that poor darling, he had no courage left. He had lost his spirit entirely.

Of course I realised that he was terminally ill. I knew in my heart that he would be dying in the not too distant future. But not yet, not yet. Meanwhile it came about that it was up to me to strive alone to support our little family and take what worries off his shoulders that I could.

He was always worried; well there was little to be happy about. I knew that, although at a distance, another tragedy was happening. He sorrowed greatly over his only daughter Maria, whose marriage was failing and he was not strong enough or near enough physically to help her by intervening in the destructive force which was systematically wearing her down until she broke.

I often told Stamos, that of all his children, Maria was the most intelligent, the one with inborn logic. Why was this happening to her of all people, why?

Several wonderful and intelligent Greek women have told me of how it is pretty commonplace in all strata of society that the relatives interfere with their young people's lives to such a degree, that they often destroy them. Could it be inadequacy, envy, or even loneliness which drives them to it? Or, a superiority complex, that NO ONE is good enough for their child, sister, brother, father or mother. So it begins in a small way with niggling little criticisms, which gradually develop into a full scale and ferocious war.

Perhaps it had finally dawned, that however cruel the onslaught directed at me, it was at last accepted that Stamos and I were too strong and loving a couple to break up. I can't believe that years of such crooked fantasy had been consciously stopped because of Stamos' illness. There simply was not the love, decency or sensitivity there. Alas no, that would be far too much to hope for.

For the moment I was left alone, while the hatred switched full force onto pastures new, providing entertainment and fresh fuel to distorted minds. Unfortunately the familiar and vitriolic barrage which was removed from me, who perhaps had got just a little used to it, was now directed at Maria. Early acceptance evaporated and her choice of spouse was not approved of, therefore must be ousted.

The word 'con-man' comes to mind. We had one in my family too, known, with hushed breath, as The Wicked Uncle. A good-looking, articulate and oh so charming man, he made his living by preying on vulnerable old spinsters, and before disappearing, relieved them of their all. It was to, (a memory from childhood) obtain diamonds from the Congo, no less. That wicked man robbed the innocent for gain.

Our con-man was of another gene, although I would soon learn that gain would play a significant part in the not too distant future. I can only assume it was either jealousy of other's happiness, or the satisfaction of causing deep distress and mayhem, which was reward to black souls. And as with my wicked uncle, I truthfully believe it is all genetic, for, and sadly, my family does have another one in our generation, exactly the same as that uncle.

Whatever it was, poor Maria just could not cope with it. Having suffered from it for so many years myself, I grieved for her, who was young and very, very fragile. It seemed as an endemic disease, to make mischief, to run down and try to destroy anyone who married into the family. It might have been even more than inadequacy; etcetera, boredom could well have been the root cause. For where there has been no completed education, no real job, merely pottering around dabbling at this and that for years, perhaps that was the reason?

Stamos' second son's marriage had failed, not surprisingly as the boy was far too young and immature. He had at least benefited enormously well from it, whereas he would have achieved nothing in Greece if he had continued the way he was going. He had reason to be hugely grateful to the two British women in the family, for without both of us, he would never have had a decent English education.

Yet how shocked I was, and how I raged inwardly to hear that excellent, hard-working ex-wife, being referred to as 'that bitch'.

At that time there was an incident which perplexed and hurt me. For no reason that I could understand, Stamos suddenly turned furiously against me for several days. While tidying up some magazines during that time, secreted within one, out fell a strange, very fat air-mail letter. It was impressive due to being Express and liberally plastered all over with British postage stamps. I was surprised that it had not been mentioned. Being curious, I pulled the leaves out to find it was a furiously hand-written letter in Greek and I did not even try to read it. However, I did note with interest it was thirteen pages long. So that sudden unpleasantness was due to the fury directed at the young English ex-wife, plus presumably the British in general. So great was the family bond, so immature the fury, so dedicated was he as a loving father, Stamos turned against me as a result, if only for a short time. Of course it goes without saying, it was all about money as I learned later.

The common Greek word for 'queer', 'gay', or homosexual, is 'Pousta'. I could not believe my ears when I heard Maria's extremely heterosexual husband so slated. Perhaps it was a language thing, like the common people casually calling but anybody 'Malaka' (masturbator!) Or the British casually calling someone a bugger.

Expression or not, the full force of hatred behind it finally broke Maria, and Stamos, who was so ill and sad, did not have the strength to intervene and help. There seemed no way he could put a STOP to this latest war, in order to protect his daughter. Any more than he had before, with other nonsenses.

455

Rocking her in my arms while she wept, I used to tell her to just keep away from them. She had chosen her husband, the father of her little daughter. He was a good man, enterprising, and fun. He was her man, her life, her future.

'Keep them in separate compartments,' I urged her. 'Your old family on one side, your new family, on the other. Keep away from them, close your door, do not be influenced by them. Remember the old saying Maria, 'when you know a mule kicks, don't walk behind its back legs'.'

But it was no use, she did not understand what was happening any more than I had. Whereas Stamos and I united in our love, had struggled against it for years, so often almost breaking under the strain, poor Maria succumbed to the destructive force which seemed all pervasive in the family. Tragically, so many lives were destroyed, one way or the other as a result of it.

What with his sorrow and weakness, I eventually understood that I had to sow the little wheat-field myself. He just wasn't strong enough to be involved in such menial tasks, even putting the spreader onto the tractor was too much for him. At last in despair, it being so very late in the season, I asked Yorgos, the good neighbouring farmer, to come and teach me how to sow by hand. But first I went to the mill and bought thirty kilos of good grain.

Both of us swathed in strong tablecloths tied at neck and waist, we began the ancient way to sow wheat. I followed Yorgos as he strode ahead. Heavily pregnant with wheat we walked, up and down, up and down. A handful at a time. Arm swinging in a full arc, a small thrust, barely opening the fingers to release half the grain. A second smaller arc, and a thrust with open fingers, released the rest. How many times did I think of that lovely old children's story, 'The Little Red Hen'. Having gone one way, we now turned and criss-crossed that tatty little field till all the grain was used up. I was so grateful to Yorgos for teaching me, helping me. I was also thrilled to have learned something new, something so ancient and basic. Now we would at least have bread for the coming year.

Next morning I could barely move, I was in agony. It took days for my neck, shoulder and arm to be free of pain.

There was no rain that winter. Miserably, I watched the dry land, a few shoots struggling up through the stones. It was one of the poorest pieces of land on the farm, and with the cows and their good manure gone, I feared it must have reverted back to worthless. Then, as sometimes happens in Greece, we had two weeks of solid rain. So the miracle happened and up it came, a surprisingly bonny little field of pure green, turning to pure gold. We had our field of wheat. Yorgos rang, alerting me that there was a friendly combine in the area who had agreed to harvest my pathetic little pocket-handker-chief field for me.

When it trundled up the drive, Stamos came to life; he must have been feeling well that day, for he generously rejoiced in my success. So despite the poorness of the soil, early lack of rain and my fears, we got over 600 kilos! Not bad at all.

I was not to know it then, but I never came to use any of that wheat for bread. When, before long, disaster struck and I was totally alone, without consultation, or even a share of the proceeds, my wheat, (and much else) was sold behind my back.

I began to realise that Stamos must have been worrying about our future without him, for he suddenly did two unexpected things. The first, he organised the government agricultural insurance for the three of us. Everyone had it to a greater or lesser degree, but he insured us for the most that he could. I understood that it was small, but with Greece now in the European Union, it might go up. At that time and most important, it meant that our medical expenses would be paid. There would be a child allowance of sorts, and on reaching sixty five, I would be entitled to an Old Age Pension. It was the only thing he did for our future, and thereafter, however poor I was, I religiously kept up paying my dues

The other thing he did was to begin proceedings to get Frederikos a Greek passport. Having been born in Britain, he had been on my

457

passport until he began travelling alone. What happened to his application, where and with whom, or whether he had paid, I never knew. Despite many efforts, I was unable to track it down. Later, when I could scarcely manage to keep us, I certainly could not afford to pay for a second passport. So the little shit remains British while I have dual nationality.

A milestone, my fiftieth birthday, had to be celebrated. We were still pretending that all was well. Many friends and neighbours came. Young Mr Philipides the lawyer, was a jazz fanatic and as a gift, he brought his talented band to entertain us. There was some pretty nifty rocking and rolling by a few braves, but unfortunately the party was not a success.

Stamos was rather deaf and with the band virtually on top of us as is the habit in Greece, he could not hear. Trying to talk with his Athenian friends and unable to hear them, he threw a regrettable tantrum and they left. That was the last party we had.

The mountain house continued to give us solace, and without livestock or young workers, we spent many calm days there. While Stamos and Fredo did their own thing, I happily took to gathering the herbs and fruits of autumn.

Purely from habit, and usually now-a-days for giving away, I jammed everything that I could find and reach. Picking fruit on steep slopes is not easy and armed with my glitsa (crook) I risked life and limb in my pursuit of nature's bounty. There were wild plums of several species, gold or pink, just dripping off the trees, and the taste was exceptional. The sheep most certainly would have eaten up the falls, but the local women never did anything with them. Perhaps they had no knowledge of jam-making, or the sugar was too expensive.

This was the time when I regularly collected rose hips to put down for the winter teas. There was a magnificent wild rose bush just below the house. Fat and glorious bright red hips as jewels were there for the picking. In no time, the blood on my hands matched them. Sitting on the veranda, always with one eye roaming over the magnificent view to Mount Killini, I smashed them up while still fresh and soft, bashing them with a pestle and mortar, before laying them out on sheets to dry. There had been a lot of fine, white netting left over from Maria's wedding which I used as little bags for storage.

Once, when Stamos was in Athens we went up to shut the house down for the winter. The beauty and serenity of that place lies deep in my heart. The healing air and the peace, was always a balm to my troubled soul. A few days up there, my equilibrium restored, I could take on windmills.

If we were lucky, if the spring had been soft, we had a fine crop of walnuts to gather. We had salvaged some very long, light poles, the traditional tree thwackers, from some ruined houses. It was quite a task, even with just one tree, for everything was on different levels with steep slopes between. Once down, the walnuts had to be found, so often hiding in nooks and crannies, perfectly camouflaged.

Having collected them, they were now peeled of their husks, if any remained, and laid out on the veranda to dry. The husks were hung up in bags on the beams in the store room for any wool-dying I might be doing in the future. It was the most simple of all natural dyes. By merely boiling up the husks in water without any mordant, I could get olive green, khaki, dark brown and black.

For years I wondered at the surprisingly black hair of some of the older women until at last, I learned their secret. The walnut husks were well boiled, strained and poured into a jar, in which permanently stood a long comb. Daily use ensured that their locks would remain as in their youth. Very clever, very natural.

Loving the curious 'triple-shelled' walnuts of our tree, I always put some to one side to use for decorations at Christmas time.

So late in the season with little work to do, the old ladies used to join me round the table on our rough-paved terrace most evenings. With the wood smoke from the foufou and magic light from the setting sun, it was a delight to have their company. I felt truly, one of them.

459

There was Haralambina, Pattifingers' wife, skinny and old, her voice being quite the biggest thing about her. His name was Haralambos, something to do with JOY, if you please. The same root as 'Hereatai', the beautiful greeting, 'Be joyful, Go with joy, Come with joy'. So she was 'wife of Haralambos', Haralambina.

Yaya, came from just along the way, Panaiotina, wife of Panaiotis. And then there was me, Tripina, wife of Tripos.

Three old witches, we sat with our little glasses of wine and mezzes, gossiping on this or that by the foufou, while my jams bubbled away. They loved it, and so did I.

'Does your master (direct translation here meaning husband) beat you?' asked the poor old Haralambina.

'Let him try,' said I stoutly. 'Only low, bad men without education or self-discipline in my country do such. Mind you,' I raised my finger for effect, 'I told him once when he was angry, if he even thought to hit me; See, see that door?' The old ladies were transfixed.

'You raise a hand to me and I am going, back to my own country and my own people.' (But of course, being a true gentleman, he never did.)

'You were right my good one,' she cackled, 'for if they start, it is like a dog stealing eggs, they get a taste for it and do not stop.' Poor, poor Haralambina.

'And does your master have a mistress?' asked Panaiotina.

'Probably,' I answered, trying to sound nonchalant. 'If so, I feel very sorry for her because he left her in a big hurry when he met me. He was always guilty about it, you know what men are. He had his way with her for years, then left her. Poor thing, let her take the crumbs from our table. For it is me he loves, of that I am quite sure.'

Some evenings we invited Pappoo and Yaya to come around. She was such a lovely person, with her hair neatly done, the thin dark-grey plaits peeping, wound around her head under her mantilla. On these occasions, Yaya always wore a new apron tied over her ragged and patched old dress. Having tidied the house in their honour, wine and eats laid out, it looked lovely and glowed by lamp-light.

'How many lamps has she got lighted?' Yaya asked Pappoo from the corner of her mouth. They counted. Seven. Scandalous!

'I have been reading to Frederikos,' I explained, quietly amused. 'I read to him every evening,' pointing to the books.They nodded, greatly relieved for an excuse for my extravagance.

'She has so many lamps lit to see well, for she has been reading to the child,' they muttered, still nodding at each other. Now that, was all right.

During the winter and spring, the dumping of oranges continued. It seemed that no one wanted them, although in my opinion they were magnificent. One of the troubles with doing anything with the EEC was waiting for the money. Most farmers had precious little behind them, we had nothing.

My regular visits to the pork processing plant behind us gave me an inspiration. Their various sausages were packed and tied in plastic net bags, mostly red but sometimes green or yellow. I bought a huge roll of the red, and we began to sell our oranges direct to Athens. It was such a good feeling actually doing something, earning immediate cash and knowing we sold a great product.

Once again using our consulship, I boldly approached several embassies and consuls. We would deliver every week. I can only suppose that with the coughs and colds rife during the winter, they all thought it a good idea. Having them delivered to the embassies meant the purchasers could take them home by car instead of the heavy chore of shopping for them.

Oh the hours I spent cutting and tying that rough plastic netting, finishing them off with our own label. My poor hands. The cutting had to be precise, so that five kilos would fit in economically, not too tight but without waste. Although it was a painful-to-the-hands and fiddly job, it was well worth it, for it was an occupation as well as being an income, which lifted our spirits.

461

We sold two types. The smaller ones were for squeezing, and they had yellow plastic ribbon handles. It was more economic as they fitted the regular squeezing machines better than the larger. The larger oranges were for the table and had red plastic handles. It was great while it lasted, but all too soon the trees were stripped and that was that.

Although as Stamos grew increasingly ill, still no mention was made of death or indeed of inheritance. We had in the past lightly talked about it.

When we had made the new headstones for his grandparents and Uncle Frederikos, he happily joked, 'And make sure that they put you on my left side so that I can hear you.'

He also told me he would leave the farm divided equally between his four children and me. Not being of a scheming nature, (unfortunately) I never asked to see evidence, I just assumed what he said would be. (A ninny.)

In early summer, I realised that 'something' was going on. We were only visited when something was wanted, never from love or to give help. There was as usual, much talk. But this time, when I entered the room, all talk ceased. It was embarrassing and hurtful so I took the hint and returned to the kitchen to my preparations for a good lunch.

They then left the house and apparently drove to town. I was not informed as to why or where, but it didn't need a great mind to understand that they were going to the lawyer about the will.

I remember exactly what happened when they returned. Or was I imagining that the hard, hating eyes, were glaring at me now, more boldly with triumph?

When Stamos came slowly in, he did not look at me. He ate his lunch too, avoiding eye contact with me, his face was so sad.

Then I knew. A Judas. A cold hand squeezed my heart, for I realised that once again he had been bullied into making a terrible mistake. It would all come out in a few months. Oh my poor, weak

Stamos. He can't have fully understood how serious it was to be, the dreadful mess that he was he was leaving us in. Yet who could blame him, a natural, loving father? He always wanted to believe the best, so poor thing, poor us, he believed all the promises made to him on that day, which were worthless, empty. He had just signed away any chance for justice for us all.

We, his wife and his little son, would be abandoned completely to a new life alone, without his love and protection as well as a life of deepest sorrow and total poverty. It would all be clear, all too soon.

Surely, if he had known, surely he would not have agreed to it? But perhaps because he was ill and fearful, he did succumb to a most wicked confidence trick.

Oh my poor lovely Stamos, he had just made his worst and last mistake.

Chapter 20

Down

When I had first met Stamos, he used to smoke thin little cigars which he broke in half. This seemed to be his one indulgence. The smell was pleasant and didn't lie heavily in the air, and I liked it, whereas I really hated cigarette smoke.

When he was diagnosed as having leukaemia, he was firmly told that he must stop smoking, and he did. For a while anyway. I puzzled slightly when he took to slipping out of the French doors to wander about in the mandarin grove. Until one day when he came in and I kissed him.

'You have been smoking!' I recoiled in shock.

'No I haven't,' he lied.

It was a very rare thing for me to rage at him but then I did.

'Everyone is working so hard to keep you well, and what are you doing? Sneaking off to smoke, disobeying your doctors!'

I was so furious, he was surprised. The next time I took him to Athens to the hospital I went in with him.

'Why?' I asked his doctor, 'are you wasting your time with Stamos? You told him that he must NOT smoke. He is.'

464

So he was taken to task and well scolded. Once more he gave up smoking.

Since then, years on, I consider that I made a mistake. He was dying anyway, what harm would it do to allow him the small pleasure of enjoying his little cigars? But while there is life there is hope. I was misguided by my love for him. I desperately wanted him to beat his illness, and to stay with us for as long as possible.

After the orange crop, life was 'thin' again and without work, I despaired. There was one corner of the land on the front northern border which was virtually useless. The soil was very sandy and poor, as well as being a very awkward shape, we never used it. I begged him to sell it; to pay off his debts, to help his children, and to ease our lives just a little. But he would not, ever fearful and weary of the violent criticisms which would inevitably follow.

'Let them do it.' They never have, and the debts have now increased fivefold.

Nonetheless, early summer that year was loving and precious. Nothing interesting took place in our lives but we were quietly contented to be together. His children came now and again, so while they talked, I dished up good meals.

They were going to the cinema one night. To my surprise Fredo was invited too. I was not keen, knowing the rubbish usually shown in town, but Stamos agreed to let him go. They returned at about eleven, and remained chattering and smoking in the kitchen. At midnight I went and hauled Fredo away to come to bed.

This was to be quite a night. No sooner asleep, than I heard him wailing.

'What is it Fredo?'

'A snake,' he sobbed, 'there was a big snake in the film.'

'Come,' said I, 'come and sleep with us.'Gladly the little chap rushed across the room and got in between us, safe at last. It was like having a large cricket in the bed. He tossed and turned, kicked and flayed his arms about. Exhausted in the morning, Stamos smiled lovingly at us.

465

'Well, that was a lovely night, wasn't it?' Fredo never forgot his saying that.

Yet again, Stamos became ill and this time he was put into a hospital on the northern outskirts of Athens. It was a pleasant place, not unlike the one where years before we had both languished with meningitis. Acres of shady pine woods had fine old buildings dotted around. Heavy ceramic-tiled roofs and broad verandas gave it a colonial air. It was, after the frenetic activity of the city, very peaceful.

He was put into what had been a single room but which now had two huge beds in it, so it was very cramped. A call came for me.

'You must come to Athens to be with and nurse him.'

I was shocked. How could I possibly leave the farm and Frederikos and go to live in Athens to look after Stamos? How could I abandon my child? This was of course, a question of what you were used to. In my book if you were in hospital, there were trained staff to nurse you. Relatives only came to visit.

Not so, of course, as everyone knows, in Greece and other Mediterranean countries. The nurses do the minimum. The relatives do everything else.

Now we began to spiral downwards into the depths of hell. Stamos' eldest son was persuaded to stay at the farm in my absence. The summer groups had begun, our only income; it was imperative that I continued with them. So I spent six days in Athens with Stamos, left on Thursday night for the farm, then returned on Friday afternoon after the group had left.

It took quite some organisation at long distance. I ordered what I could by phone or shopped at a huge supermarket en-route back to the farm. It was desperately hot, a lot of work. There were still young people helping at the farm.

One evening when I returned I called for Frederikos. Where was he?

'He is at the cinema.'

'With whom?'

'Oh he is on his own, he goes every evening. I drop him off and collect him.'

I began to tremble. I tremble now with the memory of it. My very attractive, blonde nine year old son, was dumped in one of the several cinemas in town, EVERY evening! Just to get rid of him. What kind of responsibility was that? This was a garrison town! He was alone. I began to weep, I weep now remembering it. I felt so helpless, fearing, as every mother, of all the things which could happen to him.

So shattered and distressed was I, that I did it all wrong of course. What I should have done, was to totally let go. I should have taken the stick to my stepson who was in charge, and screamed at the few foreign workers who should have known better. The stiff upper lip was quivering perilously. No longer could I 'Be strong'!

Instead, when poor Fredo came in, I took a glitsa from behind the door and beat my child. I beat him and I beat him, screaming, crying, raging. And then we held each other sobbing, and while we wept together, I begged his forgiveness. For he had been blameless, an abandoned child.

Baba was ill, Mummy was in Athens with him. His little world was crumbling all about him. There was NO ONE in that place with any sense of responsibility. Not one decent human being cared for him. As for love, with us gone, love had gone too.

Over the years I have continued to beg his forgiveness. Today, more than twelve years on, the 25th of March, 2001, Mother's Day, just when I was writing this, he phoned. He chose his moment as it happens, for once again, weeping, I told him how deeply sorry I still am for that loss of control, and again begged his forgiveness.

He laughed.

Then, remembering all the children who I had cared for, loved, nurtured, for weeks and months at a time over so many years, I began calling around. There was a debt to be re-paid to me. I desperately needed help. Surely there was someone out there who would have him in our time of need?

467

I freely admit that apart from being very lively, Fredo had become increasingly and deeply disturbed. Now, he was wild, as an abandoned, loveless child. Very half-hearted offers dribbled in. Memories are often so short. A few days here, a few days there, which made him, if possible, ever more unhappy and unstable.

Despite phoning him every day, I was increasingly ever more worried. Then, one day when he did not answer the phone, I panicked. The young people had all gone their ways. The farm was no longer a happy, organised place as of old. The cook had gone, there was little money, so why should they labour for free?

As always there was goodness, right there on our door-step. Knowing the system and that I was in Athens with Stamos, most dear Angiliki Petropolou took over. Aware of the ways of Greek men, she went across to the farm to wash up and clean every day. Most excellent friend and neighbour, how blessed we were.

It was from her that I heard that Fredo was still asleep at noon.

'Oh Mummy, Mummy, I was so frightened Mummy. I couldn't sleep,' he told me. 'Because I was all alone.'

'Why darling, why were you all alone, isn't your brother there?'

'No,' came the reply, 'he went to Athens; he said not to tell you.'

All the recent years of strife and sorrow now bubbled up inside me turning into pure hatred, because now my child was suffering. Show me one normal mother who wouldn't feel the same. With Stamos ill and out of the way, what little sense there ever had been, was now gone.

It was obvious that no one would help us. The few cousins who could have helped, kept their distance. Increasingly desperate, I called my sister in London, as a last resort. For she had recently married an elderly man who would understandably not welcome a lively kid in his lovely home. There seemed no other solution.

The memories are very vivid and precious of that last togetherness. Stamos was so proud of his handsome little son, all dressed up with his back-pack on, ready to fly away to stay with his aunt, all on his own. Together they wandered hand in hand around the building. Making introductions, shaking hands, explanations being made, everyone smiling, and all the while Stamos was brimming with pride.

New friends in the diplomatic service now offered me the use of a flat in their basement nearby, for whenever I needed it. This meant that I could go to shower and weep in private. For I still maintained a determined hold on my emotions. It wouldn't do at all to break down in front of Stamos. I was utterly miserable. Sleep was almost an impossibility and the only thing which tipped me into oblivion was a bottle of Amstel beer, which unfortunately resulted in my putting on a lot of weight.

Every evening Stamos' friends came to see him. Alison the diplomat's wife came too and he was charmed by her gaggle of lovely little fair-haired daughters.

Father Bert, the Anglican chaplin who had often visited us on the farm, came weekly. I used to ask him to hold the oxygen tubes in place while I went to wash Stamos' pyjamas. On my return I would find him, eyes shut, head in hands. This touched me so much, for here at least was someone actually praying for Stamos. No Orthodox priest ever came.

The deterioration was speeding up alarmingly. A young doctor told me quietly,

'The situation is very grave.'

Again without consultation, a night nurse was employed. A hard-faced woman who arrived at eleven and left at five in the morning. With her flask of black coffee and cigarettes, she sat outside all night and did the minimum. Stamos hated her.

I was lent a little deck-chair so that I could sit outside too. Obviously someone else used it, for one day I found that the canvas had been ripped and it was useless. Heavy disapproval came my way. A cheap deck-chair. Funny how little things stay in the mind. I bought new canvas and repaired it. It cost five hundred drax, a fortune to me at that time.

Instead of leaving Athens on Thursday evenings to do the groups, I now left at five on Friday morning to return at five at night.

It was terribly hot in July and August. The sweat used to trickle down the back of my legs and down my front as I worked. Helen, an English friend also married to a Greek, came to assist me. An efficient and fast worker, she was a great help, particularly as she spoke English with our guests.

I had to budget so carefully, because I was determined to send Eleni her monthly pittance as well as keeping us. Stamos had long given up caring for anything.

It was a big group that time, about fifty guests. As usual they were lovely and perhaps knowing my situation, were extra kind. After they left and all was tidy again, I did my accounts; it had been a good day. After I settled my bills, the profit was twenty thousand drachma. I left fifteen thousand for running the house and kept five for myself. I needed petrol, and with the poor hospital food, I would buy extra little things to tempt Stamos.

Handing over the notes, I made to leave. But I could not. As I approached the door, my way was barred. I went to the French doors and again could not get out. I ran to the hall door, and again, a solid brute stood between me and freedom. I was very shocked, abhoring violence of every kind, I had never, ever, in all my life been so roughly shoved and pushed about.

'Give me money!'

I was aghast. Was I hearing right? I had just handed over the lion's share of my day's profits. I had nothing else. What was this?

'I have given you fifteen out of the twenty profit I made today, I must keep five. I have nothing else.'

'Give me money!' like a deaf lunatic.

I sat down, I was dreadfully tired for it had been a long, very hot and hard day. What was he talking about? I had been as fair as I could, more than fair. There was no more. I tried to explain, all my own money had long gone. But it was no use.

Once again I tried to leave. Once again my way was barred. Was he mad? I had to get back to Stamos.

'Give me money, give me money, give me money,' as a parrot.

Trying to reach the door handle to the hall I tried to force my way out and was roughly thrown backwards on to the rail of Fredo's cart bed. My back hurt. Now I was really angry. Perhaps if I hadn't been so tired I would not have let go.

'Get out of my way,' and lifted my hand to deliver a slap, as to a bad child.

I don't know how long I was unconscious, but I could hear a wailing in the distance which was me. I was lying some yards away, by the fireplace. A terrible blow to the side of my head had thrown me there. My mind was screaming,

'Stamo, Stamo!'

The next thing I became aware of, was another voice,

'Don't tell my father, don't tell my father.'

It took some time to sink in. As with all bullies, this one was a coward too.

As if I would tell Stamos. How to tell a dying man who I loved, the whole awful, ugly truth? What good would it do, how could I give him more pain than he had already? But again, looking back, that is exactly what I should have done and in so doing save myself years of hardship. Theirs was a fantasy world, a Cloud Cuckoo Land. Marvellous tales were put about of how rich their father had been when I, the wicked step-mother, had arrived and spent it all. My swallowed-up small fortune was totally dismissed. They liked to believe that Stamos had always paid for everything.

Haralambina would be proved right, for this was just the beginning. I would not, in the future, be the only one to be subjected to physical violence. But at the time, I had absolutely no idea of how much worse things would get before long. I just lived for the day, and every day was Stamos'. A terrible mistake.

471

For he was dying, and we would live. There was still time to change his will, to put things properly and decently in order. But I was breaking and could not tell him.

The next day my eyes were black. I ladled the make up on, something unusual for me, but they were too bad and he noticed. Friends and relatives turned away embarrassed, they did not want to know.

'What happened?' Stamos asked me, distressed and shocked.

'I fell,' I lied.

'Where?' he demanded.

'Going up the steps on the side terrace,' I lied again.

He did not believe me, of that I am sure. But I stuck to my guns. You don't tell such a hideous truth to so sick a man. At least, and more fool me, I did not.

I called on an English doctor friend and asked her to look at me. Quite obviously I had severe whiplash for my head wobbled dreadfully, and I could not keep it still. To this day when I am tired or nervous, it still shakes.

To my sorrow and hurt, this friend, who together with friends and relations, had over the years enjoyed our hospitality countless times, informed me that she had no time to stand up in court for me.

Court? Court? What was she talking about? Whoever said anything about court? This was Greece, and she had grown accustomed to how they did things here. It wasn't a court I needed, it was medical attention, love, kindness and support. Nowadays, I hear the words 'counsellor', or 'being counselled' at every turn. That is what I needed, but there was no one.

Ruth brought me some mending to do. She had been given two small pieces of beautiful, very old Greek embroidery in poor condition. So now I sat beside Stamos every day, wondering at the glorious work and colours, carefully restoring them with backing and tiny stitches. He was so pleased. Later, Ruth gave them to me and even now I have them, hanging up, framed, a poignant memory.

Then I was told, no consultation or discussion again, just told, that Stamos was to be moved to the Intensive Care Unit in the centre. 'It costs sixty thousand drachma a day. You must pay half.' Gob-smacked again, I said absolutely nothing. Well, what could I say? If I was very lucky, our summer income for the month was sixty thousand drax. with which to keep the whole family. I had Stamos' bank book which had six hundred drax in. (I have it yet, intact.) I was sorry he was to be moved though, because Stamos was happy where he was, it was a gentle place. We had made friends with many of the other patients, it was as a loving, caring family, just what we needed.

If only I could have totally lost control and wept and wailed and told all the ghastly truths. Thirty thousand drax. a day? Laughable.

The third week in August has the biggest religious holiday of the year, apart from Easter. The feast of the Virgin. Accidents on the roads are always fearful, all the hospitals are overflowing. So it was that the Intensive Care Unit was full. Stamos didn't go after all, so I was saved the embarrassment of not being able to pay my half.

Compared with the other hospitals I had been in, I found this one quite the nicest. The staff were all kindly, the atmosphere was good. Stamos was getting better, he was to come home and we were so joyful.

Early on the morning of departure I went to kiss him and reared back in shock. He was on fire, a raging temperature. He would not be going home. 'Wired up' all the time, when the drip needed changing I would ring the bell. As well as being pleasant, this hospital was rather modern. A voice would float down from a small speaker above the door.

'What do you want?'

After I had replied, they usually took ages; very worrying.

When everything in Stamos' body began to pack up, things became worse by the day. He had had increasing prostate trouble for years and refused to do anything about it. The poor food and his sick body, caused him to be totally stopped up and he was very uncomfortable. I rang the bell.

'What do you want?'

'Please will you bring a suppository for my husband?'

We waited, and asked and waited, until on the third day I got very huffy.

'We are waiting for a male nurse to come from the main building.'

A male nurse? A MALE nurse?

'Why can't YOU come to do it?' I asked.

'It is not allowed kyria, a male nurse must do this for a male patient.'

Grief! I was incredulous, for in my knowledge, a patient is a patient, is a patient.

'Bring me the suppositories, I will do it.' So at last in some small way at least, Stamos became more comfortable. The heat was so terrible however, that I had to keep the suppositories in an ice box to prevent them from melting.

Stamos could no longer walk so I wheeled him to the bathroom every day. An English couple, acquaintances from the Anglican church, met me in the corridor on a return journey. They waited till he was settled, then took me to one side and gave me the name of a lady lawyer who they suggested I would be needing. Touched by their thoughtfulness, I was nonetheless still in ignorance of what the future would bring.

Every night, Stamos' friends and family gathered to see him although half the time he was sleeping, so they sat in the hallway to talk together. Then I would leave to go to the friend's house nearby, to shower and hopefully to sleep. At five in the morning, I was back to take over from the dreadful night nurse.

Early on the 28th of August, I went into his room to find it was stinking. Stamos, the cleanest of the clean, was lying in a bed of filth and the nurse was raging at him while he was hitting at her. Incensed, I told her to get out, and set to work to clean him up. Ill though he was, he knew it was me, and gave me the most beatific smile, 'Judaki, Judaki,' which almost broke my resolve to 'Be strong.'

I decided then, that I would never leave him alone again in her cruel hands. As the patient in the next bed had left, I determined to sleep there beside him in future. I would never leave him again. When the nightly visitors came, I rushed off for my shower and this time returned at eleven to stay with him.

To my annoyance, a couple arrived and demanded the second bed. My patience was thin, I quarrelled fiercely, babbling at them. My husband was dying, I needed the bed, we needed the room for ourselves. Of course I didn't know he was dying! I just did not want them in there. But at the word 'death' they scuttled off. We had just a little peace at last.

In the early hours of Tuesday, the 30th of August, a crowd of doctors and nurses came in. All Stamos' veins had collapsed, yet they were determined to set up his drip, and now followed a desperately distressing time. They prodded and poked needles in him; arms, legs, everywhere. And all the while Stamos groaned and called out in agony.

'Are you in pain my darling?' he nodded. 'Where?' I asked.

'Everywhere.' he replied.

'Leave him alone,' I implored, 'just let him sleep. Do it in the morning. Please, please, go away, leave him in peace.' But no, they went on and on so that he was exhausted and I became frantic. At last they found a vein; they left at one fifty.

'Come my darling,' I caressed him, 'let us get you comfy.'

Now the wretched night nurse, with probably more experience of death than I had, helped me. A sore was forming on his hip, I rubbed Magic Oil on it. We turned him.

'There my darling,' kissing his brow, 'There. Now you are more comfortable, now you can go to sleep.'

'Sleep,' said Stamos, 'Sleep.' And died.

BOOK III

Chapter 1

A Vale of Tears

Stamos died.

Perhaps I had read about it, that 'death rattle', but I had no experience of it before and this is what happened. As we turned him, there was a curious, dry rattle in his throat, and I remember crying out and quickly turning him again so that I could start trying to resuscitate him. A young doctor who had been attending him must have heard me, for he returned immediately. Firmly I was pushed to one side while nurses came running carrying equipment so I took the opportunity to go quickly to the phone in the hall where I rang my sister-in-law. I even remember what I said,

'Come at once.'

Just that, and fled back into Stamos' room. By then he was wired up it seemed everywhere, arms and legs, but there was no sign of heartbeat. They removed the apparatus and began taking it away. The doctor kindly took my hand and shook it.

So he had gone, and even though I had known he was really ill, it was a terrible shock. I remember cradling his head in my arms, seeing the sudden deathly white pallor, yet he was still warm. I closed his eyes and rocked him, telling him how sorry I was he had died. Then I went out into the night, it was the early hours, and walked through the dark, silent pine woods to the front gate to wait for my sister-in-law.

It was so peaceful, I was not afraid although I had been warned not to walk in the hospital grounds at night. But I did not feel alone for I felt both my father and Stamos walking with me. The night-nurse, that horror, who he had hated and who had not taken care of him, had at least tidied everything up and put it on the veranda.

Two porters came with a low trolley and we watched them as they lifted him onto it. That was the last time I saw Stamos. I remember stating that I wanted him buried at the farm, because that is what he wanted.

'Make sure they put you on my left side.' He used to joke, because he was so deaf in his right ear.

The next day is a jumble of sorrow and tears and being dimly aware that the family completely ignored me, I might as well not have existed. I was instructed to take the nurse to her home, and to give her five thousand drax, which I very reluctantly parted with. She had been so awful, lazy, cruel, smoking on the veranda, all night, and, she had been paid, now this, and I was so grievously short of money myself.

A dear American friend, who we always called 'Little Mary', took me in hand and trawled me around the shops till we found two very simple, black cotton dresses. I have them yet, somewhat worn. I also have Little Mary, albeit far away, still a good friend.

A sweet woman friend of the family stayed with me and drove me to the airport to meet Frederikos. I had phoned my sister in London, of course, but not to tell him his father had died as there might have been tears on the plane. All those weeks and months of BEING STRONG, now seemed to desert me. I was numb, but the tears were just under the surface and how to meet the boy in a busy airport and tell him?

So I rang the airport authorities, spoke to a young woman, explained the situation, and asked if there was a private room we could go to, and, can you believe it, she began shrieking! Now that was just what I needed! Another young woman came on the line, gentle, intelligent and, because, as she told me, she had been through exactly the same loss as a child, kindly directed me to a staircase, where at the top there was a small room. So I took Fredo up there and sat him down and told him,

'Darling, your daddy died last night.'

And his response was to shout 'No, no, no!' So we hugged each other and wept.

By then I did know the rule in Greece to bury the dead the following day, all hot countries do it and so plans were made, to bury him at the farm. This at least was done because I asked for it, but in every other way, I was ignored.

The next morning Fredo and I drove back to the farm and stopped at a huge super market as I intended to give Stamos a Wake. The funeral was to take place in the early evening and the young men set to digging the grave, just opposite the church, beside his uncle Frederikos and grandparents. It was a noisy day too, as they were using a road drill to get through the conglomerate which was just under the surface. In the kitchen, I toiled away, such a therapy to work, to do the thing I do best. This was going to be a small feast, but I welcomed Mrs Petropoulos who arrived bearing a great dish of the traditional plain, boiled wheat. Stamos would have been so pleased.

People began to arrive in their dozens. The Athenians made themselves at home in the big saloon and demanded endless Greek coffees. The locals hung about the church and admired the enormous, be-ribboned wreathes on stands which had appeared from somewhere. I noticed my name on one, but certainly I had nothing to do with it.

Father Bert Chivers, the chaplain of the Anglican church arrived wearing a simple soutane. I was so touched that he would bother.

481

Here was one of my own people coming to support me! It was he who had visited Stamos weekly, and prayed for him. I was so very grateful.

The Greek Orthodox priest arrived, and from courtesy, I introduced him to Father Bert. Now hear this – 'If he stays,' said that man of God, 'I go.'

So I burst into tears and spluttered that he was NOT a man of God and I hope he understood, the devil. Father Bert then tactfully hid himself away, but the damage was done. BE STRONG, no longer, and all I did was to weep.

The hearse obviously got lost for it was late and I could even smile for my husband who would have hooted with laughter, for it was an incredibly swanky, white affair! Apparently they open the coffin before the burial, and my sister-in-law warned me so I fled with friend Diamando into the church where she sobbed in sympathy with me.

Stamos' mistress was there, the poor little woman he had abandoned to marry me. She howled and wailed as the Greek wife, appalling, and, yes, I comforted her! What use sympathy for one such as she, a low, pathetic woman who had lost all her chances of marriage? For as she left, she came up to me, her eyes blazing with malice, 'The last time we were together was . . .'

I was numb, shocked. Of course I had known, but the man was dying, and if he took comfort from his old mistress, I would not make a scene. I turned the other way. But this declaration, at his funeral? What kind of people were these? Savages? I should have hit her, but I am not that type of woman, I just turned away again.

After everyone left for the house, Father Bert reappeared and said some lovely prayers by the grave, particularly for Frederikos and me. This made me so grateful, although sadly they did not work for many years. Then two little Swedish girl friends sang a song, and somehow, I felt better, so appealed to all Stamos' Athenian friends and close neighbours to stay to feast for him.

It was a 'gentle' evening, using one of Stamos' expressions, except the lights went out, so we sat under the walnut trees and ate by candle light. We learned that it was not just us, or a local failure, but the whole of Greece. This caused merriment, for of course, the lights had gone out for Stamos.

The funeral took place on the 1st of September, 1988, and since that evening, I have neither seen or heard from any of his 'friends'. Not one. They who came so often to feast and stay. They who left their children, (or dogs) with us, not one thought to phone me, 'Are you OK? How is the boy? Are you managing?' Not one. It was such a lesson to me which I have tried to remember. To be kind to bereaved friends, not for just a week or a month, but for always.

The very next day I began to understand my lot. I was a woman and a foreigner, despite having taken dual nationality. I was a widow. Last but not least, I was poor.

Understatement, I was destitute. Having sold my house in England, and had my considerable all, persuaded out of me by a very determined Stamos, all I had was what I earned with the tourist groups. It was September, and I had three more meals to serve. After that, nothing, no income whatsoever. No insurance, nothing in Stamos' bank but the tiny sum of Drax 600. I even tried to take that out later, but was told by them that I must have the signatures of the other three. Naturally I did not bother and still have that book, intact.

While Stamos had been ill, I had done my best with my earnings to keep the place going, and every 1st of the month, I had sent Eleni, the children's mother, her pittance. Now, I was so grateful to him for dieing on the 30th of August, so I did not have to give poor Eleni her money. It was a question of need then, I simply could not afford it, I must think of my child. Yet in the past, she had often phoned and begged help, and I had always sent her something.

After paying for the wake, I was really down to a few hundred draxs. Life had to go on, food to buy and petrol for the Datsun, the only vehicle left. Stamos had sold my Landrovers and as we plunged ever down, we had both struggled to pay monthly for the Datsun.

But I had not any idea of the barrage of abuse I would now face from the family. Of course they wanted me gone, dead too. Having all moved into the house, the children (in their 20s) together with man-friend and little Daphne, who I had been mother to for months in the past, they just took over.

My kitchen was no longer my kitchen, the cooker was no longer my cooker. My matrimonial home was certainly not mine any more. The mess was horrendous because the men left everything for Maria to clean up, as is the custom. When they were out I used to creep in to cook for us, then run.

When Mrs Petropoulous said just after the funeral, 'Don't go, Judy, don't go!' I was surprised, and even shocked. Go! Where to go and indeed HOW to go? I had NO home in England, my money had all gone into the farm and the children. This was my matrimonial home, I had no other. Even so, I was touched by her words. But, Fredo was going to school, and I had to drive him every day, and to try to keep up some normality.

I have never been an 'asker', never. So many people offered to LEND me money at that time, but remembering the mess we were in from Stamos' borrowing, I always refused. When I phoned my mother to tell her that Stamos had died, her unbelievable response was, 'You married a penniless foreigner, you made your bed, you lie on it, don't come to me for help.'

As if I ever would! But, it hurt, no sympathy at all, and the irony is that years later when she was very old and helpless, it was I, who had to look after her.

When I wept in our room, Fredo used to rage at me, 'Stop crying!' In the house I wore my old clothes; if I went out, I always wore black, for the first time in my life, but I had to obey the laws of the land.

The unpleasantness from the young people grew, and they now took away the keys of the Datsun, leaving me without any transport.

I was so shocked, it had been such a struggle to pay the monthly instalments on it. They offered me an old Mini van of theirs, a wreck (which of course I had originally paid for), which was so dangerous they wouldn't drive it, but, they wanted me dead. And what about their 9 year old half brother? I struggled to manage, hitching rides, and one day, the nicest Sarakatzani man, Kostas, drove me to town. And because we were old friends his sympathy for my plight, reduced me to tears. When he dropped me off, he gave me Five Thousand Drachma, a fortune to me, so we could live for ages on it. Years later I took his wife the gift of some good jewellery in thanks. Nothing is free in life!

Then my sister-in-law heard of the key removal, and thankfully, she reprimanded the kids, so I got them back. I was scrupulous about putting in petrol, they were not. They were as unpleasant as they could be at every opportunity, it was shocking.

If only one, decent man in our acquaintance had taken them to task and spoken to them. 'This woman did her best for your father while he was ill. This woman is grieving. Stop this wicked behaviour. Show respect for your father's widow.' But no one had the courage, otherwise my life might have been easier, and, we would not ultimately, have left Greece.

Now came the time to sell my last treasures, and it hurt. A few last pieces of jewellery, some small bits of furniture, and my beloved German, bisque doll, Susannah. With her lovely eyes, matching her hair, which had been mine, long frilly dress and little leather shoes, a nice woman bought her, but I regret it to this day. Acquaintances asked me why my head was shaking. Of course I was aware of it, but not that it was visible to other people. Obviously the vicious blow I had received had damaged my neck. I still wobble, HOW, I ask myself, did I get involved with such an awful family? It has gone on sadly, that total lack of self control, for without Stamos there to guide them, there is no guidance.

One day I went into the kitchen to find the usual mess. Appalling. No clean plate or glass stood on the dresser. The draining boards and dining table were littered with dirty crocks. My sympathy for Maria, who I had loved, took over, despite the fact she was of the three, for a short time anyway, the most vicious to me. So I cleared up, had it looking like my old kitchen, and unexpectedly, she came in. Glancing around at the order, the look of relief on her face was tangible. We did not speak and I left to go into the big room, which Stamos had arranged for us after the big earthquake of 82. Fredo slept in his lovely old cart bed under the stairs, and I slept in the far corner. The young people slept upstairs.

I was told that I must allow them to use the big room in the evenings till nine o'clock. Most of them were smokers, so I said, 'No.' I had been ousted from the kitchen, and so we had to have somewhere peaceful to sit and sleep. My sister came to support me, and some English friends lent us a little house by the sea for a week, which was just what we needed.

A new sorrow hit me, ridiculously, it caused me to weep copiously, all over again. While at the hospital, I had left the little deck chair which had been lent to me, on the veranda outside Stamos' room. A room designed for one bed had two in it, so there really was no space at all to leave anything. Well, someone must have used the chair, and I got lice!

So silly, but it opened the floodgates once more. Lice! Ridiculous.

The young people had decided, for tax reasons, that they must become farmers, so they planted a field of spinach to prove it. A cold wet job as the year waned, but they apparently did well. I was not allowed to farm at all, and having been a real working farmer, this came hard. So I took to handicrafts in order to earn money to keep us. Our needs were few, petrol and food.

I engraved glass and kind people ordered them from me. I made herbal remedies, span wool, carved, you name it, I did it. As Christmas approached, I began making 'steffania', Christmas wreathes. It was luck to spot on a rubbish bin, one of those 'big bead car backs', broken, of course. So I painted the fat wooden beads, red, for berries, indeed I still have some. Beads being so expensive, this really was a windfall. I cut out all sort of little things from tins to put on the wreathes, and this was wonderful therapy. Muriel, an English friend who toils yearly for the Anglican Church Bazaar took me to a supplier of all things Christmassy, and I bought a lot of fluffy green stuff by the metre, for the wreathes.

Meanwhile, the machinery, the bailer, the mill and goodness knows what else, was sold. Having paid for all of them, I never even received the legal one third. So too my last crop of wheat, a mere half a ton, which I had, helped by Yorgos, sown by hand, to provide bread for us. I could not believe it and the children's story of 'The Little Red Hen, came again to mind. Eventually, Stamos' beloved John Deere went, 'lost' through peculiar and incompetent circumstances. At no time was I consulted on any of this, not a drac came my way and being utterly broken and sad, I never said a word.

Now was the time to make enough money to survive through the winter. How I toiled! But what nonsense, a dream indeed. Then, placing my wreathes in big, circular baskets, the kind usually used for bread or nuts in the market, I set off. I was terrified. Selling in the street, a tall foreigner in black, too conspicuous. Yet at first, I was just looked at, or rather, gawped at. I stood in the back of the Datsun with the wreathes on my arm on a Sunday evening when everyone was coming home, held them up, and sold not a one. I had been given a red corduroy suit which I had dyed black, for it was getting chilly. In my left, top pocket, I put my Greek identity card. No go, utterly depressing.

Dear little Mary invited me to stay, she had always been so supportive and kind. Her flat was right in the centre, so I had a better chance as Christmas approached.

'Go to Bucherestion,' I was told, 'there are many artisan there.'

Christmas Eve, I went, and sure enough, there were many others as I, selling their home made wares. With my two baskets brimming with jolly wreathes, I stood, trying to catch the eye of any interesting passer by. A man I knew slightly, friend of my sister-in-law passed. 'Good day, Yorgo,' I called.

Well maybe he didn't recognise me, or maybe he was so horrified to see me standing there, a street seller, he walked on.

Bucherestiou is a handsome pedestrian street, lined with very, very smart shops. As I stood, I noticed a fine, jewellery shop, and suddenly recognised one of the owners. A pleasant woman, she and her husband had been to the farm for lunch. She did not recognise me, and, of course, I did not approach her. Her brother then came out, and looked all along the street at us riff-raff, his face stern.

So the cops arrived, he had sent for them, and we were hustled to move. Now I have said earlier how the tears were always just there, ready to fall. I fought them back, 'Be Strong, be strong'! Impossible.

'Boys,' I said tearfully, in my best Greek. 'How am I to keep my child for the winter if I do not sell my steffania?'

They were young, not unkind. They obviously observed my black clothes and my identity card. If you wear black, you are in mourning, they knew that well.

'Go to Monesteraki, kyria,' they said kindly. 'No one will bother you there.'

It was quite a trek carrying my baskets, but at least, all downhill. Still fearful of this new role of street selling, once there, I hid in a corner, and of course, no one took any notice of me. Then I decided it was time to be courageous, to move to nearer the entrance of the underground station. If my father could see me! Indeed, if my mother could see me! If Stamos could see me! The disgrace, the shame of it. 'Be strong'.

Then, a miracle happened, as they do, thank heaven. Such a miracle, to this day I can not believe it. Suddenly, through the crowds, approached one of the dear, old boys from the farm. One of our long lasting, kindest workers, from Holland, Harry.

We looked at each other incredulous, and hugged, and laughed and of course, I cried, but in happiness. Now, I was not alone, now I had support, a chum. As Gabriel, he stood on guard behind me and my courage soared and I began to sell my steffania, I even gave one to a dear little girl.

As evening fell, I had only three left, wonders, we might survive. I rang Ruth, who had the boy and asked if Harry could come for Christmas lunch, for he was on his own. Of course he could, so we parted happily and I took the underground to Kiffissia, my baskets packed on each other.

Four months since Stamos died, and here it was, Christmas. As we rattled along I had time to think, but now calmly, so grateful for the money stuffed in my bag. Then I observed the man sitting beside me. He was apparently a plumber for he had his big bag of tools at his feet, and on his lap, a thin nylon bag with, plain to see, three pork chops inside. So that was going to be his families' Christmas lunch.

As he rose to leave, I suddenly held out a wreath for him, he looked at me incredulously, and I told him, 'Good Christmas.'

Poor man, he backed out of the door, first looking at me, then the wreath looped over his hand, while the door of the train banged and opened, till finally he got out.

At Kiffissia I did the same thing, hurriedly so as not to make a scene, the driver who had already got out, and the ticket collector. They gazed at me, surprised, 'Good Christmas, Good Christmas'.

It was a good Christmas, with everyone making much of Frederikos, who, as with all children, had quickly forgotten his sorrow. He had so many presents, his excitement was amusing. Harry came, and we feasted, and my friends were so kind, and being away from the farm and all that aggression was so healing.

Back to reality, at least I had enough money for us to live for a little while. At that time, there was no help for widows. Maybe there is not now, I don't know, in Greece, the family were expected to help, and usually did. Dowries were supposed to be given back, I have yet to see mine. There was monthly money due for Fredo, but it took a year to come through, so I could not depend on that. Meanwhile, I had to pay for my agricultural insurance, known as OGA. In 1984, when Greece became aware that there were no pensions, there were two main pension schemes instigated.

IKA was for businesses, shipping etc, I think, and OGA which was entirely for agriculture so we joined OGA. This was the one thing which Stamos did for us. It meant that there would be monthly money for Fredo, eventually, and that when I reached 65, I would get a pension. It also entitled us to free medical attention and medicines.

A kindly neighbour undertook to organise everything. It goes without saying that the family having turned their backs on us, were of no help whatsoever, so I was extremely grateful to him then, and to this day. It was a struggle to pay, but I did, and in the long run it made me feel more Greek, as if I belonged, having worked as a farmer for so many years.

Immediately after Christmas, my sister called, her husband had died, just six months after Stamos. However, her situation was vastly different from mine and she organised air tickets to be collected at the airport, so that we could go to support her at the funeral. This meant I had a whole month away from the gross unpleasantness I had been subjected to. In London, I quickly enrolled with a caring agency, and did some small jobs in order to be a little independent.

Then an extra bonus, my sister took us to Florida, to Disneyworld in the USA for a week. Fredo was in seventh heaven. Somewhat restored, we made our way back to Greece, I dreading what I would find, fearing that they would have invaded our room and taken over, but I was wrong.

On my return, I was surprised to find that most of the children had left. Half an hour after we arrived, Maria came and quietly told me that they too were leaving. I could not understand what had happened, but gradually, made sense of it with the help of neighbours, who had heard the shouting.

When I first arrived at the farm, I was shocked to see and hear the violence directed at Stamos. Never in my life had I experienced children being so abusive to a parent. Then, as I have written right at the beginning of this journal, gradually the hatred was transferred to me! It was all so shocking and painful. I would never shout at my parents, indeed, following the quaint old habit, 'anyone older, is wiser', raise my voice to an elder. Indeed, I had never heard such before, and understood, in our society anyway, that only the lowest of the low who would behave thus.

So it became apparent that without me to communally hate, they had turned on each other. Unable to live and work together, they had drifted off to squat on anyone who would have them. Unfortunately the eldest and most difficult, returned now and again, so I began to live in terror for my life. Having never experienced any violent abuse, I reverted to my old tearful self, just doing what had to be done, eking out an existence, making things, coping.

Two important things happened around then, but in my state of sorrow, I can't put a date on them. The first was Stamos' will was read. He had always told me that the land would be equally divided into five parts. Well I remember his coming home from the lawyer, escorted by his eldest son. He could not even look at me, for his shame. His eyes avoided mine, he had failed us. Ill, weak, he had been bullied into writing a grossly unjust will. I never took him to task, ever the optimist, I could not believe it.

As usual, a dirty trick had been done and the eldest son got himself the lion's share of 10 parts of 32. The next three children got 6 parts of 32, and I, the widow, got 4 parts of 32. Which of, course, I have never had. I was so shocked. All my money, educating two of Stamos' children in England, all the promises that it would be returned. Well I was not the first wife to be so cheated, and will not be the last.

The one thing which was required, was for me to leave. But I had nowhere to go. So the physical abuse began again and I was always hiding, afraid to be seen. One day my third son Geoffrey rang, and foolishly I wept, told him of my anxieties, and the dear boy, he offered to come out. What a miracle. I vividly remember the occasion when he stood in front of me, his arms spread while I cowered behind him, to avoid the blows. He said later, that he knew that if he had hit out, he would have been killed.

Then my second son, Sebastian rang from the North of India where he had been for six months, teaching English to Tibetans. Should he come? Wonderful, so he arrived, very skinny, so I had a project to fatten him up, which I did. But we were a united front, and the abuse lessened. One day however, when the boys were teaching Fredo how to play cricket in front of the house, it happened again.

I was in the kitchen and the bully came in, and seeing me alone, began chasing me around the kitchen table, throwing punches. As I passed the window, I screamed, 'Boys, boys' and ran to the big room where I held onto the door handle to prevent him from hitting me. Well he did anyway, right through a pane of glass and caught me under my left breast. Shards of glass flew and my arms were covered with pin pricks of blood. Fortunately the boys arrived to see this, so since, having denied any wrong doing, there are witnesses. I was however, really sad that Fredo should have seen the shocking behaviour of his eldest brother.

The bruise was horrific and painful, and this time, I decided to do something about it. So I went to my doctor and showed him, then my lawyer, then the son's lawyer. I went to the police and showed them, but, I told them, I will not make any charge, this time, because he is the child of my husband. Such a disgrace.

By chance, Maria phoned, not for me, but for the bully who was out. Then, sudden courage filled me, and I told her what had happened. It was easier, long distance, to speak to her somehow, and I told her that for Stamos' sake, I had not made an issue of it, but. IF, he ever touched me again, I would drag him through the mud of the law courts. She must have rallied the family, for he never actually hit me again, although I understand he has continued over the years, particularly with other young female relatives. Terrible.

It was wonderful having three sons with me, we were happy together, spring was coming, and with it, Serena, my eldest Goddaughter, just returned from working in Japan, such an enterprising girl.

Of course my steffania money was fast running out with a family to feed, and when she left, that sweet girl went with the boys to the bank and deposited £1,000. in my account, without a word to me. So I was blessed, by that wonderful, generous gesture, and so we survived until the groups began again in the spring.

Chapter 2

One Mistake after the Other

Of course, and sadly, it is common the world over for families to interfere with their children's choice of spouse. Usually, alas, it is the girls who suffer most. So it seems in Greece. My only, real Greek girlfriend, was once such a victim. She fell in love with a foreigner, English, so I believe, but her parents, educated and well to do people, made sure she did not marry him. He died a few years later, she never married and Eleni slowly but surely became so lonely, and unbelievably cranky and bad tempered. She who had been a good friend, the fun we had together, completely changed. Well yes, the marriage may not have lasted, but maybe she might have had a child, or two, and given her parents joy. Instead of the utter disappointment and problems they did have.

Now my stepdaughter, Maria, had been getting the same treatment, and being very emotionally fragile, could not cope. Previously, it had been I, the only one in the family who volunteered to have her little daughter, for months on end, while she struggled to get well.

I used to tell her, 'Keep them in completely different compartments. Don't listen to all that nonsense, your husband is a good man, you love him, Amen!'

After her divorce she used to cry to me,
'I never should have left him, how stupid I was.'
Apparently the hate in our family is their life force, verbal, at highest decibel, and even violence, as I know, occurs regularly. Yet again, the family had been educated, originally well-to-do too, until incompetence lost all. The constant hatred, of someone, anyone, seemed to be a necessity and caused so much sorrow, and where it came from and why, I do not know. Sadly, it was I all too often who was the hated one.

My sons could not stay to protect me forever. It was impossible for me to remain in my matrimonial home with the threat of violence ever present. Anyone who has suffered physical violence will know the scars it leaves. You never forget. For me, mourning, exhausted and constantly anxious, it was also a shock at my age, to be beaten.

It wasn't only that they wanted me gone, I realised that they urgently needed somewhere to house their mother, Eleni, now I had stopped giving her money and there was no other income to pay for her accommodation. They did not work, at least, they did not earn. I understood that she was now in a geriatric home, probably paid for by my long suffering sister-in-law, and surely, at that time in Greece, they were very basic. Eleni (not my old friend, Eleni is a very common name in Greece), was an educated woman, who spoke several languages, well. But she was reputed to be very 'difficult'.

Now IF, the kids had been remotely civilised and pleasant to me, things might have been different. I am not an unkind woman and had a great sympathy for Eleni. I would have offered to have her in the house and look after her. Despite the constant barrage of poison she heard of me from her children, we got along well, for she was very intelligent, despite her nervous character. Many was the time when she thanked me for helping her children with their education. Indeed many was the time she phoned and begged me to send her money, because, in her perfect English, 'I have not a penny'.

We had both lived with Stamos, that charming if incompetent man. She, as I, had suffered from family disapproval, if for different reasons. We had both had to put up with the 'the mistress', but, as unlike me, she had no money, her life must have been very hard for more years than mine. My only reluctance to do this would have been because she was, whenever possible, a chain smoker.

Suddenly, I realised that I did have a source of cash, my life insurance policy. One of my oldest friend's husband left the army and until he found an occupation which suited him, he sold insurances. Out of friendship I bought one, little thinking that this would virtually save us at a wretched time.

Unfortunately, there was no one to advise me, I did not know the ropes. A nice woman at the end of the line explained to me that by breaking the insurance, two years early, I would lose considerably. But to wait till the twenty years were up? How, would we survive? Of course, now, I realise that my bank would have held my policy and lent me the money. But at that time, I was totally UNWORLD-LY. So, I broke it, and had just enough money to restore the spitaki, the little ruin where we had kept the pigs. This was the first of several major mistakes I made over the next few years.

No roof, few walls, concrete floors, but it was a start and now began a busy time, which was exactly what I needed. This was the little house Stamos had begun restoring years before, by removing the roof! So the rain came in and destroyed it all.

A good builder who I knew slightly, came every Sunday with a team. Mixalis was a delightful, jolly young man, and he organised everything while Sebastian joined the team as labourer.

So now it was the time for my wonderful, loyal neighbours to pitch in. They were all well aware of what was going on, and, bless them, they wanted me to stay. Calls came, 'We have an old barn falling down, would you like the roof tiles?' Would I!

'We know you like old things and we have some old doors and windows, take them.'

Ruth gave me an old bath with ducky legs, which despite being very worn, is still in use with a shower on top.

Friend Eleni gave me Drax 25,000 to buy a good front door. What a gift. And I did, except it looked terrible when I bought it, old red paint flaking off, ragged and beaten. Amazing what some TLC can do, and now it is so handsome, blue and white, the very heart of the house and my memory of her. The old Greek front doors are most charming, with wrought iron shutters, brass knobs and the Virgin's hand, a brass door knocker. I scoured the breakers yards for windows with bars, because being on one floor only, for sure I'd be robbed. Well I was anyway, but I tried.

Fredo was valiant in helping me collecting the roof tiles. I made a sort of wooden V shaped chute, and he climbed up on the tumble down roofs, and slid the tiles down for me to stack in the back of the Datsun. Really dangerous for a nine year old, but he was helping his mother, where there was no one else.

Then came the long job of cleaning the tiles. I sat for hours, indeed days, wearing out three strong brushes and being very un-Buddhist, squashing the hordes of mean little scorpions which emerged from every crack and crevice, tails up. It was a huge job, literally hundreds of tiles, but very therapeutic.

One day Fredo came home from school where they had been walking on the beach. He told me, eyes bright, 'Mummy, there is a marble sink on the beach!'

Poor boy, I barely took notice until the third time, such rising excitement, I went with him to the beach. Sure enough there it lay, a very solid, heavy marble sink. Thankfully I was on the best of terms with many people in town, and approached our vegetable supplier, who without hesitation, came and lifted it on to the back of the Datsun. Bravo, we now had a sink, a proud Fredo's contribution to our home. We have it yet, but with flowers growing in it.

Summer came and comparative peace, for there was little sign of the children. My matrimonial home was mine again. Of course, there was no farming being done, the spinach having been a 'five minute wonder!' And anyway, there was now little machinery left to farm with. Occasionally, dear old workers arrived, just to see us; it was almost like the good old days.

Sixth June, 1989. That night we were a small group supping under the walnut trees. Stamos had set up a handsome lamp above the table, which threw a good light about us. I was in the kitchen getting the meal ready when one of the young came in, face serious.

'Judy, Maria is here.'

Shocked, I started shaking. How awful, how stupid of me. Memories of her flashed through my head. Maria, who at fifteen had demanded to go to school in England, and had done so well. Maria's wedding, a whole day of hard labour and much joy. Maria who had stayed with us when she was pregnant and come to me, 'Judy, I don't feel well.'

Then the dreadful time after Stamos' death, when, alas, she was so wickedly influenced to be cruel to me.

Taking the meal out to the serving table, I tried to control myself, for I had heard on the grape vine that once again, Maria's fragile nerves were in a mess. Looking out into the darkness, I could see a waif in the shadows, wandering about, and my heart melted.

So believe it or not, this is what happened. I felt a hand on my shoulder, pushing me gently and Stamos' lovely voice in my head saying, 'Love my child.'

I went out and found her, embraced her and said, 'Maria, it is your birthday, darling, come, eat with us, we are all friends here.'

Hastily I went inside and found a poor little necklace, all I had to give her. She was very sweet, gentle, pleased, quite a different young woman from six months previously when I had been subjected to her terrible hatred.

We talked late, and being very intelligent, quite the brightest of Stamos' children, she told me that she must see a doctor and asked me to arrange it. Having rung an English doctor friend in town and asked her advice, an appointment was made for her at nine in the morning.

Exhausted I went to bed, but, rising at seven, I found Maria gone. Disaster. Mice and men! Indeed the beginning of a long running disaster which went on for months. A catastrophe indeed, for Maria knew she needed help, not escape. Her elder brother had arrived, very late, and presumably, she had told him her plan.

Sadly, in Greece, mental illness is not understood. It is considered a huge, family disgrace if a member is disturbed in any way. Maria was whipped out of my care, taken to Athens, where, can you believe it, he 'lost her'. She did ring me, several times, sounding dreadful, but my pleas to her to come home were apparently beyond her.

Now real disaster, for she was picked up by the police and taken to the big mental hospital in Daphne. The whole family was shattered, not least me, who had tried so hard to help her, quietly and discretely. Unbelievable that she had been taken away, to totally refute the fact that she needed help.

One day, I went to visit her, carrying the food she liked best, only to find that it had been ferociously decreed, that on no condition would I be permitted to visit her. That vicious, hatred again. Fortunately, the intelligent young doctors had noted the vehemence and hatred, and asked me to come in to speak with them. How could they treat Maria without knowing the true family history. Very gently, they asked me questions, very gently, I replied to them, giving them the whole awful story. I spoke honestly, grateful that with their intelligence they had realised that the brother who was in charge, was her main problem. Then I handed over the food to give her, with my love.

Later, I did visit her, and found her well again, and so sweet to those others more unfortunate than herself, incarcerated in that place. Gently, slowly, we became friends again, for she was at last, understanding our family situation, regaining her balance and realising that it was NOT I who was the monster.

Meanwhile, at the farm, slowly but surely, the little house grew from a total ruin to something more or less habitable. Imagining that we would live there forever, well, there was nowhere else for us to go, I planned ahead. The larger part of the house would be Fredo's, when he grew up and got married, while I would move into the small 'Granny flat' alongside, just as Stamos and I had planned years before. It was small, but convenient, and had everything necessary. Ah the best laid plans –.

When I approached the electrical supply company, I was informed by the family, that I could not have electricity officially as this would mean the house would be legally mine. And, oh dear, that would never do! They were making sure then, and to this day, that I would have nothing. So a slender line was brought from the big house, which would supply lights, a fridge and the washing machine, not sufficient for even one heater, but good, because I did not have to pay for it. I then installed the telephone.

Good friends from the school of archaeology locally, came to help me move. I was one hundred percent honest in what I took from the house and kitchen, just what we needed, and what was mine. What we could not get into the spitaki, mostly crates of books, we stored in the Kotetsi (hen house), for sadly, as with all the other creatures on the farm, there were no fowl of any sort left. At one point I was accused of taking their possessions, and they insisted on going through the kotetsi, sure that they had been robbed, to no avail. Everything was mine, and most of the books had been left by my sister when she left Greece. Really, I found such behaviour was quite embarrassing and dishonourable.

My efforts with painting the doors and shutters deep blue, and the white plastered walls, made a very pretty house, so Fredo and I moved in and we were safe.

Everything was very basic. The floors were concrete still, as they had been when it was a pig sty. The big old, wood burning, Swedish stove I had brought from England in the Landrover, thirty years before, was installed. This was our only heating and bath time was perilous. I set two huge pans of water on the stove, put a little cold water in the bath, and then, fearful of tripping and spilling boiling water, I took them very carefully through to the bathroom. We managed.

Meanwhile, and everlasting blessings to them, the tourist groups came, now to eat outside the spitaki once a week all summer. Mostly Scandinavian, they were so kind and so appreciative of my efforts. This was my only income, thus we survived.

Oh but the extra little things I did in order that we should. I made olive oil soap, a ghastly, very smelly job, outside of course. Having begged everyone's stale oil, I was taught by a neighbour. A tin barrel was set on stones with a fire underneath. The oil and lye were then stirred, and stirred, and stirred, with a big pole. The steam got into my throat and eyes and I thought it would never thicken, but my neighbour bullied me on, until, there it was.

We had made old wooden boxes ready, lined with newspaper, so, very carefully, we poured the cooling sludge into them to set. Well I loved doing that sort of country thing, and was so grateful to my neighbours, all sadly now dead, for their patience in teaching me. Their daughters being totally disinterested in the old ways, bought scented soap and despised the old stuff. So these good old women had an unusual, foreign adopted daughter to bully and bawl at for her incompetence, and we were all very happy with the situation.

After a couple of days, when the boxes were cool and almost set, came the cutting, quite a job with a huge knife, and the village way was to make big square lumps. Now I cheated, for with my lumps, I approached the butcher who supplied my groups. He, dear man, then sliced them for me with his electric saw into neat little slabs, much more acceptable to foreigners. A young friend did some labels for me, with olives drawn on, and I sealed them in little plastic bags. Much easier as small gifts to take home, and another small income.

Another thing I had done while we had apricots, was to fill huge Ali Baba pots with them, never mind if they were mushy. Then I filled them with water laced with a little vinegar, and covered them well with gauze. A year or two later, after several strainings, I had the most wonderful Apricot Vinegar. Pink, aromatic, I filled lovely little old bottles with it, corked and tied them, and then, with beeswax from the candle factory near us, sealed them. Finally, labels, and I sold them very cheaply, so they went well.

Another rather daft concoction I made was toothpowder, and I still have some, and used once a week it gives the cleanest, smoothest teeth. It still works! But messy! And so much labour! Old, past it aubergines, dried, then, baked to charcoal. Mint, sea salt and bicarb, all pounded into a fine powder. Packed in little round plastic boxes and labelled. Oh the mess to use, yes, but fun.

The moment we left the big house, the children installed their mother in it. A year after Stamos died, I had expected some sort of religious service for him, as was the norm, but nothing was said or done. No one spoke to me about his tomb, so I decided as his widow, to do it. Having saved my catering money most carefully, I thought it was time to make Stamos a headstone. Using the same design we had made his grandparents and his Uncle Frederikos, the same marble and from the same factory, it was done. It was impressive to see those three fine stones, side by side, and, a good feeling that I had paid for all of them. Our guardians, as it were.

Seeing there was no car at the big house one day, I went to see Eleni, poor, lonely woman. I found her in the kitchen at the table, trying to eat very stale bread and chipping away at a lump of ancient, very hard Mizithera (grating cheese).

'Do you have nothing else to eat, Eleni?' I asked. Then went to look in the big fridge. Deja vou! It took me back to my very first day on the farm. Totally empty. She did ask me if I had a cigarette, but being a non smoker, I had not.

We had fassolatha – bean soup, that night for supper, a great peasant standby, tasty and nutritious. Haricot beans, well soaked then simmered with a bay leaf. Water thrown away. Onions, garlic, green celery, tomatoes and carrots, pepper, added and cooked gently, forever. The salt goes in at the end with a little olive oil. I gave Fredo a goodly bowl to take to Eleni with some bread and fetta alongside. When he came back, I asked him if she was pleased, but, no!

'I will not eat Judy's food,' he relayed, which quite crushed me, but of course she must have been bombarded with poison about me, so it was understandable. However, next morning, she arrived at the spitaki carrying the beautifully washed up bowl and plate.

'Thank you so much for my supper, Judy, it was really delicious.'

So good sense and hunger had overcome the silly influences.

There was another incident when I knew Maria was coming. Very gently I said to Eleni,

'As Maria is coming, won't you let me cut your fingernails for you?'

They were truly shocking, very long, jagged and stained with nicotine.

'No,' she said, 'I'll go to town and have them done professionally.' I was incredulous, for I had no idea that there was anywhere in town, with such a service. Besides, knowing there was absolutely no money anywhere, how would she manage that? In all my life, to date anyway, I have never been so indulged. To my surprise, next morning, she arrived and happily told me she had come for me to do her nails. So I ran, collecting up bowls of warm water with washing up liquid in and sat her down outside in the sunshine with hands soaking. Then I found clippers, scissors, files, you name it, and with some soft towels, did my best to be professional, for I suppose, I had seen something of the sort on TV.

It was pleasant sitting there, chatting, two of Stamos' women, mothers of his children.

I ended by creaming her hands liberally, and by the time I had finished, they even looked quite respectable, she was so charmingly pleased.

Now to my next big mistake.

Apparently, two young Iranian couples and their children were installed in the big house, rescued from Amnesty International, by the eldest son,' to look after Eleni'. What a foolish move, for I soon became aware of screaming at the big house, and ran over. The poor things were gathered outside, 'wringing their hands' as it were, for they had been 'thrown out', Eleni did not want them, and where to go?

To cut a long and ugly story short, I took in one couple with their dear little daughter and housed them in our granny flat. Next, I went to the school to enrol Sara, a sweet, bright child who learned Greek with astonishing speed. How I envied her. Next, I then job hunted for her father. It was not an ideal situation for them, but they had a roof over their heads, and electricity, everything for free. The other couple were more lucky, for the father, a gentle man, was a chemist, and I believe found a job in Switzerland.

At first, being hospitable, I fed my new 'lodgers', but it soon became obvious that the lazy mother was too happy with this arrangement, so I had to stop it, for I certainly could not afford to keep them. If she could find the cash to drink as much she did, she could certainly feed her family.

The next mistake.

My sister phoned me from London, telling me that she had finally, since her husband's death, organised her finances. She now offered to put Fredo into a boarding school. The arrangement was, he would fly out to me every school holidays. Well, this was the first and indeed only offer of help I had from anyone. And anyway, it was not an unfamiliar situation, for we had been sent to school in England while my father worked abroad.

By then, I had become aware that I had a second, severely dyslectic child, and in the school he was at in town, there were absolutely no facilities whatsoever, to help such children.

It was too good an offer to refuse. I accepted.

So off he went, and soon, photographs came, of a very smart, little blonde boy, dressed in grey flannels and a tweed jacket. I missed him fearfully, and because he could not write English (or indeed anything) we communicated by phone. It was lonely without him, getting him off to school, feeding him, doing things with him, and I began to feel vulnerable again.

Then, I had an unexpected break. The Scandinavian Christians had left for Bulgaria, their fleet of caravans all packed up, except for one lot. A newborn, fourth if I remember correctly, had held them up. The wife was a kind if dizzy girl, while the husband was one of those excellent men who could turn his hand to anything. It seemed that he was totally exhausted with the responsibilities of his young family, so I volunteered to share the driving with him. It was a wagon and a trailer, so off we set, with me also trying to provide food as the young wife only offered her children boiled sweets, all day long. It was a strange situation, I would have stayed on as a granny, to help out, for I considered that their condition was dire.

When we met up with the rest of the group it was joyful, and some of the young I had become especially fond of welcomed my unexpected arrival. I gave a charming gold and pearl brooch to Charlotte for her wedding, and I hope she still has it. On leaving Greece, I had been allowed a mere 500 drax, so thankfully I was given my fare home or I would never have got there. It had been a good break for me, being useful, and I love driving and travelling. Although not a Christian, I did grow very fond of those batty people.

Back in the spitaki, this was the period when the matchmakers began arriving. A year had passed since Stamos' death, I was, apparently, available. Completely unaware of what was going on, totally dumb, I dutifully entertained them in the usual Greek manner, water, and a small plate with something sweet on it. But, I just did not understand. They told me that they were looking for a foreign wife for their friend. One proposed to me a policeman with a house & two young sons. Another, a small farmer, assuring me she

505

would not have to work. I said I would search for them, still not realising that I was the object of their attentions! Another, and so on. Eventually, I suppose, they gave up.

With no income for the winter months, I thought about going to England to work as a nurse/carer, for heaven knew, I had enough experience. This meant I could be with Fredo sometime. Then, the husband of my best schoolgirl friend rang from Brussels. It was strange that he kept in touch with me after her death, but then, I had been good to one of his boys, a dear lad who had stayed with us two summers. It was winter '98, and I was still grieving for Stamos and apart from his unkind family, was suffering from the careless way he had left us. I seriously needed to work, a change, and besides, Greece can be bitterly cold in winter. It was not a happy prospect being alone and very poor in the spitaki. Apart from all that, I needed to be busy, to be needed.

He suggested that I come and help his new, young wife with her four month old baby. I was delighted, for I love babies, and apart from needing to earn my living, I very much needed a change of scenery. After a brief time in London with my sister and Fredo, I took a bus to Brussels.

This was the biggest disaster of all, for I was totally emotionally crushed at a time when I seriously needed to be uplifted. It became very clear that I was not wanted, again. I wasn't even allowed to take the little boy out in the pram for walks. It was as a prison, concrete all about me, a country girl, causing me to have terrible headaches. Whatever I did was wrong, I who had reared four fine sons and nursed in the prem unit of the biggest maternity hospital in Athens.

The young woman was totally without kindness, sympathy or understanding of someone recently bereaved, and, her knowledge of bringing up a baby was nil. Apparently her mother had been similarly poorly treated, doing her best, with a mother's knowledge and love, she had left, as would I before long, in a storm. But, at the beginning, I, silly me, took her place thinking this might be a happy situation, well it was not. It was back to the inner cry, 'Be Strong, be strong'.

Always searching for tasks, I busied myself with repairing the husband's clothes and the wonderful Brussels's lace table linen. As it was a diplomatic household, there was much entertainment so I involved myself in doing the flowers which I really enjoyed. Englishwomen do flowers well. But, sadly, this was a short lived joy, for when they were admired, that was it, my flower arranging was no longer required and a professional florist was called in.

It is difficult to describe distress of real bereavement, but my sorrow was so deep, and in that place, I was so unhappy. I had, what I think, was a mild stroke, for one day my left arm simply would not function, it hung limp, and I had to cradle and massaged it. Remembering that my father had been so afflicted at my age and for many years after till his death, I requested to see a doctor but was refused. 'Be strong, be strong'.

On one occasion, the wife produced a sheet of paper and told me to sign it. It is one thing not being unworldly, and another thing signing a strange piece of paper, which was in French. I quickly understood that the embassy was paying me, the nanny, a goodly sum of money. Not that I was getting it. Unbelieving, I peered at it.

'What is this?' I asked.

'Oh just sign it.' She told me very angrily.

So I did. 'Be strong, be strong'.

Of course the husband was aware of what was going on, but like all men, was too weak to intervene. I felt very sorry for him, poor man, what a ghastly wife.

There were however, two cheerful highlights to my stay in Brussels. The MEP who had come to that happy feast at the farm, the day when Lilly the pig first gave birth, invited me to dinner. Later, when thoroughly miserable, I contacted the Anglican vicar, remembering the wonderful one in Athens, and was similarly welcomed. I even helped to make some hangings for the church. Good company and good therapy, I was so grateful to them all.

Next mistake.

Such a lovely plan it was too, Willem and chum, Bridget and baby son, and I, were going to drive together through Germany, Hungary and into Romania, recently freed of its terror. I had collected vegetable seeds from far and wide to take to distribute. A good American friend from Athens had asked me to collect a painted chest for her. The address of other friends in Bucharest had been given to me to go together with them to the North of the country for Easter.

I bought a fine, big VW van from Willem's brother for our journey, and then, can you believe it, each of my companions let me down. They would not be coming. Devastating.

One of my worst failings is inflexibility. If I say, I will do something, go somewhere, whatever it is, even if I am ill, I will do it, on my knees. More fool me, for that is what I did, because I had promised to collect the painted chest, and the other friends were waiting for me.

Crazy.

The van broke down in Germany, and I spent two days there having it repaired at great cost. It continued to break down all along the road, so my three months agony earnings quickly disappeared. By wonderful chance, I met up with some of my Scandinavian, Christian friends on the road. It was brief but again joyful, if only I had stayed with them and not continued my foolish journey.

Romania. The village where the man with the chest lived, was utterly fascinating, an education to me, of how life must have been one hundred years ago in Britain. They managed so well with entirely primitive conditions, I was impressed. The loos were totally archaic, a two compartment privy built on a slight slope, with a walled area beside to catch the solid stuff. Daily, the grandfather scattered ashes from the magnificent, ceramic stove, over it, so, it did not smell. Once a year, farmers came with their cart and dug it out for their fields.

A gulley ran through the courtyard and under the gate, taking the liquid sewage which joined another larger, communal gulley in the street, which led into the river. I believe that the river was totally dead, for I never saw any movement in it, or indeed, anyone fishing. The houses were beautiful, so lovely, with carved eaves, and fine doors. The stoves however, were the most magnificent, taking up a quarter of the room, covered with beautifully hand painted tiles. They were the most efficient and attractive form of heating I had ever seen anywhere. My hosts did their best to entertain me, but, I soon realised that despite having been paid, the chest was not painted and there was no intention to do so.

Here I distributed my seeds, and hope they were fruitful. Something good had to come out of that mad trip, one which I would have enjoyed so much better with companions, and maybe, emerge, unscathed.

Chapter 3

A Lonely and Ridiculous Journey

Having left the misery of Brussels, on arriving in Romania, I now found myself in another unhappy situation. My host was something of a 'cowboy', albeit a very charming one, and understanding that I was going to visit other friends of our mutual friend in Bucharest, he determined to come too. With a chum, what's more, but a nicer, quieter man, who I understood was more wealthy and who drove a Mercedes.

Having been told to bring a LOT of cigarettes, they being the currency in Rumania at that time, and crates of beer, I suppose it was assumed that I too was wealthy and material to be fleeced. Yes, I did accept hospitality from them, although I still slept in the van outside in the courtyard. They asked me for dollars, and foolishly I handed over what I had, with no exchange, not that Rumanian money was worth anything anyway.

Thinking to travel back to Greece through Bulgaria, which I knew and liked, I was persuaded to do a detour through Turkey, where he wanted to do 'business'. By then, all I wanted, was to get home to my little house in Greece and I began to feel very pressured. Women,

510

I understood, did what the men said, and this was a very determined, macho male.

They asked me most seriously, what 'business' they could do in Greece. All I could think of was bees wax, for church candles, and those magnificent ceramic stoves. Apparently, they were not impressed with my reply, for they arrived with all sorts of very odd things, probably very scarce in Romania at that time, but abundant and inexpensive in Turkey and Greece.

Two things come to mind, sewing machine needles and plastic dolls. The cowboy was in such a state of excitement over this trip, and said he had a friend in Bucharest who had a garden where we could park safely. It was apparently well known that thieves abounded and I would bitterly find out about this in no time.

Meanwhile, the other people who I was to visit said they could not go to the North for Easter after all, another let down, so I spent Easter with the first family. This was quite an experience, not dissimilar to Easter midnight service in Greece. Throngs of people attended and the stink of bodies, sheep, garlic and incense rose with the communal warmth. There were no wax candles to buy and light as in Greece, just great stands of tiny electric candles, many being 'on the blink', but the service, very well attended, was most interesting and beautiful.

My host's wife, (his second) was an intelligent young woman who spoke good English, and had two dear little children. She was the curator of the local folk museum, a wonderful place, a feast for my eyes, all that handwork. As far as I could understand, my host made his living by painting the typical Romanian pictures on glass as well as chests. A small crate of pictures was put in the van and I was asked to sell them for him in Greece. I wondered how on earth I would manage that, it was getting more depressing.

It was some sort of holiday so I was delighted by the national costumes which suddenly blossomed in the village. Wonderful clothes, all black and white, of course all hand-spun, hand-woven

511

and hand made. Pleased with my admiration, they were excited that I took photographs of them, and later I did send copies to my hostess but never had any acknowledgement.

Finally, we were off and driving in convoy through Romania I saw the beauty and potential, but also the dead rivers, from so much ignorance and neglect. The tyranny having just fallen, there were high hopes of a better life ahead. Bucharest too, was totally shabby and run down, but one could see that originally the architecture of many of the buildings had been glorious with their stucco designs.

Sadly, I noticed that many of the pretty young women had very poor teeth, therefore did not smile, from poor nutrition I suppose. It seemed that everyone carried a little handbag of cigarettes to trade or to bribe with and I was sorry that I had parted with all my loot.

The friend with the garden was not to be found, probably away for Easter. Or, just not wanting a group of squatters in his yard. Never mind, the other friends were tracked down, they would do just as well, I was horrified.

The next mistake.

For the first time since I left Holland, I accepted and slept in a bed in their apartment. My hostess was charming and tried to make us all comfortable. We went to the market where in huge excitement, she bought spinach and lots of half rotten apples. It had become very apparent to me just how scarce food was, and fresh vegetables and fruit almost nil. It was moving to see that nice woman proudly place the apples in a bowl on the table, apples I would have given to the pigs.

That night she made a tasty dish of the spinach, mixed with flour, I think, which we ate with bread. There was some heavy drinking later so I soon went to bed. In the early morning, worried about the van, I got up and going into the kitchen, found the pan of left over spinach, uncovered and alive with the most enormous cockroaches I have ever seen.

Unfortunately, I could not get out of the building as it was locked from inside, and assuming they were sleeping it off, I had to wait.

When finally I got out, I found the worst had happened, the van had been broken into and everything I possessed had gone, including the crate of paintings.

Twenty-first of April, 1990. My birthday, never to be forgotten. Worst of all, my extra wash bag, under my seat in the car. In it, my most precious earrings, not only family, but exquisite and rare. To this day, I look for them. Police came, I did drawings of my earrings, descriptions of what I could remember had gone. All my clothes, my best clothes too, having foolishly thought life in Brussels might offer some entertainment. Utterly fruitless.

My companions were sympathetic, but I sensed impatience, for they were determined to continue on their selling journey. As we left, I gave all my Rumanian money to my hostess, for it was of no use to me, or indeed anyone else, and I was so cast down, I had no intention to ever return there.

On the border, I got talking to some nice Bulgarians who asked me to exchange some dollars. As I had foolishly given all my dollars to my host, I could not, but they were far more sympathetic about my plight and invited us to stay with them for the night. They even organised a friend to repair the small, side window which had been smashed. Good people, to whom I still send Christmas cards.

The cowboy became ever more excited as we approached Turkey, apparently he smelt huge profits on the goods he was going to sell. I seriously had my doubts over these ignorant dreams and pathetic merchandise. The constant breaking down of the van was a worry, holding us up and highly irritated him, and he was most scathing about it. When it came to sales, where I could, I helped them with my schoolgirl French, but their prices were so ludicrous, the Turks went away laughing.

Now it really was time for me to leave them, I had had enough. The van was the main problem, stopping regularly, I thought perhaps a block in the petrol feed. How Willem's brother could have sold me that wreck, I do not know, indeed, how could Willem have let him!

One of my problems was that I had no change of clothes, just what I stood up in. So every night I washed out my undies in a petrol station loo or wherever, and hung them in the van to dry. They were usually still damp in the morning, but, who cared.

Knowing I was very close to the Greek border, I determined to get there as soon as possible but simply could not see any signpost to indicate it. Desperately I asked people,

'Greece? Grechia? Ellada? Ellas?'

No one knew what I was talking about. So I pulled into a petrol station and looked at the huge, stained map on the wall and there it was, 'YUNANISTAN.' Fancy that?

Now I made a run for it to get to the border, praying the van would keep going. It was a most charming border post, reminiscent of small Indian railway stations. Music blared, top decibel, Lambatha. My mood light at finally nearing Greece, I was highly amused.

They told me that I would have to hurry as the border closed at four and it was almost that. So I made a dash for it, and of course, you might have known there would be a water-splash of disinfectant. And needless to say, the damned van broke down right in the middle of it. What a journey.

Tall, good looking Greek boys approached me dubiously. A lone woman in a Dutch VW van sitting in the middle of the water-splash. I called to them, at least being able to communicate.

'Oh boys, boys, I am so glad to be home.'

And managed to jump the beast forward by using the starter, until I reached them and Greece.

Exhausted by now, I blurted out my troubles with the van, gave them my identity card and passport, and thankfully drove a little way into Greece before pulling in for the night.

I have never calculated the mileage I did on that trip, it must have considerable. Holland through to Germany, where I spent days having the van so-called-fixed. Romania, Bulgaria, Turkey, mostly driving on my own. How on earth I had got into that ridiculous situation, I still don't know. Basic inflexibility, being too trusting of friends, being an idiot. What ever money I had earned in Brusselles just slipped away, a thankless, miserable time followed by a lunatic drive.

After breaking down several more times, I found a VW garage, where I spent three more days while they worked on the poor brute. This at least gave me the chance to walk into town, to explore a totally unknown part of the North of Greece. Chancing upon a ladies lingerie shop, I asked for six pairs of cotton panties and one bra. Now I have said earlier on in this journal, how inquisitive Greeks are. The good woman was fascinated.

'Six pairs?' she enquired, 'are they all for you?'

So out came the miserable story about my stay in Bucharest and having everything stolen. With just the clothes I was standing up in, which of course, meant one pair of panties not forgetting the breaking down van, now being repaired, again. She was incredulous. Suddenly I had a chum, who insisted that she put an extra pair in, for free. From one pair of panties to eight! I was home.

Happily, I called on her each day and we chatted, ate gleeko and she called in friends and customers to hear the scandalous story. The fact I had also been widowed and my husband had been Greek earned me unexpected kindness. Manna from heaven indeed, after the past horrible months. It certainly happily passed the time and I did send her a postcard from Corinth later, to say I had arrived safely.

Dreading my return to the farm and the expected unpleasantness, I felt my heart sinking with every kilometre. Unfortunately, my home-coming was worse than usual, it was utterly miserable. For I quickly discovered that most of my dear dogs were dead, or dying. I rushed the few survivors to the vet, to find that due to poor food, they had been consumed by ticks, and had an animal version of leukaemia. Most of them died, it was heart breaking. For the four and a half months I had been away, they had been so neglected, totally without care and nutrition, just the odd pig's trotter thrown at them. I was furious and upset that after the years of struggling to feed them, scrounging from tavernas, butchers and abattoir, cooking up great pans with garlic against ticks. Even dear little Trixie died. She who had arrived with her broken leg on the day when the Dutch Queens changed places. Such a loyal, valiant little dog. It was a bitter time, to see the neglect of the animals, yes gone were the happy old days, nothing had changed.

Well yes it had. For anything to do with me had been removed. The sign above the fine big lean-to the boys had built outside the kitchen, 'The Cheopery', had gone. So too 'The Kotetsi', on the hen house. Neatly painted in blue, innocent, amusing, no harm to anyone. I wondered why the Cheopery itself, the Kotetsi and the beehive oven, all my doing, had been allowed to remain standing. Too useful to demolish I suppose. The children's tree house had been ripped down, pathetic!

Another very silly thing had happened which distressed me to a ridiculous degree. It concerned the beautiful, big white, swan of a pram, which friend, Annie had given me, and which we had brought to Greece on the roof of the Landrover when Fredo was born. Stored in the barn, covered with a cloth, I thought it would be safe, but no. The hatred and spite directed towards me was bent on any inanimate object to do with me. Insane. Apparently anything to do with me was so hated, it was thrown out. I found the pram, apparently wheeled out of the barn and left in the middle of the field for months, in sun, wind and rain. Ruined of course, despite my later efforts to restore it. Such a shame, for now grandchildren are arriving it would have been useful again. Now we only have photographs of Fredo sitting in it, a lovely little blonde baby, occasionally even with a chum alongside. Shocked, upset, I never said a word and just retreated into my little house to pick up the pieces there.

The tourist groups began again and were as always charming and appreciative. No longer living in my matrimonial home, the big house, I served their meals in front of the spitaki, the little house. Sadly now, we did without the 'theatre' of the wonderful big beehive oven we had built and in which I cooked their meals, to their general amazement. This must have been the most photographed oven in Greece, and I always blessed Stamos for his extravagant size of it. This was my livelihood, and I strove to serve them the best meal possible, as well as to make money. In fact they often told me that it was, the best meal they had had in Greece. It was a time when Greeks had become careless about their catering, and mainly produced, 'Brissoles and patatoulis and Greek salad'. Chops and chips and the simplest salad.

Then, when the tourists began going to Turkey and further a-field, the authorities made a fuss, the press waded in and things got a lot better.

Otherwise my life was quiet, no one called, no one rang, but my neighbours were then, as now, ever constant.

With summer my sons came and finally that dreadful old van behaved itself, after so much work and money spent on it, so it should. But this gave us freedom to go swimming every day, and weekends to the mountain house, a paradise.

I recall one day when Sebastian had gone off in the van with Fredo and whoever else was staying, two members of the family arrived, and not realising I was inside, walked around the house, peering here and there, talking loudly. Fearfully, behind the closed shutters, I crept from room to room and watched their progress and listened to them. The word 'bulldozer' reached me.

Horrified, I realised the severity of their vendetta against me. I had moved from my matrimonial home to please them, and by dint of breaking my life insurance policy prematurely, had restored the spitaki from a pigsty. Well I thought, if they did knock my house down, I would just move back into the big house. It never happened,

I suppose they wouldn't dare, public opinion would surely go heavily against them. A friend, who knew them well, advised me to remove anything precious to me or of value, in case it did. Alas, some time later, I did just this, taking my treasures to the mountains for safe keeping. Again a disaster. But that is another ugly story. A paradise lost.

Since the death of Stamos, quite honestly, Greece was not kind to me, there was no moral or financial support from anywhere. A woman, a widow, a foreigner and no longer with any money, I was a fourth class citizen.

When the tourist groups finished, I worked on my handicrafts and herbs, so that I could get to England in the winter to be with Fredo and to work. For despite efforts, I could not find work in our area and being alone, cold and afraid through the winter, was not really an option.

Things for my little son were not too good either, except when he was at school where he was very happy. While he had half terms with my sister, he phoned me, and we both ended up weeping. It was so hard for a young boy to lose his father, his home and his country, and now, his mother. It was so hard for me too. At least he had come home for holidays when we were both happy.

Believing it to be the correct thing to do, I had signed some papers giving my sister, who was, after all, paying his school fees, full authority over him. Alas, I was totally unworldly, believing it to be the wisest thing to do, but as things turned out, it was not. Fredo was struggling to learn to read and write English. Being severely dyslectic, he had, in his four years of school in Greece, learned little. Yes, he was completely bi-lingual, but the only way we could communicate was by phone. Perhaps, seeing the close attachment we had, and the tears, my sister decreed that we could not speak to each other any more, and we were desolate.

With winter coming, suddenly, breaking again, I found myself at another cross road. With no Stamos to support and defend us, no powerful friends or relations to take his place, I had to make the decisions. Having sold my house in England, I had nowhere to go. My mother was totally unsympathetic and indeed, patently did not even like my fourth son. So, I sold the van and made the painful decision to leave Greece, to move back to England and regain my child. I would find work, any work, and without either Greek or British family help, I determined we would survive .

Thinking back, really I was as my sister claimed, a 'ninny', for I never asked anyone for help, although many offered me loans. By the time I had paid my fare, I had the noble sum of £200. And, I felt rich!

It was painful leaving my home of eighteen years, and actually, I could not believe that I was doing it. I think that the constant fear of abuse had worn me down to half my usual self. My courage and optimism had just evaporated. It had been such a sorrowful few years. Bereavement is almost an illness, a time to be loved by friends and family, to be supported. So much for that. Anyway, not really believing that it would be permanent, I locked up my little house and left.

Chapter 4

London/Greece/London/Greece

After a few days staying with my sister, it became very clear that I was not wanted. She had decided that I had relinquished Fredo to her, was determined to keep him and just wanted me gone. So I began taking live in jobs with ill, elderly or Alzheimer's patients. It was often not easy work, but it gave me back my equilibrium.

My favourite employer was a viscountess, a delightful, eccentric lady. I sat in her front garden waiting for my interview when she finally arrived with the butler, so late I had almost given up. No interview was required, so the butler drove me to my digs to collect my things, and kindly informed me of the lie of the land before driving off to the seat in the North. He also showed me how her ladyship liked her table napkins folded, and this put me in very good stead later for she was surprised and pleased. There I was, in an exquisite town house, with a supposedly ill lady, for whom I had been employed as a nurse. Nothing doing, she had a dinner party that night, and despite having pleurisy, had a happy evening. Having cooked and catered for hundreds of people, I now realised that I had never been a waitress, and simply had to try to remember how I had been served, in order to do things properly. I'm afraid that I didn't do too well occasionally in my flap to get things done.

Having read Monica Dickens books years previously, I was amused to find myself in a similar situation. I was nurse, cook, bottle washer, shopper, cleaner, driver, you name it. But I was busy, and I was appreciated, food for the gods! When I wasn't working, I attacked the cellar which had shelves upon shelves of broken yet wonderful china. Horrified, I set to gathering them together, each little piece wrapped in kitchen paper, then put all together and labelled. Miessen, Crown Derby, Worcester, Delft, Bow, you name it. It was my fervent hope that one day, someone would repair them.

We got along so well, perhaps I was an enigma, but it might have been my real appreciation of her lovely house which helped. My love of beautiful things drove me to repair everything I could find which was broken, so satisfying, for there were very many sadly broken and neglected things in that splendid home. The lovely, huge oval dining table had a bell push, Fabergé no less, with a little cabochon amethyst button, lovely, and I got that one going, to my lady's delight. I also gathered up all her broken spectacles and finding the name of the optician in a case, took them to be repaired.

One night, she had a big dinner party and I really was the kitchen maid this time. Having peeled the broad beans, I was instructed to peel them again. I was tired and dumbfounded, and stood for ages at the sink, getting the outer casing off the wretched beans for her. They were then tossed in butter, and no doubt delicious. It was rather a grand do, with a Duke and Duchess, and an Arch Duke, and the odd Honourable. A jolly evening with much talk, I would have been pleased. The little bell rang constantly, she was obviously enjoying that.

Then I forgot myself completely for I was not accustomed to being a servant. Apparently you must not have eyes, ears or mouth, unless spoken directly to, but I was 100% inexperienced in such matters. Probably gathering up plates, I heard Her Ladyship say, 'And who was Bishop Odo, anyway?'

Horrors, big mouth who loves history, totally without thinking, promptly replied,

'He was half brother to William of Normandy, Lady –.'

To which she graciously thanked me.

Oh dear!

Toiling in the kitchen, clearing up very late after they had all gone, the intercom rang.

'Well!' she said, poor lonely lady, 'How did you think the dinner went?'

I assured her from the volume of the chatter, it had been a huge success.

But oh dear, again, I forgot myself, 'That duchess, what a messy feeder. You should just see the mess under her place, just like feeding the birds in the park!'

'Nooo' she said, 'Reeeally!' I shall never forget that incident and always smile over it.

Sadly, a proper ladies maid was found, so I left, which I had to anyway as Fredo had half term and I determined to see him. At least I was solvent and very careful with my earnings. I called in at the bank to check my account, confident that it would be good which it was. Until the girl told me rather snootily, that it was 'OD'. I was so shocked.

I rang her ladyship and asked if I might call by. From her tone, I understood all was not well and when I arrived she closeted me in a corner and poured out her woes about the ladies' maid, who was an arrogant horror. When she was called to the phone, the maid nobbled me, and I got her side of the story. But my loyalties were firmly with my ex-employer, we had got along so well, I really liked her. However, it was hardly the time to inform her ladyship that her cheque had bounced. Had I come all that way for nothing? Writhing inside with uncertainty, I hesitated. So embarrassing for her and me.

Then, on the doorstep she kissed me, and I had the courage to tell her the problem. Her cheque had bounced. Furious, she dragged me back into the house, rang her bank, gave them hell, and gave me an extra cheque for £50 for my trouble, full of apologies.

Sadly, I never saw her again although she did ask me to return to work for her, but I had taken on another job which I would keep, on and off, for five years. Happily, we did speak on the phone occasionally.

Not having a single reliable, loving relative to help me out in school holidays was hard. One half term, Fredo came to stay with me in the live-in job I had at the time, a huge house, and only one, very confused old lady. It soon became apparent that long term, this would not work, for I was constantly saying, 'Ssh' or 'Not now' or 'don't go in there'. No fun for the boy, and painful for me not to be free to be with him, to do things for him.

A kindly daughter of the house who visited daily, told me I should ask for help. Being a widow with a child, apparently I was entitled to it. This did not appeal at all. I had been independent for so long, managed to cope despite so many obstacles, this seemed like charity. So what was the option? Facing up to the fact that we truly were a charity case, I decided to go for it.

Now I had to go through endless trials to see if I was deserving, it was awful. I felt, what I suppose in truth I was, a real pauper. There were many such as I, in that huge hall, every race, every creed. Smoke and fag ends. Empty drink cans. Babies in pushchairs, sucking bright pink liquid or tea from bottles. And shouting. Oh my goodness, the shouting, I was appalled. This was a scene from hell.

The interviewers were safely barricaded behind thick glass windows at one end of the hall and our names were called in turn, so we waited. One applicant really began abusing the poor thing behind the glass. Ghastly. I would soon have to learn the limitations of our beautiful language in my new life, for the expletives were mainly Fs.

Alas, will I never learn? I was so horrified by the barrage of abuse, top decibel, I stood up and added my voice.

'Stop shouting at her. Stop it. She is only trying to do her job. Don't you see, you only make it worse for the rest of us!'

Then the wrath of the gods fell on me, now everyone yelled at me. Except one, young black girl. Charming, kindly, she yelled back at them that I was right, he was holding up things, he was making us wait. As a sudden storm, it was over. They all fell silent and murmurs of agreement filled the hall. Suddenly I had a new friend and she came and sat beside me. We exchanged our stories, she told me she had been born in England, but had sickle cell anaemia, and I told her my tale of woe.

Then suddenly, unbelievably, out of the corner of my eye, I saw a familiar figure coming in through the door, my sister. I felt faint, and wrapped my scarf around my head like a Muslim woman. So she had found out that I was seeking accommodation, and had crossed London to do her mischief. Always a nervous person, I began to tremble, and my young friend ran to fetch a glass of water and comforted me. Mercifully, nothing came of that attempt to sabotage my plans, for it was getting late and the staff must have had more than enough. She was told to come back tomorrow, but I understood, she did not.

We were given a wonderful flat with a housing association. It was on the fifth floor however, the previous tenant of my flat had not only super-glued my lock, but had made a fire in the lift, so it was a climb. Another similar, beautiful flat next door was shown to me, so I accepted with great pleasure. A locksmith was found and the keys were sent to me. Horrors, I had never seen such desecration and filth anywhere. A couple with a baby and two dogs, (not allowed) had lived there. The floors were strewn with dirt, used nappies and dog mess. There was an open tin of dog food on a window sill full of blue bottles and the pretty small balcony was high with rubbish, dirty nappies, you name it. I closed the door and ran.

'I am sorry,' I told them, 'I simply cannot take that flat, it is so, so filthy.'

Unfortunately they were unused to honest people, for they did not believe me.

'Can't you people even do a little cleaning!' shouted the indignant woman.

'Go and see it,' I said equally crossly, 'you just go and tell me if YOU, would accept a flat in such a terrible, filthy and unhygienic condition.'

Well they must have, for professional cleaners were called and did their best.

It was a lovely flat with one large and one small bedroom, and with the help of good friends, we moved in struggling up all those stairs. I soon began noticing shot lodged in the walls, had the man been insane? Then neighbours told me that he had shot a worker on a nearby scaffold, and a woman walking her dog. The carpets were stained forever, and the fine washing machine had been deliberately broken which I never did afford to have mended, But, we had a home, we were independent, joy.

I was able to visit Fredo, a tiresome journey by public transport, but so good to see him happy. He loved his school, but in no time at all, my sister informed me that she could not afford to keep him there, and had given the school notice.

Her idea was that he would get a scholarship in a charity school, so booked several appointments for his interviews. I was appalled, knowing of his dyslexia and that he could barely read or write English and with past knowledge of the schools, was well aware of their very high standards. Just one school however, seemed a possibility. In the country with 300 acres of land, it was very well endowed and took children, like mine, who had lost one or both parents. Or whose parents were blind. Or Service children. I applied, we went and were accepted, but meanwhile, they had been informed that I was wealthy, had property in Greece (half true) and that I could afford the full fees, which I certainly could not. My only sibling was out for full battle now to remove my child from me.

The following weeks were a nightmare of trying to explain, all over the place, that I was just a normal, loving, widowed mother who for no reason of her own, found herself totally destitute. I was not, as written here there and everywhere, 'an alcoholic, rich, a bigamist, violent and totally unsuitable to be a mother'.

Then a miracle happened. A woman solicitor, who had received all this information in an attempt to part me from my young son, actually wrote to me, sending copies of the letters she had received, and explaining kindly that she felt I should know about them – 'As I feel that your sister is trying to harm you.' What a sensitive woman, I am eternally grateful to her.

Shamelessly now, I made photocopies of those vitriolic letters and instead of the unpleasantness of trying to explain, just sent them everywhere.

Suddenly the blessed wheels of kindness began turning, and a couple of trusts paid for the cancelled term which I had been landed with. I did, however, have to find £700, a fortune at that time when I earned £100. a week. But, it was paid, slowly, and we were safe.

A new problem hit me. Having broken my life insurance policy, I had absolutely nothing to fall back on. Say if I became ill, or died. Who would bury me? How could I allow my older sons to take on the responsibility of all that plus caring for their youngest brother? It was imperative that my sister be kept out of it. A new life insurance policy was bought, a poor thing, but, better than nowt.

Then another anxiety. Somehow, I must keep up Fredo's Greek, it was important, and mine was so poor, I was hardly the person to speak with him. At that time, the papers began offering two flights for the price of one, if you collected their tokens. This I did avidly, so we often managed to get to Greece for school holidays and it was wonderful for him to be home again.

The Iranian family were still living in part of the little house and begged me to re-connect my telephone. They were planning to emigrate to Canada and constantly wanted to speak with their family in Iran. Those were, alas, the days before mobiles. Despite a niggle of doubt, and, yes, being a 'ninny', I did. Well I had been right to doubt them because when they left, they also left a hefty bill.

The little annexe was also a mess, the dirty fridge closed and full of flies. Behind the house lay a mountain of bottles, non returnables of course, which I had to dispose of. The wife must have been an alcoholic, for she was forever calling her little daughter to fill up her glass.

Their reply to my letter asking them to pay their phone bill was that, I, being a wealthy woman, owning that big farm, etc I could pay it, for they were poor and could not. So much for two years of free accommodation, and much kindness.

It took quite some time to arrange to re-connect the phone, and having finally paid their bill, we returned to England without it having been done. Things moved very slowly in Greece.

Around that time, one of my American archaeological friends, who I am very fond of, accused me of playing the victim. I was deeply hurt. Yes, I did seem to be the victim, but truthfully, none of it was my fault, I just had too many bad people in my life.

So it was that our next trip to Greece, expecting to find the phone working, it was not. I went to OTE, the telephone exchange, to ask them to re-connect. They informed me that as I had not paid the bill, they would not. Dumbfounded, I argued with them, even showed them the receipt, but no, they informed me, that was the previous bill, now, it was much more than that. This was another bill. In despair, I asked to see the director who was a friend.

'Andrea,' and held out the old bill and the new one. 'What is all this about?'

Dear man, he smiled and explained. Apparently after we had left, the engineer had arrived at the farm to re-connect. Apparently due to total lack of funds, the phone at the big house had been disconnected, the bill unpaid. So the poor ignorant engineer was instructed not to connect up to the little house, but directed to connect MY phone up at the big house. When that bill was not paid, they disconnected that one too. Hence I had received another even bigger bill, for calls I had not made.

'We know what is going on Mrs Judith,' said the kindly Andreas, 'don't you worry, your phone will be connected immediately.' And it was.

Victim, yes, that was me!

We flew out on our 'two for the price of one' tokens for Christmas, it was cold but joyful to be home. For many years, we had had a Carol Service in the little church of Saint Nicholas, it had become an annual event for ex-pats in the area, and for all our neighbours. I laid out thick flokatia on the floor, those natural coloured woolly rugs for the kids to sit on. Eats were arranged. Carol sheets handed out. Every candle stick and lamp was lit. Oh but it was so beautiful, a wonderful memory. The talented Theresa came with her guitar which really helped the singing along. It was a particularly happy time as Maria was there, happy, helpful, loving. I remember telling her, 'Sing, sing!' For she had been to school in England, and knew the carols. I was not to know that it would be the last of the carol services. Or that it would be Maria's last Christmas.

Every day she came up to the spitaki to be with me. I tidied, we talked, and talked and all the ugly memories of after Stamos' death faded.

In less than two months, came another tragedy in our family. A neighbour rang me, Maria had died, she knew little else. Shocked, I rang Fredo's housemaster and asked if he could have some days off. Maria was killed in a car crash with her new fiancé on Saint Valentines Day.

I was nursing at the time and clocked off at 6 p.m. Somehow, we got night flights and Fredo, step granddaughter Kas and I flew out, arriving at the farm at midnight. It was bitterly cold and the neighbours had built a good fire outside the church to sit around.

There she lay, in the little church where she had been married, serene in her coffin, just a small scratch on her nose. Somehow I could not sit outside with the others, so I just sat close beside her till dawn.

The loss of Maria, the most intelligent of Stamos' children, was a bitter blow for all the family. For she had been the one with logic, sensitivity and might have made such a difference to all our lives. For me it was the most bitter loss, having so recently mended our relationship, I would be bereft of her support for ever more.

Confused, the poor Eleni told me that her mother had died, and indeed latterly, Maria had been as a mother to her. I had no answer. Then she asked me later if it had been Maria who had died. I felt so sorry for her, to lose a child must be terrible, but in her situation, to lose her daughter, a disaster. Who would look after her now? I told her yes, her dear Maria had died and tried to comfort her, but I knew that her lot would be appalling now without the love and care of her daughter, her really caring child.

After the Iranians left, a Bulgarian family moved into the annexe, a mother and two sons. The mother, Vicky, was supposed to be looking after Eleni in the big house as well as working on the land which had been let. Having done my best to make them comfortable, it turned out to be the same old story, over the top gratitude at first, which certainly evaporated with time.

'You are my mother and father!' she said, kissing my hands. And when she too eventually left, she took my fridge, a very expensive item in those days. Ha!

By now, we had been moved from our wonderful flat to an entirely different area. Rough! It was fearful, I went to a surgery of our MP, a charming woman and famous actress. I implored her to help me not to move there, but she could not. Ghastly! The hallways of the block were littered with needles and beer cans. The flat itself was fine, except it had been built at a time when working people were so undernourished, they were all small. We were big, and everything was as a doll's house. The first day there, my tools were stolen, and this is how it went on for three years.

Above us lived a family from Glasgow, and their grandsons were the torment of the neighbourhood and certainly, our lives. They stole Fredo's wonderful new bike, given him by his aunt. Next day, we bought another through a newspaper which I could ill afford. It seemed that most of the teenagers were thieves, bored, just out for trouble. Parents were either absent, drunk or on drugs. How we had sunk. I longed to catch one kid particularly, tie him to the railings, tar and feather him. Then ring up the newspapers! A nice dream. But I did make friends, some who I still have.

Fredo hated the place, a country boy in that concrete jungle. All my efforts therefore were for us to spend as many holidays as possible away somewhere, or in Greece. Whenever we went out, I took Eleni clothes, for how she loved them, and although they were from charity shops, as were mine, she was thrilled. It was sad to see her condition deteriorating, and the sloppy care she was receiving. The woman did the minimum, the family were generally absent, and that poor old woman was ever alone in a tiny room upstairs, unable even to come down in the end.

So she died too, alone and in squalor, and it was left to the dear neighbours, Petropoulos to find the sons and to run about organising things. By now there was a handsome row of fine tombstones in front of the dear little originally Byzantine church which I had paid to have restored. With Maria's beside Stamos, they put Eleni beside Maria. But not knowing a thing about how to be correct, they had her grave facing North/South, totally un-Christian where of course they must face to the East.

Years on, all the tomb stones were removed. No one was consulted, we didn't count, even if we had paid for them. The eldest son was so afraid of death, he hated to see them. Scandalous, wicked, unlawful. And so there are no tombstones to mark that family. Everyone is shocked, horrified, scandalised. It just is not done. But with a tyrant there, no one has the courage to do anything about it, yet, anyway.

In the summer, we went to Spiti Sebastian and enjoyed the glory of the mountains. Ah but that was the happiest place, no bad memories, just peace and fun and coping happily with the limitations of simple mod cons, few facilities. We made xelopittes (little pasta squares) mizithra, (fresh cheese) bread on the fou-fou in a frying pan. I taught Fredo to drive, to his delight, and years later when he took his test, he got it first time.

The house always needed attention, which I could not give it. But it had a great charm, with the simple furniture, Fredo's old cart bed from Argos, hand woven rugs and some exceptional hangings. The peace and beauty of the mountains was ever healing, and our neighbours a delight. We got electricity, wow. I did it very simply, just a few power points for lights. We had no electric appliances, as we had a small gas cooker, and of course the wonderful wood burning fou-fou.

One day, I heard a great deal of shouting from below us. Patty Fingers was beating his wife.

'You are bad,' she shrieked, 'Bad!' Awful man, poor old girl. The following day he arrived looking sheepish. Could he have a lamp? He had made a mistake! Oh, thought I, a mistake, by beating your wife, you broke the lamps, eh? Well, now we had electricity, I gathered up all our lamps, wicks, fuel and so forth, and gave them to him. Some were tall and elegant, I imagine poor old Athena would be delighted.

Next day, and the next three days, a large demijohn of sheep's milk sat outside our door. This happy time I had Fredo and one of the nice Swedish girls, Sofia, with me so we laboured long and hard making xelopites (pasta) cheese, yoghourt, a wonderful memory never to be forgotten.

But, this brings me to the next tragedy.

Dear friends decided that I must get up out of this widow woman's attitude. My step daughter-in-law, Liz, gave me some condoms, which greatly amused me. I wonder what happened to them. But an original gift, dear girl.

Ruth gave me an introduction to a marriage bureaux. Such a generous gift, £200. It was very superior, top drawer, and indeed I got along very well with the owner, a charming woman. The few men I met through her must have been so horrified by my situation, I saw them but once. Then, fool me, I mentioned the mountain house, that I would like to LET it for a tiny sum and to cut a long story short, I agreed to lend it to her daughter and four friends. The £100 a week was put aside, because they were young, and nice. So I thought.

They collected the key, hung on a lovely old bronze sheep's bell, and every detail of how to get there, what to expect, how to cope. They saw the grim place we now lived in, which must have shocked them, as it had shocked me.

The next thing I heard was on the phone, the nice girl, 'The house has burned to the ground.'

For a moment I was speechless and asked her to repeat herself. She did.

'The antiques in the cellar? The cradle, the high chair, the hangings?

'All gone,' she said.

That much loved old house, which had given so much happiness to so many people, gone. Fredo's cart bed. The old painted chests, the old oak carved chest, the superb hanging in the cool, dark cellar. I thought of all these things, I still do, unbelieving.

The girl was distraught of course, and being so poor, of course I had no insurance although since then I have been assured no one would have insured it, being in the mountains so often devoured by fire.

'We will all give you our insurance.' The nice daughter told me. Well, of course, they never did. Neither did they give me back the key with the little bronze bell. Inevitably, being foreigners, they had awful trouble with the authorities who wanted to put them in jail. I understood too that some of the firemen were making romantic overtures, appalling.

Sebastian, whose house it was, and I phoned here and there instructing the authorities to let them go. We did our best for them, aching, for it surely must have been a horrible experience, but we, we had lost a precious if ramshackle house.

I wrote to them, kindly, quoting an old Greek saying, which goes something like this, 'One day, we might be able to laugh at this'. And ended, 'Keep in touch'.

I never heard from them again. This was so shameful, unbelievable. This I think hurt most of all, and one day, when I have some money, I will contact them and tell them to pass the hat, so we can re-build it.

There was much discussion on how they burnt it down. Albanians lived in the village, good boys who worked locally, but Albanians get blamed for everything. However, yes they do steal, but they do not fire, ever, for if they did, they could not go back to steal again.

It was a disastrous fire, probably started in the cellar, for the huge beams were totally burnt out. The villagers told me there were a couple of explosions, the gas bottles no doubt. The mercy was that there was no wind, or the village would have been consumed. Every year there are terrible forest fires in Greece, and thank heaven, this catastrophe of ours did not spread and involve anyone else.

Finally, after long examination and discussion, together with the revelation from the mother, that the young people were smokers, we understood. We were not smokers, any of us, so there were no ashtrays anywhere. Probably, a young person had left their cigarette sitting on the edge of a piece of furniture. They were in a hurry to get three of their friends to the airport, so no doubt were, rushing.

All the floors were covered with thick, woollen, hand woven rugs. A cigarette would fall, ignite, and the fire would creep, slowly, slowly, until it came to something really inflammable. Anyone who knows anything about wool knows it does not burn, it smoulders until it meets up with something, then, whoof, maybe hours later. Whichever of those young people left that cigarette, will know it in their hearts.

I never heard from them again, and that was so painful. Having thought that they were respectable, decent people, I wonder if they have any conscience, and remember. Now, years later, I see in the papers that they are still in business. I have heard from an acquaintance, the enormous sums they now charge for their marriage brokering, but thousands.

I continue to dream that one day we will re-build. I feel such guilt for lending it to them, so Sebastian lost his house, I lost a refuge, and sadly, faith in people who I thought were good, honest people. Truly a bitter disappointment.

Chapter 5

Picking up the Pieces

It was four years after the trauma of Stamos' death when I came to life again. Yes we were living in a terrible place, although the flat was nice. Somehow I managed by doing little nursing jobs in term time, to keep us going. But the pain went, and I felt as if I could now go forward.

An old friend, half Greek, half English came to live in Highgate, not so far away, and this was a truly warm friendship with reciprocal entertaining. Freddie became the Baba of our home, he loved the boys and they loved him.

Number three son came to live with me, because his digs had been burnt down (including his landlady). Unaware that I could not have my children to stay, it caused huge upset because as a widow with child, my rent was low. Suddenly it went UP. I rang and was told that as I had 'an individual' living with me, that was how it was. I erupted.

'Is one not allowed to have a child staying, or do you want another homeless young man on the streets?'

End of problem. Later, also in need, another son came to stay, it was wonderful, quite like old times and they helped me with collecting Fredo from his school when I was working.

Whenever possible we went to Greece, for I was determined that Fredo should keep up his Greek. We were always welcomed by the neighbours and townsfolk, just as ever, the family did not care to be friendly and we hardly saw them.

But the mistakes were not yet over, would I never learn? I gave in kindness, the key of the spitaki, our home, to the big house. This, just in case there was another big earthquake, when for sure, the big house with its heavy roof would collapse.

'If there is an emergency, you are welcome to use it.' HA!

They put in, Bangladeshis, Bulgarians, an idiot Brit, Iranians, a Greek, latterly, a Pakistani, furniture for storage, you name it, all, without first asking my permission. Everything was broken, even the loo pan! As usual, I coped and had everything repaired, and then I took the key back.

A call came, indeed several calls came. Neighbours who had been good friends and who had been particularly kind to Fredo after Stamos died, were being evicted. Vassilis was the caretaker for the smart villa and small farm alongside ours. They lived in two rooms with three children. They had numerous animals, dogs, sheep, goats, the ones I had delivered in the night, and begged to move into the spitaki. I was appalled; I just wanted our house for ourselves, not once again to be foisted out to the annex. They begged, they pleaded. Apparently the owner had died and the place was divided between his two daughters. The elder was married, the usual story, and the husband demanded they be given the cash, so it was being sold and Vassilis and family had to move. The new people did not want them there. Sadly, I eventually relented.

As usual, gratitude evaporated very quickly and complaints and demands poured down on me. The ceilings were not good enough, the archway from the hall into the dining room was not nice, and so on. Imagine? Such nonsense!

Vassilis, a scruffy individual who never shaved, criticised my house when all he had to do was to spend a few drax to buy a throw away razor. I was fed up with them. But they did pay rent which went into Fredo's bank account.

While they were there, the eldest son of the big house walked in and took things, which he considered were his, a thief. A desk of Stamos' father, my most beautiful old English bow fronted commode, now worth a fortune, which was left, goodness knows why, outside so that wind and rain ruined it. A painting which my sister-in-law had given us and which Fredo always said was the road to the mountain house. He neither asked the little family or me.

Then one day I heard that Vassilis had moved out, without a word, leaving a dreadful mess. Truly, I was in despair. What was the matter with people to be so thoughtless. I was so offended, having done them a favour. But there it was again, a lone woman, a widow, a foreigner.

But this was not the end of the story, what I tell next is rather awful, but funny too.

The calls started again, they needed my help – cheek! Vassilis had been an Agricultural Policeman. These chaps have an idyllic life wandering from village to village being given hospitality, which being Greek, was always forthcoming and generous. So they might referee a dispute over land, a tree, or a donkey! And they had a gun. Status.

Now some time after Vassilis' family moved into the spitaki, the new owner of the neighbouring property, a gangster by all accounts, was shot dead through the fence.

Naturally Vassilis was suspect, and the police went through MY house with a fine tooth comb. Various things were removed, including a hammer, shovel, etc, etc, and then, damn them, they found my little box of treasures. Bits and pieces I had found on the land, shards, obsidian cores, glass. Having worked for archaeologists, I knew that you just did not remove such from the scene. Here was evidence of what lay under the soil, and let's face it, everywhere you put your foot in Greece, you find something. These were my little treasures, safe in a box in the big chest of drawers in the bathroom.

Story has it that the then chief of police was a keen antiquarian and had told his boys to look out for and bring him anything of interest. My junk was hardly interesting to the likes of him who wanted whole antique vases and so on. Story has it, and I do not know if it is true, that he was eventually found out and charged.

Back to the calls. Vassilis was going to court, charged with – now hear this, stealing – from me, EIGHTY-EIGHT – 88, amphora. Well!

I have no amphora, indeed I have never ever had any amphora, let alone eighty eight.

It was laughable. I felt hard, very hard, they had let me down and now they were begging me to help them, again, to hell with them. I ignored the calls, but they went on, and on and yes, of course eventually I relented.

I wrote a letter to the court saying that my very small box of artefacts and bits and pieces where nothing, whatsoever to do with Vassilis or his family who were tenants. The person to blame for all this was the over zealous young policeman who had gone through MY personal things and there certainly were NO amphora amongst them. The fault lay with that young man who made the gross mistake of removing evidence from our land. You see, I still get heated about all this, particularly as I never got back my little collection of treasures. Or the hammer, etc!

Apparently my letter did work, and Vassilis got off. When I met him next I told him that he owed me at least some olive oil. But, the miserable mean man, he never came up with any and I still feel sore at him.

Worse was yet to come, would I never learn? Yet this was different, or so I thought. Some of the Scandinavian Christians who I had befriended, reappeared. The mother, of whom I was very fond, suggested that her elder daughter and husband rent the spitaki to continue their philanthropic work with children. I was delighted, here were Northern Europeans with a totally different standard of behaviour, perhaps now the little house would be cherished and enjoyed.

Again, I was too generous, I offered them six months without rent, and thereafter, just £100. a month. We were friends after all, and I would never overcharge them. Such a mistake, and in no time I realised that things had gone badly wrong, for a start, I could not contact them, they seemed to have disappeared.

My treasures were locked in the study. The four poster (and hangings) in which I had given birth to my children. The few old good pieces of furniture, yes, all needing attention but antique and potentially valuable were carefully stacked. I had put down loads of rat poison, because the farm was growing maize and rats were everywhere.

Finally, I went to see what was going on. The sheer scale of devastation far outdid anything all the previous 'tenants' had left. The walls of the bedrooms were demolished and the doors were stacked in a corner. The bathroom wall and basin and kitchen sink behind, all knocked down. The study had been opened and all my treasures had been thrown away by that totally ignorant fool. Finding him to get it restored was the difficulty. I emailed Israel where his father and entire group of pilgrims were now settled. No response. I emailed Sweden and Denmark, begging for help in this appalling story. I even approached the bishop there who said that sadly he could not help as they were not under his jurisdiction. No one wanted to know or claim responsibility. It took over a year, with no help from anyone. Finally, with photocopies of snaps taken of the destruction, I reached the innocent and kindly mother who had made the original suggestion, she was horrified, so at last we came to an agreement, a pitiful sum of money was handed over so that I could get the place re-built. Never again!

Life went on with us living in London and going to Greece whenever possible. I have said we lived in a very rough area, and so now, having been broken into and robbed, something much worse happened.

Fredo, home from school, was out with a little chum when he was set upon, shoved down some steps by eight boys who then proceeded to kick him in the head. He arrived gasping at the flat, battered, filthy with a thick lip, but worse, emotionally shattered, which I so understand. If only that nice MP had helped us not to move there. It was wrong of the authorities to move single mothers to such a bad place. We had enough troubles without having to cope with any extra difficulties. No more could I ask him to pop around the corner to buy milk or bread. He flatly refused to go out, poor boy, it had been a vile experience.

Shortly after this, I went to buy whatever and came face to face with the gang leader who had attacked Fredo. Will I never learn? I just stood in front of him, my eyes hard.

'So, here he is, the bully, who needs lots of little chums to do his dirty work for him eh? You could not take my boy on one to one, could you – coward.'

There was not a soul about. He lifted his fists, jumping up and down, circling me and replied.

'Come on then, I'll fight you.'

'Bravo you,' I replied, 'so you'll fight a lone woman will you? Shame on you, I wonder what your mother would think if she could see you now?'

I was unaware that windows overlooking us were filled with eyes. I was different yes, but, I had friends. He turned tail and fled just as the police came around the corner.

There was a court case, he was charged and eventually Fredo had recompense.

BUT! Little did I know that this was to be the turning point in our lives. He did not die, and he did not become a cabbage, probably because he was strong and at least one foot taller than his attackers and had made his good escape. He was different. We were different, we did not belong there although I have to say I shall be ever grateful to the powers that be who gave us shelter.

What was I doing here? Why had we come to this? Stamo, oh Stamo, how could you have left us in such dire circumstances? How to cope with the horrors of living in such a place? We had to get away.

North, to the glorious open spaces and sheer beauty of the North. My mind made up, I began the tentative steps to get us out of London, and to the North. A cousin gave us a dear old car, bless her, for this meant freedom. There was a little house, very primitive, which I wanted to buy. We had known and loved it for years, so now was the time to move the world and it was as if my life just changed.

Having been really poor for the eight years since Stamos died, strange things happened. I began to attract money. A couple of older friends died, a family trust folded, I was offered a sum to move out of the flat, which I was leaving anyway, even my mother, for the first time ever, gave me £1,000. For a small sum, I bought it, almost a ruin, but with huge potential and certainly a possibility for toughies as we, to camp in. Then someone told me that being a widow with a child, I might get grants from the authorities to do up the little house.

It was miles from anywhere, up on the fell, so pretty nestling into the hillside. It was, looking back, a huge undertaking, because I foolishly thought with my new found wealth, I could manage. Being unworldly had become a habit, I always took off more than I could chew.

It had nothing, no electricity, no running water, because one hot summer the spring had died. There was a chemical loo, and an ancient privy, which I thought, as in Romania, I could get going again. All sort of makeshift arrangements were possible, tanks in the roof to catch the rainwater. Halogen lighting, a gas cooker and fridge, not least, a range. We, who were used to the simple life in the Greek mountains, would manage brilliantly. Or so I thought, for here there was a welfare state. I went to the authorities, a silly move as I realised later because now, we were ON the map. They hadn't even known of the little house, but now they did and my fate was sealed. I had to do things their way, I could not camp with a kid in a freezing old house, oh well, we all make mistakes and certainly I was a specialist and right then, then, right at the beginning, I understood this was a big one.

I investigated all the alternative solutions. A small windmill on the roof for electricity, the kind they have on boats. A generator, although I certainly knew nothing about them. We had managed so well in the Greek mountains with our oil lamps, our fou-fou on which I cooked all our meals and bread and coped well enough with our simple but good sewage system.

Then, a miracle happened, at the Boat Show, of all places. Kind men advised me, I struggled with the decision as to whether to buy a windmill or a generator. That problem was solved by the authorities who firmly told me that as the house was in an area of exceptional natural beauty, NO windmill. It was a very cold and damp house. I told the men about it, how, over the centuries, the earth had built up at the back of the dairy, and I urgently needed a bulldozer to clear it. As I was still working in London, just dashing North in holidays and half term, how on earth to find a bulldozer?

So to the miracle.

'I have an acquaintance up there, who is a civil engineer,' said the young man selling generators, he sought out his address book and gave me a phone number. 'Try him, he has lots of bulldozers.'

So I rang, and was thoroughly put out because the stranger was so curt, I would before long realise that this was his way and that he hated the phone.

'My bulldozers are twenty miles away,' said he very sternly.

The mat was pulled from under my feet.

'Sorry, sorry,' said I, 'Forgive me for bothering you, so I'll say goodbye.'

But he relented, thank heaven.

'Wait a minute.' he said, 'Give me your phone number and I'll call you when I have time.'

Which I did, which he did.

So that is how I met Andrew, who had recently been widowed and was desperately sad and lonely. We made friends over the phone, and it was a joy to come home from work exhausted and have someone wanting to speak with me. We married two years later. All because of a bulldozer, and anyway, I actually found one up there working on a neighbours' property who took away the soil behind the dairy.

Now there was a dear man in my life again, who took on all my practical problems with relish. A civil engineer who knew the ropes, and loved a challenge.

We moved North.

Life was sweet again with a gentle companion who tried his hardest to help me with my cranky, impossible teenager. There were so many problems though, no school or college near the little house for Fredo, I was in despair. But Andrew had the solution for that too, we moved in with him, a mere sixty miles from the little house so I could be working on it whenever possible.

There was horrible disapproval from his 'friends' and some of the neighbours. They were actually rude to me, or in my hearing. Happily his charming daughter welcomed me, a companion for dad. But generally, I was a scarlet woman, it was painful, but then, I was used to that. Years of unpleasantness must have smoothed my sensitive corners off. We were very content.

Andrew took us away for a wonderful six weeks. He told me later, it was to find out what sort of person I was on holiday!

Over the years, I had made many friends all over the world to whom I had given much hospitality. Now I took them up on their offers of return hospitality. We went to Syria, and loved it. My friends made our trip easy and wonderful. Funny how one has preconceived ideas of a country, so it was a delight to find really good people everywhere, kindness, assistance, giving us wonderful memories. Then, on to Jordon, more friends, more fun, and my friends, all so joyful to be with and they were so happy for me, and all approved of Andrew.

Then I took him to Greece and we stayed in my little house which, unknown to me, shocked him sorely. The floors were still just rough concrete, as they had been when the pigs lived there. Everything was very, very simple and ordinary, despite being pretty on the outside.

It was actually a shock when he suddenly announced he was going to pay to have marble tiles put down! Suddenly this was a proper little house which was clean and very easy to keep so. I remember with humour a row between him and the 'masteros', the marble layer. He had not put tiles under the little bath, very Greek. Water and all sorts of nasties would eventually thrive there.

'Tell him,' said Andrew looking fierce, 'I will not pay him until he has finished the job, properly.'

Uproar.

Here was I, translating, two very angry men raising their voices at me. Aghast, I tried.

'We are in Europe now,' I told the brute, 'you really have to do your work to a higher standard now, and be sure, he will not pay you until you do so.'

More uproar, the masteros was furious. How dare these foreigners tell him how to do his job?

'Listen' I said, 'Andreas was a BIG shot in his work, a civil engineer, building roads, bridges, harbours, all that kind of thing. It was his job to always make sure everything was done Alfa Ena (A1). If it was not done properly, the bridges would fall down, the roads would break up and the harbours would be useless. We (I used the Greek WE) 'must now try to join Europe in every sense, not just because of politicians and pieces of paper.'

He eventually, with a very poor grace, did it, and Andrew, having peered under the bath to check it was done properly, paid him immediately.

Now something new came about, the step-children viewed me with a different light. No more alone, no more the easy subject to be bullied, I had my knight in shining armour. It was wonderful. And, they liked him.

Of course, he was scandalised by all I told him. How badly I had been treated. That in all those years, we had not received a penny from Stamos'will. Years on, he still is incredulous, because nothing has changed. The laws in Greece are very different from Britain. The men in Greece are mostly as Ali Pasha, they want it all. So forget it, women and children, second class citizens.

Aged sixty five, hurray, I got my Agricultural pension, with a struggle. Having paid for it since Stamos died in '88, there was now a battle to not let me have it. Despite my having dual nationality, which I had thought would help, another struggle with the authorities ensued. Kind Yorgos to the fore, more battles, and eventually we won. Why oh why does everything have to be such a headache? It is not a great deal of money, but it is something and I feel gratified after so many years of struggling to pay up, there is return.

A new crisis hit me, would it never end? My lawyer received a huge bill from the tax office. They were charging me, and only me, death duties for Stamos, because, according to the family, I had never been a farmer. I, the only one who actually had been, who had slaved away day after day, year after year, in all weathers. Why? Who? The children had been ever conspicuous by their absence, except when they wanted something. I felt myself once more crumbling. When would this vile abuse end?

Andrew paid the bill, thousands of pounds, with the assurance from my excellent lawyer, that we would fight this and get it back. I can't remember how many times I flew out over this story. Still in good health, I always chose to take economy flights, which were overnight and exhausting. Once, I arrived for the court case, at nine o'clock for ten, only to be told it had been cancelled. I burst into tears then, to the horror of my companions, exclaiming that I had had enough, enough!

My wonderful neighbours came to my help and all got up in court to say that, of course I had been a farmer, everyone knew that. Nothing is free in life, so I tell my sons, so now I bought splendid M&S thick jumpers, a lovely blue dressing gown and a neat jerkin for them in thanks. They were all so pleased.

Not only had I been a hard working farmer, I believed that I had been a good one. I strove to help my neighbours, brought in pure breeds (with their documents), eggs to hatch, hens, geese and ducks, and they did very well. One interesting point I must tell, is that when I knew I was flying with eggs, I used to phone the customs at the airport and explain what I was doing. Generally they were helpful, I suspect perhaps, a little amused. Then, just once, with a batch of Light Sussex eggs, there was a little Hitler who insisted that they went through the x-ray machine. Disaster. For when they hatched, half were seriously deformed, and of course had to be killed. Thereafter, I really laboured the point, opened up the egg boxes, let them SEE and handle them. No hand grenades, no bombs. Those kindly people must have been born country folk, for I never had to put them through the machine again.

The last time I flew out for a court case, is memorable. I was of old, used to the court house in Corinth. Handsome, airy, but a bit like a market place, with people wandering in and out.

This was a courtroom I had not been in before. Memories of all those kids I had helped in the past were of another, larger one. Here, extremely heavy benches were shoved right to the back of the room so you had to clamber over to get a seat. My lawyer told me what to do and say, I had my identity card ready.

The judge came in, a woman with very dyed black hair. Beside her, the advocates and scribes, four younger women, all peroxide blondes. I stood up and bowed as was correct. It was a crowded court and our case came rather to the end. When my name was called, I stood up and tried to scramble out of my seat, but my lawyer wisely intervened and I was merely asked for my identity card which was handed over the heads of the crowd. It was difficult to hear what was being said, because they were speaking to the judge, away from me. First my lawyer spoke, then, and bless him, Yorgos.

I heard bits and pieces, but I was caught by the emotions on the faces of the five women sitting on the dais. They were actually smiling at Yorgos. Quite charming.

'She was a very good farmer,' he said. 'She brought in pedigree animals, cows, with papers of course. She brought in excellent breeds of duck eggs, goose eggs and hen eggs. She has contributed to our area by raising the standard of our animals. She was a very good and generous farmer for she shared them with us, her neighbouring farmers.'

He must have elaborated a little, but I could not hear it all.

Big smiles.

He sat down.

'Why?' the judge turned and addressed the tax officer, 'Has this case been brought against this woman?'

Wait for it now – here it comes!

'I don't know,' came the reply! Imagine?

Well I did know, it came because of spite, of the continual intention to harm me. We eventually got our money back, and everything on that score is peaceful once more.

Chapter 6

Another Wedding

He had grown up, Stamos and my son, Fretherikos. 6 foot 5 inches tall and at 27 years old, marvellously handsome. Despite his dyslexia, he had with Andrew's help, completed his education, gone through college and was an independent, working man. Louise, he brought her to see us, the prettiest fair girl with the bluest eyes. Clever, independent, and a good match for him.

Should they get married in Greece? Well why not. Fredo had been baptised in our little church of Saint Nikolas, where his father and I had had our religious marriage. It had been a long time since the little church had been used properly, sadly, the last occasion had been for Maria's funeral, but, we must look ahead. It would be FUN. Word went out to the four corners of the globe, invitations in both Greek and English to adorn many mantelpieces.

Sadly, Andrew would not come, for he was feeling frail and thought, probably rightly, that it would be too hectic for him.

A miracle had occurred. The family had at last, for the time being anyway, forgotten their miserable attitude towards me and truly excelled themselves. The 'little' half brother was going to have a splendid send off, and they were going to be a big part of it, bravo!

A wedding, a wedding, with two lovely young people. The church was painted purist white, inside and out, like a little wedding cake. The surroundings had been ploughed and glorious new green grass emerged, a back drop for the wonderful spring flowers of Greece. They had done an excellent job and I was so grateful.

I went out two weeks before the big day and stayed for one week after. An old girlfriend, Gail, came from the States to help me, and we began the enormous job of getting organised for the mob, to make the little house spick and span.

What a task, for the little house, the spitaki, would be the place for the wedding, or rather the area beyond, in front of the cave.

We began whitewashing, then, gave up, two old girls, exhausted, and called in the excellent Ali, a Pakistani who had lived in Greece for thirty years. He was much better at it than we were anyway and in no time the house gleamed.

I called the tsingania, the Rom, my old friend Xrysoula and her family. How we toiled, it seemed endless, washing, painting, clearing weeds, and it rained and rained. All to the good in fact as the flowers erupted from their winter sleep, a carpet of tiny, wild calendula, with yellow corn daisies and blue cornflowers everywhere. They began to arrive then, the 'young' who had been young twenty plus years ago, but who were just the same. Two from New Zealand, little Sue, of the earthquake night, and Dave, who had taken beautiful photographs at Fredo's baptism. Three from America, son, Antony and the two grandsons, my special foster son, Jack, from Canada. Harry came all the way from India, and five from Eire. Philip, one of the main builders in the restoration of the mountain house, with his wife and two children and Bridget, she who lost her precious flute on the bus; bless them all, for we never lost each other. Last and certainly not least, hordes of Brits, old friends, childhood friends, all precious and wildly happy to be with us and together.

My little house had three bedrooms. Gail and I slept in the granny annexe next door so we at least had some space and peace. My pension had been mounting up and now I went wild and splashed out, everything to make a happy, comfortable time.

I bought new mattresses, and lots of smart new camp beds plus pillows galore. I went to see all my old friends who had supplied me for the tourist groups and I gave my orders, for it was my intention to do the feast. Of course we would have to hire tables and chairs, plates, glasses etcetera. But I had laboured over making twelve handsome, all enveloping aprons, for my helpful girls to wear.

The plan was to have the traditional mezzes, with a vengeance. Tsatsiki, terama, aubergine salad, cheese and spinach pies, olives of course, fetta, good bread, thin sliced spicy salami and bowls of good salad. Next, lamb, rice and more salads. Clare, who had lain next to me in the Royal Free Hospital, also trying to hang on to her baby, arrived with that baby, now an elegant young woman. So wonderful, to have kept up friends like that. She, poor soul, brought the wedding cake on the plane, and, typical of the Korinthian taxi drivers, because of the rain and mud on the drive, they dumped her at the gate so she had to walk carrying all their luggage plus the cake.

Then, sadly, once again the mat was whipped from under my feet. I KNOW it was meant kindly, but I was so shocked. As usual, the 'ninny' again, I acquiesced, said not a word, because believing they were doing me a big favour, the family offered to do the feast.

Back to town, to cancel everything, the huge tub of yoghourt, for the tsatsiki, the lamb, the boxes of cucumbers, tomatoes onions, the fetta, the bread, you name it. But the young people meanwhile had joyfully driven to Nemea and bought huge boxes of wine, which they attacked gleefully, so at least it was merry.

Then, an amazing piece of chance again, I was ringing up some of Stamos' old friends, the ones I liked, who had always been courteous to me, to invite them. They were pleased, after twenty years to be in touch, to be invited to Fredo's wedding. Joseph, who had been a boy when we knew each other, greeted me warmly, and when I told him of the event, he told me that he was in the wedding business and offered any help I needed. Miracles do happen!

The rain! Oh my goodness but it poured, like the monsoon, and I was fearful it would continue and carry on for the big day.

Strange, because that is exactly what had happened for Maria's wedding, it had deluged with rain, the weekend before and the weekend after. But that weekend had been magical for her.

I spoke to Andrew in England three times a day, telling him the progress, or not, and how Joseph had offered help. So, bless him, Andrew offered to pay for a vast marquee. It was arranged and arrived and the sun came out and more and more young people arrived, trailing up the drive, and it was so joyful, a reunion of so many good old friends. How they laughed at each other, twenty years older, but, just the same.

Now we had to accommodate everyone. Five girls slept in my bedroom in the spitaki, literally elbow to elbow, we could not get another camp bed in if we had tried. Across the hall in Fredo's room, slept the American/Canadian contingent, four of them. In the sitting room, Clare and daughter slept on camp beds, and in the study, Sebas and Alice. In the little courtyard behind the sitting room, two tents sprouted with the two New Zealanders, and Harry, from India. Thankfully, still being friends with all my neighbours, next door offered us the use of a little old house, so four, no, it was five more slept there but came to us for meals. We were either twenty two or twenty four all told, and everyone got along famously and helped wherever it was needed. Neighbours arrived with handsome loaves of special wedding bread, demijohns of wine, gifts for the bridal couple, it was hectic.

My eldest step son then excelled himself by ordering a grader to come and smooth the drive and lay flat the field alongside, for a car park. A porto loo arrived too, because and sadly, my dream of erecting 'bush' loos just did not materialise due to the Rom boys being unwilling to do the work! Everything possible was thought of, the family did their very best for their young half brother, that baby giant who made them smile, because he was so tall.

My extensive research into Saint Nikolas of Bari, now would be used. For some reason, I had known and stored that title from Stamos. Saint Nicholas, saint of children, sailors and goodness knows who else, is in fact, our Santa Claus, Father Christmas. Then, I recalled that the Bishop who married Maria had told me about him. It was a good thing our church was well known locally as that, for the family pooh poohed my wording on the invitations, but then, they just did not know. Fortunately, there had been quite some publicity to that old saint in Britian, so I was able to borrow from the papers and the TV and wrote up a sheet with all the information I could find. A young neighbour wrote a translation beautifully for me, so we had it in Greek and English and I had one hundred photo copies made to hand out.

Son Antony decided his gift for the feast would be to make BAKLAVA, which he surpassed at. Huge tins, 'merinas' were borrowed from the baker in the village, and Antony was assisted with the gang of girls, all happily wearing THE aprons. They worked outside the spitaki and there they were, ready to be baked at the fournos (baker) and in due course, found to be most excellent.

Gail's husband arrived from the USA so they moved to Ancient Corinth while a Scottish friend arrived and took her place with me in the annex. The ever warm bed! The girls all went out to collect wild flowers, but again, the mat. So although it was not the same as Maria's wedding with the church entirely decorated with wild flowers in little bags, it was very smart, with bought flowers which I have to admit, were magnificent.

The day before the wedding, the girls all sat and made up bunches of wild flowers which they did hang in the church after all. Then they tied up the bonboniera, hankies which daughter-in-law, Alice, brought from China. A neighbour, Soula, who had been tremendously helpful in many ways, had organised the purchase of kilos of sugared almonds, so seven were tied in each hanky, to be handed out after the ceremony, as is the way.

Each day Xrysoula arrived and I had to find some tasks for her to do in order to pay her. Finally, in despair I asked her to scrub the tombstones, for lack of any other jobs. I had been completely unaware that the stones had been removed. Apparently my eldest stepson had had them taken down because he did not like seeing them every day. We will all die, it is inevitable, and we were so privileged to have the little church with the six tombs standing to attention, being part of it, as it were. Well apparently the second step son insisted, rightly, that they be put back. Well, they were not put back securely in that sandy soil.

I was horrified when I saw one huge marble stone lying down, flat on its face, and thought that it was my fault, for telling Xrysoula to scrub them. For as usual, Xrysoula, given a hose, went to town. So I ran to the eldest son and told him to have it put up properly, as we did not want any broken legs. It was done, but sadly, only for the time being, the moment the wedding was over, they were removed again!

It was, as with Maria's wedding, very much a village affair with all the friends and neighbours arriving, from far and near.

Just before the ceremony, the Icelanders arrived, Sigurdur, who had been our best man at our civil marriage in Reykjavik, and naughty son, Sigi Palli. Wonderful, such a compliment to have them all, from far and wide, truly a joyful day before even it started. Father Nick, from Solomos, who spoke English and who we had known for years, indeed had been to our Panaieri before and baptised my Goddaughters Anastasia and, Marianna, he came with a young monk and together they stood outside the church door and held the ceremony under the sky in the bright Greek sunshine.

I had been to the village and bought 5 kilos of rice from Voula, which was handed round. Poor young couple, they were pelted with vigour as is the custom, while they walked three times around the small table which served as the outside altar.

Everyone was there, Louise's family and all, ours including my older sister-in-law who came specially from Athens. Missing were Stamos and Maria, our lost ones, and grand daughter, Daphne and my dear Andrew.

The floral crowns were put on their heads, there was laughter because the groom had to duck in order for the best man to reach up. The service, out in the open with crowds watching from the ridge above and all around, was short and sweet and lovely.

After the ceremony we all stood in line and kissed and shook hands, endlessly, this time, unlike with Maria's wedding, I was right there. There was absolutely no ill feeling directed towards me. Then we all drifted to the huge tent in front of the cave where tables were laid and the party began.

A disco had been engaged and a valiant young woman pleased everyone with her choice of music, top decibel. A proper Rom band arrived to add to the fun, and our Rom women got up and hands raised, did their strangely slow and elegant dance to the wild music. The dancing, or perhaps better put, gyrating, went on long into the night. At one point, the bride, Louise threw her bouquet, as is the custom. And hurray, grand daughter, Kassandra, caught it! So who knows, maybe we'll have another wedding before long.

My goodness, what a party! As it should be.

Chapter 7

A New Beginning?

I gave the young couple the quaint and beautiful little blue 'steffanothiki'. The charming village tin case, round and painted blue with two little love birds centre top. For years the steffania (crowns) which Stamos and I, and Maria and David, had worn for our marriages were safely kept in there. I am a foolishly sentimental woman, and was glad to give Daphne her mother's steffania.

Now there were still two sets of crowns, a glass window on the front to protect them and two love birds on the top, a little battered, to indicate what it was. It is, very rustic and quite charming.

The days after the wedding, the young people began to leave, to revisit old places and new. It was sad to suddenly feel the evaporation of joy, but, it lingered. It had been a huge privilege having so many from all over, unforgettable indeed, a time to remember. Let us hope there will be some baptisms in the future, so we can, in a smaller way at least, repeat it. The marquee was taken away, and we cleared up.

Elie, my Scottish friend wanted to be driven to the airport. I was not due to fly home till the next day and really did not want to go as I still had a lot of work to do. So the last days were frantic trying to get the spitaki tidy and clear the annexe. During my three weeks in Greece for the wedding, I had two mobile phones, one for Greece, for local calls, and one for abroad for Andrew. The former was ancient, the latter, quite smart and new.

In the hurry to make order, the smart phone disappeared, got buried, or so I thought. I sent off the Rom with endless gifts, clothes, food and the old fridge from the annexe. They had done really well over the weeks, earning cash and having a good midday meal, quite a good time for them really.

So I locked up the little house and said my goodbyes to everyone. Off we went to the airport and I for one last night with Ruth and Em. Who had been the original cause of all this, so many years previously.

Back home, I went through my luggage still searching for the smart moblile. Then, oh the shock, the sorrow, I opened my jewel box to find that my lovely earrings which I had worn for the wedding, were not there. So I knew exactly who had taken them, Varvara, Xrysouls's daughter, at twenty eight years old, expecting her eighth child. Painfully thin, poor, her husband had just come out of prison yet they had all benefited from Fredo's wedding. I was so upset. On my last run up to the gypsy village, I had waved to another daughter, a beautiful girl who I was good friends with. I wondered at the shadow which crossed her face, the worried look she cast in the direction of Varvara's house.

So I rang the eldest stepson, who was still on a high and immensely cheerful. I told him my fears. That both phone and earrings had been taken by Varvara and he said he would go immediately to see Xrysoula. Which he did, and phoned me that evening to say she was not there and that her house was all locked up.

Now it is the norm, when the Rom steal from you, they run for it. They go and squat on relatives in another gypsy village, their relatives sell the goods, they share out the bounty and eventually, they come back. But this was not the case, as, Xrysoula must have

thought that she was wanted for work, for she arrived next morning. My stepson told me it was pitiful how she wailed, 'No, no, no! It is not possible.' And left, to walk or hitch a ride the two miles home.

I would have liked to be a fly on the wall then, for I can imagine Xrysoula's wrath. Within two hours she was back, with the phone and earrings. Poor thing, mortified, because she knows that I am good to her, and because I give the baker money so that at least they always have bread, a bonus. So, there was another miracle. And together with the huge success of the wedding, the stepson and I were at last, civil to each other.

By chance, two stragglers, the Oliver boys, who I have known since they were little, were to fly home that day and they brought the phone and earrings back. Peace was restored and all was well. Of course, Varvara had tried to get the phone working, but, because it was for abroad, she did not. When next I saw her, she had a sweet new baby daughter, and, as is the custom, I gave a money gift. Varvara was shame faced, but I told her it was 'finished' only she must never do that again. As a precaution, she is not invited to the spitaki any more, a shame from my point of view, as she is a very good worker.

It is thirty-eight years since I first went to the farm, a life time. So many memories, mostly good, many just wonderful, sadly, some really bad, and they are all written here in this journal. And now, 2009, it is twenty plus years since Stamos died. Dear, mad, man, who lived a life not without its problems, and left us, his family, in a total mess. Even now, twenty years on, we have not a penny from his will. Or is it a drac, or a euro? Everything I put into the farm and children, gone, forgotten. I am told by the pessimists that I will never get anything back, but maybe my children will. I sincerely hope so.

For I am an old lady now, my needs are few, but I have my memories. There are times when I remember lying under the great beams in the ceiling of the cellar in the mountain house, the coolness and the sheer beauty of the place. Lost, by the foolishness of my own countrymen.

I remember the kindness of my excellent Greek neighbours, and am grateful for their real and continued friendship, their delight in my appreciation of their ways. I can never forget the sheer joy and fun which I had most of the time.

Now I live peacefully, busily, in the English countryside with gentle Andrew. I run a small Cottage Industry, making Pothies that first pair for Stamos' birthday, so many years ago. My take go to three charities, including the bread for Xrysoula.

My contribution to the community is to demonstrate spinning, never forgetting where it all began in the '60s, on Siphnos. Where, because of the storms, we could not leave. Kaliopi, our landlady, was spinning with a drop spindle and I was totally fascinated, so, somehow, I asked her to teach me. Together we walked into the village to the woodworker, who made me a spindle, the whorl, from a bun handle off an old chest of drawers, I have it yet. I learnt, and was so thrilled, felt that I could rule the world. The natural progression was to get a wheel, so while touring Scotland with Stamos thirty plus years ago, I bought a fine Shetland, still my workhorse, an upright wheel, neat, handsome. So now I have six wheels, ridiculous, and I teach, passing on my skill to the young, the daughters I never had. So of course, that was not all in vain!

Well now to end this journal, by saying, that because of all the joys and in spite of the many sorrows, half my heart still remains in Greece.

P.S. 26th May 2009. Born to Louise and Frederikos, a son – Theo Stamos.

Na za zissi.